# The History and Chronology of Ancient India

# The History and Chronology of Ancient India

## Undoing Distortions from Colonial Rule

**Anil J. Mehta**

Satyam Press

Published by
Satyam Press, Missouri City, Texas 77459
www.SatyamPress.com



First Edition

Library of Congress Control Number: 2024905745

ISBN: 979-8-9874369-0-5 (Hardcover)
ISBN: 979-8-9874369-1-2 (e-book)
ISBN: 979-8-9874369-2-9 (Paperback)

Line and Copy Editor: Rima Kar Ghosh
Book Design and Artwork: Pradeep Aeri and Ravi Narain
All photographs, unless mentioned otherwise,
are by Anil J. Mehta

Printed and bound in the United States of America.

*Dedicated to*
*Mother India and truth in history*

*In the year,*
*Kaliyuga Śaka 5126*
*Saptarṣi Samvat (Kashmirābda) 5100*
*Vikrama Samvat (Chaitri-North India) 2081*
*Vikrama Samvat (Kārtiki-Gujarat) 2080*
*AD 2024*
*Śālivāhana Śaka 1946*

# CONTENTS

## Chapter 11



## Chapter 12

# Chapter 13

# Chapter 14

# Chapter 15

# Chapter 16

# Appendix I

## Appendix II



## Appendix III



## Appendix IV



## Index | 351

# List of Figures and Tables

## Figures

## Tables

# PREFACE

History gives us identity and defines who we are. The fact that you have picked up this book means that you are curious to know more about the history of India. I appreciate your time and hope you will journey with me through the authentic history of ancient India. I believe that as we learn more about India, we will also understand our own identity better.

History teaches us many things. It is often said that those who don't learn from or forget history are doomed to repeat it. Indians have lost wars only when not united. The colonial British did not win a single battle in India without the help of the Indians.

I was born and brought up in India and studied Chemical Engineering as a profession. My destiny brought me to the United States of America where I was fortunate to have a satisfying career. Though I do not have a degree in history, I have been deeply interested in it since childhood, and have dedicated the later years to reading and learning more about history.

I had never suspected that the history, which we were taught in school, may not be all true until 1998. I learned from the late Robert Arnett (1996), the author of *India Unveiled*, about the paper titled, *'The Myth of the Aryan Invasion of India'* published by David Frawley (1998), an American Indologist. Ten years later, in 2008, I read about huge distortions made in the chronology of ancient India in the book, *The True History and the Religion of India*, by Swami Prakashananda Saraswati (2006). At first, I questioned whether this could even be possible! I became obsessed with unearthing the truth and ultimately, I retired early from my profession to dive into the research of ancient India's history and chronology. True chronology is the foundation of true history.

This book is my humble attempt to share with you, in a concise and cogent manner, what I have learned from my research. I have focused my research primarily on the chronology of ancient India from about 3100+ BC to AD 1192. I have provided many references, duly acknowledged, that helped me get a better sense of our history. I have utilized what I considered historical reliable data from multiple sources. If I have been able to kindle your interest in the history of India, I will find great fulfillment. Kindly write to me with your views, I will welcome them with gratitude. You can contact me through my blog at www.satyampress.com.

Anil J. Mehta
Houston, Texas
April 2024

# ACKNOWLEDGMENTS

I am deeply grateful for the blessings from Śrī Gaurang Nanavaty and the late Smt. Darshana Nanavaty, direct disciples of the great saint Swami Chinmayananda, my spiritual guides, and Acharyas of Chinmaya Mission Houston, as I embarked on this journey. My courage to pursue this challenging project likely came from listening to and reflecting upon the weekly spiritual discourses by the Acharyas for over twenty years.

I owe a huge gratitude to the late Dr. Kalkivayi Mahankali (K. M.) Rao whose blog led me to learn about Pandit Venkatachelam's outstanding work. In his blog, Dr. K. M. Rao summarized the lifetime work of Pandit Venkatachelam on restoring the true chronology and history of ancient India. My thanks to Michel Danino, guest professor at IIT Gandhinagar, for sharing his copies of Pandit Venkatachelam's books, especially, Chronology of Ancient Hindu History Part I and II. I am immensely grateful to the Internet Archive, a non-profit organization, for their website www.archive.org which has been my primary source of invaluable, out-of-print books and journals. Additionally, gratitude goes to my friend, the late Pushpak Pandya, for sharing with me his copy of Panchānga (traditional Indian almanac).

Knowledge of Sanskrit is helpful in researching the history of ancient India. Free and remote, but live Sanskrit classes conducted by volunteers of Samskrita Bharati, a non-profit organization, could not have come at a better time for me. I am very grateful to my Sanskrit teacher Smt. Ramapriya for teaching Sanskrit every week for four years and still continuing. The Sanskrit knowledge I have gained through these classes has been very helpful in understanding the historically relevant Sanskrit verses of the Purāṇas.

My deep gratitude to those who read full drafts along the way and provided invaluable feedback and suggestions – my nephews Hemal Mehta and Sachin Mehta, my music gurus Pandit Suman Ghosh and Smt. Shashikala Ghosh, the founders of the Center for Indian Classical Music of Houston (CICMH), and Bharat Raval. They have been very supportive of the project. I am also grateful to my niece's husband Devanshu Patel, Smt.

Pratima Banik, and my friends from Indian Institute of Technology (IIT) at Kharagpur—Vilas Koleshvar and Suranjan Chatterjee, for reading substantial portions of drafts and providing their invaluable suggestions. Thank you to Ravishankar for thoroughly proofreading the book in the final stage and providing valuable suggestions. There have been many others, not mentioned here, who have provided valuable feedback. I am ever thankful to them.

I thank the Independent Book Publishers Association (IBPA) which has been a useful source of information and new contacts for me. Thank you to Pradeep Aeri and Ravi Narain for their brilliant talent in graphics and book design, and to Rima Kar Ghosh for polishing the manuscript with her fine line and copy editing.

I am immensely grateful to my children Neha, Kajal, and Jignesh, and my sons-in-law, Samit Patel and Jay Brahmbhatt, for their invaluable insight, constant support, and encouragement. I am deeply indebted to my wife Nita for thirty-nine years of generous support and for raising three outstanding children with me. My gratitude to the Almighty for recently blessing us with our first grandchild, Ishaani, bringing us good luck. I am grateful to my extended family, my sister, brothers, and their families for their love and support. I am indebted to my late parents, Shantaben and Jethalal Mehta, for raising me with love, instilling good values, and showering their blessings.

# Transliteration and Pronunciation Guide

The Devanāgarī (देवनागरी) characters in this book are transliterated according to the ISO 15919 international standard on the romanization of many Brahmic scripts. Each Devanāgarī character has a specific sound value.

| | | *(sounds like)* | | | *(sounds like)* |
|---|---|---|---|---|---|
| अ | a | o in son | ठ | ṭha | th in ant-hill |
| आ | ā | a in class | ड | ḍa | d in dog |
| इ | i | i in is | ढ | ḍha | ** |
| ई | ī | ee in bee | ण् | ṇ | n in under |
| उ | u | u in put | त | ta | t in tabla |
| ऊ | ū | oo in cool | थ | tha | th in thumb |
| ऋ | ṛ | in Kṛṣṇa | द | da | d in divine |
| ए | e | e in egg | ध | dha | th in then |
| ऐ | ai | i in high* | न | na | n in no |
| ओ | o | o in oh | प | pa | p in pen |
| औ | au | ow in now* | फ | pha | ph in phone |
| अं | ṁ | m in simple | ब | ba | b in but |
| अ: | ḥa | h in aha | भ | bha | bh in abhor |
| क | ka | k in key | म | ma | m in mother |
| ख | kha | kh in khan | य | ya | y in yes |
| ग | ga | g in girl | र | ra | r in run |
| घ | gha | gh in ghee | ल | la | l in love |
| ङ् | ṅ | n in single | व | va | v in van |
| च | ca | ch in churn | श | śa | sh in shine |
| छ | cha | ** | ष | ṣa | sh in show |
| ज | ja | j in jug | स | sa | s in Sun |
| झ | jha | jh in Jhansi | ह | ha | h in hug |
| ञ् | ñ | n in punch | क्ष | kṣa | ctio in action |
| ट | ṭa | t in toy | ज्ञ | jña | gn in gnostic |

** Do not have an exact English equivalent, an approximation is given here.*

*** Doesn't have an English equivalent sound.*

## Abbreviations

| | | |
|---|---|---|
| YS | = | Yudhiṣṭhira Śaka |
| BK | = | Before Kaliyuga |
| BL | = | Before Laukikābda |
| VS | = | Vikrama Samvat |
| BC | = | Before Christ |
| AD | = | Anno Domini (Latin for 'in the year of the Lord') |
| n.d. | = | no date |
| p. | = | page number |
| rpt. | = | reprinted |

# 1

# INTRODUCTION

## India – One of World's Oldest Civilization

Archaeological excavations in the Sindhu (Indus) valley in the early 1920s discovered the large well-planned cities of Harappa and Mohenjo-daro dating back to 3300–3200 BC. According to the then Director General of the Archaeological Survey of India, John Marshall (1931, Preface), 5,000 years ago, Panjab and Sindh, if not other parts of India as well, were enjoying an advanced and singularly uniform civilization of their own, closely akin to, and in some respects even superior to that of contemporary Mesopotamia and Egypt. For instance, the quality of the drainage system in these towns which included brick-lined sewers complete with man-holes was not seen in Europe until the time of the Roman Empire 3,000 years later (Johnsen, 2009, p. 20).

These and other discoveries led to India being acknowledged as one of the oldest civilizations in the world. Since then, numerous sites of similar or even older eras have been unearthed, encompassing a wide expanse from Jammu and Kashmir in the north to Gujarat in the south, and Baluchistan in the west to Uttar Pradesh in the east (Amarendra Nath, 2014). This enormous area, at least 700 miles from north to south and 800 miles from east to west, is much greater than the combined area of the contemporary Egyptian and Mesopotamian civilizations (Johnsen, 2009, p. 20).

## Contradiction in the Currently Accepted History of India

It is a paradox that while India is acknowledged as one of the four oldest civilizations in the world at more than 5,000 years old, in the currently accepted history, the earliest kingdoms in India are dated to only around 600 BC, with the birth of Gautama Buddha dated to 563 BC (Barraclough, 2001, p. 82). Of the other three oldest civilizations of the world, Egypt's earliest monarch, King Menes, is dated to 3100 BC (p. 58); the Sumerian city-states, the earliest political entities of Mesopotamia, are dated to 3000–2500 BC (p. 54), and the Shang kings, the earliest rulers in China, are dated to 1523 –1028 BC or 1751–1111 BC (p. 62). This prompts the following questions:

- Why are the earliest kings or political entities in India dated to no earlier than 600 BC?
- What happened in the period from around 3200 to 600 BC, a span of about 2,600 years?
- Who were the rulers/political entities during this time?
- What philosophy were they guided by?
- How did their contributions shape true Indian history?

## Intent of this Book

This book seeks to answer these questions, elucidate the true chronology and history of India, and explain how the original was distorted. It is not common knowledge, even within India, let alone the world, that the widely presented history and chronology of ancient India, is not the one recorded by Indians, but a distorted version created by European Indologists (mainly British and German) during the British colonial rule of India from the late 1700s to 1947. The next question that naturally springs to mind is—what motivated those historians?

## A Glance at the Distortions in History

The colonial era European Indologists were steeped in the biblical (Christian) version of world history wherein the world originated with Adam in 4006 BC as discussed in detail in Chapter 2. These Indologists could not accept the chronology of India going back to 3100+ BC. In an effort to perpetuate their convictions, the Indian chronology had to be repudiated and altered to no earlier than the Greek chronology which starts at about 600 BC. Additionally, the colonial rulers had a vested interest in showing Indians in a poor light to help them perpetuate their rule.

The colonial Indologists wrongly identified Chandragupta Maurya of

1534 BC, instead of Chandragupta I of the Gupta Dynasty of 327 BC, as a contemporary of Alexander which shrank ancient India's chronology by over 1,200 years. They made this wrong identification the basis for rewriting India's chronology and dated everything before and after Chandragupta Maurya in relation to him being the ruler around 326 BC. As the final result, these Indologists shrank India's chronology from 5,000 years to its last 2,500 years as discussed at length in Chapter 2. Table 1 and Figure 1 show some of the major distortions made to the chronology and history of ancient India.

**Table 1: Major distortions in the chronology of ancient India's history**

| Key Events or Persons | True Dates | False Dates | Antiquity Reduced by (Years) |
|---|---|---|---|
| Mahābhārata War | End of 3139 BC | Called mythical | |
| Writing of the Vedas | 3100+ BC | 1200–400 BC | 1900+ |
| Gautama Buddha | 1887–1807 BC | 563–483 BC | 1324 |
| Maurya Dynasty | 1534–1218 BC | 322–185 BC | 1212 |
| Kaniṣka | 1298–1234 BC | 120–144 AD | 1418 |
| Ādi Śaṅkarāchārya | 509–477 BC | 788–820 AD | 1297 |
| Gupta Dynasty | 327–82 BC | 320–550 AD | 647 |
| Varāhamihira | 123–41 BC | 6th century AD | About 600 |
| Vikramāditya | 82 BC–18 AD | Existence denied | |
| Śālivāhana | 78–138 AD | Existence denied | |

Their chronological misrepresentations moved the Maurya Dynasty of 1534–1218 BC to 322–185 BC, the Gupta Dynasty of 327–82 BC to AD 320–550, and Gautama Buddha's time from 1887–1807 BC to 563–483 BC (Venkatachelam, 1957a; Smith, 1914). Ādi Śaṅkarāchārya's antiquity was similarly reduced from 509–477 BC to AD 788–832.

These Indologists erased two great emperors of ancient India from history: Vikramāditya of Ujjain, the founder of the Vikrama *Samvat* (era) in 57 BC, and Śālivāhana, the great-grandson of Vikramāditya and the founder of the Śālivāhana *Śaka* (era) in AD 79. Both these calendars are still active in India, the Vikrama Samvat primarily in western and northern India as well as Nepal, while the Śālivāhana Śaka in much of the rest of India.

After denying the existence of Vikramāditya, these Indologists then declared that the Vikrama Samvat was named after Chandragupta II of the

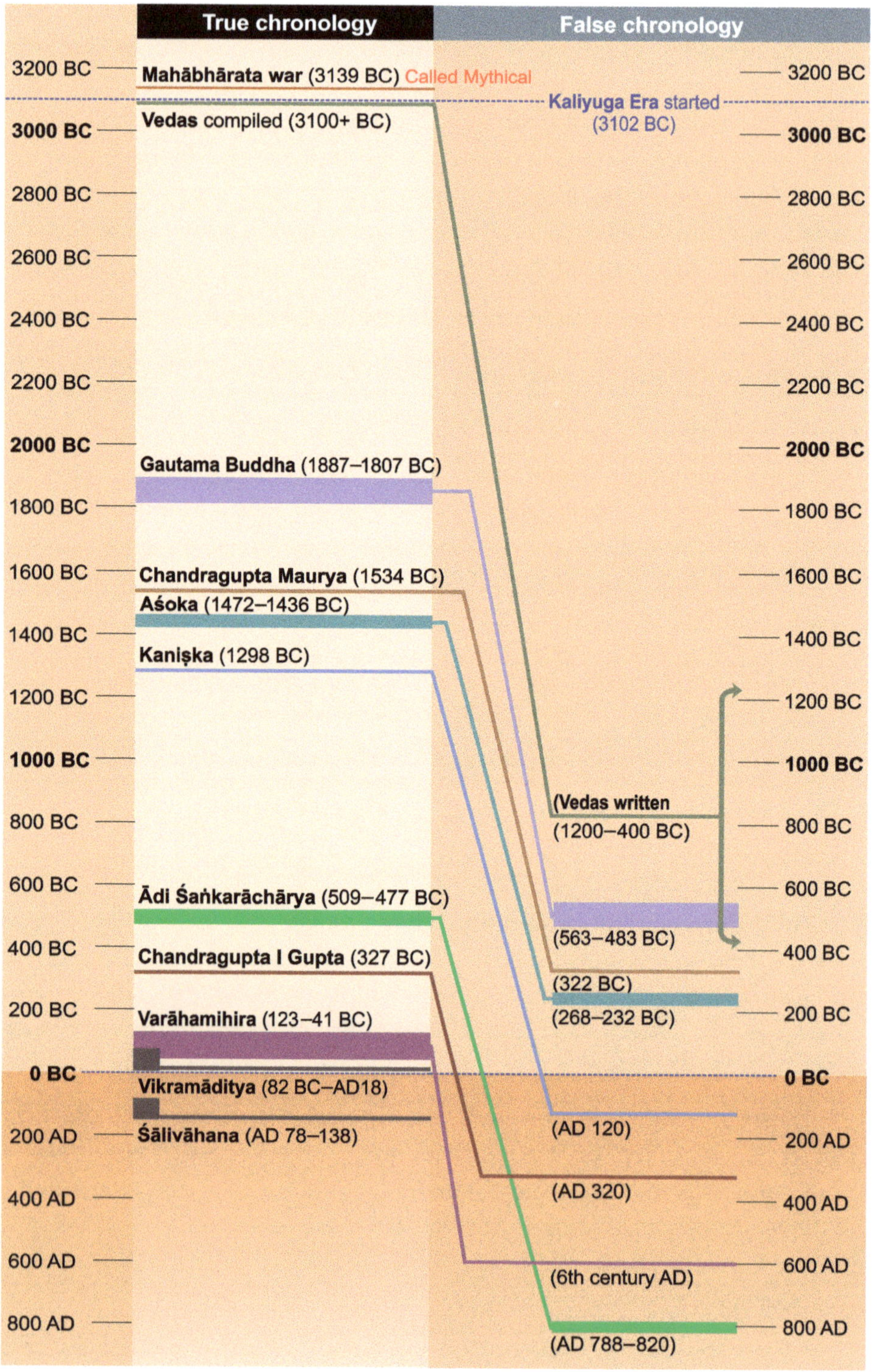


**Figure 1: Major distortions in ancient India's chronology and history**

Gupta Dynasty who also held the title of Vikramāditya, and supposedly reigned from AD 375 to 415. The history written from the colonial era is, therefore, strife with contradictions as seen below:

| Contradiction 1: | Contradiction 2: |
|---|---|
| If Vikramāditya ruled from AD 375–415 then why did the Era named after him start in 57 BC? | If Adi Śaṅkarāchārya repelled Buddhism and revived Hinduism during AD 788–820, and Gupta Emperors ruled from AD 320–550, then how is it that Gupta Emperors followed Hinduism? |

## Distortion of History Called Out

The 19th century British Indologist, William Hunter (1893, p. 5), who worked for decades in India for the British colonial government, recognized India's history written by Englishmen to be distorted. He wrote:

> “Short Indian histories, as written by Englishmen, usually dismiss the first two thousand years of their narrative in a few pages, and start by disclosing India as a conquered country. This plan is not good, either for Europeans in India or for the Indians themselves ; nor does it accord with the facts.”

The American Indologist, Linda Johnsen (2009, Ch. 2), has described at length in her book, *The Complete Idiot's Guide to Hinduism,* how "the westerners have gotten India's history completely wrong." Regarding Buddha's true birthdate, she states:

> “No less an authority than the sixteenth Dalai Lama has appealed to Western scholars to get together, clear their minds, and straighten the mess once and for all!” (p. 22)

## Past Attempts to Restore True History

In the course of my research, I came across the work of two great Indian historians of the 20th century who have worked exhaustively to restore the true chronology of Indian history—T. S. Narayana Sastry and Pandit Kota Venkatachelam.

After 20 years of intense research into the chronology of Ādi Śaṅkarāchārya and ancient India, T. S. Narayana Sastry published a biography of Ādi Śaṅkarāchārya, titled *The Age of Śankara,* in 1916, establishing his true chronology and history. He had planned to publish much more but his work was cut short when he passed away in the prime of his life. Manuscripts containing his invaluable research were lost, 'without a trace' as stated by his son, T. N. Kumaraswamy, in the preface to the second edition of his father's book released in 1971.

Pandit Kota Venkatachelam (1957a, p. vii) paid the following tribute to the work of T. S. Narayana Sastry in his book:

> “ The material discovered and unearthed by him and presented to us by Sri. T. S. Narayana Sastry is really invaluable for the reconstruction of the true history of Bharat. The enormous cost of his researches may be estimated from the regrettable fact that after his demise in 1917, his residence at Madras was sold for Rs. 1,25,000 to repay the debts he had contracted, with the interest accrued thereon, for acquiring the library and other equipment he needed for his researches. His scholarship, devotion to research, readiness to sacrifice for it and persistence in his endeavour deserve adequate recognition and the gratitude of the nation which he has not received so far, presumably due to the indifference and lukewarmness of the modern historical research scholars, which is very much to be regretted. We, for our part, hasten to tender to his memory, our heartfelt appreciation and gratitude.
>
> His writing may not be quite free from all errors but if we find a few such, it is our duty to correct them and allow for the errors and use his writings. We, for our part, have so amended and used them in this volume. ”

Pandit Kota Venkatachelam clocked four decades of painstakingly thorough research and published 24 books in the 1950s, some in Telugu and some in English. He set down in detail the actual timelines, encompassing a complete list of the kings, and their periods of reign, major dynasties, and their influence. Thus, he reestablished ancient India's true chronology and history, thoroughly refuting the altered history created during the British colonial rule. The following is a list of the books published in English by Pandit Kota Venkatachelam.

1. Historicity of Vikramāditya and Sālivāhana, 1951
2. Chronology of Nepal History Reconstructed, 1953
3. The plot in Indian Chronology, 1953
4. Chronology of Kashmir History Reconstructed, 1955
5. Age of Buddha, Milinda & Amtiyoka and Yugapuraṇa, 1956

6. Indian Eras, 1956

7. Chronology of Ancient Hindu History Part I, 1957

8. Chronology of Ancient Hindu History Part II, 1957

9. Age of the Mahabharata War (published posthumously), 1991

Since the beginning of the distortion in the late 18th century, numerous eminent Indologists have challenged the distortions in our history and its foundation. These include the 19th century French Sanskritist M. A. Troyer (1840), K. T. Telang (1875, p. cxviii) who was a Bombay High Court advocate and a Sanskrit scholar, Swami Vivekananda (Advaita Ashrama, 1964, p. 534), T. S. Narayana Sastry (1916/1971), N. Jagannadha Rao (1931), M. Krishnamachariar (1937), D. S. Triveda (1947), Pandit Venkatachelam, K. D. Sethna (1989), David Frawley (1991, 1998), Michel Danino and Sujata Nahar (1996), Francois Gautier (1996), Rajendra Singh Kushwaha (2003), Vedveer Arya (2015), and many others.

## Time to Reinstate our True History

It is disheartening that even after 75 years of India's independence, the distorted history written by her past colonial masters pervades the curricula in the schools and colleges within and outside of India. It is a tremendous injustice to the people of the Indian subcontinent, and humanity in general. Another misconception spread by those same European Indologists is that Indians did not record their history when in fact, the opposite is true. There is no dearth of historical material in and of India, as discussed in Chapter 3.

It is high time indeed, and also our responsibility to uproot the false chronology, restore the true history of ancient India, and pass it on to the future generations. If this is not done soon, the false timeline and history which is only 150–200 years old will become permanent. It has been getting institutionalized over time and will be even more difficult to uproot as the years pass. For example, a TV series, *Chakravartin Ashok Samrat (2015)*, shows Chandragupta Maurya and Chāṇakya as contemporaries of Alexander when, in reality, they existed 1,200 years before Alexander's time! True chronology is the foundation of true history. Without it, history is a story without foundation.

## A Glance at the Book

This book describes the true, continuous, and connected history and chronology of India from before the time of the Mahābhārata War in 3139

BC to AD 1192. It includes great personalities, rulers, and dynasties of the major political centers of ancient India such as Magadha, Hastināpura, Ujjain, Kashmir, Nepal, and more.

The chronology and history described in this book is a unique synthesis of the research by T. S. Narayana Sastry, Pandit Kota Venkatachelam, and K. D. Sethna. Each of these outstanding 20th century historians delved deep to find the truth with extensive supporting literature. Pandit Venkatachelam, alone, has cited hundreds of references, most of which I was able to obtain, study carefully, and verify.

T. S. Narayana Sastry, Pandit Kota Venkatachelam, K. D. Sethna, and other historians acknowledged in this book deserve our sincere recognition and gratitude for their dedication to restoring India's true chronology and history. Had it not been for their lifelong dedication to its truth, we might not have been able to learn our true history.

New research literature available since the publication of books by Pandit Venkatachelam in the 1950s, has enabled me to refine his work, sometimes with a different conclusion. K. D. Sethna's book, *Ancient India in a New Light* (1989), has helped resolve critical questions including the implication of the bilingual inscription in Kandahar on its dating. Other historians cited in this book have shed more light on the history, laying a firm foundation for factual accounting. I have built on that by including significant additional material.

Restoring true history is like putting together a puzzle of a thousand pieces where each puzzle piece must connect on all its sides, bound by the corners. The history of India written under British rule is discontinuous; the corners of the puzzle do not connect with other events of the same time. The true history and chronology of ancient India established in this book is continuous, connected, and fits well with the surrounding pieces. I recognize the limitations of uncovering thousands of years of history and also admit that some of the history and chronology presented in this book may be further refined in the future. If this book inspires the readers to further investigate, dive deeper, and push the boundaries of our knowledge, my joy will know no bounds.

Figure 2 shows in one chart the true history and chronology of the major dynasties and personalities of India from 3400 BC to AD 1192, a span of about 4,600 years.

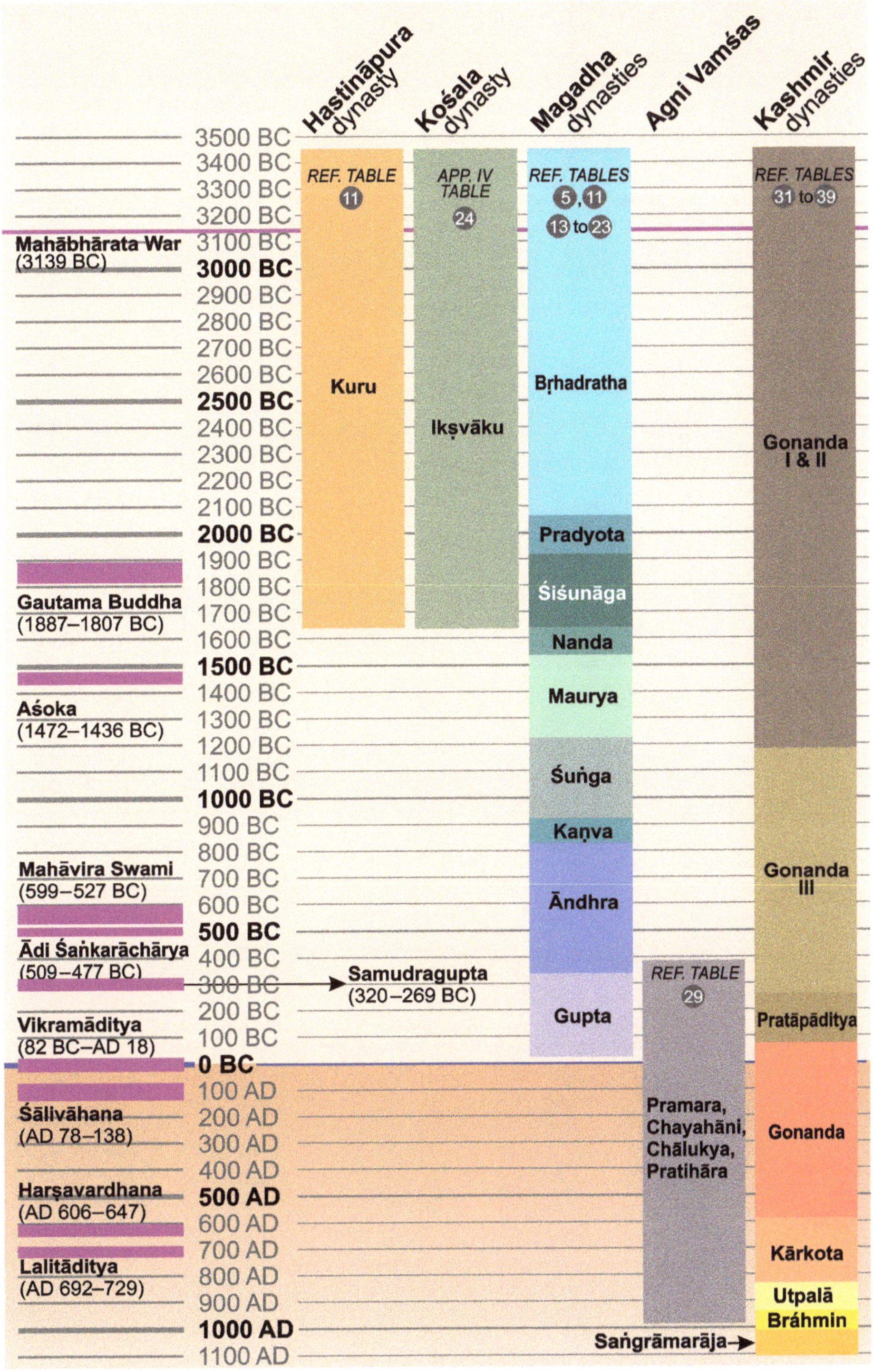


**Figure 2: True history and chronology of ancient India at a glance**

The next chapter details step-wise, the journey of when, why, and how the history of ancient India was rewritten into a false narrative during the British rule of India. Chapter 3 provides a variety of sources containing the true history of India from the vast literature of ancient India. Chapter 4 introduces the major calendars that were either used in the past or continue to be used and discusses some of those in detail. Knowledge of these calendars is essential to learning the true chronology of ancient India. Reading and understanding the information provided in Chapters 2 to 4 first will help in understanding the rest of the chapters better.

Chapters 5 through 13 narrate the true history and chronology of the various major centers and great personalities of ancient India. Chapter 14 discusses the key inscriptions and archaeological evidence supporting the great antiquity of India. Chapter 15 debunks the myth of the Aryan Invasion of India. Finally, Chapter 16 concludes with a summary of the key points and provides a conclusion.

## References

1. Advaita Ashrama (1964). 'The East and the West.' in *The Complete Works of Swami Vivekananda: Mayavati Memorial Edition* (8th ed., Vol. 5). Calcutta.
2. Amarendra Nath, Dr. (2014). *Excavations at Rakhigarhi: 1997–98 to 1999–2000.* Archaeological Survey of India.
3. Arnett, Robert (1996). *India Unveiled.* Columbus, GA: Atman Press.
4. Arya, Vedveer (2015). *The Chronology of Ancient India: Victim of Concoctions and Distortions.* Hyderabad: Aryabhata Publications.
5. Barraclough, Geoffrey (Ed.) (2001). 'The early empires of Mesopotamia c. 3500 to 1600 BC, p. 54; Ancient Egypt and her empires, p. 58; The beginnings of Chinese civilisation to 500 BC, p. 62; India: the first empires, p. 82.' in *Harper Collins Atlas of World History* (2nd rev. ed.). Michigan: Borders Press & Harper Collins.
6. Danino, Michel, and Sujata Nahar (1996). *The Invasion that Never Was.* New Delhi: Song of Humanity.
7. Frawley, David (1991). *Gods, Sages and Kings: Vedic Secrets of Ancient Civilization.* Twin Lakes, WI: Lotus Press.
8. Frawley, David (1998). *The Myth of the Aryan Invasion of India.* https://www.academia.edu/64378583/The_myth_of_the_Aryan_invasion_of_India (Accessed on February 1, 2023).
9. Gautier, Francois (1996). *Rewriting Indian History.* New Delhi: Vikas Publishing House.
10. Hunter, William Wilson (1893). *A Brief History of the Indian Peoples* (20th ed.). Oxford: Clarendon Press.
11. Jagannadha Rao, Nadimpalli (1931). *The Age of the Mahabharata War.*
12. Johnsen, Linda (2009). *The Complete Idiot's Guide to Hinduism* (2nd ed.). Alpha Books.
13. Krishnamachariar, M. (1937). *History of Classical Sanskrit Literature: Being an elaborate account of all branches of Classical Sanskrit Literature, with full Epigraphical and Archaeological Notes and References, an Introduction dealing with Languages, Philology and Chronology, and Index of Authors and Works.* Madras.

14. Kushwaha, Dr. Rajendra Singh (2003). *Glimpses of Bhāratiya History*. New Delhi: Ocean Books.

15. Marshall, Sir John (Ed.) (1931). *Mohenjo-daro and The Indus Civilization: Being an official account of the Archaeological Excavations at Mohenjo-daro carried out by the Government of India between the years 1922 and 1927* (Vol. 1). London: Arthur Probsthain.

16. Narayana Sastry, T. S. (1916). *The Age of Śankara* (2nd ed. 1971, edited by T. N. Kumaraswamy). Madras: B. G. Paul & Co.

17. Prakashananda Saraswati (2006). *The True History and the Religion of India: A Concise Encyclopedia of Authentic Hinduism*. New Delhi: MacMillan.

18. Sethna, K. D. (1989). *Ancient India in a New Light: I. The Challenge of India's Traditional Chronology, II. The Momentous Evidence of Megasthenes, III. A Reconstruction of Ancient Indian History: Aśoka – and Before and After*. New Delhi: Aditya Prakashan.

19. Smith, Vincent A. (1914). *Early History of India: From 600 B.C. to the Muhammadan Conquest including the Invasion of Alexander the Great* (3rd ed.). Oxford: Clarendon Press.

20. Telang, Kāshināth Trimbak (1875). 'Introductory Essay.' in *The Bhagavadgita: Translated into English Blank Verse with Notes and an Introductory Essay*. Bombay: Atmaram Sagoon & Co.

21. Triveda, Dr. D. S. (1947). 'The Date of Lord Buddha, 1793 B.C.', *Bhāratīya Vidyā: A Monthly Research Organ of the Bhavan on all subjects connected with Indology*, Vol. 8 (8, 9 & 10, Aug–Sept–Oct), 220–238. Bombay: Bharatiya Vidya Bhavan.

22. Troyer, M. A. (1840). *Rādjataranginī: Histoire Des Rois Du Kachmīr*. Paris: L'Impremerie Nationale (MDCCCXL).

23. Venkatachelam, Pandit Kota (1955). *Chronology of Kashmir History Reconstructed*. Arya Vijnana Series, Publication 18. Vijayawada.

24. Venkatachelam, Pandit Kota (Kali 5052, AD 1951). *The Historicity of Vikramāditya & Sālivāhana [A Great Research work]*. Arya Vijnanam 10, Publication 15. Vijayawada.

25. Venkatachelam, Pandit Kota (Kali 5054, AD 1953a). *Chronology of Nepal History Reconstructed (Nepalraja Vamsavali)*. Arya Vijnana, Publication 16. Vijayawada.

26. Venkatachelam, Pandit Kota (Kali 5054, AD 1953b). *The Plot in Indian Chronology*. Arya Vijnana, Publication 17. Vijayawada.

27. Venkatachelam, Pandit Kota (Kali 5057, AD 1956a). *Indian Eras*. Arya Vijnana Grandhamala. Vijayawada.

28. Venkatachelam, Pandit Kota (Kali 5057, AD 1956b). *The Age of Buddha, Milinda & Amtiyoka and Yugapurana*. Arya Vijnana Series, Publication 20. Vijayawada.

29. Venkatachelam, Pandit Kota (Kali 5058, AD 1957a). *Chronology of Ancient Hindu History Part I*. Arya Vijnana Grandhamala, Publication 23. Vijayawada.

30. Venkatachelam, Pandit Kota (Kali 5058, AD 1957b). *Chronology of Ancient Hindu History Part II*. Arya Vijnana Grandhamala, Publication 24. Vijayawada.

31. Venkatachelam, Pandit Kota (Kali 5092, AD 1991). *Age of The Mahabharata War*. Arya Vijnana Grandhamala, Publication 25. Vijayawada.

# 2

# WHEN, WHY, AND HOW THE FALSE HISTORY WAS WRITTEN

It is necessary to understand in a stepwise manner when, why, and how the false history of ancient India was written. This will enable us to effectively correct the distortions by European Indologists under the patronage of the British rule in India from the late 1700s to 1947.

## Beginning of the False History

Bengal was the first region of India to fall to the British East India Company in AD 1757, after the battle of Plassey. In 1784, William Jones, a British scholar and judge, founded the Asiatic Society in Kolkata, Bengal, under the patronage of Warren Hastings, the then governor-general of India for the British East India Company. From the beginning of the society in 1784 to 1828, only Europeans were elected as members of the society. Indians were first admitted as members in 1829 (Britannica, 2023). The name was later changed to The Asiatic Society of Bengal in 1832 and its works were published under the name of Asiatic researches.

William Jones had heard of the high antiquity of India's history from his conversations with the pandits in Bengal. He could not believe that the antiquity of India's history spanned several thousand years and was dismissive of it from the beginning. As president of the Asiatic Society, William Jones presented a paper, *On the Chronology of the Hindus*, in January 1788. He stated (1799a, p. 111; 1807a, p. 1):

> “The great antiquity of the *Hindus* is believed so firmly by themselves, and has been the subject of so much conversation among *Europeans*, that a

short view of their Chronological system, which has not yet been exhibited from certain authorities, may be acceptable. ... I propose to lay before you a concise account of *Indian* Chronology, extracted from *Sanscrit* books, or collected from conversations with *Pandits*, and to subjoin a few remarks on their system, without attempting to decide a question, which I shall venture to start, " whether it is not in fact the same with " our own, but embellished and obscured by the fancy of their poets and " the riddles of their astronomers ?" ”

In the same paper, William Jones, presented the chronology of the kings of Magadha as he understood it which is shown in Table 2. He had extracted the chronology from the *Purānārtha Pracāśa (The Purāṇas Explained)*, composed in Sanskrit by Pandit Rādhākānt Sarman who was 'a *Pandit* of extensive learning and great fame among the *Hindus* of this province', in the words of William Jones (1799a, p. 119, 137).

**Table 2: Purānic chronology of Magadha as understood by William Jones, AD 1788**

| Kings of Magadha | Starting Year, BC |
|---|---|
| The family of Jarāsandha: (Sahadeva, Mārjari, Srutasravas, Ayutāuysh, Niramitra, Sunacshatra, Vrihetsena, Carmajit, Srutanjaya, Vipra, Suchi, Csema, Suvrata, Dhermasutra, Srama, Dridhasena, Sumati, Subala, Sunita, Satyajit), Total 20 Reigns = 1000 years | 3100 |
| Pradyota Kings (Pradyota, Pālaca, Visāchayupa, Rājaca, Nandiverdhana), Total 5 Reigns =138 years | 2100 |
| Siśunāga Kings (Siśunāga, Cācaverna, Cshemadherman, Cshetrajnya, Vidhisara, Ajātasatru, Darbhaca, Ajaya, Nandiverdhana, Mahānandi), Total 10 Reigns = 360 years | 1962 |
| Nanda Kings = Total 100 years | 1602 |
| Maurya Kings (Chandragupta, Vārisāra, Aśocaverdhana, Suyaśas, Deśaraťha, Sangata, Sāliśūca, Somaśarman, Satadhanwas, Vrihadraťha), Total 10 reigns = 137 years | 1502 |
| Sunga Kings, 10 Reigns =112 years | 1365 |
| Canna Kings, 4 Reigns = 345 years | 1253 |
| Āndhra Kings, 21 Reigns = 456 years | 908 |
| Death of Chandrabija, the last Āndhra king | 452 |

Although there are significant errors in the chronology presented by William Jones (Table 2), which starts from 3100 BC and ends in 452 BC, it is still not too far from the true chronology which starts from 3138 BC and ends in 327 BC. However, this chronology was just not acceptable to William Jones. The following paragraphs show, step by step, how this near-truth chronology was distorted and shrunk by thousands of years from this point in time onwards as the decades passed and the British grip on India tightened.

The significant errors in the chronology are as follows. In the first dynasty hailing from the family of Jarāsandha, there were 22 kings, starting from Mārjari. However, William Jones arbitrarily reduced the number of kings in the dynasty from 22 to 20, that too, starting with Sahadeva who was the predecessor of Mārjari. Thus, William Jones effectively reduced the number of kings in the dynasty from the original 22 starting from Mārjari to 19. Moreover, the years of reign for all the dynasties from the Maurya Dynasty onwards are wrong. This is further discussed in Chapter 7. After presenting this chronology, William Jones (1799a, p. 142) stated:

> “ After the death of CHANDRABĪJA, which happened, according to the *Hindus*, 396 years before VICRAMĀDITYA, or 452 [= 396 + 56] B. C. we hear no more of *Magadha* as an independent kingdom ; but RĀDHĀCĀNT has exhibited the names of seven dynasties. … ”

Jones concluded (1799a, p. 142–143), saying:

> “ On the whole we may safely close the most authentic system of *Hindu* chronology, that I have been able to procure, with the death of CHANDRABĪJA. Should any farther information be attainable, we shall, perhaps, in due time, attain it either from books or inscriptions in the *Sanscrit* language ; … and that the *fourth*, or *historical*, age cannot be carried farther back than about two thousand years before CHRIST. ”

By the term *'fourth*, or *historical*, age' in the preceding sentence, William Jones meant *Kaliyuga*, the fourth age in the sequence of the Satyayuga, Tretāyuga, Dvāparayuga, and Kaliyuga cycle. Jones added that he was not willing to accept the beginning of this fourth age (Kaliyuga) before about 2000 BC. We will see later that this was because of his strong belief in the biblical version of world chronology. He then conjectured a shortened chronology (1799a, p. 144) as shown in Table 3.

In the first line of Table 3, we see 'Abhimanyu, *son of* ARJUN'. William Jones accepted Abhimanyu and Arjun as historical and guessed Buddha's date to be 1027 BC which is in contrast to the currently taught date of 563–483 BC. As shown in the second last line of the table, William Jones did not doubt the existence of VIKRAMĀDITYA in 56 BC whom the colonial Indologists of

**Table 3: Shortened chronology conjectured by William Jones, AD 1788**

| | Y. B. C. |
|---|---|
| Abhimanyu, *ſon of* Arjun, | 2029 |
| Pradyóta, | 1029 |
| Buddha, | 1027 |
| Nanda, | 699 |
| Balin, | 149 |
| Vicrama'ditya, | 56 |
| De'vapa'la, *king of* Gaur, | 23 |

the later time declared non-existent. William Jones' conjecture continued as follows. He stated further (1799a, p. 144):

> “If we take the date of Buddha's appearances from ABU'L FAZAL, we must place ABHIMANYU 2368 years before CHRIST, unless we calculate from the twenty kings of *Magadha,* and allow *seven hundred* years instead of *a thousand,* between ARJUN and PRADYOTA, which will bring us again very nearly to the date exhibited in the table ;”

Further reading of the paper shows that Jones, thus, continued to play with the original chronology to shrink it according to his imagination and preconceived notions.

## Behind the Thinking of William Jones

The next table showcases the beliefs and thinking of William Jones which brought about his reasoning that distorted the actual chronology of Hindu kings and thereby, our ancient history. Table 4 shows the chronology presented by William Jones (1799a, p. 147) in the same paper referred to earlier.

Note that the table starts with ADAM in the first column titled CHRISTIAN and MUSELMAN; the middle column titled HINDU shows MENU I as the first historical person. The last column shows the number of years *'of our era'* elapsed before the year AD 1788, the year in which William Jones prepared the table. Thus, Table 4 shows that William Jones was comparing the chronology of India with the biblical (Christian) version of history which believes that the world started with Adam 5,794 years before AD 1788, i.e. in the year 4006 BC (= 5,794 – AD 1788). Jones was trying to fit India's history within the biblical

**Table 4: Chronological table by William Jones, AD 1788**

A CHRONOLOGICAL TABLE,

ACCORDING TO ONE OF THE HYPOTHESES INTIMATED IN THE PRECEDING TRACT.

| CHRISTIAN and MUSELMAN. | HINDU. | *Years from* 1788 *of our era.* |
|---|---|---|
| ADAM, | MENU I. Age I. | 5794 |
| NOAH, | MENU II. | 4737 |
| Deluge, | | 4138 |
| *Nimrod,* | *Hiranyacaſipu.* Age II. | 4006 |
| *Bel,* | *Bali,* | 3892 |
| RAMA, | RAMA. Age III. | 3817 |
| *Noah*'s death, | | 3787 |
| | *Pradyóta,* | 2817 |
| | BUDDHA. Age IV. | 2815 |
| | *Nanda,* | 2487 |
| | *Balin,* | 1937 |
| | *Vicramáditya,* | 1844 |
| | *Dévapála,* | 1811 |
| CHRIST, | | 1787 |
| | *Náráyanpála,* | 1721 |
| | *Saca,* | 1709 |
| *Walíd,* | | 1080 |
| *Mahmúd,* | | 786 |
| *Chengiz,* | | 548 |
| *Taimúr,* | | 391 |
| *Babur,* | | 276 |
| *Nádirſháh,* | | 49 |

T 2. ON

timeline of history. This clearly shows that William Jones was highly guided by the biblical chronology of world history prevalent in Europe in his time, the late 18th century.

According to the biblical (Christian) version of the history, as shown in Table 4, the 'Deluge' (third line in the table) occurred in 2350 BC (= 4,138 – AD 1788). Therefore, according to the biblical version which William Jones believed in, none of the dynasties could have existed before 2350 BC. This date was against the antiquity of the Indian history documented in the Purāṇas, including the fact that the Kaliyuga Era started in 3102 BC. In 'The Tenth Anniversary Discourse' delivered to the Asiatic Society on February 28, 1793, as president, William Jones (1799b, p. 3) stated:

> "In the first place, we can not surely deem it an inconsiderable advantage, that all our historical records have confirmed the *Mosaic* accounts of the primitive world ; and our testimony on that subject ought to have the greater weight, "

Thus, we see in William Jones' own words that he was strongly guided by his deep conviction in the biblical version of the history that the world started in 4006 BC, and in the white man's superiority complex that Indian history could not be older than European history. Jones did not even shy away from using power to rewrite history as follows in the same paper (1799b, p. 5–6):

> "The numerous *Purānas* and *Itihāsas*, or poems mythological and heroick, are completely in our power ; and from them we may recover some disfigured but valuable pictures of ancient manners and governments ;"

Yet, further in the same paper (1799b, p. 6), Jones stated:

> "It is now clearly proved, that the first *Purāna* contains an account of the deluge ; between which and the *Mohammedan* conquests the history of genuine *Hindu* government must of course be comprehended ; but we know from an arrangement of the seasons in the Astronomical work of PARASARA, that the war of the PANDAVAS could not have happened earlier than the close of the twelfth century before CHRIST ; and Seleucus [who attacked India around 300 BC] must, therefore, have reigned about nine centuries after that war. Now the age of VIKRAMADITYA is given ; and if we can fix on an *Indian* prince contemporary with SELEUCUS, we shall have three given points in the line of time between RAMA, or the first *Indian* colony, and CHANDRABIJA, the last *Hindu* monarch who reigned in *Behar*; so that only eight hundred or a thousand years will remain almost wholly dark ;"

In this way, the newly fabricated chronology of ancient India began to take shape as shown in Table 4, according to the belief and fancy of William Jones. He moved the Mahābhārata War to no earlier than the 12th century BC.

The sense of superiority of Europeans over Asians exhibited by William Jones is glaringly obvious further down in the same paper (1799b, p. 8) where he states:

> "To that cause he would impute the decided inferiority of most *Asiatic* nations, ancient and modern, to those in *Europe* who are blest with happier governments ;"

## The Monumental Misidentification – The Sheet Anchor of the False History

The greatest mistake and the harm done to the chronology and history of ancient India is the misidentification of *'Sandracottus'*, the Indian king referred to by the ancient Greek writers of Alexander's time, with Chandragupta Maurya of 1534 BC instead of Chandragupta I of the Gupta Dynasty of 327 BC. After all, Alexander invaded India in 326 BC. Unfortunately, with this wrong identification, India's history was cut short by more than 1,200 years.

It was William Jones (1799b, p. 11) who first suggested during his presidential address in 1793 his so-called discovery of the identity of Chandragupta Maurya with *'Sandracottus'* of the classical Greek writers of Alexander's time, as follows:

> "This discovery led to another of great moment ; for CHANDRAGUPTA... was no other than that very SANDRACOTTUS who concluded a treaty with SELEUCUS NICATOR ; ... and may in round numbers consider the twelve and three hundredth years before CHRIST as two certain epochs between *Rāma*, who conquered *Silān* a few centuries after the flood, and *Vicramadiya*, who died at *Ujjayini* fifty-seven years before the beginning of our era."

William Jones did not give his arguments for this so-called discovery and passed away shortly after in 1794. Subsequently, Captain Francis Wilford (1799, p. 262), a fellow member of the Asiatic Society, took up the subject and continued the misidentification using false arguments, stating:

> "*Chandra-Gupta*, or he who was saved by the interposition of *Lunus* or the *Moon*, is called also *Chandra* in a poem quoted by SIR WILLIAM JONES. The Greeks call him *Sandracuptos, Sandracottos*, and *Androcottos*. *Sandrocottos* is generally used by the *historians of Alexander* ; and *Sandracuptos* is found in the works of *Athenacas. Sir William Jones*, from a poem written by *Somadeva*, and a tragedy called the coronation of *Chandra* or *Chandra-Gupta*, discovered that he really was the *Indian* king mentioned by the *historians of Alexander*, under the name of *Sandracottos*."

Francis Wilford (1799, p. 262), then explicitly linked the name *'Sandracottus'* with Chandragupta Maurya instead of Chandragupta I of the Gupta Dynasty as follows:

> "The history of *Chandra-Gupta* is related, though in few words, in the *Vishṇu-purāna*, the *Bhāgawat*, and two other books, one of which is called *Brahatcatha*, and the other is a lexicon called *Camandaca* : the two last are supposed to be about six or seven hundred years old.
>
> In the *Vishṇu-purāna* we read, "unto *Nanda* shall be born nine sons ; *Cotilya*, his minister shall destroy them, and place *Chandra-Gupta* on the throne.""

Talking about Nanda, Wilford (p. 263) stated further:

> "by *Mura* he had *Chandra-Gupta*, and many others, who were known by the general appellation of *Mauryas*, because they were born of *Mura*."

Thus, *'Sandracottus'* of the ancient Greek writers was identified as Chandragupta Maurya instead of Chandragupta I of the Gupta Dynasty. It may be possible that neither William Jones nor the followers of his theory knew of the existence of Chandragupta I, who founded the Gupta Dynasty in 327 BC succeeding the Āndhra Dynasty to the throne of Magadha. However, this misidentification became the sheet anchor of the false history and chronology of India written by the colonial era Indologists as follows.

## Max Müller Concretized the Misidentification and the False Chronology

Though Professor Lassen (1800–1876), a Norwegian-born orientalist, subsequently attempted to further bolster William Jones' conjecture, it was Friedrich Max Müller (1859/1926), a German Sanskritist, who declared that *Sandracottus* of the ancient Greek writers was identical with Chandragupta Maurya.

Max Müller (1823–1900) was initially employed in Britain in 1847 by the British East India Company to translate the *Rig-Veda-Sanhita of Sayanacharya* (Max Müller, 1849) from Sanskrit to English at a salary of 200 pounds a year by preparing 50 sheets to print each year. Max Müller was pleased with the offer (Max Müller, G., 1903/2005, p. 64, 73). Later, he was appointed a professor at the University of Oxford. Max Müller lived the rest of his life in Britain and never visited India.

Max Müller denounced the chronology of India preserved in the Purāṇas to be vague and unsystematic and proceeded to change the dates of chief events of ancient India's history. The following excerpts show Max Müller's thinking. He stated (1859/1926, p. 143–144):

“ **Everything in Indian chronology depends on the date of Chandragupta,** Chandragupta was the grandfather of Aśoka, and the contemporary of Seleucus Nicator. Now, according to Chinese chronology, Aśoka would have lived, to waive minor difference, 850 or 750 B. C., according to Ceylonese chronology, 315 B. C. **Either of these dates is impossible, because it does not agree with the chronology of Greece, and hence both the Chinese and Ceylonese dates of Buddha's death must be given up as equally valueless for historical calculations.**

**There is but one means through which the history of India can be connected with that of Greece, and its chronology be reduced to its proper limits.** Although we look in vain in the literature of the Brāhmans or Buddhists for any allusion to Alexander's conquest, and although it is impossible to identify any of the historical events, related by Alexander's companions, with the historical traditions of India, one name has fortunately been preserved by classical writers who describe the events immediately following Alexander's conquest, to form a connecting link between the history of the East and the West. This is the name of Sandracottus or Sandrocyptus, the Sanskrit Chandragupta.

We learn from classical writers, Justin, Arrian, Diodorus Siculus, Strabo, Quintus Curtius and Plutarch, that in Alexander's time there was on the Ganges a powerful king of the name of Xandrames, and that soon after Alexander's invasion, a new empire was founded there by Sandracottus or Sandrocyptus. ” [Emphasis added]

The statements highlighted in bold in the preceding paragraphs show how Max Müller believed that the chronology of Greece was the standard to which the chronology of India must fit. This approach left no room for the chronology of India preceding Greek history. Max Müller (1859/1926, p. 145–146) stated further in the same book:

“ There is in the list of kings of India the name of Chandragupta, and the resemblance of this name with the name of Sandracottus or Sandracyptus was first, I believe, pointed out by Sir William Jones : Wilford, Professor Wilson and Professor Lassen have afterwards added further evidence in confirmation of Sir W. Jones's conjecture ; and although other scholars, and particularly M. Troyer, in his edition of the Rājataraṅgiṇi, have raised objections, we shall see that the evidence in favour of the identity of Chandragupta and Sandrocyptus is such as to admit of no reasonable doubt. It is objected that the Greeks called the king of the powerful empire beyond the Indus, *Xandrames,* or *Aggramen.* Now the last name is evidently a mere misspelling for Xandrames, and this Xandrames is not the same as Sandracottus. Xandrames, if we understand the Greek accounts rightly, is the predecessor of Chandragupta or rather the last king of the empire conquered by Sandracottus. ”

Thus, Max Müller (1859/1926, p. 146) recognized that the name *'Xandrames'* was not matching with Chandragupta. Still, he continued with the conjecture as shown below:

> “ If, however, it should be maintained, that these two names were intended for one and the same king, the explanation would still be very easy. For Chandragupta (the protected of the moon), is called Chandra, the Moon ; and Chandramas, in Sanskrit, is a synonym of Chandra. ”

Interestingly, Max Müller admitted (p. 146):

> “ Xandrames, however, was no doubt intended as different from Chandragupta. Xandrames must have been king of Prasii [Magadha] before Sandracottus, and during the time of Alexander's wars. ”

In the line below, comes a far-fetched conjecture of Max Müller (p. 146):

> “ If this Xandrames is the same as the last Nanda, the agreement between the Greek account of this mean extraction, and the Hindu account of Nand being a Śudra, would be very striking. ”

How could *'Xandrames'* be the same as the last Nanda? *Xandrames* of the Greek writers does not sound similar to Nanda by any stretch of the imagination! Max Müller was forced to admit that the identification of *Sandracottus* of Greeks with Chandragupta of the Maurya Dynasty could be erroneous, for, he said (1859/1926, p. 146):

> “ It is not, however, quite clear whether the same person is meant in the Greek and Hindu accounts. ”

A little further in the same book (p. 146), confirming his doubts, he said:

> “ Plutarch says distinctly that Sandracottus reigned soon after, that is soon after Xandrames, and we know from Justin, that it was Sandracottus, and not Xandrames, who waged wars with captains of Alexander. ”

Therefore, Max Müller knew that the identification of *'Sandracottus'* of the Greek writers as Chandragupta Maurya was likely wrong as it did not match up with their accounts. *Xandrames* (Chandramas or Chandrasri) was the emperor preceding Chandragupta I of the Gupta Dynasty. However, Max

Müller ignored his doubts and moved on with this misidentification blunder, reducing the antiquity of Chandragupta Maurya by more than 1,200 years. He made this greatest misidentification the 'Sheet Anchor' for dating the rest of ancient India's history.

The wrong sheet anchor was then blindly followed by all European Indologists of the 19th and 20th centuries and their Indian followers. Everything else in ancient India's history, forward and backward, was dated in relation to Chandragupta Maurya's newly assigned date of 321 BC. The beginning of the reign of Emperor Aśoka, Chandragupta Maurya's grandson, was assigned the year 269 BC; the nirvana of Gautam Buddha was assigned the year 483 BC, 214 years before Aśoka's time. The entire Bṛhadratha and Pradyota dynasties, and the kings of the Śiśunāga Dynasty preceding Gautam Buddha's time were discarded.

Thus, the chronology of Magadha, and thereby, of ancient India was shrunk from its original date of 3138 BC (Krishnamachariar, 1937, p. lxxii ; Venkatachelam, 1957a) to about 600 BC as shown in Table 5 and Figure 3. In keeping with the same tradition, Vincent Smith (1914, p. 31) an eminent Indologist of the early 20th century who worked for the British colonial government in India from 1871 to 1900, begins his book, *Early History of India,* from about 600 BC. The history and chronology of Kashmir and Nepal were shrunk similarly.

**Table 5: Puranic (True) vs. Colonial (False) chronology of Magadha**

| | Years of Reign (Dates) | |
|---|---|---|
| **Dynasty Name** | **Purāṇic Chronology (True)** | **Colonial Chronology (False)** |
| Bṛhadratha (बृहद्रथ) | 1006 (3138–2132 BC) | Discarded |
| Pradyota (प्रद्योत) | 138 (2132–1994 BC) | Discarded |
| Śiśunāga (शिशुनाग) | 360 (1994–1634 BC) | 230 (602–372 BC) |
| Nanda (नन्द) | 100 (1634–1534 BC) | 50 (372–322 BC) |
| Maurya (मौर्य) | 316 (1534–1218 BC) | 137 (322–185 BC) |
| Suṅga (शुंग) | 300 (1218–918 BC) | 112 (185–73 BC) |
| Kaṇva (कण्व) | 85 (918–833 BC) | 45 (73–28 BC) |
| Āndhra (आन्ध्र) | 506 (833–327 BC) | 253 (28 BC–225 AD) |
| Gupta (गुप्त) | 245 (327–82 BC) | 230 (320–550 AD) |

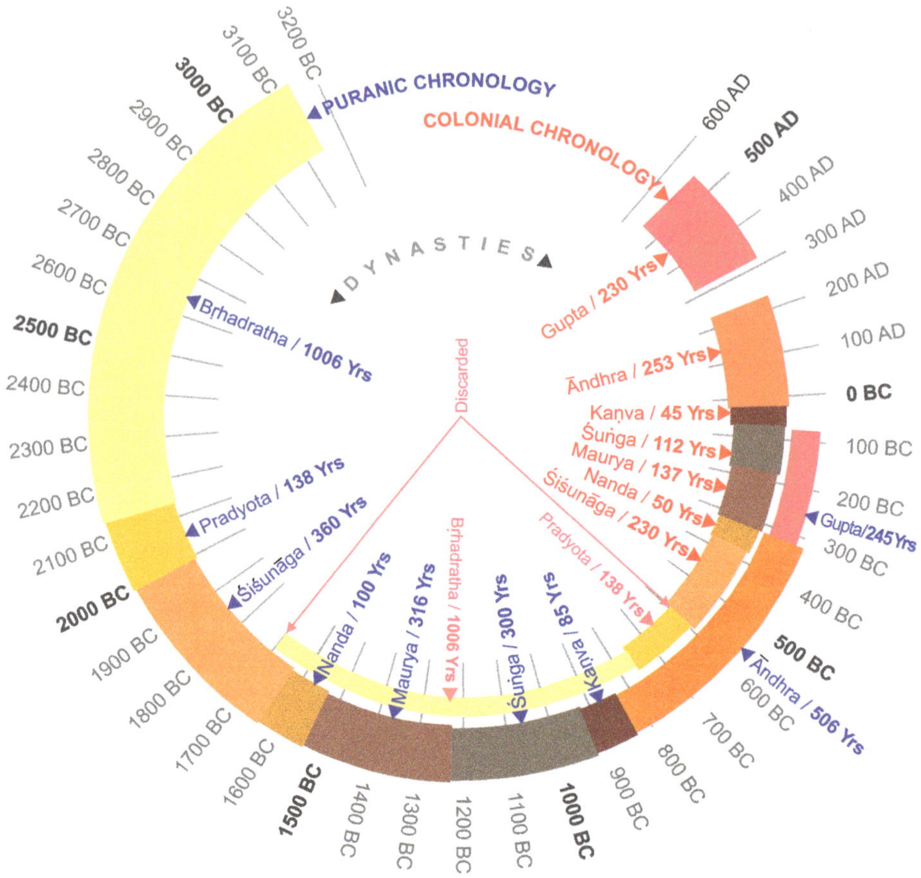


**Figure 3: True vs. False chronology of Magadha**

## How was the Date for the Vedas Determined?

Max Müller (1891), later in his life, recognized that it was extremely difficult to determine the date of composition of the Vedas, as follows:

> “Whether the Vedic hymns were composed 1000, or 1500, or 2000, or 3000 years B.C., no power on earth will ever determine.” (p. 91)

> “If then we place the rise of Buddhism between 500 and 600 B. C., and assign provisionally 200 years to the Sūtra period, and another 200 years to the Brāhmana period, we should arrive at about 1000 B. C. as the date when the collection of the ten books of the ancient hymns [Ṛgveda] must have taken place.” (p. 96)

However, Western historians completely ignored this uncertainty and ran with the 1000 BC date as if it was a definite determination.

The misidentification blunder and the false timeline based on it have caused great harm to the history of the Indian subcontinent and the world. The following section explains in detail why the identification of *Sandracottus* with Chandragupta Maurya is completely wrong.

## Why is the Identification of Sandracottus as Chandragupta Maurya Wrong?

Many accounts prove the identification of *Sandracottus* as Chandragupta Maurya wrong. In addition, a plethora of distortions has resulted from this blatant error.

1. The identification of *Sandracottus* as Chandragupta Maurya is against all Hindu, Buddhist, and Jain traditions and historical records. According to all Indian traditions, Chandragupta I Gupta (founder of the Gupta Dynasty), usurped Magadha from Chandrasrī, also called Chandramas or Chandrabija, the last king of the Āndhra Dynasty, around the time Alexander invaded India in 326 BC. This matches with the accounts of the ancient Greek writers which state that *Xandrames* preceded *Sandracottus* as the king of Prasii (Magadha) (Max Müller, 1859/1926, p. 145). On the other hand, Nanda was the king who preceded Chandragupta Maurya, and *Xandrames* of the Greek writers bears no resemblance in sound to Nanda.

2. Alexander was told that King *Aggramen* or *Xandrames* kept in the field an army of 20,000 cavalry, 200,000 infantry, 2,000 chariots, and 3,000 (or 4,000) elephants (Rapson, 1922, p. 468). In this light, Chandramas would be equivalent to *Xandrames* of the Greek writers. Identifying *Xandrames* as Nanda does not make sense.

3. There is no mention of the name 'Maurya' in any of the Greek writers' accounts. Neither is there any mention of Chāṇakya or Kautilya who was responsible for getting rid of the Nandas and installing Chandragupta Maurya on the throne. Kautilya, also called Chāṇakya or Viṣṇugupta, was a key figure in the court of Chandragupta Maurya. If the identification of *Sandracottus* of the Greek writers with Chandragupta Maurya is correct, then why isn't there a mention of Chāṇakya or Kautilya in any of the fragments of Megasthenes' *Indika* (McCrindle, 1877) or any of the classical Greek writer's writing?

4. Plutarch (McCrindle, 1877, p. 10) stated that:

   > "not long after, Androkottos, being king, presented Seleukos with five hundred elephants, and with six hundred thousand men attacked and subdued all India."

Further, Pliny (McCrindle, 1877, p. 139; *The Natural History of Pliny*, p. 45) stated:

> " Their king has in his pay a standing army of 600,000 foot-soldiers, 30,000 cavalry, and 9000 elephants ... "

Other such descriptions given by the Greek and Roman writers apply to Samudragupta of the Gupta Dynasty, and not to Chandragupta Maurya. Nowhere in the Hindu or Buddhist texts (or in the inscriptions or coins) do we find that Chandragupta Maurya led an army of six lakhs and conquered the entire country. It is said that Chandragupta Maurya was a puppet in the hands of Chāṇakya and no such deeds are attributed to him (Jacobi, 1932, Canto 8, 253–278, p. lxxv).

5. Megasthenes who was sent on an embassy by Seleucus Nicator to *Sandracottus* in around 300 BC stated that there was no slavery in India as follows (McCrindle, 1877, p. 40):

   > " Of several remarkable customs existing among the Indians, there is one prescribed by their philosophers which one may regard as truly admirable : for the law ordains that no one among them shall, under any circumstances, be a slave, but that, enjoying freedom, they shall respect **the equal rights to it which all possess :** " [Emphasis added]

   Megasthenes (McCrindle, 1877, p. 68–69) stated further:

   > " all the Indians are free, and not one of them is a slave. ... the Indians do not even use aliens as slaves, much less a countryman of their own. "

   In contrast to the above statements of Megasthenes, we find definite references to the existence of slavery in Kautilya's *Arthaśāstra*, where Chapter 65 titled *Dasakalp* is solely devoted to the status of slaves among the Aryas and Mlecchas. Hence, it can be safely concluded that Megasthenes was not in the court of Chandragupta Maurya whose contemporaneity with Kautilya is questioned by none (Venkatachelam, 1953b, p. 108).

6. Chāṇakya has described the system of administration in the time of Chandragupta Maurya who ruled from 1534–1500 BC (See Chapter 7). There is no similarity between the system of administration described by Chāṇakya and the system of the city administration described by Megasthenes who was in the court of *Sandracottous* (McCrindle, 1877, p. 86).

7. K. D. Sethna, an Indian poet, scholar, writer, and philosopher writes in his book, *The Ancient India in a New Light* (1989, p. 218):

   > " We find Jarl Charpentier informing us that, according to Jain

records, at the time when Chandragupta Maurya "took possession of the throne ... a dreadful famine lasting for twelve years devastated the region of Bengal". From Megasthenes-Diodorus we do not quite learn that "famine has never visited India": what we gather is that conditions were such in the age of Sandrocottus as to render famine extremely unlikely. But under these conditions, what the Jain records convey is almost incredible – unless the age of Chandragupta Maurya was not at that of Sandrocottus. ”

8. Ancient Greek writers also wrote that Seleucus Nicator gave to *'Sandrokottos'* a large part of Ariane (region from the middle Indus to western Afghanistan) and entered into a marriage relationship with him (McCrindle, 1877, p. 10). There is nothing to prove that Chandragupta Maurya married a Greek princess. The Prayāg pillar inscription of Samudragupta's conquests states that Samudragupta received a daughter in marriage and administration of provinces from kings in the northwest as discussed under Samudragupta in Chapter 7. Hence, the Greek writer's accounts apply to Samudragupta.

9. Captain Francis Wilford (1799, p. 285) of the Asiatic Society, who took up the subject after William Jones passed away, states:

   > “ The Greek historians say, the king of the Prasii (Magadha) was assassinated by his wife's paramour,... ”

   This account matches perfectly with the Purāṇic accounts for Chandragupta I Gupta but not for Chandragupta Maurya. The same point has also been made by A. Somayajulu (Krishnamachariar, 1937, cii–cv).

10. Captain Wilford (1799, p. 286) states further:

   > “ The son of *Chandra-Gupta* is called *Allitrochates* and *Amitrocates* by the Greek historian. *Seleucus* sent an ambassador to him ; and after his death, the same good intelligence was maintained by *Antiochus* the son or the grandson of *Seleucus*. ”

   Again, the names *'Allitrochates'* or *'Amitrocates'* can sound a little similar to Samudragupta who was the successor to Chandragupta I Gupta but not even remotely similar to Bindusāra who succeeded Chandragupta Maurya to the throne.

11. “ The Greek historians also wrote that Sandrocottus quarreled with his father and left Magadha and having collected armies, he invaded Magadha, killed his father, and became king of Magadha. This account

does not refer to Chandragupta Maurya at all but applies to Samudragupta exactly. ” (Venkatachelam, 1953b, p. 109)

12. All the kings of the Gupta Dynasty adopted a second name, each one ending with Aditya, e.g. Chandragupta I was called Vijayāditya, Samudragupta was called Aśokāditya, Chandragupta II was called Vikramāditya, and so on. One of the statements of Megasthenes (McCrindle, 1877, p. 66–67) was:

    > “ The king, in addition to his family name, must adopt the surname of the Palibothros, as Sandrakottos, for instance, did, to whom Megasthenes was sent on an embassy. ”

    This is found true if *Sandracottus* of the Greek writers is Chandragupta or Samudragupta of the Gupta Dynasty but not Chandragupta Maurya. None of the kings in the Maurya Dynasty had a second name or a title.

13. We can see from the chronology summary given by William Jones, as shown in Table 2 in this chapter, that he knew that Chandragupta Maurya lived in 1502 BC according to the Purāṇas. Still, he made Chandragupta Maurya the contemporary of Alexander from 327 BC because he believed in the biblical version of history and did not accept the high antiquity of India's history.

14. The reference to Pāṭaliputra as the capital of the Mauryas in the Sanskrit drama *Mudra Rakṣasa,* on which William Jones and other colonial Indologists placed a lot of emphasis, has misled the colonial era historians into believing that Mauryas ruled from Pāṭaliputra. Viśākhadatta, the author of this drama, might have been either ignorant of the fact or selected Pāṭaliputra as the scene of action on account of the prominence of Pāṭaliputra in his time. Around 21 or 26 centuries had elapsed from the time of the Mauryas (16th century BC) to the time of Viśākhadatta (6th or 11th century AD) and 9 or 14 centuries had passed from the time of the Guptas (4th century BC) to the time of the author. These periods are long enough to render the anomaly possible (Venkatachelam, 1953b, p. 99).

15. Fa-hsien (Giles, 1923), the Buddhist pilgrim from China, who lived in India from AD 399 to 415 and visited Pāṭaliputra, never mentioned the Gupta emperors who supposedly ruled from AD 320 to 550. According to the colonial Indologists, Chandragupta II was supposedly ruling at that time! Vincent Smith (1914, p. 294) admitted in his book, *Early History of India,* the lack of mention of the Gupta emperor's name by Fa-hsien and justified it as follows:

> “The worthy pilgrim, it is true, was so absorbed in his search for Buddhist books, legends, and miracles that he had little care for the things of this world, and did not trouble even to mention the name of the mighty monarch in whose territories he spent six studious years.”

The truth is that Chandragupta II of the Gupta Dynasty reigned from 269 to 233 BC, more than 600 years before Fa-hsien's visit. However, Vincent Smith kept believing in his conjecture.

16. Hiuen-Tsiang, the later Buddhist pilgrim from China who visited India from AD 629 to 645, has described the Nalanda University in detail, including how it began (Beal, 1888, p. 110–112). According to his description, the institution was started by King *Śakarāditya*. After his death, his son Buddhagupta came to the throne and continued the vast undertaking; he built another *Saṅghārāma* towards the south. Then his son built another *Saṅghārāma* to the east followed by his son, Bālāditya, who built a *Saṅghārāma* to the northeast; then his son, Vajra, built another to the north, and after him, a king from mid-India built another by its side. Thus, six kings in a succession added to the university buildings.

Hiuen-Tsiang added that it had been 700 years since the foundation of the institution (by the time of his visit).

The list of the kings described by Hiuen-Tsiang resembles the emperors of the Gupta Dynasty. *Śakrāditya* may be Skandagupta who ruled by the title of Parākramāditya. Translation of an Indian name into Chinese and then back into Indian correctly can be a significant challenge. Bālāditya was second to the last emperor of the Gupta Dynasty who ruled from 161 to 126 BC according to the true chronology of the Gupta Dynasty described in Chapter 7. After the last emperor of the Gupta Dynasty, Vikramāditya came to the throne in 82 BC in Ujjain in central India and became the emperor of the whole of India; he easily fits the description of 'the king from mid-India' in the preceding paragraph. Thus, Hiuen-Tsiang's statement that it has been 700 years since the foundation of Nalanda University, matches with the end of the Gupta Dynasty in the first century BC which was about 700 years before Hiuen-Tsiang's time of AD 629–645.

17. Megasthenes reported:

> “From the days of Father Bacchus to Alexander the Great their

kings are reckoned at 154, whose reigns extend over 6451 years and 3 months. ” (McCrindle, 1877, p. 115)

> “ From the time of Dionysos to Sandrakottos the Indians counted 153 kings and a period of 6042 years, but among these a republic was thrice established * * * * and another to 300 years and another to 120 years. ” (McCrindle, 1877, p. 203)

As analyzed in detail by K. D. Sethna (1989, p. 61) under the section, The *Momentous Evidence of Megasthenes,* if we count the number of kings from the very beginning of the Chandra Dynasty given in Appendix I, the number of kings from the beginning to Chandragupta Maurya is only 96. K. D. Sethna could get a maximum of 113 by going farther back to the maximum extent. However, the number of kings from the beginning in Appendix I to Chandragupta I of the Gupta Dynasty comes to 155 which is very close to 153 or 154 stated above by Megasthenes.

The above points prove without a doubt that the identification of *Sandracottus* of the classical Greek writers with Chandragupta Maurya is baseless and completely wrong. This wrong identification and the chronology based on it has been challenged since its inception by numerous Indologists as follows.

## Numerous Oppositions to the Misidentification and the False History

Eminent Indologists and Sanskrit scholars have challenged the misidentification and the resultant chronological distortion since its inception. The undisguised reluctance in admitting the proofs and recognizing the true high antiquity of Indian history is shocking.

1. Prof. M. Troyer (1840), a French Sanskritist, in his *Introduction* to the French translation of Kalhaṇa's *Rājataraṅgiṇī,* disputed the identification of *Sandracottus* of Greek writers with Chandragupta Maurya. Max Müller (1859/1926, p. 146) admitted Troyer's objection to the identification but ignored it.

2. Indignant to the prevalent trend of reducing the antiquity of India's history and literature, Kāshināth Trimbak (K.T.) Telang (1875, p. cxvii-cxviii), a Bombay high court advocate and a Sanskrit scholar, observed in his English translation of *Bhagavadgītā:*

   > “ And now, I trust, I may allow myself here one general remark, suggested not merely by Dr. Lorinser's essay, but by various writings

of the most celebrated Sanskrit scholars of Europe. It appears to me that in these days, there has set in a powerful tendency in Europe, to set down individual works and classes of works of our ancient Sanskrit Literature to as late a date as possible. ”

“ Yet I submit with all respect, but with very great confidence, that they betray a frame of mind which is the reverse of scientific. ”

3. Later, an Āndhra scholar Kuppaiah (or Kuppayya) (*Kuppayya's Ancient History*, p. 198–199), exposed the fallacy in the basic assumption of Max Müller but he also did not receive any attention (Venkatachelam, 1953b, p. 63).

4. Vincent Smith (1914, p. 135), an eminent British Indologist, admitted that there was no archaeological evidence supporting the identification of Chandragupta Maurya as a contemporary of Alexander as follows:

   “ Unfortunately no monuments have been discovered which can be referred with certainty to the period of Chandragupta or his son, and the archaeologist is unable to bring the tangible evidence afforded by excavation to support the statement of the Greek observers. ”

   However, Vincent Smith ignored his own concern and used this misidentification in rewriting the colonial version of India's history.

5. T. S. Narayana Sastry (1916/1971), after extensive research over 20 years, disproved the false identification of Chandragupta Maurya as *'Sandracottus'* in his book, *The Age of Śankara.*

6. Prof. V. Rangacharya (1929, p. 216), professor of history at Presidency College in Madras, wrote in his book, *History of Pre-Musalman India*:

   “ Max Muller, in 1890, was careful enough to warn students that his intervals of 200 years [for writing of the Vedas] were purely arbitrary, that it was only the *terminus ad quem*, that it was impossible to fix the earliest date ; that *"whether the vedic hymns were composed in 1000, or 1500, or 2000, or 3000 B.C., no power on earth could ever fix."* This extremely important caution, however, was ignored as Winternitz points out, by most writers ; ... the vast majority took the suppositions of Max-Muller as proved facts, and held that the date 1200–1000 B.C. for the Rig-Veda was quite proved. ”

7. N. Jagannadha Rao (1931), an Āndhra scholar, also called out the mistaken identity and the subsequent false chronology in his book, *Age of the Mahabharata War.*

8. M. Krishnamachariar (1937, p. ii), M.A., M.L., Ph.D., a scholar and member of the Royal Asiatic Society of London, stated in his book, *History of Classical Sanskrit Literature:*

> “In the hands of many Orientalists, India has lost (or has been cheated out of) a period of 10–12 centuries in its political and literary life, by the assumption of a faulty Synchronism of Candragupta Maurya and Sandracottus of the Greek works and all that can be said against that *"Anchor-Sheet of Indian Chronology"* has been said in this Introduction.”

9. Dr. D. S. Triveda, M.A., Ph. D. (1942, p. 584), a 20th century historian, called out the misidentification of *Sandracottus* in his paper titled, *The Sheet Anchor of Indian History,* stating:

> “The identification of Candragupta Maurya with Sandracottus of Greeks seems to have been the greatest mistake ever committed in the field of Indian chronology, literature and history.”

10. Next, Pandit Kota Venkatachalam who spent over forty years researching and restoring the true chronology of ancient India presented a paper titled, *The Pre-determined Plot in Indian Chronology Exposed,* at the 17th 'All India Oriental Conference' held in Ahmedabad in 1953 (p. 79). In the 1950s, he published a series of books (listed in Chapter 1) describing the true history and chronology of India. He stated (1953b, p. 6):

> “In fact, these orientalists could not produce any inscriptions, coins, buildings or any genuine historical evidence for their theory of the contemporaneity of Alexander with Chandragupta Maurya. Yet, they made it the foundation of Indian history and from that point they are counting backwards and forwards, the reigns of kings as given in our Puranas, ignoring that starting point in the Puranas was the time of the Mahabharata war, i.e. 3138 B.C.”

11. K. D. Sethna (1989, p. viii), an Indian scholar, poet, writer, and philosopher has disproved systematically in his book, *Ancient India in a New Light,* the identification of *Sandracottus* with Chandragupta Maurya, stating:

> “The utter wrong-headedness of the current historical view can be proved by sheer reasoning, without the need of any documentary of archaeological prop, at only one point: the substitution of Chandragupta I, founder of the Imperial Guptas, in place of Chandragupta Maurya in the time of Alexander and the years immediately following his invasion.”

12. Francois Gautier (2002, Foreword), a French journalist, based in India says:

> "But the British, who were the Masters in India, had a vested interest to show that Indian civilization was not as ancient and as great as it was earlier thought. For, up to the 18th century, philosophers and thinkers in Europe, such as Voltaire, Hegel and even as late as Nietzsche, kept referring to Indian philosophy and science, as the mother of all philosophies and sciences."

Despite such strong and persistent questioning of the gravely erroneous identification of *Sandracottus*, the false history set in motion by William Jones and concretized by the later colonial Indologists, especially Max Müller, continues to be taught in the schools and colleges in India and the world after 75 years of India's independence. This is a great injustice to the people of the Indian subcontinent and great harm to the true history of the world.

> William Jones not only cut down the antiquity of India's history by more than 1,200 years but also accused the ancient Indian authors of falsely propagating the antiquity of their history!

## Did European Historians Know the True Antiquity of India's History?

Amidst such opposition to the misidentification which was pruning the true chronology of ancient Indian history, the possibility arises that William Jones and other European Indologists and historians were in fact, aware of the truth. Based on the chronology presented by William Jones, shown in Table 2, Jones knew that Chandragupta Maurya reigned in around 1500 BC and Chandrabīja was the last Āndhra king who died in 452 BC (327 BC is the true date but not so far off in the bigger picture). Nevertheless, he ignored this and set in motion Chandragupta Maurya as a contemporary of Alexander, reducing the antiquity of India's history by more than 1,200 years. Why would Jones deviate from his own chronological table?

Since Jones was looking to identify *Sandracottus* described by Megasthenes, it is evident that he was familiar with the works of classical Greek writers such as Pliny, Arrian, Strabo, etc. which cited *Indika* of Megasthenes. How else would Jones have heard of *Sandracottus*? Megasthenes also reported (McCrindle, 1877, p. 115):

> “From the days of father Bacchus to Alexander the Great their kings are reckoned at 154, whose reigns extend over 6451 years and 3 months.”

Since Alexander invaded India in 326 BC, going backward by 6,451 years as reported above, takes the beginning of India's chronology to 6777 BC. Keeping track of an exact number of years and months elapsed is possible only with a calendar that must have started at least in 6777 BC. Despite such strong evidence of time tracking by Indians, colonial Indologists claimed that ancient India did not have a system of reckoning time!
See in **Chapter 4**, at the end of the section on **Saptarṣi Śaka**, how we arrive at the same year from a different angle.

## The 18th and 19th Century European Mindset

As discussed earlier, William Jones was steeped in the biblical belief that the world originated in 4006 BC and he was trying to fit Indian history within that time frame. Jones was not alone in this belief which was widely prevalent in 18th century Europe. The preface of Asiatic Researches (Asiatic Society, 1799, p. viii) states:

> “Thus the accounts of MOSES and the Hindu Scriptures concerning the creation may be easily reconciled to each other. But it is not our intention to support the Hindu writings in preference to the Hebrew Pentateuch ; all we desire is, that truth may be investigated, and that error may be exploded.”

The same notion that the world began with Adam in 4006 BC is seen continuing in *Remarks on the Principal Eras* and *Dates of the Ancient Hindus* by John Bentley, a member of the Asiatic Society in Bengal. Table 6 and Table 7 show a copy of the table prepared by John Bentley (1799, p. 318). Table 7 is a continuation of Table 6.

In the first column of the two tables, labeled *'Poetical Eras'*, Bentley divided the total 5,803 *'Years of the World'*, starting from ADAM'S first year, into 1,728 years of *Satya Yug, or Golden Age,* followed by 1,296 years of *Treta Yug,* or *Silver Age,* followed by 864 years of *Dwapar Yug, or Brazen Age,* followed by 432 years of *Cali Yug, or Iron Age,* and then restarting the cycle from *Satya Yug or the second Divine Age*. In the middle column of the two tables, Bentley shows

**Table 6: Chronology presented by Bentley based on biblical belief, Part I**

CHRONOLOGICAL TABLE OF ANCIENT ÆRAS, &c.

| | *Poetical Æras.* | | *Year of the World.* | | *Astronomic Æra.* | |
|---|---|---|---|---|---|---|
| *Satya Yug, or Golden Age.* | | 0 | ADAM | 0 | CALI YUG | 0 |
| | | 1 | | 1 | * | 1 |
| | | 130 | SETH born | 130 | | 151 |
| | | 905 | | 905 | | 751 |
| | | 906 | | 906 | | 823 |
| | | 1056 | NOAH born | 1056 | | 824 |
| | | 1656 | Flood | 1656 | | 882 |
| | | 1728 | | 1728 | PRADYOTA | 1000 |
| | | | | 1729 | BUDHA I. | 1002 |
| *Treta Yug, or Silver Age.* | | 1 | NIMROD | 1787 | | 1043 |
| | | 59 | | 1905 | | 1101 |
| | | 177 | | 1907 | SISUNGA | 1139 |
| | ICSCHWACHU and BUDHU | 179 | ABRAHAM | 1948 | NANDA | 1409 |
| | | | NOAH's death | 2006 | CHANDRA GUPTA | 1509 |
| | | 220 | | 2044 | PUSHPAMITRA | 1736 |
| | | 278 | | 2404 | VASUDEVA | 1848 |
| | | 316 | | 2504 | | 1853 |
| | | 676 | | 2641 | | 1920 |
| | | 776 | | 2753 | | 1920 |
| | | 913 | | 2758 | | 1925 |
| | | 1025 | PARASARA | 2825 | | 1930 |
| | RAMA | 1030 | YUDHISHTHIR | 2825 | | 2075 |
| | | 1097 | VYASA | 2830 | | 2119 |
| | | 1097 | PARICSHIT | 2835 | | |
| | VALMIC | 1102 | | 2980 | | |
| | | 1107 | | 3024 | | |
| | | 1152 | | | | |
| | | 1296 | | | | |

* The *Cali yug* commenced in February, in the 906th year of the world.

chronology in the biblical *'Year of the World'* beginning with ADAM in the year 0 (zero) and ending at 5803 as the 'Current Year of the World', at the time of his writing (October 2, 1796) stated at the end of the paper. Therefore, the 'Year 0 of the World' works out to 4007 BC (= 5803 – AD 1796) according to Bentley's belief in the biblical version of world history.

Further, in the middle column, Bentley shows NOAH born in the biblical *'Year of the World'* 1056 which works to 2951 BC (= 4007 BC – 1056), and NOAH'S death in the *'Year of the World'* 2006 which converts to 2001 BC i.e. NOAH must have lived for an incredible 950 years! Next, in the middle column, he shows PARASARA, YUDHISTHIR, VYASA, and PARICSHIT, respectively, assigned to *'Year of the World'* 2825, 2825, 2830, and 2835 which translate into years 1182

**Table 7: Chronology presented by Bentley based on biblical belief, Part II**

CHRONOLOGICAL TABLE OF ANCIENT ÆRAS, &c. continued.

| | *Poetical Æras.* | | *Year of the World.* | | *Astronomic Æra.* | |
|---|---|---|---|---|---|---|
| *Dwapar Yug, or Brazen Age.* | CUSHA | 1 | | 3025 | | 2120 |
| | | 74 | | 3098 | BALIN | 2193 |
| | | 530 | | 3554 | CHANDRABIJA | 2649 |
| | | 576 | | 3600 | | 2695 |
| | | 676 | | 3700 | | 2795 |
| | | 776 | | 3800 | | 2895 |
| | | 864 | | 3888 | | 2983 |
| *Cali Yug, or Iron Age.* | | | | 3889 | | 2984 |
| | | 1 | | 3950 | VICRAMADITYA | 3045 |
| | | 62 | | 3983 | DEVAPALA | 3078 |
| | | 95 | CHRIST | 4007 | | 3102 |
| | | 119 | | 4073 | NARAYANPALA | 3168 |
| | | 185 | | 4085 | SACA | 3180 |
| | | 197 | | 4088 | | 3183 |
| | | 200 | | 4188 | | 3283 |
| | | 300 | | 4320 | | 3415 |
| | | 432 | | 4321 | | 3416 |
| *Satya Yug, or the IId Divine Age.* | | | | 4505 | VARAHA | 3600 |
| | | 1 | | 4520 | | 3615 |
| | | 185 | | 4624 | | 3715 |
| | | 200 | | 4720 | | 3815 |
| | | 300 | | 4920 | | 4015 |
| | | 400 | | 5120 | | 4215 |
| | | 600 | | 5320 | | 4415 |
| | | 800 | | 5520 | | 4615 |
| | | 1000 | | | | |
| | | 1200 | | | | |
| | Current year | 1483 | Current year | 5803 | Current year | 4898 |

BC, 1182 BC, 1177 BC, and 1172 BC, respectively. Thus, Bentley brought down the Mahābhārata age from its actual date of 3139 BC to about 1182 BC.

In the last column in the two tables, labeled *Astronomic Era,* Bentley shows in the "CALI YUG" years, the chronology of India as he understood it — BUDHA in the CALI YUG year 1002 (2100 BC) and VICRAMADITYA in the CALI YUG year 3045 (57 BC). Kaliyuga Era started in 3102 BC. Bentley's note at the bottom of Table 6—"The *Cali Yug* commenced in February, in the 906th year of the world"—demonstrates his belief that the world started in 4007 BC. Thus, most of the colonial era European Indologists were trying to fit India's history into the constraint of the biblical version of world history.

## Macaulay's Thinking

Thomas Macaulay was responsible for introducing English education in India in 1835. Before that, education in India was in Sanskrit and Arabic. Macaulay's *Minute on Education* (1835) shows that he argued forcefully for funding English-only education in India. The following are some of his arguments that formed the foundation of the colonial education system in India and other British colonies. You can judge for yourself Macaulay's mindset and motivation behind these arguments.

1. “Dialects commonly spoken among the natives of India, contain neither literary or scientific information, and are, moreover, so poor and rude that, until they are enriched from some other quarter, it will not be easy to translate any valuable work into them.” (p. 3)

2. “A single shelf of a good European library was worth the whole native literature of India and Arabia. The intrinsic superiority of the western literature is, indeed, fully admitted by those members of the committee who support the oriental plan of education.” (p. 3)

3. “All historical information which has been collected from all the books written in the Sanscrit language is less valuable than what may be found in the most paltry abridgements used at preparatory schools in England.” (p. 3)

4. The English language was superior in metaphysics, morals, government, jurisprudence, and trade. The literature extant in English is of far greater value than all the literature that three hundred years ago was extant in all the languages of the world together (p. 4).

5. “We must at present do our best to form a class who may be interpreters between us and the millions whom we govern ; **a class of persons, Indian in blood and colour, but English in taste, in opinion, in morals, and in intellect.**” (p. 9) [Emphasis added]

## Insight into Max Müller's Thinking

The title of the book written by Max Müller, *A History of Ancient Sanskrit Literature – so far as it illustrates – The Primitive Religion of the Brahmans*, speaks volumes about what he thought of the Indians and the Hindu religion early in his career. He stated in this book (1859/1926, p. 9):

> “No wonder that a nation like the Indian cared so little for history ; no wonder that social and political virtues were little cultivated, and the ideas of the Useful and the Beautiful scarcely known to them.”

The following quotes from Max Müller leave little doubt that he too, like many Europeans of his time, was eager to convert Indians to Christianity. In a letter dated August 25, 1856, to Chevalier Bunsen, with whom he was in frequent correspondence, Max Müller wrote (Max Müller, G., 1903, p. 191):

> " After the last annexation, the territorial conquest of India ceases – what follows next is the struggle in the realm of religions and of spirit, in which, of course, center the interests of the nations. **India is much riper for Christianity than Rome or Greece were at the time of St. Paul. The rotten tree has for some time had artificial supports, because its fall would have been inconvenient for the government. But if the Englishman comes to see that the Tree *must* fall, sooner or later, then the thing is done, and he will mind no sacrifice either of blood or of land.** " [Emphasis added]

## Considerable Change in Max Müller's Views

Max Müller, in the later part of his life, in the 1880s and 1890s, gave a series of lectures that reflected a more nuanced and often admiring view of Indians. After working with Indians and experiencing their work firsthand, Max Müller (1883, p. 63) said the following on the reliability and regard for truth on the part of the Indian scholars:

> " During the last twenty years, however, I have had some excellent opportunities of watching a number of native scholars under circumstances where it is not difficult to detect a man's character, I mean in literary work and, more particularly, in literary controversy. I have watched them carrying on such controversies both among themselves and with certain European scholars, and I feel bound to say that, with hardly one exception, they have displayed a far greater respect for truth, and a far more manly and generous spirit than we are accustomed to even in Europe and America. They have shown strength, but no rudeness ; nay I know that nothing has surprised them as much as the coarse invective to which certain Sanskrit scholars have condescended, rudeness of speech being, according to their views of human nature, a safe sign of not only of bad breeding, but of want of knowledge. When they were wrong, they have readily admitted their mistakes ; when they were right, they have never sneered at their European adversaries. There has been, with few exceptions, no quibbling, no special pleading, no untruthfulness on their part, and certainly none of that low cunning of the scholar who writes down and publishes what he knows perfectly well to be false, and snaps

> his fingers at those who sill value truth and self-respect more highly than victory or applause at any price. …
>
> Let me add that I have been repeatedly told by English merchants that commercial honour stands higher in India than in any other country, and that a dishonoured bill is hardly known there. ”

Despite this drastic change in Max Müller's views, his earlier disparaging views of Indians had, unfortunately, taken hold and already done their damage.

## Tampering of the Purāṇas

Once the misidentification of Chandragupta Maurya as '*Sandracottus*' was made the sheet anchor for rewriting India's history, European Indologists and their Indian followers of the 19th and 20th centuries found that nothing in the Purāṇas and history books made sense for their new chronological theory. They started making conjecture upon conjecture on when and what might have happened and proceeded to edit the Purāṇas to support their new chronological theory. Chapter 7 shows specific examples of tampering with the Purāṇas. Pandit Venkatachelam (1953b, p. 76–77) describes the tampering in detail, for example:

> “ In addition to the damage perpetrated in deliberately and wrongly identifying the names of the kings, these European orientalists ventured to meddle even with the texts of our Puranas to obtain and show support to their wrong determination of time. In the verse in the Vishnu Purana which says that the princes of the Maurya dynasty ruled for 337 years the letter (3) was replaced by (1) so that the period comes to 137 years only. The verse in the Matsya Purana which specifies 316 years is altered to mean 137 years. But there are other manuscripts of the Matsya Purana still extant which unequivocally give the figure 316. The text of the Kaliyuga Raja Vrittanta gives the figure 316 only. The period of reign of the Sunga dynasty of kings is given in the Puranas as 300 years. This has been altered by these orientalists into 112 years but they have not been able to make this alteration in the texts of all the Puranas.
>
> After the Mahabharata War, according to all our Puranas, among the kings of Magadha, the Brahadratha dynasty (22 kings) ruled for 1000 years, the Pradyota dynasty (5 kings) ruled for 138 years, the Sisunaga

dynasty for 362 years, the three dynasties together for 1000 + 138 + 362 = 1500 years. But this figure has been amended in the texts of some Puranas by a slight change in one single letter into 1050 ('Pancha Sata' into 'Panchasath'). But even now in a larger number of manuscripts of our Puranas the figure is 1500 only. But Prof. Pargiter preferred the figure 1050 which he found in his copy of the manuscript text, instead of correcting the mistake in his copy and if necessary in the hypothesis as the basis of his wrong conclusions. The trend of the Western orientalists as well as their devoted Indian followers had been consistently thus to correct the texts of the Puranas with a view to reduce the periods of the reigns of kings as far as possible and in consequence, on the whole, to reduce the antiquity of our entire history and to bring it down to within the Christian era. ”

## Tampering of the Bhaviṣya MahāPurāṇa

The *Bhaviṣya MahāPurāṇa's* Pratisarga Parva (3rd Parva) which narrates the history of ancient India appears highly tampered. The following is a sample of the genealogy for the kings of Magadha and Gautama Buddha given in the currently available copy of *Bhaviṣya MahāPurāṇa* (Pratisarga Parva, Khanda 1, Adhyay 6, Shloka 36 (3.1.6.36) onwards).

> 'Kāśyapa → Gautama (ruled for 10 years in Paṭṭaṇa) → Śākyamuni (ruled for 20 years) → Śuddhodana (ruled for 30 years) → Śakyasiṁha → Buddhasiṁha → son Chandragupta who married a daughter of Sulūvasya, the king of Persia and ruled for 60 years' (Shlokas 36–43).

This genealogy appears completely made up and makes no sense. None of the other Purāṇas or any ancient historical text of India gives such genealogy or states that Chandragupta's father was Buddhasiṁha and that Chandragupta married Seleucus's daughter. Such changes in the Purāṇa could have taken place only during the colonial rule of India, after wrongly identifying Chandragupta Maurya as Alexander's contemporary.

The following are a few of the verses which appear to have been inserted into the *Bhaviṣya MahāPurāṇa* (3.3.2.22–24) during the colonial rule.

हूणदेशस्य मध्ये वै गिरिस्थं पुरुषं शुभम् । ददर्श बलवान्राजा गौराङ्गं श्वेतवस्त्रकम् ।। २२
को भवानिति तं प्राह स होवाच मुदान्वितः । ईशपुत्रं च मां विद्धि कुमारीगर्भसंभवम् ।। २३
म्लेच्छधर्मस्य वक्तार सत्यव्रतपरायणम् । इति श्रुत्वा नृपः प्राह धर्मः को भवतो मतः ।। २४

These verses, describing Emperor Śālivāhana, state:

> "On the mountain in the middle of the Huṇa Deśa, he saw a fair-skinned auspicious man dressed in white clothes. Upon his [Śālivāhana's] inquiring who he was, he was pleased and replied, I am Iśaputra born from a virgin. I preach Mleccha dharma and follow the path of truth."

## Vandalism of the Purāṇas

Admittedly, this was a planned vandalism of the Purāṇas. There was a concerted effort by missionaries and foreign corporations to destroy the ancient Sanskrit literature of India. The oldest and the most authentic manuscripts were preferentially destroyed so no one could use those in the future to contest the falsehood being propagated. Louis Jacolliot (1870, p. 321) writes in his book, *Bible-Le-Indi,* on the vandalism of the Purāṇas by missionaries in India during the colonial rule:

> "The rev. fathers, Jesuits, Franciscans, stranger-missions, and other corporations, unite with touching harmony in India to accomplish a work of Vandalism, which it is right to denounce as well to the learned world as to Orientalists.
>
> Every manuscript, every Sanscrit work that falls into their hands, is immediately condemned and consigned to the flames. Needless to say that the choice of these gentlemen always falls from preference upon those of highest antiquity, and whose authenticity may appear incontestable."

> "Oh! they well know, and especially the Jesuits, the value of the works they destroy. Every new arrival receives a formal order, so to dispose of all that may fall into his hands. Happily the Brahmins do not open to them the secret stores of their immense literary wealth, philosophic and religious."

# Summary of the Chapter

Rewriting of India's history began with the founding of the Asiatic Society in Kolkata in 1784 by William Jones, a Britisher working for the East India Company. Until 1829, only colonials were allowed to be members of the society. Jones, like most Europeans of his time, firmly believed in the biblical version of history that the world began in 4006 BC. Therefore, he dismissed the traditional high antiquity of India's chronology recorded in the Purāṇas and started shortening it arbitrarily to fit it into the biblical timeline. He laid the foundation of the false chronology by misidentifying *'Sandracottus'* described by ancient Greek writers, a contemporary of Alexander, with Chandragupta Maurya of 1534 BC instead of Chandragupta I of the Gupta Dynasty of 327 BC, erasing over 1,200 years of India's chronology.

Later European Indologists (mainly British and German) followed in Jones's footsteps. Max Müller, a German Sanskritist hired by the British East India Company in 1847 to translate a *Rig-Veda-Sanhita,* concretized the false identification around 1859 and made it the basis for rewriting the entire history of India. The wrong basis was blindly followed by all European Indologists and their Indian followers over the next 50–60 years. Everything else in India's history (Emperor Aśoka, Gautam Buddha, etc.) was dated in relation to Chandragupta Maurya's new date of 321 BC. The kings and dynasties preceding Gautam Buddha's time were discarded. Thus, India's chronology was shrunk from 3138 BC to 600 BC and this is the history still taught all over the world.

## References

1. Asiatic Society (1799). *Asiatic Researches; or Transactions of the Society Instituted in Bengal for inquiring into the History and Antiquities, the Arts, Sciences, and Literature of Asia, Vol. 5, Advertisement, iii–xi.* London.

2. Beal, Samuel (1888). *The Life of Hiuen-Tsiang: by the Shamans Hwui Li and Yens-Tsung, With an Introduction containing an account of the work of I-Tsing.* London: K. Paul, Trench, Trübner.

3. Bentley, John (1799). 'Remarks on the Principal Eras and Dates of the Ancient Hindus.' *Asiatic Researches; or Transactions of the Society Instituted in Bengal for Inquiring into the History and Antiquities, the Arts, Sciences, and Literature of Asia, Vol. 5,* 315–343 (Calcutta, October 2, 1796). London.

4. *Bhaviṣya MahāPurāṇa: (Sanskrit) with Hindi translation* by Pandit Baburam Upadhyay (2006). Prayāg: Hindi Sahitya Sammelan.

5. Britannica (n.d.). *Asiatic Society of Bengal: Oriental studies society.* https://www.britannica.com/topic/Asiatic-Society-of-Bengal (Accessed February 11, 2023).

6. Gautier, Francois (2002). *Rewriting Indian History (Rev. Ed.).* New Delhi: Bahri & Sons.

7. Giles, Herbert A. (Re-trans.) (1923). *The Travels of Fa-hsien (399–414 A.D.), or Record of the Buddhistic Kingdoms.* Cambridge University Press.

8. Jacobi, Hermann (Ed.) (1932). *Sthavirāvalicarita or Pariśiṣṭaparvan: an Appendix of the Triśaśti-Śalākāpuruṣacarita by Hemacandra (Bibliotheca Indica Work No. 96, 2nd ed.).* Calcutta: Asiatic Society of Bengal.

9. Jacolliot, Louis M. (1870). 'A Work of Jesuitism in India (Ch. XII).' in *The Bible in India: Hindoo Origin of Hebrew and Christian Revelation (Translated from La Bible Dans L'Inde of M. Louis Jacolliot).* London: John Camden Hotten, 74 & 75, Piccadilly.

10. Jagannadha Rao, Nadimpalli (1931). *The Age of the Mahabharata War.*

11. Jones, William (1799a). 'On the Chronology of the Hindus, written in January 1788 by the President.' *Asiatic Researches; or Transactions of the Society Instituted in Bengal for inquiring into the History and Antiquities, the Arts, Sciences, and Literature of Asia, Vol. 2,* 111–147. London.

12. Jones, William (1799b). 'The Tenth Anniversary Discourse, delivered on 28 February 1793, by the President, on Asiatic History, Civil and Natural.'

*Asiatic Researches; or Transactions of the Society Instituted in Bengal for inquiring into the History and Antiquities, the Arts, Sciences, and Literature, Vol. 4,* 1–18. London.

13. Jones, William *(1807a)*. 'On the Chronology of the Hindus: written in January 1788 by the President.' in Lord Teignmouth (Ed.), *The Works of Sir William Jones with the Life of the Author (Vol. 4, 1–47)*. London.

14. Krishnamachariar, M. (1937). *History of Classical Sanskrit Literature: Being an elaborate account of all branches of Classical Sanskrit Literature, with full Epigraphical and Archaeological Notes and References, an Introduction dealing with Languages, Philology and Chronology, and Index of Authors and Works.* Madras.

15. Macaulay, T. B. (1835, February 2). *Macaulay's Minute on Education.*

16. Max Müller, Dr. (1849). *Rig-Veda-Sanhita, The Sacred Hymns of the Brāhmans; together with the commentary of Sayanacharya* (Vol. I), published under the Patronage of the East-India-Company. London: W. H. Allen & Co.

17. Max Müller (1859). *A History of Ancient Sanskrit Literature: So far as it illustrates the Primitive Religion of the Brahmans* (Allahabad ed. 1926). London: Williams and Norgate.

18. Max Müller, F. (1883). *India: What Can it Teach Us? A Course of Lectures Delivered Before the University of Cambridge.* London: Longman, Green & Co.

19. Max Müller, F. (1891). *Physical Religion: The Gifford Lectures Delivered Before the University of Glasgow in 1890.* London: Longman, Green & Co.

20. Max Müller, Georgina (1903). *The Life and Letters of The Right Honorable Friedrich Max Müller: Edited by his Wife* (rpt. ed., Vol. I, 2005). New Delhi: Asian Educational Services.

21. McCrindle, J. W. (1877). *Ancient India as Described by Megasthenes and Arrian: a translation of the Fragments of the Indika of Megasthenes collected by Dr. Schwanbeck, and of the First part of the Indika of Arrian.* London: Trübner & Co.

22. Narayana Sastry, T. S. (1916). *The Age of Śankara* (2nd ed. 1971, edited by T. N. Kumaraswamy). Madras: B. G. Paul & Co.

23. Rangacharya, V. (1929). *History of Pre-Musalman India (in Nine Volumes): Vol I. Pre-historic India.* Madras: Huxley Press.

24. Rapson, E. J. (1922). *The Cambridge History of India: Vol I. Ancient India.* Cambridge University Press.

25. Sethna, K. D. (1989). *Ancient India in a New Light: I. The Challenge of India's Traditional Chronology, II. The Momentous Evidence of Megasthenes, III. A Reconstruction of Ancient Indian History: Aśoka – and Before and After.* New Delhi: Aditya Prakashan.

26. Smith, Vincent A. (1914). *Early History of India: From 600 B.C. to the Muhammadan Conquest including the Invasion of Alexander the Great* (3rd ed.). Oxford: Clarendon Press.

27. Telang, Kāshināth Trimbak (1875). 'Introductory Essay.' *in The Bhagavadgita: Translated into English Blank Verse with Notes and an Introductory Essay.* Bombay: Atmaram Sagoon & Co.

28. *The Natural History of Pliny: Translated with Copious Notes and Illustrations* by John Bostock & H. T. Riley (MDCCCLV or 1855) (Vol II, Book VI, Ch. 22: The Ganges). London. (Originally written in the 1st century AD).

29. Triveda, Dr. D. S. (1942). 'The Sheet Anchor of Indian History.' *The Annals of the Bhandarkar Oriental Research Institute, Vol. 23*(1–4), 582–591. Poona.

30. Troyer, M. A. (1840). *Rādjataranginī: Histoire Des Rois Du Kachmīr.* Paris: L'Impremerie Nationale (MDCCCXL).

31. Venkatachelam, Pandit Kota (Kali 5054, AD 1953b). *The Plot in Indian Chronology.* Arya Vijnana, Publication 17. Vijayawada.

32. Venkatachelam, Pandit Kota (Kali 5058, AD 1957a). *Chronology of Ancient Hindu History Part I.* Arya Vijnana Grandhamala, Publication 23. Vijayawada.

33. Venkatachelam, Sri Kota (1953). 'The Pre-determined Plot in Indian Chronology Exposed.' *Proceedings and Transactions of the All India Oriental Conference: 17th session, Ahmedabad, October-November 1953* (V: Papers accepted for different Sections: Section VIII: History, No. 27). Ahmedabad: Gujarat Vidyasabha.

34. Wilford, Capt. Francis (1799). 'On the Chronology of the Hindus.' *Asiatic Researches; or Transactions of the Society Instituted in Bengal for inquiring into the History and Antiquities, the Arts, Sciences, and Literature, Vol. 5*, 241–295. London.

# 3

# SOURCES OF TRUE HISTORY AND CHRONOLOGY OF ANCIENT INDIA

India possesses a vast amount of historical literature, contrary to what Indians and the world have been led to believe by the colonial era European Indologists. Massive destruction of ancient India's literature took place when most of the ancient universities of India such as Nalanda, Vikramaśila, Odantapuri, etc. were destroyed and their libraries were burned by invaders like Mohammad Bakhtyar Khalji in the 12th and 13th centuries AD (Singh, 2017, p. 41). Despite the colossal destruction, there is still a huge amount of ancient literature available. The literature containing historical information includes Purāṇas, Mahābhārata, Rāmāyaṇa, Kaliyuga Rājavṛttānta, and Rājataraṅgiṇī among other texts written over the millennia. The literature of ancient India can still fill libraries. The Purāṇas, Mahābhārata, and Rāmāyaṇa are not mythologies as taught since the colonial times but are primarily *Itihāsa* (history) with poetic embellishment. Perhaps, no other country in the world has as much written history and literature as India if there is a willingness to look for it.

Numerous *Vaṁśāvalis* (genealogies) of royal dynasties such as those of Nepal, Mewad, Jaisalmer, and many others, as well as chronological lists of the heads of religious institutions such as various *Pīṭhas* and *Maṭhas*, are found all over India. Another source of invaluable historical information is the records of foreign travelers who visited India and wrote travelogues. Besides all these, there are numerous inscriptions and archaeological evidence available all over India. Each of these sources of historical information is described in varying details in this chapter.

## Purāṇas

Of the various historical sources available, Purāṇas hold the foremost position as the source of ancient India's history and chronology containing a treasure trove. The Sanskrit word Purāṇa is defined by the phrase *'purā api navāh'* (पुरा अपि नवाः) which means 'though old, yet ever new'. There are 18 major Purāṇas which were written by Śrī Krishna Dvaipāyana Vyāsa, known as Maharṣi Veda Vyāsa, the author of the epic Mahābhārata. Perhaps, he had a team working with him. Purāṇas cover many branches of knowledge such as astronomy, geography, description of many cities, places of pilgrimage and their significance, flora, and fauna of various places, philosophy, rituals, and history. For example, the following verse from *Viṣṇu Purāṇa* (2nd Aṁśa, Adhyay 3, Shloka 1 (2.3.1) described the boundaries of India millennia ago.

उत्तरं यत्समुद्रस्य हिमाद्रेश्चैव दक्षिणम् ।
वर्षं तद्भारतं नाम भारती यत्रा सन्ततिः ।।

Uttaraṁ yatsamudrasya Himādreścaiva dakṣiṇam ।
Varṣaṁ tad-Bhārataṁ nāma Bhāratī yatrā santatiḥ ।।

Translation:

> What lies north of the seas and south of the Himalayas is called Bhāratavarṣa and the people living there are called Bhāratiya.

Significant portions of some of the 18 Purāṇas, as well as the Mahābhārata, describe *vaṁśāvalis* (genealogies) of numerous royal dynasties of ancient India such as the *Sūrya Vaṁśa* (Sūrya Dynasty), *Chandra Vaṁśa* (Chandra Dynasty), their branches, sub-branches, and many other dynasties. Five of the Purāṇas – the *Matsya* (मत्स्य), *Viṣṇu* (विष्णु), *Vāyu* (वायु), *Brahmāṇḍa* (ब्रह्मांड), and *Śrīmad Bhāgavata* (भागवत) Purāṇa, narrate numerous genealogies including those of the kings who ruled Hastināpura, Ayodhya, Magadha, and more before and after the Mahābhārata War in 3139 BC.

Appendix I–III and Chapter 5 show about 50 generations long genealogies of the Chandra Dynasty and a few of its many branches—the kings of Hastināpura, Pāñcāla, and early eastern kings. Chapter 6 shows about 50 generations long genealogy of Śrī Krishna, Devaki, and Kaṁsa. Chapter 7 describes the genealogy of the kings of Magadha. Appendix IV describes the 96 generations long genealogy of the Sūrya Dynasty, and Chapter 8 contains the genealogy of the kings of Kośala, a branch of the Sūrya *Vaṁśa*. The *Bhaviṣya* (भविष्य) Purāṇa describes in detail the four *Agni Vaṁśas* (dynasties) of Ujjain and other parts of northern India. Such extensive and connected genealogies cannot be a figment of someone's imagination.

The Purāṇas give a connected and continuous account of the kings of Magadha from the time of the founding of the Magadha kingdom, centuries before the Mahābhārata War in 3139 BC to the Gupta Dynasty of 327–82 BC. This is a period of over 3,000 years and the account has the names of the kings, their reigning periods as well as the total years of reign for each dynasty. Even the colonial era Indologists rewrote India's history based on the list of the dynasties and kings contained in the Purāṇas, albeit shortening various reigns and discarding some dynasties and kings arbitrarily to fit them into a much-shortened chronology adhering to their biblical timeline of history, as discussed in Chapter 2. See *The Purāṇa Text of the Dynasties of The Kali Age* (Pargiter, 1913). Pandit Venkatachelam (1957a, p. v– vi) states:

> “It is an error to presume that they [the colonial era Indologists] had constructed their histories of Ancient India solely or mainly on the basis of inscriptional and other such evidences only. From the time of the Mahabharata war to the end of the Gupta dynasty, their lists of the rulers of Magadha conform to the accounts in the Puranas, on the whole. They have omitted only two princes of the Maurya dynasty and two princes of the Aandhra dynasty from the Puranic list, and the tenth dynasty, the Panwar dynasty of 21 kings (of Ujjain) altogether.”

## Remarks from European and Indian Historians on the Value of the Purāṇas

### Horace Hayman Wilson (AD 1786–1860)

H. H. Wilson came to India in 1808 as an assistant surgeon for the British East India Company. He was appointed secretary to the Asiatic Society of Bengal in 1811 and was a member of the Royal Asiatic Society and its director from 1837 till his death. Wilson became deeply interested in Sanskrit and the ancient literature of India and was the first person to translate Ṛgveda into English. In 1832, he was appointed the first chair of Sanskrit at Oxford University. In his introduction to the English translation of the third *Aṁśa* (book) of Viṣṇu Purāṇa, Wilson (1840, p. 58) observed that a very large portion of the contents of the Purāṇas is genuine and old. He wrote:

> “The arrangement of the Vedas and other writings considered sacred by the Hindus, being in fact the authorities of their religious rites and belief, which is described in the beginning of the third book [of Viṣṇu Purāṇa], is of much importance to the history of Hindu literature, and of the Hindu religion. The sage Vyāsa is here represented, not as the author, but the arranger or

compiler of the Vedas, the Itihāsas, and Purāṇas.

His name denotes his character, meaning the 'arranger' or 'distributor' and the recurrence of many Vyāsas, many individuals who new modelled the Hindu scriptures, has nothing in it that is improbable, except the fabulous intervals by which their labours are separated. The rearranging, the refreshening, of old materials, is nothing more than the progress of time would be likely to render necessary. The last recognized compilation is that of Krishṇa Dvaipāyana, assisted by Brahmans, who were already conversant with the subjects assigned to them. ”

“ it is therefore as idle as it is irrational to dispute the antiquity or the authenticity of the greater portion of the contents of the Purāṇas, in the face of abundant positive and circumstantial evidence of the prevalence of the doctrines which they teach, the currency of the legends which they narrate, and the integrity of the institutions which they describe, at least three centuries before the Christian era. ”

Wilson (1840, p. 60) wrote in the introduction to the translation of the fourth *Aṁśa* (book) of Viṣṇu Purāṇa:

“ The fourth book contains all that the Hindus have of their ancient history. It is a tolerably comprehensive list of dynasties and individuals; it is a barren record of events. It can scarcely be doubted, however, that much of it is a genuine chronicle of persons, if not of occurrences. That it is discredited by palpable absurdities in regard to the longevity of the princes of the earlier dynasties must be granted, and the particulars preserved of some of them are trivial and fabulous: still there is an inartificial simplicity and consistency in the succession of persons, and a possibility and probability in some of the transactions which give to these traditions the semblance of authenticity, and render it likely that they are not altogether without foundation.

At any rate, in the absence of all other sources of information, the record, such as it is, deserves not to be altogether set aside. It is not essential to its credibility or its usefulness that any exact chronological adjustment of the different reigns should be attempted. Their distribution amongst the several Yugas, undertaken by Sir Wm. Jones or his Pandits, finds no countenance from the original texts, farther than an incidental notice of the age in which a particular monarch ruled, or the general fact that the dynasties prior to Krishna precede the time of the great war, and the beginning of the kali age; both which events we are not obliged, with the

Hindus, to place five thousand years ago. To that age the solar dynasty of princes offers ninety-three descents, the lunar but forty-five, though they both commence at the same time.

Some names may have been added to the former list, some omitted in the latter; and it seems most likely, that, notwithstanding their synchronous beginning, the princes of the lunar race were subsequent to those of the solar dynasty. They avowedly branched off from the solar line; …

Deducting however from the larger number of princes a considerable proportion, there is nothing to shock probability in supposing that the Hindu dynasties and their ramifications were spread through an interval of about twelve centuries anterior to the war of the Mahābhārata, and, conjecturing that event to have happened about fourteen centuries before Christianity, thus carrying the commencement of the regal dynasties of India to about two thousand six hundred years before that date.

This may or may not be too remote; but it is sufficient, in a subject where precision is impossible, to be satisfied with the general impression, that in **the dynasties of kings detailed in the Purāṇas** we have a record which, although it cannot fail to have suffered detriment from age, and may have been injured by careless or injudicious compilation, **preserves an account, not wholly undeserving of confidence, of the establishment and succession of regular monarchies amongst the Hindus, from as early an era, and for as continuous a duration, as any in the credible annals of mankind.** ” [Emphasis added]

Wilson's favorable views of the Purāṇas did not prevail, as by his time, the views of William Jones, who came much before him, had taken hold among the Indologists.

## Frederic Eden Pargiter (AD 1852–1927)

Justice F. E. Pargiter was a British civil servant who worked in India, for the British colonial government, from 1875 to 1906. He was also an eminent Indologist of the early 20th century. While discussing the numerous genealogies given in the Purāṇas, Pargiter (1910, p. 5) remarked in his paper, *Ancient Indian Genealogies and Chronology*:

“ These old genealogies, therefore, with their incidental stories, are not to be looked upon as legends or fables, devoid of basis or substance, but contain genuine historical tradition, and may well be considered and dealt with from a common-sense point of view. They give us an opportunity of viewing ancient India from the kṣatriya standpoint. The kṣatriyas played a very great part in those early days, and a consideration of the literature that they originated is essential to a right understanding of those distant times. ”

## Vincent Arthur Smith (AD 1843–1920)

Vincent Smith (1914), who worked for the British colonial government in India from 1871 to 1900, and wrote several books on the history of India after his return to England, said this about the Purāṇas:

> “ The most systematic record of Indian historical tradition is that preserved in the dynastic lists of the Purānas. Five out of the eighteen works ... namely the Vāyu, Matsya, Vishṇu, Brahmānḍa and Bhāgavata contain such lists. The Matsya is the earliest and most authoritative. ” (p. 11)

> “ Modern European writers have been inclined to disparage unduly the authority of the Purānic lists, but closer study finds in them much genuine and valuable historical tradition. ” (p. 12)

> “ I may add that *Purāṇas* in some shape were already authoritative in the fourth* century B. C. The author of the *Arthaśāstra* [economics] ranks the *Atharvaveda* and *Itihāsa* as the fourth and fifth Vedas (Bk I, ch. 3) ; and directs the king to spend his afternoons in the study of *Itihāsa*, which is defined as comprising six factors, namely, (1) *Purāṇa*, (2) *Itivritta* (history), (3) Ākhyayika (tales) (4) *Udāharaṇa* (illustrative stories), (5) *Dharmaśāstra,* and (6) *Arthaśāstra* (Bk. I, ch. 5). ” (p. 23)

> *According to the chronology discussed in Chapter 7, the author of the Arthaśāstra, Kautilya, (i.e. Chānakya or Viṣṇugupta), who orchestrated the overthrow of the Nanda Dynasty and installed Chandragupta Maurya to the throne, lived in 1534 BC, not in the fourth century BC as stated above by Vincent Smith. Therefore, the Purāṇas were authoritative in the 16th century BC.

## Dr. Haraprasad Shastri (AD 1853–1931)

Dr. Haraprasad Shastri, also known as Haraprasad Bhattacharya, was a Sanskrit scholar and historian of Bengali literature. He was a professor of Sanskrit and head of the Sanskrit department at Presidency College, Kolkata. He held various positions in the Asiatic Society and was its president for two years. Dr. Shastri (1928, p. 325–326) wrote:

> “ In the eighties my European friends advised me not to touch the Rāmāyaṇa, the Mahābhārata, and the Purāṇas for the purpose of getting

Indian history from them. They worked hard with the coins, inscriptions, notices of foreign travellers, archaeology, sculpture, architecture for extracting chronology and history from them. In fact they studied everything but the Purāṇas. But lo! Mr. Pargiter and Mr. Jayaswal now produce a chronology from the Purāṇas themselves which agreed in the outline prepared with so much of toils of nearly 150 years by the Orientalists.

The last work of Mr. Pargiter is on the reliability of Indian traditions, i.e., on the Purāṇas generally. He says that there is nothing in the Purāṇas to show that the Kṣatriyas came from the west. ... But this is not the place for going into detail of what Mr. Pargiter and Mr. Jayaswal say. All that the present address is concerned with is that they rescued the Purāṇas from the disrepute in which they were placed and heightened the respect for them.

As a consequence, the study of the Purāṇas has commenced in Europe, and the idea of editing passages on particular subjects has taken root. ”

### Nadimpalli Jagannadha Rao

N. Jagannadha Rao (1931, p. 21, 20), an early 20th century Indologist, states in his book, *The Age of the Mahabharata War*:

> “ Even the orientalists who had contemptuously disregarded the ancient Hindu literature such as Puraṇas, Ithihasas etc. as mere traditional records, had to depend upon the same for the history of any period anterior to the invasion of Alexander the Great in 327 B.C. ” (p. 21)

> “ From the materials supplied to us by the Ancient Hindu Literature, the Ancient History of India may conveniently be divided into two periods for all chronological purposes and they may be called as Pre-historic and Historic periods. The dividing line between these two periods may be taken as the date of the Mahabharata war. ... The period prior to this Great War may be taken as prehistoric period and the one after that date as Historic period; for, all the Puraṇas and Ithihasas of the Hindus give the chronology and history of all the Hindu dynasties of Magadha from the Mahabharata War and from the beginning of this Kaliyuga. ” (p. 20-21)

## Kaliyuga Rājavṛttānta (कलियुग राजवृत्तांत)

The most unique and authoritative source of the chronology of ancient India is Kaliyuga Rājavṛttānta. It is considered a portion of the *Bhaviṣyottara* Purāṇa, which is an extension of the Bhaviṣya MahāPurāṇa. Pandit Venkatachelam (1953b, p. 38) describes Kaliyuga Rājavṛttānta as follows:

> “An attempt was made centuries back in our country to study critically the accounts of the dynasties of the kings of Kali given in our Puranas, to detect and amend the errors due to ignorant scribes, and misreading and misinterpretation by malicious and biased interpreters, and to evolve a valid and authoritative account of the dynasties of the Kings of Kali based on the maximum agreement among the varying texts of the different Puranas. The result of this exhaustive and critical enquiry was published in the Sanskrit language in the form of a treatise entitled "Kali Yuga Raja Vrittanta". In this treatise a connected and consistent account of the history of our country down to the eighth century after Christ has been given in detail based upon our Puranas and in agreement with the references in them to the movement of the Great Bear [Big Dipper]. This Great book has been rejected and sneered at by some as a mere forgery and despised and neglected by others as belonging to the tenth or the sixteenth or even the eighteenth century. ... Let us remind them that all their histories were written at the end of the 19th century.”

> “The western historians did not accept for a long time the existence of Aandhra kings. ... Afterwards, when some inscriptions and coins of the Aandhra kings were found, they could not but believe the existence of the thirty Satavahana kings and their titles. The titles of these kings were found in the Puranas even before the inscriptions were found out. In a similar way the names of the Gupta kings and their titles are found in Kaliyugaraja-Vrittanta irrespectively of the inscriptions.” (1957b, p. 169–170)

Dr. B. Bhattacharya, M.A., Ph.D. (1944, p. 4), a 20th century historian, writes on Kaliyuga Rājavṛttānta in his paper, *New Light on the History of the Imperial Gupta Dynasty*:

> “I shall show here how a neglected Purāṇa throws a flood of light on the history of the Guptas in less than 30 stanzas, and sets at rest most of the controversies that now are raging amongst the Gupta historians.
>
> Detailed information on the subject comes from a work called the *Kaliyuga-rāja-vṛttānta* which is a part of the *Bhaviṣyottara Purāṇa*. Although I have not got an opportunity to consult the work in *extenso* as yet, I read some of the extracts quoted in the introduction to his *History of the Classical Sanskrit Literature* (Madras, 1937) by M. Krishnamachariar, and was struck by the wealth and originality of the information contained therein.”

Unfortunately, R. C. Majumdar (1944, p. 345), a 20th century Indian historian who followed the colonial historians, called Kaliyuga Rājavṛttānta 'a forged Purāna-text'. Pandit Venkatachelam (1957b, p. 167) called Dr. Majumdar's criticism illogical with detailed arguments.

M. Krishnamachariar (1937, p. xlviii–lvi) and Pandit Venkatachelam (1957a) have quoted in their books extensively from Kaliyuga Rājavṛttānta. Despite searching widely, I was not able to locate a copy of the Kaliyuga Rājavṛttānta. Pandit Venkatachelam (1957a, p. vii) describes in his book how he learned about Kaliyuga Rājavṛttānta, in possession of T. S. Narayana Sastry:

> “The manuscript of this volume was composed in 1948 but I had been waiting for clearing a few doubts that remained before publishing it. During this interval I happened to come across the publication "The Age of Sankara" by Sri T.S. Narayana Sastry, B.A., B.L., High court Vakil, Madras. I found that he had in his possession, in addition to the editions of the puranas examined by me in connection with the composition of my book, an ancient manuscript edition of the Matsya Purana in Tamil Grantha script and the Kaliyuga Raja Vrittanta, a rare ancient historical treatise still unpublished, and the extracts quoted by him from these precious documents were so indisputable and conclusive and setting at rest all possible doubts the matters dealt with, I had to revise my book in the manuscript form, incorporating verses from his ancient manuscript edition of Matsya purana and the Kaliyuga-Raja-Vrittanta, quoted by him

इत्येते दशच द्वेच ये भोक्ष्यन्ति वसुन्धराम् ।

शतानि त्रीणि वर्षाणि तेभ्यः श्रृङ्गान् गमिष्यति ।। ३० ।।

This version of Matsya Purana tolerably agrees with that given in the manuscript copy of the **Kaliyuga Rājavrittānta** in my library which also I add below for easy reference.

द्वादशैते नृपामौर्याश्चन्द्रगुप्तादयो महीम् ।

शतानि त्रीणि भोक्ष्यन्ति दश षट् च समाः कलौ ।।

Dvādaśaite nṛpāMauryāśCandraguptādayo mahīm ।
Śatāni trīṇi bhokṣyanti daśa ṣaṭ ca samāḥ kalau ।।

**Figure 4: Reference to Kaliyuga Rājavṛttānta**

as the authority for his views and the chronological determinations. ”

Figure 4 shows one of the many verses quoted by T. S. Narayana Sastry from the manuscript copy of Kaliyuga Rājavṛttānta (Venkatachelam,1957a, p. 89–90). The first verse is from the Matsya Purāṇa, and it is compared with the similar verse from the Kaliyuga Rājavṛttānta. The first verse in the figure means that the 12 kings will enjoy the earth for 300 years and then (the earth) will go to Śuṅgas. The second verse means that the 12 Maurya kings starting from Chandragupta will reign for a total of 316 years.

## Rājataraṅgiṇī (राजतरंगिणी)

Rājataraṅgiṇī, written by Pandit Kalhaṇa (कल्हण) in AD 1148 (Wilson, 1825; M. A. Stein, 1900), gives the history and chronology of the kings of Kashmir starting from about 3400 BC (about 250 years before the Mahābhārata War in 3139 BC) to Kalhaṇa's time. Vincent Smith (1915, p. 54) wrote on Rājataraṅgiṇī:

> “ The Sanskrit book which comes nearest to the European notion of a regular history is the *Rājatarangiṇī* of Kalhaṇa, a metrical chronicle of Kashmir, written in the twelfth century by the son of a minister of the Rājā. ”

P. Gwasha Lal, B.A. (1932, p. 8) stated in his book, *A Short History of Kashmir*:

> “ Kalhaṇa's Rājatarangini is almost a revelation. Among the master pieces of the world his history is also one. ”

M. A. Stein (1900, p. 3) writes in his English translation of Kalhaṇa's Rājataraṅgiṇī:

> “ It has often been said of the India of the Hindus that it possessed no history. The remark is true if we apply it to history as a science and art, such as classical culture in its noblest prose-works has bequeathed it to us. But it is manifestly wrong if by history is meant either historical development or the materials for studying it. India has never known, among its Śastras, the study of history such as Greece and Rome cultivated or as modern Europe understands it. Yet, the materials for such study are equally at our disposal in India. They are contained not only in such original sources of information as inscriptions, coins and antiquarian remains, generally ; advancing research has also proved that written records of events or of traditions concerning them have by no means been wanting in ancient India. ”

## Historical Texts

There is no dearth of other Sanskrit texts containing historical information and dates, for example, Kālidāsa's *Jyotirvidābaharaṇa*, *Harṣacharitam* written by Bāṇabhatta in about AD 620 for Harṣavardhana, the emperor of North India from AD 606 to 647. Lt. Col. James Tod (1829, p. viii), an early 19th century officer of the British East India Company and an Indologist, argued that Rājataraṅgiṇī clearly demonstrates that regular historical works were once less rare in India than at present, and further search may bring more relics to light. He added:

> " Immense libraries, in various parts of India, are still intact, which have survived the devastations of the Islamite. The collections of Jessulmer and Puttun, for example, escaped the scrutiny of even the lynx-eyed Alla, who conquered both these kingdoms, and who would have shewn as little mercy to those literary treasures, as Omar displayed towards the Alexandrine library. Many other minor collections, consisting of thousands of volumes each, exist in central and western India, some of which are private properties of princes, and others belong to the Jain communities. "

## Unreliable Books

Buddhist Sanskrit text *The Aśokāvadāna* (1960) and Simhalese Buddhist texts, such as *The Dīpavaṁsa* (1879/2006) and *The Mahāvaṁsa* (1912), which the colonial era Indologists relied on extensively are very unreliable. Krishnamachariar (1937, p. lxxxvii) wrote:

> " The Buddhists accounts of Aśoka, as given by two great schools of Buddhism—*Mahāyāna* and *Hinayāna*—not only differ from each other but also from the accounts given of Aśoka, ... "There is a good deal of confusion in these Buddhistic works as regards the very family and genealogy of Aśoka, the Buddhistic king ; and one can easily trace that the life and time of Aśoka must have been constructed by the Buddhistic writers who flourished several hundreds of years after him, by jumbling up the lives of three different Indian kings, viz. (1) of Aśoka ... of Kashmir ..., (2) of Aśokavardhana, the grandson of Chandragupta Maurya ..., and (3) of Samudragupta or Aśoka the Great. "

Pandit Venkatachelam (1957a, p. 91) wrote:

> " The Asokavadana (according to the prose version in the Divyavadana)

omits Chandragupta, and Bindusara, the father of Asoka, is represented as being the son of Nanda. The metrical Asokavadana, on the other hand, substitutes Mahipala for Ajatasatru, and exhibits numerous other variations, which make their Buddhistic accounts absolutely worthless and untrustworthy. ”

The Buddhist accounts (Aśokāvadāna, Dīpavaṁsa, and Mahāvaṁsa) make a mess of things between Udayana and Nandivardhana as discussed in Chapter 7. The Dīpavaṁsa and Mahāvaṁsa give genealogy only from Chandragupta to Aśoka. *Mahāvaṁsa* (5.21, p. 27) states that Aśoka had 99 brothers and he had slain them all!

## Religious Institutions

Countless religious institutions in India, since ancient times, have a tradition of maintaining a record of the heads of their institutions along with their respective dates. Kānchi Kamkoti Maṭha, Śāradā Pīṭha at Dvārakā, and Govardhana Maṭha at Jagannātha Puri have maintained complete chronologies of their *Pīṭhadhiipatis* (head of the Pīṭha) from their beginnings to the present time as shown in Chapter 9.

## Vaṁśāvalis (Genealogies)

It has been a tradition from ancient times for all institutions and royal dynasties in India to maintain their *vaṁśāvalis* (genealogies). Many vaṁśāvalis are available all over India, such as the dynasties of Eastern Chalukyas, and Eastern Gangas of Kaliṅga (Krishnamachariar, 1937, p. xlii). The Nepal Rāja Vaṁśāvali (Wright, 1877/1990) stands out among these. It begins six or seven centuries before the Mahābhārata War and gives an unbroken list of the kings of Nepal and dates of important events in the Kaliyuga Era. Pandit Venkatachelam (1957b, p. 187) has described many manuscripts of ancient royal dynasties of various parts of India, from Kāmarūpa (Assam) to Indraprastha (Delhi) and more, spanning thousands of years.

Figure 5 shows a picture of the genealogy, from the museum at the Jaisalmer Fort, starting from the time of Śrī Krishna to the beginning of the Jaisalmer kingdom, and continuing to very recent times. Figure 6 shows a picture of the genealogy and chronology of the kings of Mewad from the Mahārānā Pratāp Museum at Udaipur, the former capital of Mewad, from the beginning of the dynasty in Vikrama Samvat 623 (AD 566) to the 20th century.

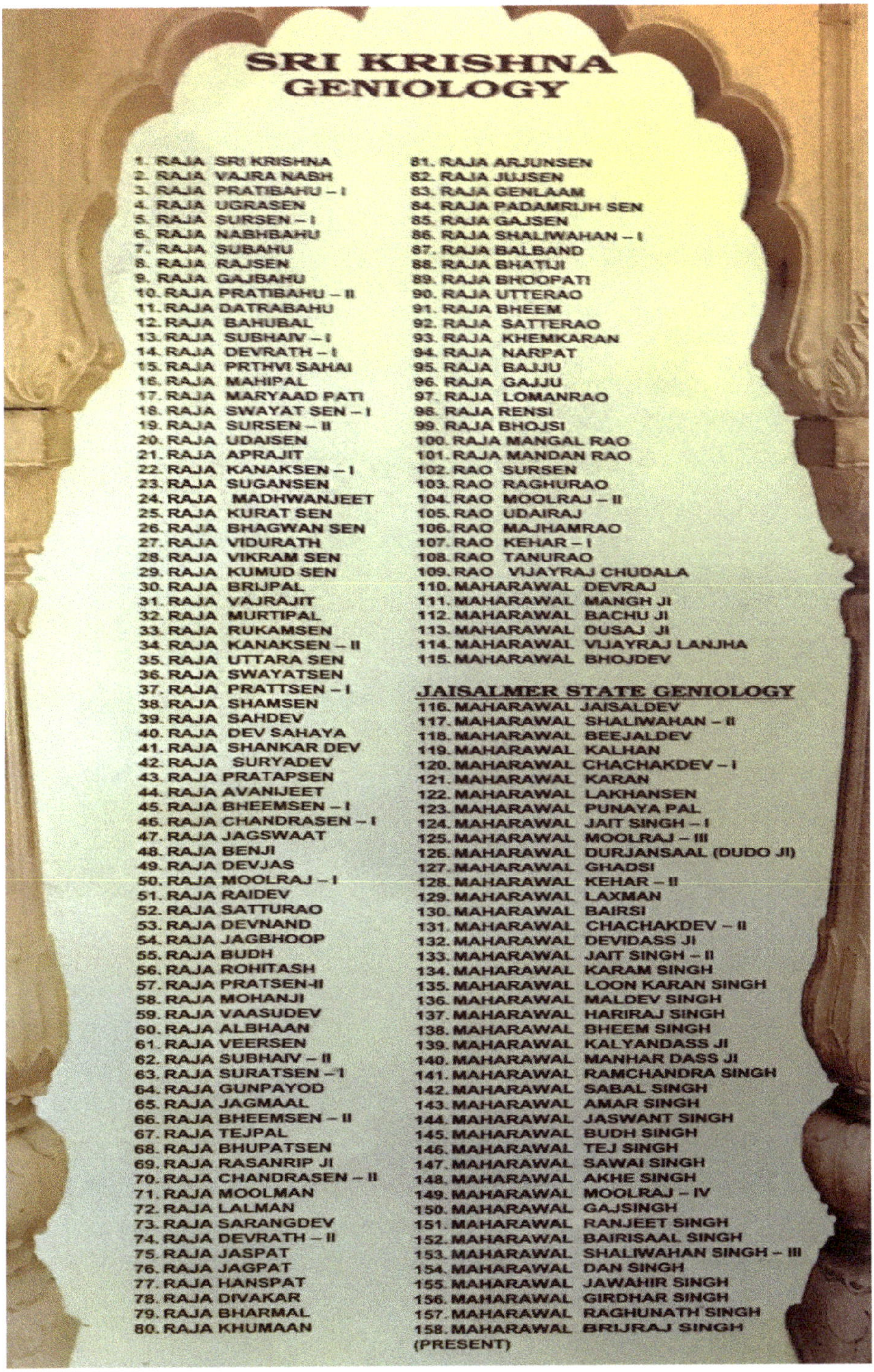

SRI KRISHNA
GENIOLOGY

1. RAJA SRI KRISHNA
2. RAJA VAJRA NABH
3. RAJA PRATIBAHU – I
4. RAJA UGRASEN
5. RAJA SURSEN – I
6. RAJA NABHBAHU
7. RAJA SUBAHU
8. RAJA RAJSEN
9. RAJA GAJBAHU
10. RAJA PRATIBAHU – II
11. RAJA DATRABAHU
12. RAJA BAHUBAL
13. RAJA SUBHAIV – I
14. RAJA DEVRATH – I
15. RAJA PRTHVI SAHAI
16. RAJA MAHIPAL
17. RAJA MARYAAD PATI
18. RAJA SWAYAT SEN – I
19. RAJA SURSEN – II
20. RAJA UDAISEN
21. RAJA APRAJIT
22. RAJA KANAKSEN – I
23. RAJA SUGANSEN
24. RAJA MADHWANJEET
25. RAJA KURAT SEN
26. RAJA BHAGWAN SEN
27. RAJA VIDURATH
28. RAJA VIKRAM SEN
29. RAJA KUMUD SEN
30. RAJA BRIJPAL
31. RAJA VAJRAJIT
32. RAJA MURTIPAL
33. RAJA RUKAMSEN
34. RAJA KANAKSEN – II
35. RAJA UTTARA SEN
36. RAJA SWAYATSEN
37. RAJA PRATTSEN – I
38. RAJA SHAMSEN
39. RAJA SAHDEV
40. RAJA DEV SAHAYA
41. RAJA SHANKAR DEV
42. RAJA SURYADEV
43. RAJA PRATAPSEN
44. RAJA AVANIJEET
45. RAJA BHEEMSEN – I
46. RAJA CHANDRASEN – I
47. RAJA JAGSWAAT
48. RAJA BENJI
49. RAJA DEVJAS
50. RAJA MOOLRAJ – I
51. RAJA RAIDEV
52. RAJA SATTURAO
53. RAJA DEVNAND
54. RAJA JAGBHOOP
55. RAJA BUDH
56. RAJA ROHITASH
57. RAJA PRATSEN-II
58. RAJA MOHANJI
59. RAJA VAASUDEV
60. RAJA ALBHAAN
61. RAJA VEERSEN
62. RAJA SUBHAIV – II
63. RAJA SURATSEN – I
64. RAJA GUNPAYOD
65. RAJA JAGMAAL
66. RAJA BHEEMSEN – II
67. RAJA TEJPAL
68. RAJA BHUPATSEN
69. RAJA RASANRIP JI
70. RAJA CHANDRASEN – II
71. RAJA MOOLMAN
72. RAJA LALMAN
73. RAJA SARANGDEV
74. RAJA DEVRATH – II
75. RAJA JASPAT
76. RAJA JAGPAT
77. RAJA HANSPAT
78. RAJA DIVAKAR
79. RAJA BHARMAL
80. RAJA KHUMAAN
81. RAJA ARJUNSEN
82. RAJA JUJSEN
83. RAJA GENLAAM
84. RAJA PADAMRIJH SEN
85. RAJA GAJSEN
86. RAJA SHALIWAHAN – I
87. RAJA BALBAND
88. RAJA BHATIJI
89. RAJA BHOOPATI
90. RAJA UTTERAO
91. RAJA BHEEM
92. RAJA SATTERAO
93. RAJA KHEMKARAN
94. RAJA NARPAT
95. RAJA BAJJU
96. RAJA GAJJU
97. RAJA LOMANRAO
98. RAJA RENSI
99. RAJA BHOJSI
100. RAJA MANGAL RAO
101. RAJA MANDAN RAO
102. RAO SURSEN
103. RAO RAGHURAO
104. RAO MOOLRAJ – II
105. RAO UDAIRAJ
106. RAO MAJHAMRAO
107. RAO KEHAR – I
108. RAO TANURAO
109. RAO VIJAYRAJ CHUDALA
110. MAHARAWAL DEVRAJ
111. MAHARAWAL MANGH JI
112. MAHARAWAL BACHU JI
113. MAHARAWAL DUSAJ JI
114. MAHARAWAL VIJAYRAJ LANJHA
115. MAHARAWAL BHOJDEV

JAISALMER STATE GENIOLOGY

116. MAHARAWAL JAISALDEV
117. MAHARAWAL SHALIWAHAN – II
118. MAHARAWAL BEEJALDEV
119. MAHARAWAL KALHAN
120. MAHARAWAL CHACHAKDEV – I
121. MAHARAWAL KARAN
122. MAHARAWAL LAKHANSEN
123. MAHARAWAL PUNAYA PAL
124. MAHARAWAL JAIT SINGH – I
125. MAHARAWAL MOOLRAJ – III
126. MAHARAWAL DURJANSAAL (DUDO JI)
127. MAHARAWAL GHADSI
128. MAHARAWAL KEHAR – II
129. MAHARAWAL LAXMAN
130. MAHARAWAL BAIRSI
131. MAHARAWAL CHACHAKDEV – II
132. MAHARAWAL DEVIDASS JI
133. MAHARAWAL JAIT SINGH – II
134. MAHARAWAL KARAM SINGH
135. MAHARAWAL LOON KARAN SINGH
136. MAHARAWAL MALDEV SINGH
137. MAHARAWAL HARIRAJ SINGH
138. MAHARAWAL BHEEM SINGH
139. MAHARAWAL KALYANDASS JI
140. MAHARAWAL MANHAR DASS JI
141. MAHARAWAL RAMCHANDRA SINGH
142. MAHARAWAL SABAL SINGH
143. MAHARAWAL AMAR SINGH
144. MAHARAWAL JASWANT SINGH
145. MAHARAWAL BUDH SINGH
146. MAHARAWAL TEJ SINGH
147. MAHARAWAL SAWAI SINGH
148. MAHARAWAL AKHE SINGH
149. MAHARAWAL MOOLRAJ – IV
150. MAHARAWAL GAJSINGH
151. MAHARAWAL RANJEET SINGH
152. MAHARAWAL BAIRISAAL SINGH
153. MAHARAWAL SHALIWAHAN SINGH – III
154. MAHARAWAL DAN SINGH
155. MAHARAWAL JAWAHIR SINGH
156. MAHARAWAL GIRDHAR SINGH
157. MAHARAWAL RAGHUNATH SINGH
158. MAHARAWAL BRIJRAJ SINGH (PRESENT)

**Figure 5: Genealogy record at Jaisalmer Museum**

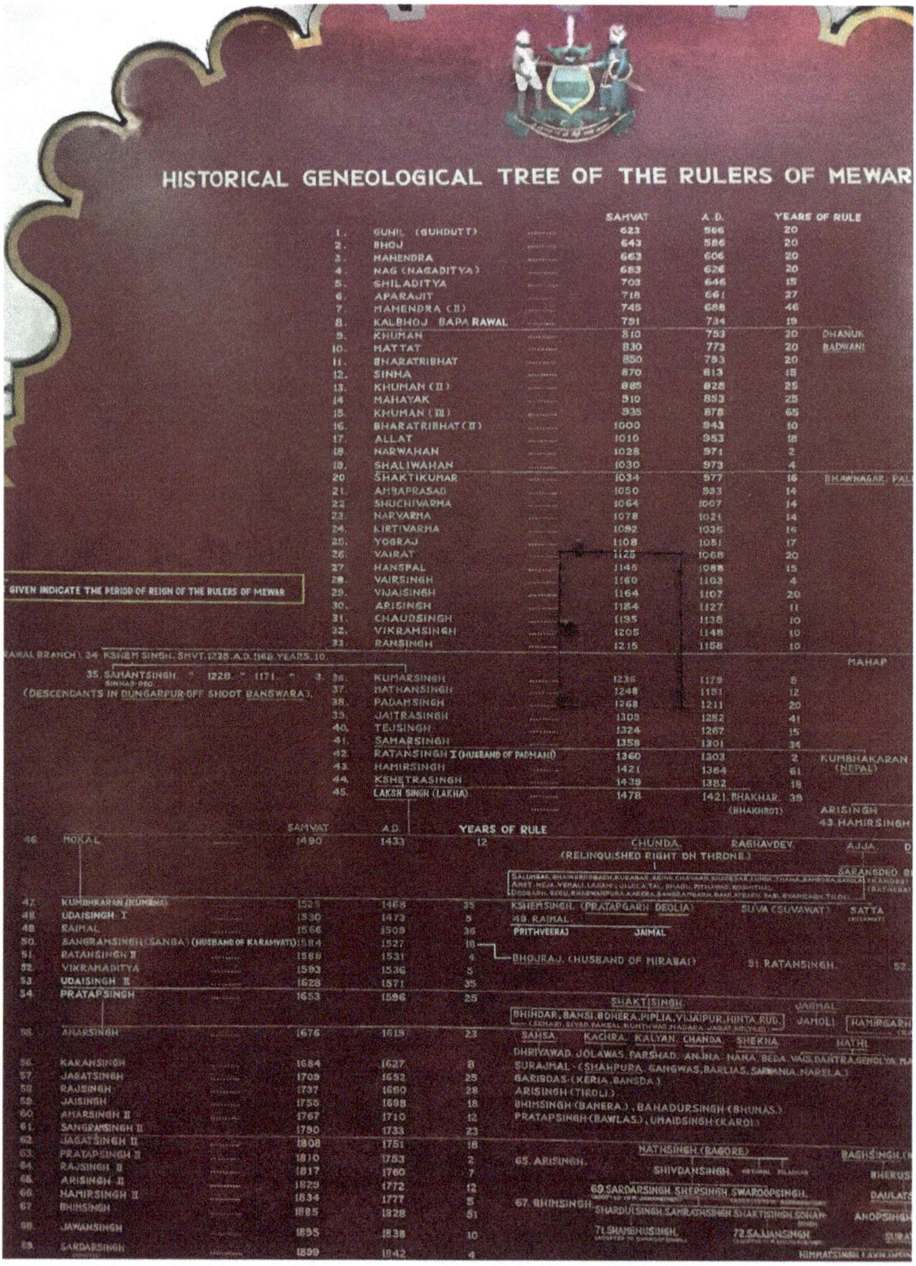


**Figure 6: Chronology of Mewad rulers at Udaipur Museum**

The photograph of the genealogy shown in Figure 6 was taken in January 2018. A revisit to the museum in March 2022 found this genealogy removed from the display!

## Accounts of Foreign Travelers

Several travelers from other countries have visited India in the past and left accounts of their visit. Here are a few well-known visitors and their accounts of contemporary history.

### Megasthenes

The earliest known account of India from a foreign traveler is that of Megasthenes, a Greek ambassador of Seleucus Nicator in the court of *Sandrakottus* in India around 300 BC. The book *Indika* written by Megasthenes has not survived but has been quoted extensively by ancient Greek writers such as Strabo (ca. 60 BC–AD 19), Plutarch (ca. AD 100), Diodorus Siculus (ca. AD 100), Arrian (ca. AD 200), and Roman historian Justin (ca. AD 500), etc. in the subsequent centuries. Therefore, we have a fair knowledge of Indika's contents. Indika's fragments from these various subsequent works are available in J. W. McCrindle's (1877) *Ancient India as Described by Megasthenes and Arrian*.

### Buddhist Pilgrims from China

Several Chinese Buddhist pilgrims, who regarded India as their holy land, came and stayed in India for many years and returned to China. Fa-hsien (or Fa-hien) visited India from AD 399 to 415.

> Fa-hsien walked from central China across the Gobi Desert, over the Hindukush mountains, through India down to the mouth of Hoogly, where he boarded a ship and returned by sea to China after many hairbreadth escapes.

Fa-hsien has not mentioned the name of Chandragupta II or Vikramāditya even once in his notes (Giles, 1923). As discussed in Chapter 2, there is no basis for Vincent Smith's assertion (1910, p. 54) that Fa-hsien remained for six years in the dominions of Chandragupta II or Vikramāditya.

Hiuen-Tsiang, another Buddhist pilgrim from China, visited India from AD 629 to 645 (Beal, 1888). He mentions in his notes that he became a friend of Emperor Harṣavardhana (Smith, 1951, p. 70). Hiuen-Tsang visited Kapilvastu, Buddha's birthplace, and found it in ruins. He has described the ruins and old foundations of the various palaces in detail. He described the population of Magadha as highly learned and virtuous. Pāṭaliputra was thriving when Fa-hsien visited but was in ruins when Hiuen-Tsang visited it.

### Alberuni

Abu Raihan Mohamad Ibu Ahmed Al-beruni, known as Alberuni, a Mumhammedan scholar, came to India, learned Sanskrit, and wrote *Tarikh-al-Hind* (*Alberuni's India*) which he finished in AD 1031 (Sachau, 1910). This work has been quoted and discussed in Chapter 4.

## Inscriptions and Archaeological Evidence

Inscriptions and archaeological evidence can serve as a means of confirming the written history as well as providing additional information. However, they can't take the place of the written history that has been passed down. Several relevant inscriptions are described in various chapters of this book. Chapter 14 describes some of the most important inscriptions and archaeological findings.

## Astronomical Positions

The Vedas, Rāmāyaṇa, Mahābhārata, and the Purāṇas are full of astronomical positions which existed at the time of various ancient events. These positions can be and are being used, to determine the year of the event. Several astronomical positions described in the Mahābhārata are given in Chapter 4 as examples.

## Transfer of Ancient Manuscripts to Europe

During the colonial rule of India, hundreds to perhaps thousands of ancient manuscripts from India were collected and sent to libraries in Europe. For example, Daniel Wright (1877/1990, Preface) mentions in his book, *History of Nepal,* that he procured several manuscripts for the university library of Cambridge. Lt. Col. James Tod (1829, p. xvi) wrote:

> “The large collection of ancient Sanscrit and Bakha MSS., which I conveyed to England, have been presented to the Royal Asiatic Society, in whose library they are deposited. The contents of many, still unexamined, may throw additional light on the history of ancient India.”

Similarly, Dr. Bühler (1876, p. 28) wrote:

> “Very soon after the beginning of my search, a great many ancient MSS. were offered to me for sale, out of which I selected upwards of 160, more than forty of which were written on birch bark. As I also increased the number of MSS. to be copied to more than one hundred, the total of books which I finally took with me from Kashmir is considerably over 270.”

## References

1. *The Aśokāvadāna: Sanskrit Text compared with Chinese Versions* (Edited and partly translated by Sujitkumar Mukhopadhyaya, 1960). New Delhi: Sahitya Akademi.

2. Beal, Samuel (1888). *The Life of Hiuen-Tsiang: by the Shamans Hwui Li and Yens-Tsung, With an Introduction containing an account of the work of I-Tsing.* London: K. Paul, Trench, Trübner.

3. *Śrīmad Bhāgavata MahāPurāṇa: (Sanskrit) with Hindi translation*, 2 vols. (81st ed., Vikrama Samvat 2071; 1st ed., Samvat 1997). Gorakhpur: Gita Press.

4. Bhattacharya, Dr. B. (1944, March). 'New Light on the History of the Imperial Gupta Dynasty.' *The Journal of the Bihar Research Society, Vol. 30, Article I.*

5. *Bhaviṣya MahāPurāṇa: (Sanskrit) with Hindi translation* by Pandit Baburam Upadhyay, 3 vols. (2006). Prayāg: Hindi Sahitya Sammelan.

6. *The Brahmāṇḍa MahāPurāṇam: (Sanskrit) With English Introduction, Verse-Index and Textual Correction.* Dr. K. V. Sharma (Ed.) Krishnadas Sanskrit Series 41, Madhyama bhāga. Varanasi: Krishnadas Academy.

7. Bühler, Dr. G. (1876). 'Sanskrit MSS: Extract from Dr. G. Bühler's preliminary Report on the results of the search for Sanskrit MSS. in Kaśmīr.' *The Indian Antiquary: A Journal of Oriental Research in Archaeology, History, Literature, Language, Philosophy, Religion, Folklore, etc., Vol. 5,* 27–31. Bombay: Thacker, Vining & Co.

8. *The Dīpavaṁsa: An Ancient Buddhist Historical Record* (English translation by Herman Oldenberg, 2006). New Delhi (First published: Berlin, 1879).

9. Giles, Herbert A. (Re-trans.) (1923). *The Travels of Fa-hsien (399–414 A.D.), or Record of the Buddhistic Kingdoms*. Cambridge University Press.

10. Gwasha Lal, P. (1932). *A Short History of Kashmir: From the Earliest Times to the Present Day* (3rd ed.). Kashmir Research Institute.

11. Jagannadha Rao, Nadimpalli (1931). *The Age of the Mahabharata War.*

12. Kalhaṇa (1148). *Rājataraṅgiṇī (Chronicle of the Kings of Kashmir) (Sanskrit text), edited with Hindi translation* by Shri Ramtej Shastri Pandey (Vikrama Samvat 2017 (AD 1960), rpt. ed. 1985). Delhi & Varanasi: Chaukhamba Sanskrit Pratishthan.

13. Krishnamachariar, M. (1937). *History of Classical Sanskrit Literature: Being an elaborate account of all branches of Classical Sanskrit Literature, with full Epigraphical and Archaeological Notes and References, an Introduction dealing with Languages, Philology and Chronology, and Index of Authors and Works.* Madras.

14. *Mahābhārata: (Sanskrit) with Hindi translation* by Pandit Rāmanārāyaṇadatta Śastri Pāṇdeya, 6 vols. Gorakhpur: Gita Press.

15. *The Mahāvaṁsa:* or *The Great Chronicle of Ceylon* (English translation by Wilhelm Geiger, 1912). The Pali text Society, Oxford University Press.

16. Majumdar, R. C. (1944). 'A forged Purāna-text on the Imperial Guptas.' *The Indian Historical Quarterly, Narendra Nath Law (Ed.), Vol. 20,* 345–350. Calcutta.

17. *Matsya Purāṇa: (Sanskrit) with Hindi translation.* Gorakhpur: Gita Press.

18. McCrindle, J. W. (1877). *Ancient India as Described by Megasthenes and Arrian: a translation of the Fragments of the Indika of Megasthenes collected by Dr. Schwanbeck, and of the First part of the Indika of Arrian.* London: Trübner & Co.

19. Pargiter, F. E. (1910). 'Ancient Indian Genealogies and Chronology.' *The Journal of the Royal Asiatic Society of Great Britain and Ireland,* January 1910, Article I. London.

20. Pargiter, F. E. (1913). *The Purāṇa Text of the Dynasties of The Kali Age: with Introduction and Notes.* Oxford: University Press.

21. Sachau, Dr. Edward C. (Ed.) (1910). *Alberuni's India: An Account of the Religion, Philosophy, Literature, Geography, Chronology, Astronomy, Customs, Laws and Astrology of India, about A.D. 1030* (English ed., 2 vols.). London: Trübner & Co.

22. Shastri, Mahamahopadhyaya Dr. Haraprasad (1928, September). 'The Maha-Puranas.' *The Journal of the Bihar and Orissa Research Society (J.B.O.R.S.), Vol. 14(3),* 323–340. Patna.

23. Singh, Sahana (2017). *The Educational Heritage of Ancient India: How an Ecosystem of Learning was Laid to Waste.* Chennai: Notion Press.

24. Smith, Vincent A. (1910). *The Oxford Student's History of India* (2nd ed.). Oxford: Clarendon Press.

25. Smith, Vincent A. (1914). *Early History of India: From 600 B.C. to the Muhammadan Conquest including the Invasion of Alexander the Great* (3rd ed.). Oxford: Clarendon Press.

26. Smith, Vincent A. (1915). *The Oxford Student's History of India* (5th ed.). Oxford: Clarendon Press.

27. Smith, Vincent A. (1951). *The Oxford Student's History of India* (15th ed. Revised by H.G. Rawlinson). Oxford University Press.

28. Stein, M. A. (1900). *Kalhaṇa's Rājataraṅgiṇī: A Chronicle of the Kings of Kashmir, English translation with an Introduction, Commentary and Appendices,* Vol. I. Westminster (MDCCCC).

29. Tod, Lt. Col. James (1829). *Annals and Antiquities of Rajasthan or the Central and Western Rajpoot States of India* (Vol. 1). Oxford: University Press.

30. *Vāyu Purāṇam: (Sanskrit)* (Śālivāhana Śaka 1905, AD 1983). Ānandāśrama Sanskrit Granthāvaliḥ, No. 49.

31. Venkatachelam, Pandit Kota (Kali 5054, AD 1953b). *The Plot in Indian Chronology*. Arya Vijnana, Publication 17. Vijayawada.

32. Venkatachelam, Pandit Kota (Kali 5058, AD 1957a). *Chronology of Ancient Hindu History Part I*. Arya Vijnana Grandhamala, Publication 23. Vijayawada.

33. Venkatachelam, Pandit Kota (Kali 5058, AD 1957b). *Chronology of Ancient Hindu History Part II*. Arya Vijnana Grandhamala, Publication 24. Vijayawada.

34. *Viṣṇu Purāṇa: (Sanskrit) with Hindi translation by* Śrī Munilāl Gupta (6th ed., Samvat 2024; 1st ed., Samvat 1990). Gorakhpur: Gita Press.

35. Wilford, Capt. Francis (1799). 'On the Chronology of the Hindus.' *Asiatic Researches; or Transactions of the Society Instituted in Bengal for inquiring into the History and Antiquities, the Arts, Sciences, and Literature, Vol. 5,* 241–295. London.

36. Wilson, Horace Hayman (1825). 'An Essay on the Hindu History of Cashmir.' *Asiatic Researches; or Transactions of the Society Instituted in Bengal for inquiring into the History and Antiquities, the Arts, Sciences, and Literature of Asia, Vol. 15,* 1–119.

37. Wilson, Horace Hayman (Trans.) (1840). *The Vishṇu Purāṇa: A System of Hindu Mythology and Tradition*. London.

38. Wright, Daniel (1877). *History of Nepal: with an Introductory Sketch of the Country and People of Nepal* (Translated from Parbatiya by Munshi Shew Shunker Singh & Pandit Śhrī Gunanand, rpt. 1990). New Delhi: Asian Educational Services.

# 4

# CALENDARS AND ASTRONOMY OF ANCIENT INDIA

To understand the history of ancient India, it is essential to be familiar with the calendars that were being used in ancient India. Indians were the first to have calendars and it is no surprise that the word 'calendar' comes from the Sanskrit word '*kālāntara* (कालांतर)' which is a combination of the two Sanskrit words, *kāla* (काल) and *antara* (अंतर). *Kāla* means time and *antara* means gap. Thus, *kālāntara* means the interval or gap between two events or periods in time. In other words, it means the tracking of time (Jarsha, 2010).

The use of calendars in the Indian subcontinent can be traced back to Vedic times (more than 5,000 years ago). Many calendars have been used in India over the millennia due to its long history and vast area. Indian calendars are lunisolar (employing the combined motions of the Sun and the Moon) in which months are based on the lunar motion and are 29 ½ days long. The year is a solar year on average, accomplished by having a 13th month every third year. A lunar month is divided into two parts–*Śukla Pakṣa* or *Suda* (waxing Moon), and *Kṛṣṇa Pakṣa* or *Vada* (waning Moon).

## Evidence of Great Antiquity from Astronomy of Ancient India

Dr. B. G. Sidharth (1999), director of India's B. M. Birla Science Centre, proves in his book, *The Celestial Key to the Vedas*, that the earliest portions of the Ṛgveda, the world's oldest teachings, can be dated to ten thousand years before the present. He has provided evidence that advanced astronomical concepts such as precession, heliocentrism, and the eclipse cycle were first discovered by Vedic astronomers. He states in his book:

> “Toward the end of 1990 it became apparent to me that many of the astronomical references in the Ṛg Veda could be meaningfully interpreted if they were set against a date of 7300 B.C., and at first sight this appeared to me completely absurd.” (p. 7)

> “Composition of portions of the Ṛg Veda as early as 7300 B.C. would imply that Vedic civilization would have extended to several centuries before 7300 B.C., because the Ṛg Veda already contains the results of a long astronomical tradition. This would take us into the last great Ice Age, which according to geophysicists, ended about ten thousand years ago.” (p. 67)

> “Once the antiquity of the Ṛg Veda beyond 7000 B.C. is recognized, several incomprehensible hymns and references in the Ṛg Veda and Vedic literature fall into place very meaningfully. For example, the list of *nakshatras* or lunar asterisms in Taittirīya Brāhmaṇa (1.5.2) starts with Kṛittikā or the Pleiades, as the first of the divine stars, that is, the star at the winter solstice, and ends with Visākha (Libra) as the last, that is, the star at the summer solstice (cf. Taittirya Samhita, 6.5.3). … originally Rohiṇī was at the winter solstice that then shifted around 8500 B.C. to the Pleiades, Kṛittikā. In fact, in the Mahābhārata story, there is a terrible battle and Kārttikeya (literally "born of Kṛittika") is split asunder, the second part becoming diametrically opposite Viśakha (in Libra), which indeed was the summer solstice in that epoch. (Viśakha literally means "split.")” (p. 73)

While discussing the *calendric astronomy* of the Vedas, Dr. Sidharth writes:

> “Thus, the wheel of time has 12 parts and 360 spokes or days or 720 pairs of day-nights, with a remainder of about 5 days (ṚV 1.164). This is evidently a solar calendar.” (p. 86)

> “From time immemorial, Vedic Indians have been using a luni-solar calendar. The origin of this calendar is again to be found in the Ṛg Veda. … He also knows the moon of "later birth" (that is, the thirteenth intercalated month, added periodically to reconcile the lunar year of 354 days with the solar year of 365 days [ṚV 1.25]). …
>
> A primitive society cannot be expected to calculate the year or the lunar month or other astronomical periodicities to any great degree of accuracy.” (p. 86)

Vṛddha Garga was an ancient Indian astronomer whose work in astronomy is described in *Mahābhārata* (Vol. 4, Śalya Parva 37.14–16). This suggests that Vṛddha Garga lived at least by the time of Mahābhārata. India's excellence in astronomy continued till the early AD 1700s. William Hunter (1893, p. 64), the 19th century British Indologist, wrote in his book:

> “The Brāhmans had advanced far in astronomy before the Greeks arrived in India in 327 B.C. ... The fame of the Brāhman astronomers spread westward, and their works were translated by the Arabs about 800 A.D., and so reached Europe. ... An Indian astronomer, the Rājā Jai Singh [the king of Jaipur], was able to correct the list of stars published by the celebrated French astronomer De la Hire in 1702.”

William Hunter (1799, p. 177) wrote the following in the paper, *Some account of the Astronomical Labours of Jayasinha, Rajah of Ambhere, Or Jayanagar:*

> “The name of Jayasinha is not unknown in *Europe* ; it has been consigned to immortality by the pen of the illustrious Sir WILLIAM JONES : but yet, the extent of his exertions in the cause of science is little known ; ...
>
> JEY-SING or JAYASINHA succeeded to the inheritance of the ancient Rajahs of Ambhere, in year *Vicramaditya* 1750, corresponding to 1693 of the *Christian era*. ... he appears to have particularly attached himself to the mathematical sciences, and his reputation for skill in them stood so high, that he was chosen by the Emperor MAHOMMED SHAH to reform the calendar, which, from the inaccuracy of the existing tables, had ceased to correspond with the actual appearance of the heavens. JAYASINHA undertook the task, and constructed a new set of tables, which in honour of the reigning prince he named *Zeej MahommedShahy*. By these almanacks are constructed at *Dehly*, and all astronomical computations made at the present time.”

M. Elphinstone (1874, p. 144) who worked for the British East India Company and later as the Governor of Bombay, wrote on the originality of 'Hindu science':

> “In the first part of their progress, all other nations were in still greater ignorance than they, and in the more advanced stages, where they were more likely to have borrowed, not only is their mode of proceeding peculiar to themselves, but it is often founded on principles with which

no other ancient people were acquainted, and shows a knowledge of discoveries not made, even in Europe, till within the course of the last two centuries. ”

Table 8 and Figure 7 show major calendars which were in substantial use in ancient India. Some of these are still in use in most parts of India. It must be noted that the list of calendars is not exhaustive; several more calendars have been used.

**Table 8: Main calendars of ancient India**

| Sr. No. | Name of the Calendar | Event | Started in | |
|---|---|---|---|---|
| | | | Kaliyuga Year | Christian Year |
| 1 | Yudhiṣṭhira Śaka | Coronation of Yudhiṣṭhira after the Mahābhārata War | 36 BK* | 3138 BC |
| 2 | Kaliyuga Śaka | Śrī Krishna passed away | 1 | 3102 BC |
| 3 | Saptarṣi, Laukikābda, or Yudhiṣṭhira Kāla Śaka | *Swargarohana* (passing away) of Yudhiṣṭhira | 26 | 3076 BC |
| 4 | Mālava-gaṇa Śaka | Mālavā attained independence | 2377 | 725 BC |
| 5 | Cyrus Śaka or Śaka Nṛpa Kāla | Beginning of the Persian Empire by Cyrus | 2552 | 550 BC |
| 6 | Śrī Harṣa Samvat | Śrī Harṣa Vikramāditya of Ujjain drove away the Śakas | 2646 | 457 BC |
| 7 | Gupta Yuga | Beginning of the Gupta Dynasty | 2775 | 327 BC |
| 8 | Vikrama Samvat | Vikramāditya of Ujjain became the emperor of India | 3046 | 57 BC |
| 9 | Śālivāhana Śaka | Śālivāhana drove away Śakas and became the emperor of India | 3181 | 79 AD |

*BK = Before Kaliyuga

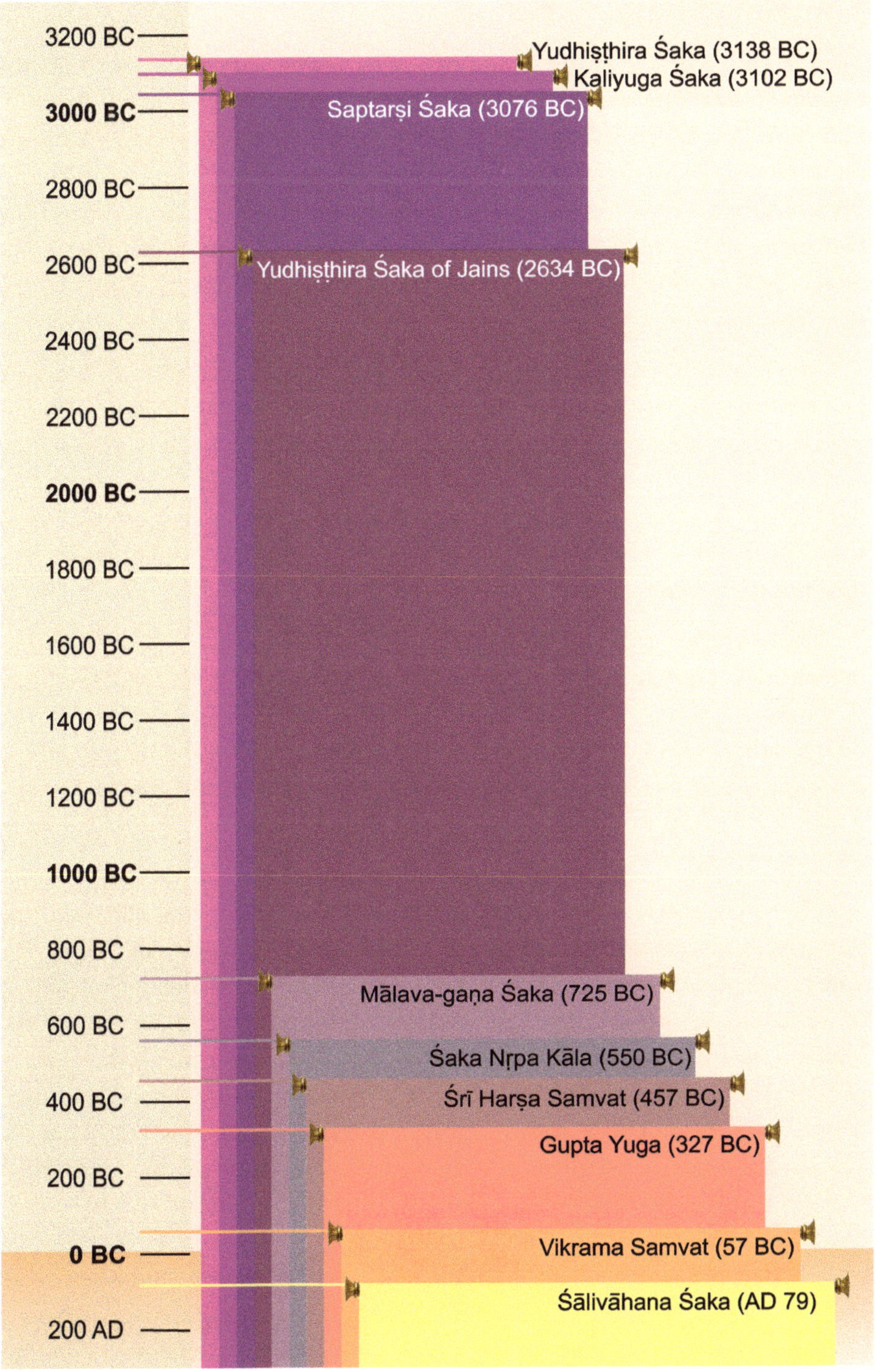


**Figure 7: Main calendars of ancient India**

## The Mahābhārata War

The early colonial Indologists did not doubt the historicity of the Mahābhārata War. William Jones listed Abhimanyu (Chapter 2, Table 3) and John Bentley listed YUDHISHTHIR, VYASA, and PARICSHIT (Table 6); all these people are from the Mahābhārata age. H. H. Wilson's remarks on Viṣṇu Purāṇa, shown in Chapter 3, demonstrate that he also accepted the historicity of the Mahābhārata War and conjectured it to have taken place about 1,400 years before Christianity. The war was called a myth only by the later colonial Indologists.

The Mahābhārata War between Kauravas and Pāṇḍavas took place 36 years before the beginning of the Kaliyuga in 3102 BC as described in the epic itself (*Mahābhārata*, Vol. 4, Stri Parva 25.43-46, etc.). This puts the war near the end of 3139 BC. The great war started on *Mārgaśīrṣa Suda* 11 and ended on the *Mārgaśīrṣa Amāvasyā*, after 18 days. Mārgaśīrṣa Suda 11 is celebrated as *Gita Jayanti* since Śrī Krishna gave Gita *upadeśa* (sermon) to Arjuna on this day before the war started.

The war took place at Kurukṣetra (located 170 km north of Delhi) in present-day Haryana. The various places associated with the war, such as Brahma Sarovar, Jyotisar, Bhishma Kund, etc. are located there. The Bhagavadgītā is believed to have been delivered there for the first time. The ancient mound measuring about 650 x 250 meters is in the nearby village, Amin. According to the local tradition, the name, Amin, is derived from Abhimanyu, the son of Arjuna.

The Mahābhārata War is vouched by the great epic Mahābhārata, the Purāṇas, Rājataraṅgiṇī (the chronicle of the kings of Kashmir), Nepal Rāj Vaṁśāvali and numerous ancient texts. As discussed in detail in Chapter 11, *Rājataraṅgiṇī* (Kalhaṇa, 1148/1985; Stein, 1900) describes that at the time of the Mahābhārata War, Gonanda II, the nominal king of Kashmir, under the regency of his mother, was only a year and a half old. Therefore, Kauravas and Pāṇḍavas did not seek his support in the war. As discussed in Chapter 12, Nepal Rāj Vaṁśāvali describes that Jitedāsti, the seventh king in the Kirāta Dynasty of Nepal, fought on the side of the Pāṇḍavas and was killed in the war; thereafter, his son Gali was crowned as the next king of Nepal. Similarly, as stated in Chapter 5, Sahadeva, son of Jarāsandha and the king of Magadha, died in the war and his son Somādhi was installed on the throne of Magadha. As discussed in Chapter 8, Bṛhadbala, the king of Kośala, was killed by Abhimanyu, and his son Bṛhatkṣaya was crowned as the next king of Ayodhya.

The epic *Mahābhārata* which consists of about one hundred thousand verses describes the war and the history before it in great detail. The date of the Mahābhārata War is important for the chronology of ancient India as the chronology given in the Purāṇas stands in relation to the date of the war. Nonetheless, scores of books have been written on determining the exact year of the Mahābhārata War.

## Date of the War from Astronomical Positions

The epic Mahābhārata contains hundreds of astronomical positions recorded which can be used to verify the date of the Mahābhārata War. In the words of Professor K. Srinivasa Raghavan (1969, p. 15), "The Maha Bharata is teeming with plenty of astronomical information regarding its own age" and "which are all consistent". The following are a few examples of the many astronomical positions described in the *Mahābhārata*:

1. Śrī Krishna left Upaplavya (उपप्लव्य) for Hastināpura for the peace mission in the *Maitra muhurta* (third muhurta of the morning from 7.36 am to 8.24 am) in the *Revati* Nakṣatra (lunar asterism), in the month of *Kumuda* (Kārtika). It was the end of the *Sharad Ṛtu* (autumn) and the beginning of *Hemant Ṛtu*. The fields were green, full of fresh crops (Vol. 3, Udyoga Parva 83.6–29).
2. After the failure of the peace mission, Krishna left Hastināpura on the day of *Uttara Phālguni*. Karṇa accompanied him in the chariot and had a long conversation. Krishna advised Karṇa that *Amāvasyā* will fall after the seventh day from the present one (in the *Jyeṣṭa* asterism), presided over by *Śakra* (Indra) *Devata*, and the war be started then (Udyoga Parva 142.16–18).
3. Pāṇḍavas left for the battlefield in Kurukṣetra in the *Puṣya* Nakṣatra (Vol. 4, Śalya Parva 35.10, 15).
4. Balarāma did not want to take part in the war. He left for pilgrimage in the *Puṣya* Nakṣatra and returned in the *Śravaṇa* Nakṣatra (Śalya Parva 34.6).
5. Duryodhana gave orders to his armies to march to the battlefield in Kurukṣetra in the *Puṣya* Nakṣatra (Udyoga Parva 150.3).
6. Bhīṣma, who had been on the bed of arrows from the tenth day of the war, breathed his last on the *Māgha Śukla Ashtami* in *Rohiṇi* Nakṣatra at Noon (Vol. 5, Śanti Parva 47.1–4). This was the day of *Uttarāyaṇa* (the beginning of the Sun's northward journey) for which Bhīṣma had waited. On his last day, he told Yudhiṣṭhira that it was the bright half of the month of Māgha

and one-fourth of Māgha was over (Vol. 6, Anuśāśana Parva 167.26–28).

## A Few Estimates of the Date

Here are some estimates of the date of the Mahābhārata War by various scholars.

1. N. Jagannadha Rao (1931, p. 90–94) has described in detail the calculations by which he obtained 3139 BC as the year of the Mahābhārata War, based on the astronomical positions described in the Mahābhārata.

2. Based on plenty of astronomical positions given in the Mahābhārata, Prof. K. S. Raghavan (1969, p. 23) estimated the date of the Mahābhārata War to be November 3067 BC. Prof. Raghavan estimated the dates of several events which occurred before and after the war and all the dates fell in a proper sequence within a reasonable range.

3. Over thirty years later, Dr. B. N. Narahari Achar (2003, 2012), Professor Emeritus in the Department of Physics at The University of Memphis, obtained an identical 3067 BC date using Planetarium software. The 3067 BC date derived by Prof. Raghavan and Achar is only 71 years away from the end of the 3139 BC date given in the Purāṇas, relatively, a small difference for the large span of 5,100 years.

4. Saroj Bala (2021) has dated sequentially many astronomical references extracted from the Mahābhārata by using the Planetarium software. All sky views observed sequentially fall between 3153 BC and 3102 BC and the date of the war falls exactly in 3139 BC.

5. Saroj Bala adds that in the Mahābhārata days, nakṣatras (lunar asterisms) were being counted from Rohiṇi, as the equinox fell on that one. Now, the spring equinox is in the third quarter of Purva Bhādrapada Nakṣatra;

### What is a Nakṣatra?

Ancient Indian astronomers from the Vedic age (before the Mahābhārata time) divided the 360 degrees circle of the Moon's orbit around the Earth into twenty-seven parts, called nakṣatras, each part covering 13 degrees, 20 minutes of the circle. The nakṣatras are named after a prominent star or constellation in the respective part of the sky.

thus, the equinox has moved by more than 5.25 nakṣatras (Krittikā, Bharaṇi, Aśvini, Revati, and Uttara Bhādrapada). See the list of nakṣatras in Table 9. The movement is in reverse order, starting from number 4.

**Table 9: Names of the nakṣatras according to Vṛddha Garga and the Purānas**

| Names of the Nakṣatras | | |
|---|---|---|
| 1. Aśvini | 10. Maghā | 19. Moola |
| 2. Bharaṇi | 11. Purva Phālguni | 20. Purvāṣāḍhā |
| 3. Krittika¯ | 12. Uttara Phālguni | 21. Uttarāṣāḍhā |
| 4. Rohiṇi | 13. Hasta | 22. Śravaṇa |
| 5. Mrigaśirṣa | 14. Citrā | 23. Dhaniṣṭhā |
| 6. Ārdrā | 15. Svāti | 24. Śatabhiśā |
| 7. Punarvasu | 16. Viśākhā | 25. Purva Bhādrapada |
| 8. Puṣya | 17. Anurādhā | 26. Uttara Bhādrapada |
| 9. Aśleṣā | 18. Jyeṣṭhā | 27. Revati |

## Yudhiṣṭhira Śaka (3138 BC)

Pāṇḍavas were victorious in the Mahābhārata War and Yudhiṣṭhira, the eldest of the Pāṇḍavas, was coronated as the emperor of Bhāratavarṣa (Indian subcontinent) on the 28th day after the war started, in 3138 BC. Yudhiṣṭhira Śaka was started to mark this historic event. The Yudhiṣṭhira Śaka used by Jains and Buddhists is a little different, starting 468 years after the beginning of the Kaliyuga or in 2634 BC. As discussed in Chapter 9, *Jina Vijaya* uses the Yudhiṣṭhira Śaka of Jains in giving the birth year of Kumārila Bhatta, a contemporary of Ādi Śaṅkarāchārya (Narayana Sastry, 1916/1971, p. 22, 149).

### Evidence for Use of Yudhiṣṭhira Śaka

There are many scriptural and archaeological proofs of the contemporary use of the Yudhiṣṭhira Śaka by the people. An inscription found by Francis Buchanan (1807/1988, p. 231) in the temple of Madhukeswara in the village of Banavasi in the North Canara district is dated year 168 of the Yudhiṣṭhira Śaka, which translates to 3138 BC + 168 = 2970 BC. See Chapter 14 for details

1. The inscriptions in the Belgaum district of the Karnataka state are dated in the Yudhiṣṭhira Śaka. Francis Buchanan (p. 231) writes:

> "The next most ancient inscription, of which he gave me a copy, is at *Balagami*, a place south-east from hence in the *Mysore* territory. *Yudishtara* or *Dharma Rāja*, dwelt at it one year ; and afterwards, during the reign of *Vira Belalla*, it was for some time the capital of *Karnata*. The ruins are said to contain an immense number of inscriptions. Two of these are dated in the reign of *Yudishtara* ; and the others are all in the reign of *Jain* princes."

2. In Chapter 9, the evidence for use of Yudhiṣṭhira Śaka is given as follows:
   a. In his Bṛhat-Śaṅkara Vijaya, Chitsukha informs us that Śaṅkara took the permission of his mother to become a sannyāsī on the 11th day of the bright half of the month of Kārtika of the year 2639 of Yudhiṣṭhira Śaka (500 BC), and was ordained as a regular sannyāsī by Govinda Bhagavatpāda on the 2nd day of the bright half of the month of Phālguna of the year 2640 of Yudhiṣṭhira Śaka (499 BC).
   b. The dates of the establishment of the five Pīṭhas by Śrī Ādi Śaṅkarāchārya are recorded in the Yudhiṣṭhira Śaka.
3. The dates of the Pīṭhādhipatis (heads of the pīthas) preserved at the Dvārakā Maṭha, from its beginning to starting of the Vikrama Samvat in 57 BC, are in the Yudhiṣṭhira Śaka (Narayana Sastry, 1916/1971, p. 219).
4. The copper plate inscription of Sundhanva is dated in the Yudhiṣṭhira Śaka 2663 (Narayana Sastry, p. 220).

## Kaliyuga Śaka (3102 BC) and Astronomical Knowledge of Ancient India

Kaliyuga, the present age, commenced in 3102 BC, on February 20 (by extrapolating the current Gregorian calendar) which was the first day of the bright half of the *Chaitra* month, 36 years after the Mahābhārata War (Narayana Sastry, 1916/1971, p. 17). Kaliyuga is reckoned in the 60-year cycles of Jupiter (described later) beginning from the first day of *Chaitra* of the year *Pramādi* according to the Southern astronomers.

Dvāparayuga ended and the Kaliyuga started when Śrī Krishna left the earth (Matsya Purāṇa 273.49). At that time, the Saptarṣi (Big Dipper) were in the *Maghā* Nakṣatra (*Bhāgavata Purāṇa*, Skandha 12, 2.29–31; *Viṣṇu Purāṇa*, 4th Aṁśa, 24.106–107). Yudhiṣṭhira had ruled for 36 years when he heard that Śrī Krishna had left the earth. Upon hearing the news, Yudhiṣṭhira gave up the throne and installed Parīkṣit, the grandson of Arjuna, as the emperor in Hastināpura, and Vajra, the son of Aniruddha and the grandson of Śrī Krishna, as the king of the surviving *Yādavas* in Indraprastha (*Mahābhārata,* Vol. 4, Stri Parva 25.43–46, etc.). T. S. Narayana Sastry (1916/1971, p. 11, 12 footnote 10) states in *The Age of Śankara:*

> “The Mahābhārata and all the important Purāṇas uniformly hold that Sri Krishṇa who was a contemporary of the Pāṇḍavas and Kauravas and who had witnessed the Mahābhārata War fought between them lived for a period of over 100 years, that he passed away from this earth 36 years after the said Mahābhārata War and that the Kali Yuga commenced on the same day on which the Lord left this earth. … (*vide,* for instance, Mahābhārata : Stri parva, XXV. 39-45 ; Mausala Parva, I. 13, II. 19-21, III. 25-41, IV. 12–24, VI. 23, VII. 10–12, VIII. 26–28 ; and Mahāprasthānika Parva, I. 1–45; Viṣṇu Purāṇa, Fourth Aṁśa : XX, XXIV, 38–40, 105–115, Fifth Aṁśa : XXXVII. 18–20, XXXVIII. 8–9 ; Devi Bhāgavata Purāṇa, Skandha II. Ch. VIII, Skandha III, Ch. xxiii ; Srimad Bhāgavata Purāṇa, Skandha XI. Ch. VI. 23–26, Skandha XII. Ch. II ; Brahma Purāṇa, Ch. CCXII. 9–10; Garuda Purāṇa, Ch. CI ; Harivamsa, III. 47–48 ; Sūrya Siddhānta, Ch I.)”

The Kaliyuga is the most widely quoted era in all the Purāṇas and the ancient astronomical works such as Sūrya Siddhānta. It is still being tracked in all *Panchāngas* (India's traditional annual calendars since ancient times). Figure 8 shows a photo of the cover page of a Panchānga published in Marathi in AD 1993. The cover page shows the current year in several contemporary eras—Kaliyuga Śaka 5095, Śrī Śālivāhana Śaka 1915, Vikrama Samvat 2049–50, Christian Era 1993–94, Pārsī Era 1362–1363, Hijari Era 1413–1414, and more, all in the Devanāgarī script.

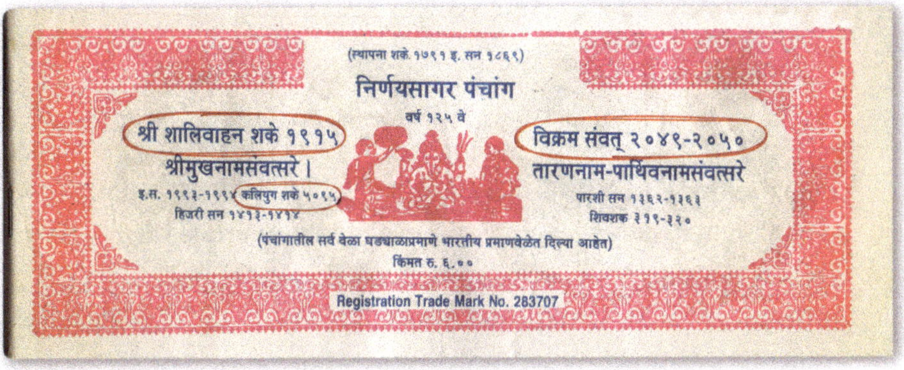


**Figure 8: Panchānga cover page showing the current Kaliyuga year**

1. Pandit Kota Venkatachelam (1956a, p. 17–18) states in his book, *Indian Eras*, that the seven planets ('planet' used as a generic term)—Saturn, Jupiter, Mars, Venus, Mercury, the Sun, and the Moon were in conjunction (together) in *Meśa* at 2 hours, 27 minutes and 30 seconds on February 20, 3102 BC. The Kaliyuga is reckoned from that moment. Our Panchāngas have been prepared year after year, based on the Kaliyuga.

2. Count Björnstjerna (1779–1847), a Swedish lieutenant general, Swedish envoy in the court of Great Britain, and author of several books on a variety of topics such as politics, economy, and history, wrote (1840, p. 23–26):

> " Kali-Yug, the actual period of the world's existence, begins, according to the astronomical calculations of the Hindoos, 3,102 years before the birth of Christ, on the 20th of February, at 27 minutes 30 seconds past two o'clock (so precisely is the date of this event given).
>
> They say that there was at that time a conjunction of the planets, and their tables show this conjunction. Bailly [the famous French astronomer], in his Essay on the Astronomy of the Hindoos, says that Jupiter and Mercury were then in the same degree of the ecliptic, Mars only eight, and Saturn seven degrees from it : whence it follows, that at the time assigned by the Brahmins for the commencement of the Kali-Yug, those four planets must have been successively hidden by the beams of the Sun, first Saturn, then Mars, then Jupiter, and last Mercury ; they appear, therefore, in conjunction, and though Venus was not visible at that time, it was natural to say that a conjunction of the planets then took place.
>
> The calculation of the Brahmins agrees with our European tables, which proves that it is the result of actual observations. ...
>
> Bailly further informs us that Laubere, who was sent by Louis XIV as ambassador to the king of Siam, brought from that country, in the year 1687, astronomical tables and calculations of solar eclipses ; other tables were sent home by Patouillet, a missionary in India, who had procured them in Krischnapooram, a town in the Carnatic. M. Gentil also brought some tables to Europe from the Brahmins at Tirvalore.
>
> Several other astronomical tables have been subsequently brought to Europe by the English ; and all agree in their calculations, though they originate with different persons in India, in ages very distant from each other, and in widely separate places.

Bailly makes the following remarks on these tables :—

"The motion calculated by the Brahmins does not differ, during the long space of 4,383 years, (which had elapsed between these observations and those of Bailly,) so much as a single minute from the tables of Cassini and Meyer. It cannot be denied that the tables brought to Europe by Laubere, in the year 1687, under Louis XIV., came at a time when neither Cassini nor Meyer's tables were in existence, and we must, therefore, allow that the coincidence between them and the calculations of the Brahmins can be no other than the result of accurate astronomical observations by both parties. We may appeal likewise to another fact, namely, that the Indian tables indicate an annual variation in the moon, the same that was discovered by Tycho Brahe, and which was unknown both to the school of Alexandria and to the Arabs, who followed the calculations of that school." (p. 25)

These several facts may suffice to prove the remote antiquity and great extent of astronomical knowledge among the ancient Hindoos. ”

“ But, if the Hindoos, as we have seen above, had attained such a high degree of astronomical and geometrical knowledge 4,400 years before Bailly wrote (about 1780), how many centuries further back must the beginning of their civilization have been? For the human mind can advance only step by step, and very slowly, in the career of science. This carries us so far back into the abyss of ages that the mind is lost in astonishment. ” (p. 26)

Jean-Sylvian Bailly (1736–1793), quoted by Bjorstjerna in the preceding paragraphs, was a mathematician, astronomer, and historian of astronomy. He was elected a member of the French academy of sciences in 1763. He wrote the *Traité de l'astronomie indienne et orientale (A Treatise on Indian and Oriental Astronomy).* Later in his life, he got involved in the early part of the French revolution and was executed.

3. Har Bilas Sarda (1922), F.R.S.L., who was a member of the Royal Asiatic Society of Great Britain and Ireland, a fellow of the Royal Statistical Society of London, and a member of the Statistical Association of Boston, U.S.A. and author of several history books writes:

> "The quantities which the Indian tables assign to other astronomical elements, viz., the mean motions of Jupiter and Saturn, have been found to agree almost exactly not with what is observed at the present time, but with what the theory of gravity shows would have been observed at the beginning of the Kaliyug. Laplace discovered it after the publication of the *Astronomie Indien* and inserted it in the *Journal des Savane.*" (p. 285)

> "The length of the Hindu tropical year as deduced from the Hindu tables is 365 days, 5 hrs, 50 minutes, 35 seconds, while La Callie's observation gives 365-5-48-49. This makes the year at the time of the Hindu observation longer than at present by 1'46". It is, however, an established fact that the year has been decreasing in duration from the time immemorial and shall continue to decrease. In about 40 centuries, the time of year decreases by *about 40 ½"*. This, then, is *an unmistakable proof of the very high Antiquity of Indian astronomy.* The observation by the Hindus must have been in the Dwapur (more than 5,000 years ago)." (p. 286)

## Evidence for use of Kaliyuga Era

1. The great Sanskrit poet and dramatist, Kālidāsa, one of the nine gems in the court of Emperor Vikramāditya (Ujjain), states in his book, *Jyotirvidābharaṇa* (22nd Aswasa), that he began its composition in Vaiśākha month after 3,068 years of Kaliyuga had passed (Venkatachelam, 1957a, p. 252):

   वर्षे सिंधुरदर्शनांबरगुणैर्याते (३,०६८) कलेस्सम्मिते।
   मासे माधवसंज्ञिके च विहितो ग्रंथक्रियोपक्रमः ।।

   Varṣe sindhuradarśanāṁbaraguṇairyāte (3,068) kalessammite ।
   Māse mādhavasaṅjñike ca vihito granthakriyopakramaḥ ।।

2. The great astronomer and mathematician, Bhāskarāchārya, in his *Siddhānta Śiromaṇi*, chapter Kālamānādhyāya, verse 28, gives Kali Śaka in the following manner (Arkasomayaji, 1980, p. 14):

   > "Six Manus have elapsed in this Kalpa, thereafter 27 yugas, as well as three yugapādas namely Kṛita, Tretā and Dwāpara. Further 3179 years of this fourth yugapāda namely Kali have elapsed by the end of the Śaka king (which moment was the beginning of the Śaka era.)"

   Meaning:

   3,179 years of Kaliyuga had elapsed (Kaliyuga 3180 was the current year) when the Śaka king was destroyed (by Śālivāhana).

3. Āryabhaṭa states in his book, *The Āryabhaṭīya* (499/1930, p. 54–55):

> “10. When three *Yugapādas* and sixty times sixty years had elapsed (from the beginning of the *yuga*) then twenty-three years of my life had passed. …
>
> 11. The *yuga*, the year, the month, and the day began all together at the beginning of the bright fortnight of Caitra. Time which has no beginning and no end, is measured by (the movement of) the planets and the asterisms on the sphere.”

Quote 10 above means that when Āryabhaṭa was 23 years old, 3,600 years of Kaliyuga had passed, and the current Kaliyuga year was 3601 (AD 499). Thus, we know that Āryabhaṭa was born in AD 476, his widely accepted birth year.

4. According to Abhayankar and Ballabh (1996), following Āryabhaṭa, it is traditionally assumed that the Sun, the Moon, and the five planets were at Meshadi, the first point of the Hindu zodiac, on midnight at Ujjain between February 17 and 18, 3102 BC, which represented the beginning of the Kaliyuga. The Mohenjo-daro Seal No. M430 represents the actual planetary configuration at the beginning of the Kaliyuga on February 7, 3104 BC.

5. Alberuni, the Arab historian, states (Sachau, 1910, p. 4):

> “Regarding the time which has elapsed since the beginning of the *kaliyuga*, there exists no difference amounting to whole years. According to both Brahmagupta and Pulisa, of the *kaliyuga* there have elapsed before our gage-year 4132 years.”

Alberuni states further (p. 7):

> “Now, the year 400 Yazadajird, which we have chosen as a gauge, corresponds to the following years of the Indian eras :—
>
> (1) To the year 1488 of the era of Śrī Harsha,
>
> (2) To the year 1088 of the era of Vikramāditya,
>
> (3) To the year 953 of the Śakakāla”

The Śrī Harṣa Vikramāditya Era above (1) converts to 1488 – 457 BC = AD 1031, as discussed under Śrī Harṣa Samvat.

The Vikrama Samvat above (2) converts to 1088 – 57 BC = AD 1031.

The Śālivāhana Śaka (3) converts to 953 + 78 = AD 1031.

Subtracting AD 1031 from the corresponding Kaliyuga year 4133 (4,132 years have elapsed) gives 3102 BC as the beginning year of the Kaliyuga.

6. Kalhaṇa (1148/1985), in his *Rājataraṅgiṇī* (1.51), used Kaliyuga besides the Kashmir Era (i.e. Laukikābda or Saptarṣi Era or Yudhiṣṭhira Kāla Śaka) which started in Kaliyuga 26 (3076 BC).

7. The Nepal Rāja Vaṁśāvali (the history of Nepal) followed the same Kaliyuga calendar that started in 3102 BC (Indraji and Bühler, 1884, p. 411).

8. Aihole inscription shown in Figure 9 is the stone inscription in Sanskrit in the old Kannada script on the wall of a Jain temple, on top of the hill at Aihole, in the Karnataka state, recording a gift deed. The inscription is by Pulakeshi II, the famous emperor of the Chalukya Dynasty in South India who stopped Harṣavardhana's advance south of the Vindhya mountains.

**Figure 9: Aihole inscription, Karnataka**

*Photo courtesy: Dineshkannambadi at English Wikipedia, CC BY-SA 3.0*

त्रिंशत्सु त्रिसहस्त्रेषु भारतादाहवादितः ।
सप्ताब्दशतयुक्तेषु श(ग)तेष्वब्देषु पञ्चसु (३७३५)।।
पञ्चाशत्सु कलौ काले षट्सु पञ्चशतासु च (५५६)।
समासु समतीतासु शकानामपि भूभुजाम् ।।

Triṁśatsu trisahasreṣu Bhāratādāhavāditaḥ ।
Saptābdaśatayukteṣu śa(ga)teṣvabdeṣu pañcasu ।।
Pañcāśatsu kalau kāle ṣatsu pañcaśatāsu ca ।
Samāsu samatītāsu śakānāmapi bhūbhujām ।।

The text of the inscription has been published in the Indian Antiquary (Fleet, 1876, p. 67–71) and The *Prāchīna-Lekhamālā* (Durgāprasād and Parab, 1892, p. 68–72). Two verses towards the end of the inscription state the date of the inscription in the Kaliyuga and the Śālivāhana Śaka as follows. The second line of the verse in the *Prāchīna-Lekhamālā* contains a suggestion for an alteration. As discussed by Pandit Venkatachelam (1957b, p. 50), additional alteration in the verse made by some people is unnecessary and only this alteration, ***Śateṣu*** to ***Gateṣu*** as shown in the parentheses in the verse, is sufficient to get a meaningful date.

Translation:

> From the Bharata war, and after 3,735 (30 + 3,000 + 700 + 5) years had elapsed in the Kali Era and 556 (50 + 6 + 500) years after the destruction of the Śakas (this temple was constructed).

When 3,735 years of the Kaliyuga had elapsed, 556 years of the (Śālivāhana) Śaka had passed. Therefore, 3735 – 556 = 3,179 years of Kaliyuga had elapsed (Kaliyuga 3180 was the current year) when the Śālivāhana Śaka began. The Śālivāhana Śaka began after 78 years of the Christian Era. Hence, the Kaliyuga began in 3180 – 78 = 3102 BC. See Chapter 14 for further discussion on interpreting this inscription.

## Acknowledgment of Kaliyuga Era by European Indologists

1. Dr. G. Bühler (1876, p. 28), in his commentary on Nepal history and the manuscript of Rājataraṅgiṇī (History of Kashmir), accepted and adopted 3102 BC as the starting point of Kaliyuga Era, and Kaliyuga 26 or 3076 BC as the starting point of Saptarṣi Era, as follows:

> “They also led to the discovery of the real nature of the Kaśmirian era which has been used by Kalhaṇa in the last three books of his chronicle, and is still in use among the Brāhmaṇs of Kaśmir. Its true name, derived from the supposed secular procession of Ursa major, is the era of the Saptarshis. It began on Chaitra Sudi 1st of the 26th [*] year of the Kaliyuga, or March-April 3076 B.C. In using it, the Kaśmirians usually leave out the hundreds, though there are instances in which they have been added. The year 24, stated by Kalhaṇa to be equal to Śaka 1070, is really the year 4224 of the Saptarshi era. With this key it will become possible to fix the chronology of the later Kaśmirian kings with perfect accuracy. I may add that General Cunningham's dates very closely agree with those obtained by reducing Kalhaṇa's Saptarshi years to years of the Christian era.”

*26th year of Kaliyuga corresponds to 3077 BC and 26 years elapsed of Kaliyuga corresponds to 3076 BC.

2. Major General Alexander Cunningham (1883, p. 12–17), a British Indologist and archaeological surveyor for the British government of India, acknowledged in his *Book of Indian Eras* that the starting point of the Kali Era lies in 3102 BC, and the Saptarṣi Era, or the Laukikābda, starts in Kaliyuga 26 or 3077 BC.

3. William Jones (1807b, p. 52) knew when the Kaliyuga Era began and wrote the following about it:

> “ Now, the Hindu astronomers agree, that the 1st *January* 1790 was in the year 4891 of the *Caliyuga*, or their *fourth* period, at the beginning of which, they say, the equinoctial points were in the first degree of *Mesha* and *Tula* ; but they are also of opinion, that the vernal equinox oscillates from the third of *Mina* to the twenty-seventh of *Mesha* and back again in 7200 years, which they divide into four *pādas*, and consequently that it moves in the two intermediate pādas, from the first to the twenty-seventh of *Mesha* and back again in 3600 years : the colure cutting their ecliptick in the first of *Mesha*, which coincides with the first of *Aswini*, at the beginning of every such oscillatory period. ”

## Saptarṣi, Laukikābda, Kashmirābda, or Yudhiṣṭhira Kāla Śaka (3076 BC)

The Saptarṣi Śaka is named after the *Saptarṣi Mandala* (Big Dipper) of the Great Bear constellation shown in Figure 10. It is a bright and easily recognizable cluster of stars in the sky.

The Saptarṣi cycle is based on the movement of this *Mandala* through the 27 nakṣatras (lunar asterisms) listed in Table 9 and is fully described in all the Purāṇas (Krishnamachariar, 1937, p. lxxvi). The Saptarṣi Kāla, also called Kashmirābda or Laukikābda, has been in use in India, particularly in Kashmir, Ladakh, and present-day Himachal Pradesh. This is the main calendar used in the Rājataraṅgiṇī. As mentioned in the first point quoting Dr. Bühler in the preceding section, the Laukikābda began on Chaitra Sudi 1 after 26 years of Kaliyuga (March-April 3076 BC) in commemoration of Yudhiṣṭhira's ascendance to Heavens (Jagannadha Rao, 1931, p. 54).

Purāṇas and other ancient Indian texts mention the movement of the Saptarṣi, through the 27 nakṣatras, staying in each nakṣatra for 100 years (*Matsya Purāṇa* 273.40; *Viṣnu Purāṇa*, 4th Aṁśa 24.106; *Vāyu Purāṇa* 99.421–422; *Brahmāṇḍa*

**Figure 10: Saptarṣi Mandala (Big Dipper)**
*Image adapted from: Notthebestusername, Wikimedia Commons, CC BY-SA 4.0*

*Purāṇa* 74.230–231). For example, see the following verse from Matsya Purāṇa.

सप्तर्षयस्तु वर्तन्ते यत्र नक्षत्रमण्डले ।
सप्तर्षयस्तु तिष्ठन्ति पर्यायेण शतं शतम् ।। ४० ।।

Saptarṣayastu vartante yatra nakṣatramaṇḍale ।
Saptarṣayastu tiṣṭhanti paryāyeṇa śataṁ śatam ।। 40 ।।

*(Matsya Purāṇa 273.40)*

When the saptarṣi's two stars rise first in the east in the night, and whichever nakṣatra is seen in line with the middle of those two stars, the Saptarṣi are said to reside in that nakṣatra for a hundred years (*Matsya Purāṇa* 273.42–43; *Viṣṇu Purāṇa,* 4th Aṁśa 24.105; *Bhāgavata Purāṇa,* Skandha 12, 2.27–28). See the following verses from Matsya Purāṇa.

सप्तर्षीणां च यौ पूर्वौ दृश्येते ह्युदितौ निशि ।। ४२
तयोर्मध्ये तु नक्षत्रं दृश्यते यत्समं दिवि ।
तेन सप्तर्षयो ज्ञेया युक्ता व्योम्नि शतं समाः ।। ४३

Saptarṣīṇāṁ ca yau pūrvau dṛśyete hyuditau niśi ।। 42
Tayormadhye tu nakṣatraṁ dṛśyate yatsamaṁ divi ।
Tena Saptarṣayo jñeyā yuktā vyomni śataṁ samāḥ ।। 43

*(Matsya Purāṇa 273.42–43)*

Alexander Cunningham (1883, p. 15) argues that the Saptarṣi cycle likely started in 6777 BC. It is noteworthy how we arrived at the same year in **Chapter 2**, under 'Did European Historians Know True Antiquity of India's History?'

The Saptarṣi complete one cycle through the 27 nakṣatras in 2,700 years as stated in the Purāṇas (*Brahmāṇḍa Purāṇa* 74.230–231). According to the information received by Alexander Cunningham (1883, p. 12) from the Brahmans of Kangra (in Himachal Pradesh) in AD 1859, the Saptarṣi had been in the Maghā Nakṣatra for 75 years at the beginning of the Kaliyuga and remained in it for another 25 years. Thus, the Saptarṣi entered Maghā in 3177 BC and left it in 3077 BC, entering the next nakṣatra. Therefore, the Saptarṣi cycle must have been in use even before Kaliyuga.

Varāhamihira (1st century BC/1946, 1959) states in the *Brihat Samhita* (13.3) that by adding 2,526 years to the Śaka kāla (of 550 BC), we get the time of Yudhiṣṭhira (his passing away) as shown in the following verse. The same verse is also found in Kalhaṇa's *Rājataraṅgiṇī* (1.56).

आसन्मघासु मुनयः शासति पृथ्वीं युधिष्ठिरे नृपतौ।
षड्द्विकपञ्चद्वियुतः शककालस्तस्य राज्ञश्च।। ३।।

Āsanmaghāsu munayaḥ śāsati Pṛthvīṁ Yudhiṣṭhire nṛpatau
Ṣaḍdvika-pañcadviyutaḥ śakakālastasya rājñaśca ।। 3 ।।

Translation:

The Saptarṣi (Big Dipper) were in Maghā (nakṣatra) when Yudhiṣṭhira was ruling over the earth. The interval between his time and the Śakakāla is 2,526 years.

The cycle of the Saptarṣi movement through the nakṣatras has been used as another method to document the chronology of important historical events as shown by examples in Chapter 7. This cycle is described in *Indian Eras* (Venkatachelam, 1956a, p. 40). The sequence of the nakṣatras in it is given in the reverse order since the Saptarṣi move through the nakṣatras in the reverse direction. According to Pandit Venkatachelam, Alexander Cunningham (1883) missed the retrograde motion of the Saptarṣi in his otherwise excellent *Book of Indian Eras*.

## Dr. Bühler's Acceptance of the Saptarṣi Era

Dr. Bühler (1877/1984, p. 268) accepted the origin of the Saptarṣi Era conclusively as discussed earlier, and claimed that it helps establish the origin of the Kali Era indisputably in 3102 BC. He stated:

> "The beginning of the Saptarshi era is placed by the Kaśmirians on Chaitra Sudi 1 of the twenty-fifth year of the Kaliyuga, and the twenty-fourth year, in which Kalhaṇa wrote [Rājataraṅgiṇī], is consequently the Saptarshi year 4224. For
>
> | | |
> |---|---|
> | From Kaliyuga 25 to the beginning of the Śaka era is | 3154 |
> | From Śaka Saṁvat 1 to Kalhaṇa's time | 1070 |
> | Total – Saptarshi years | 4224 |
>
> My authorities for placing the beginning of the Saptarshi era in Kali 25 are the following. First, P. Dayarām Jotsī gave me the subjoined verse, the origin of which he did not know: …"

Dr. Bühler (1877/1984, p. 268) concluded:

> "Paṇḍit Dayarām explained the verse as I have done in the above translation, and added that each Saptarshi year began on Chaitra Sudi1, and that its length was regulated by the customary mixing of the *Chāndra* and *Saur mānas*.
>
> The correctness of his statement is confirmed by a passage in P. Sāhebrām's *Rājataranginisaṁgraha* where the author says that the Śaka year 1786 (A.D. 1864), in which he writes, corresponds to Kali 4965 and to Saptarshi or Laukika Saṁvat 4940. One of the copyists, too, who copied the *Dhvanyāloka* for me in September 1875, gives in the colophon, as the date of his copy, the Saptarshi year 4951. These facts are sufficient to prove that P. Dayarām's statement regarding the beginning of the Saptarshi era is not an invention of his own, but based on the general tradition of the country. I do not doubt for a moment that the calculation which throws the beginning of the Saptarshi era back to 3076 B.C. is worth no more than that which fixes the beginning of the Kaliyuga in 3101 B.C. But it seems to me certain that it is much older than Kalhana's time, because his equation 24 = 1078 agrees with it. It may therefore be safely used for reducing with exactness the Saptarshi years, months and days mentioned in his work to years of the Christian era. The results which will be thus obtained will

always closely agree with those gained by General Cunningham who did use the right key. ”

### Gross Distortions by the 19th Century European Indologists

As discussed earlier, William Jones (1807a, p. 17–20) knew of the Kaliyuga Era of 3102 BC, and Dr. Bühler and Alexander Cunningham had unequivocally accepted the Kaliyuga and the Saptarṣi eras. Other European historians of the 19th century such as Prof. Wilson, Prof. Max Müller, Dr. Hultzsch (1889, p. 65), and Dr. Stein (1900, p. 58) had also accepted that the Kaliyuga Era began in 3102 BC (Satyanarayana, 1953, p. V). However, the colonial Indologists ignored the three eras (Yudhiṣṭhira Śaka of 3138 BC, Kaliyuga Śaka of 3102 BC, and the Saptarṣi Śaka of 3076 BC) and declared that India had no system of reckoning time that could be made the basis of Indian history! Elphinstone (1874, p. 11) wrote:

> “ No *date* of a public event can be fixed before the invasion of Alexander, and no *connected* relations of the national transactions can be attempted until after the Mahometan conquest. ”

This is a glaring misrepresentation by the colonial era European Indologists.

## Bārhaspatya-chakra or the 60-year Cycle of Jupiter

The Bārhaspatya-chakra or Samvatsara is a 60-year cycle of Jupiter or five revolutions of Jupiter around the Sun. Each of these years has a different name as shown in Table 10 (Cunningham, 1883, p. 18, 25; Balachandra Rao, p. 58).

The years named after the cycle of Jupiter will be encountered in Chapter 5 and Chapter 9. Therefore, without going into the details at this point, suffice it to say that there are three modes of reckoning the cycle. The mode of reckoning used in North India is different from the mode used in South India.

## Mālava-gaṇa Śaka (725 BC)

The Mālava-gaṇa Śaka was started by the people of Mālavā in commemoration of achieving their independence from the Magadha Empire in 725 BC (Venkatachelam, 1955, p. 123; 1956a, p. 41). See Chapter 10 in this book for details.

### Distortion of the Mālava-gaṇa Śaka by Colonial Era Historians

The colonial era European Indologists deliberately ignored the above fact of Mālava-gaṇa Śaka and wrongly identified it with the Vikrama Samvat of 57 BC. Consequently, they brought down all inscriptions dated in the Mālava-

**Table 10: Samvatsara names**

| Name of the Year | Name of the Year | Name of the Year |
|---|---|---|
| 1. Prabhava (प्रभव) | 21. Sarvajit (सर्वजित्) | 41. Plavaṅga (प्लवंग) |
| 2. Vibhava (विभव) | 22. Sarvadhāri (सर्वधारि) | 42. Kīlaka (कीलक) |
| 3. Śukla (शुक्ल) | 23. Virodhi (विरोधि) | 43. Saumya (सौम्य) |
| 4. Pramoda (प्रमोद) | 24. Vikṛta (विकृत) | 44. Sādhāraṇa (साधारण) |
| 5. Prajāpati (प्रजापति) | 25. Khara (खर) | 45. Virodhakṛt (विरोधकृत्) |
| 6. Aṅgirasa (अंगिरस) | 26. Nandana (नंदन) | 46. Paridhāvi (परिधावि) |
| 7. Śrīmukha (श्रीमुख) | 27. Vijaya (विजय) | 47. Pramādi (प्रमादि) |
| 8. Bhāva (भाव) | 28. Jaya (जय) | 48. Ānanda (आनंद) |
| 9. Yuvan (युवन्) | 29. Manmatha (मन्मथ) | 49. Rākṣasa (राक्षस) |
| 10. Dhātṛ (धातृ) | 30. Durmukha (दुर्मुख) | 50. Anala (अनल) |
| 11. Iśvara (ईश्वर) | 31. Hemalamba (हेमलंब) | 51. Piṅgala (पिंगल) |
| 12. Bahudhānya (बहुधान्य) | 32. Vilambi (विलंबि) | 52. Kālayukta (कालयुक्त) |
| 13. Pramāthī (प्रमाथी) | 33. Vikāri (विकारि) | 53. Siddhārthi (सिद्धार्थि) |
| 14. Vikrama (विक्रम) | 34. Ṣārvari (शार्वरि) | 54. Raudra (रौद्र) |
| 15. Vṛṣa (वृष) | 35. Plava (प्लव) | 55. Durmati (दुर्मति) |
| 16. Citrabhānu (चित्रभानु) | 36. Śubhakṛt (शुभकृत्) | 56. Dundubhi (दुन्दुभि) |
| 17. Subhānu (सुभानु) | 37. Śobhakṛt (शोभकृत्) | 57. Rudhirodgārī (रूधिरोद्गारी) |
| 18. Tāraṇa (तारण) | 38. Krodhi (क्रोधि) | 58. Raktākṣī (रक्ताक्षी) |
| 19. Pārthiva (पार्थिव) | 39. Viṣvavasu (विश्ववसु) | 59. Krodhana (क्रोधन) |
| 20. Vyaya (व्यय) | 40. Parābhava (पराभव) | 60. Akṣaya (अक्षय) |

gaṇa Śaka by about seven centuries. Therefore, the period of the Gupta Dynasty which was identical to the age of the inscriptions was brought down to the fourth and fifth centuries AD. Thus, the Gupta Yuga which commenced in 327 BC was brought down to AD 319–320.

An inscription found in Mandasar (Insc. No. 163) contains the following verse (Fleet, n.d., p. 50; Venkatachelam, 1955, p. 123–124):

पंचसु शतेषु शरदां यातेष्वेकोननवतिसहितेषु ।
मालवगणस्थितिवशात् कालज्ञानाय लिखितेषु ।।

Pañcasu Śateṣu Śaradāṁ Yāteṣvekonanavatisahiteṣu ।
Mālavagaṇasthitivaśāt kālajñānāya likhiteṣu ।।

J. F. Fleet (1886, p. 228) interpreted this as:

> “five hundred and eighty-nine autumns having elapsed from *(the establishment of)* the supremacy of the tribal constitution of the Mālavas, *(and)* being written down in order to determine the time;”

The interpretation 'the tribal constitution of the Mālavas' has no basis. The word *gaṇa* means 'collection' and *Mālava-gaṇa* means 'collection of Mālava people'. The correct and complete translation of the verse is (Venkatachelam, 1956a, p. 42):

> “five hundred and eighty nine years elapsed, since the period fixed, for calculation of time, to be in traditional use, among the Mālava people.”

Therefore, it is proper to call the era the Mālava-gaṇa Śaka as noted in the inscription, and not Vikrama Śaka. Accordingly, the year 589 of Mālava-gaṇa Śaka is 136 BC, and the Gupta Yuga year 191.

## Cyrus Śaka or Śaka Nṛpa Kāla (550 BC)

The people of Persia were called Śaka by ancient Indians. The Śaka Kāla was started in commemoration of the founding of the Persian Empire by Cyrus in 550 BC. Encyclopedia Britannica (1885, Vol. 18, p. 565) states:

> “The date of the overthrow of Astyages [Ishtuvegu in Persian (Saney, 2011, p. 18)] and the taking of Ecbatana [present day Hamadan in Iran] is, according to the Babylonian tablet, the sixth year ; and, as it is in the highest degree probable that the years in this memorial are those of the Babylonian king Nabunaid, we must place these events in the year 550.”

A question may arise about why this era (the Śaka Kāla) would be used in India. The following paragraphs shed some light on this. India was acknowledged as a great power by the Persian, Median, Babylonian, and other kings in the region, who courted assistance and mediation of Indian kings in the various disputes as quoted in the following by M. Rollin (1850, p. 21):

> “Cyrus, understanding that there was a frequent intercourse and communication between the Indians and Chaldeans, desired that the latter would send persons to accompany and conduct the ambassador,

> whom he was preparing to send to the king of India. The support of this embassy was, to desire some succours in money from that prince, in behalf of Cyrus, who wanted it for the levying of troops in Persia, and promised that, if the gods crowned his design with success, the king should have no reason to repent of having assisted him. ... The ambassador set out the next day, accompanied by some of the most considerable persons of Chaldea. ”

Rollin (p. 12–13) states further:

> “ One day, as Cyrus was reviewing his army, a messenger came to him from Cyaxares [Huvakshatara in Persian (Saney, 2011, p. 17)], to acquaint him, that some ambassadors being arrived from the king of Indies, he desired his presence immediately. 'For that purpose (says he) I have brought you a rich garment, for the king desires you would appear magnificently dressed before the Indians, to do the nation honour.' ...
>
> Cyaxares, satisfied with this answer, ordered the Indian ambassadors to be introduced. The purport of their speech was, that they were sent by their king their master, to learn the cause of the war between the Medes and the Babylonians, and that they had orders, as soon as they had heard what the Medes should say, to proceed to the court of Babylon, to know what motives they had to allege on their part ; to the end that the king their master, after having examined the reasons on both sides, might take part with those who had right and justice on their side. This is making a noble and glorious use of great power : to be influenced only by justice, to seek no advantage from the division of neighbours, but declare openly against the unjust aggressor, in favour of the injured party. Cyaxares and Cyrus answered, that they had given the Babylonians no subject of complaint, and that they willingly accepted the mediation of the king of India. It appears, in the sequel, that he declared for the Medes. ”

M. Rollin describes in further detail the assistance Cyrus received from the Indians. The alliance of the Persians and Medians defeated the Babylonians, in which Cyrus took the help of the Indians. It was natural for the Indians (especially of northwestern India) to honor the victory of Cyrus by adopting the era started by him.

As discussed under the Saptarṣi Śaka, the Śaka Kāla started after 2,526 years of the Saptarṣi Śaka, which started in 3076 or 3077 BC. Therefore, the Śaka Kāla's starting year is 3076 or 3077 BC + 2,526 = 550 or 551 BC. See the arguments by K. D. Sethna (1989, p. 50–55) in support of the starting of the Śaka Era in 550 or 551 BC.

Varāhamihira has given his time in Śaka Kāla in Pañcasiddhāntikā, as shown in the following shloka, stating that he was writing it in the year 427 of the Śaka Kāla (of 550 BC) which is 550 BC + 427 = 123 BC (Venkatachelam, 1955, p. 242; 1991, p. 36).

सप्ताश्विवेदसंख्यं शककालमपास्य चैत्रशुक्लादौ ।
अर्धास्तमिते भानौ यवनपुरे सौम्यदिवसाध्ये ।।

Saptāśvi-vedasaṅkhyaṁ Śakakālamapāsya caitraśuklādau ।
Ardhāstamite bhānau yavanapure Saumyadivasādhye ।।

Translation:

> Subtract 427 from Śaka Kāla, when the Sun is half-setting at Yavanapuri at the beginning of the Chaitra Śukla Pratipadi, it is the beginning of Wednesday.

### Distortions by the Colonial Era Orientalists

In almost all cases where the dates of the events are given in the Śaka Kāla, the colonial era orientalists wrongly identified every such Śaka Kāla year with the year of Śālivāhana Śaka which started in AD 79 and caused a great deal of confusion.

The word 'Śaka' has two distinct meanings. The 'Śaka people' are those who lived in the west of the River Sindhu including Persians. The other meaning of 'Śaka' is the 'era' or 'kāla' as in the Mālava-gaṇa Śaka, Śālivāhana Śaka or Yudhiṣṭhira Śaka.

## Śrī Harṣa Samvat (457 BC)

A good deal of confusion was introduced into the chronology of the kings of Nepal, by Fleet and other 19th century orientalists. They mistook the Harṣa Era given in some of the copper plate inscriptions as referring to an era supposed to have originated with Harṣavardhana Śiladitya of Kannauj who ruled from AD 606 to 647 but never started any era.

Alberuni, the Arab historian (Sachau, 1910, p. 5, 7), describes the existence of the Harṣa Era in Nepal and other northern kingdoms in his time (AD 1031). As mentioned earlier in this chapter, under the fifth point in the section 'Historical Evidence for Use of Kaliyuga Era', Alberuni states that the year

400 of Yazdajird, his gauge year, corresponds to the year 4133 of Kaliyuga (AD 1031) and the year 1488 of Śrī Harṣa Era. This means that (4133 – 1488 =) 2645 years of Kaliyuga had elapsed when the Harṣa Samvat started in Kaliyuga year 2646 (457 BC). Alberuni also states that between Śrī Harṣa and Vikramāditya, there are 400 years, as told by some of the inhabitants of that region (Mathura and Kannauj). The Vikrama Samvat started in 57 BC, exactly 400 years after the Śrī Harṣa Era started, which matches Alberuni's statement. The detailed history of Śrī Harṣa Vikramāditya is discussed in Chapter 10.

## Gupta Yuga (327 BC)

The Gupta Yuga began with the founding of the Gupta Empire by Chandragupta I of the Gupta Dynasty around the time of Alexander's invasion of India. Pandit Kota Venkatachelam (1956a, p. 59) writes on the Gupta Yuga:

> "The Western historians discussed at length about the beginning of the Gupta Era and each one arrived at his own date. Dr. Fleet said it was 319–320 A.D.; M.A. Pai fixed it as 272–273 A.D.; D. N. Mukherji guessed it to be 419–20 A.D.; Pandit Sharma Sastri refuted the above three dates and settled it as 200–201 A.D.; Alberuni thought it to be 319–320 A.D. Cunningham surmised it as 167 A.D. … *But none of these scholars took in to account the date of the Bhārata War and the genealogy of the kingly dynasties mentioned in our Puranas.* The difference of opinion arose from the mistaken impression of Maurya Chandragupta to be contemporary king of Magadha in 326 B.C." [Emphasis in italics in the original]

## Vikrama Samvat (57 BC) and Śālivāhana Śaka (AD 79)

Vikrama Samvat and Śālivāhana Śaka are still widely used in India. See the current year of both calendars on the Panchānga cover page in Figure 8. Vikrama Samvat is used in the western and northern parts of India, and Nepal. The starting date of the new year in Vikrama Samvat varies from region to region, e.g., in Madhya Pradesh and Nepal, the new year starts from Chaitra Suda 1 (March/April), whereas in Gujarat, it starts 7 months later, from Kārtik Suda 1 (October/November).

As discussed under Kaliyuga in this chapter, Alberuni has stated in his book (Sachau, 1910, p. 4–5, 7) that the year 400 of the Yazdajird, the gauge year, corresponds to the year 953 of Śakakāla (Śālivāhana Śaka), the year 1088 of Vikramāditya Era, the year 1488 of Śrī Harṣa Era, and the year 4133 of

Kaliyuga. The new year's date on this gauge year 400 fell on AD March 9, 1031. According to Alberuni's reckoning:

1. Vikrama Samvat started when (4133 – 1088 = ) 3045 years of Kaliyuga had elapsed, i.e. on the first day of Kaliyuga 3046 (57 BC).
2. Shalivāhana Śaka started when (4133 – 953 = ) 3180 years of Kaliyuga had elapsed, i.e. on the first day of Kaliyuga 3181 (AD 79).

Vikrama Samvat was started in Kaliyuga 3046 (57 BC) by Emperor Vikramāditya of Ujjain after expelling the Śakas from India and after the last remaining king of the Indian subcontinent, the king of Nepal, accepted his sovereignty (See Chapter 12). The previously existing Mālava-gaṇa Śaka then went out of use.

The Śālivāhana Śaka was started in Kaliyuga 3181 (AD 79) by Emperor Śālivāhana, the great-grandson of Vikramāditya, after expelling the Śakas to the west of the Sindhu and conquering the whole of India. It is used in most parts of India. It is called the Indian national calendar for it is the official calendar of the Government of India and is mentioned along with the Gregorian calendar for the communications issued by the government.

## Distortions by the Later Colonial Era Indologists

William Jones (1799b, p. 6) never doubted the historicity of Vikramāditya and considered him one of the pivotal emperors of ancient India as discussed in Chapter 2. It is also obvious from the presence of Vikramāditya in the charts presented by William Jones (see Table 3 and Table 4) and his statement:

> “ Now the age of VIKRAMADITYA is given ; and, if we can fix on an *Indian* prince contemporary with SELEUCUS, ... ”

See 'VIKRAMADITYA' also in the table presented by Bentley (Table 7). The historicity of Vikramāditya and Śālivāhana was denied by the later European Indologists of the second half of the 19th and the first half of the 20th century, such as Vincent Smith, F.E. Pargiter and their Indian followers. The conjectures of Vincent Smith on the Vikrama and Śālivāhana Eras are as follows:

> “ The popular belief which associates the Vikrama era of 58–57 B.C. with a Rājā Vikramāditya or Bikram of Ujjain at that date is erroneous. There was no such person then. But the era really arose in Mālwā and probably was invented by the astronomers of Ujjain. The first name of it was the Mālwā era. The term *vikrama-kāla* used by poets to express the autumn season when kings went to war, may, perhaps, have been

transferred from the season to the year, which began with autumn in some parts of India. People then seem to have fancied that Vikrama must be a king, who founded the era, and probably a vague recollection survived of King Chandragupta II Vikramāditya, the conqueror of Ujjain. ” (1910, p. 53)

> “ The Gupta and Saka eras changed their names similarly, becoming known in after ages as Valabhī and the Śālivāhana eras respectively. ” (1951, p. 69)

Thus, Vincent Smith made conjecture upon conjecture without any basis. Rapson (1922, p. viii), too, followed a similar path. In response to questioning by several historians such as Rao Bahadur, C. V. Vaidya, and Haraprasad Shastri, on the omission of Vikramāditya, D. R. Bhandarkar (1917/1976, p. 189), following in the footsteps of the European Indologists, wrote:

> “ The theory that Vikramāditya was the originator of the Vikrama Saṁvat must, therefore, be given up, and the sooner we consign it to the region of oblivion, the better. ”

Vincent Smith (1914, p. 22) also wrote:

> “ Mr. F.E. Pargiter in his valuable work, *The Dynasties of the Kali Age* (Clarendon Press, 1913), has succeeded in obtaining more definite results. He proves that the *Bhavishya Purāṇa* in its early form was the original authority from which the *Matsya* and *Vāyu Purāṇas* derived their dynastic lists. The versions of those lists as now found in the *Matsya, Vāyu,* and *Brahmand Purāṇas* 'grew out of one and the same original text.' ”

Based on these statements from Vincent Smith, it is impossible that the colonial era European Indologists were not aware of the two Emperors Vikramāditya and Śālivāhana described extensively in the Bhaviṣya MahāPurāṇa. As expressed by Pandit Venkatachelam, it appears that they purposely ignored the four dynasties of Agni Vaṁśa which covered about 1,300 years, from 101 BC to AD 1192 i.e. from the time of Vikramāditya to the time of Prithvirāja Chauhan.

These omissions were necessitated by the wrong basis used by the colonial era Indologists in rewriting ancient India's history. The wrong basis was identifying Chandragupta Maurya of 1534 BC instead of Chandragupta I of the Gupta Dynasty of 327 BC as the contemporary of Alexander. This grave error had shrunk the chronology of the Indian subcontinent by over

1,200 years, and there was no room left in it for Vikramāditya of the first century BC and Śālivāhana of the first century AD.

## Evidence Contradicts the Later Indologists

Figure 11 and Figure 12 show evidence for use of Vikrama Samvat in the third century AD in the inscription of the two pillars in Barnala, Rajasthan. One pillar bears the date Vikrama Samvat 284 (AD 227) and the other pillar, Vikrama Samvat 335 (AD 278). These pillars are said to be currently preserved in the Amer museum.

An even earlier inscription dated in the year 96 of Vikrama Samvat is described in Chapter 14. Even yet earlier evidence is found in the chronology of the Dvārakā Maṭha which used to be recorded in the Yudhiṣṭhira Śaka. However, the chronology has been recorded in the Vikrama Samvat since Vikrama Samvat 9; see Table 26 in Chapter 9. Additional evidence to this effect is given under the Thākuri Dynasty section in Chapter 12.

The ample evidence completely contradicts the myth propagated by the colonial era Indologists that the era which started in 57 BC came to be known as Vikrama Samvat only after AD 375. The colonial Indologists wrongly assigned the year AD 375 to the beginning of the reign of Chandragupta II, also called Vikramāditya, of the Gupta Dynasty.

**Figure 11: Barnala pillar inscription, Rajasthan**
*Photo adapted from: https://rootshunt.com/aryans/indiairanandaryans/throneofkings/vikramsamvat.htm*

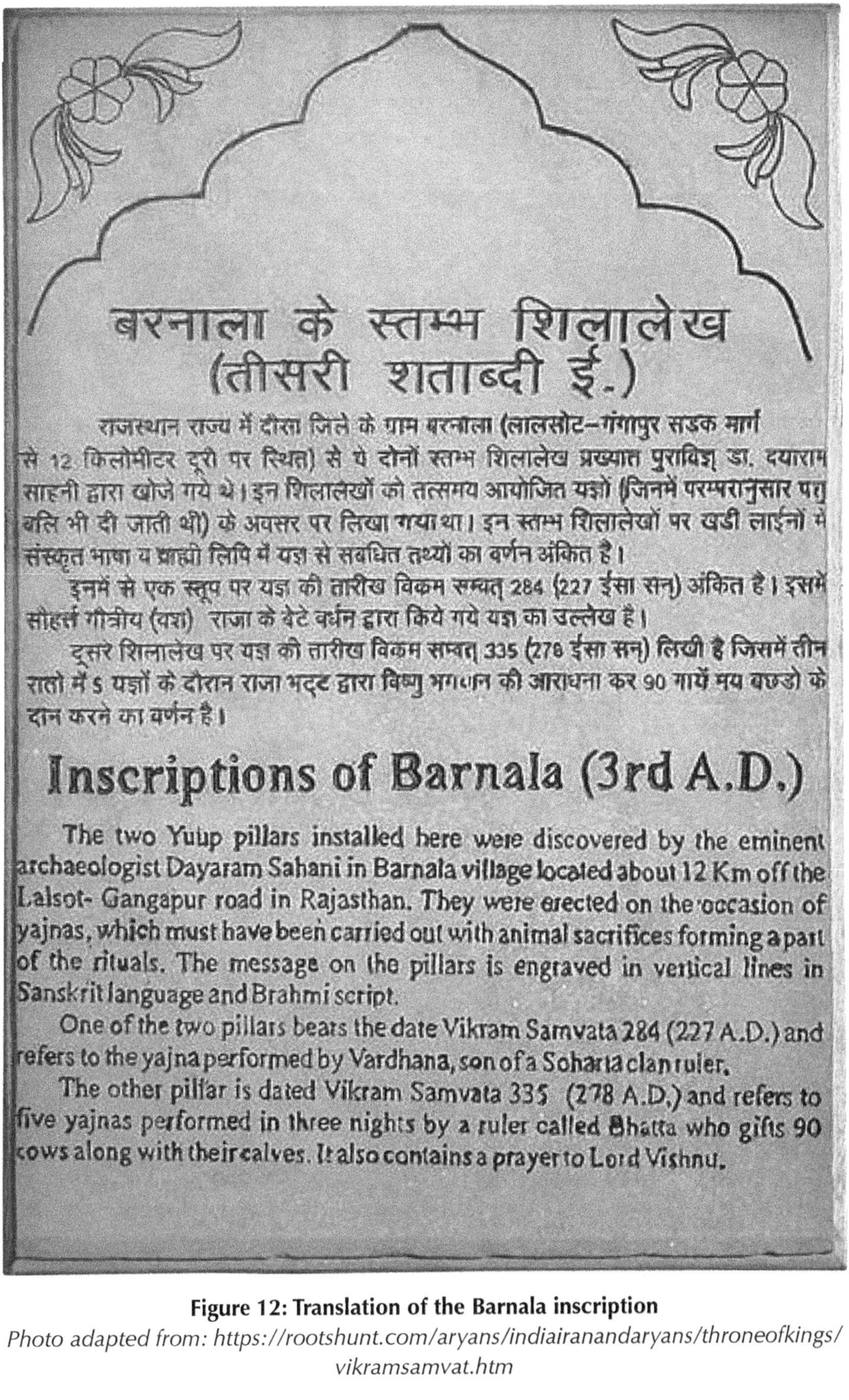
बरनाला के स्तम्भ शिलालेख
(तीसरी शताब्दी ई.)
राजस्थान राज्य में दौसा जिले के ग्राम बरनाला (लालसोट–गंगापुर सडक मार्ग से 12 किलोमीटर दूरी पर स्थित) से ये दोनों स्तम्भ शिलालेख प्रख्यात पुराविद् डा. दयाराम साहनी द्वारा खोजे गये थे। इन शिलालेखों को तत्समय आयोजित यज्ञों (जिनमें परम्परानुसार पशु बलि भी दी जाती थी) के अवसर पर लिखा गया था। इन स्तम्भ शिलालेखों पर खडी लाईनों में संस्कृत भाषा व ब्राह्मी लिपि में यज्ञ से संबधित तथ्यों का वर्णन अंकित है।
इनमें से एक स्तूप पर यज्ञ की तारीख विक्रम सम्वत् 284 (227 ईसा सन्) अंकित है। इसमें सोहर्त गौत्रीय (वंश) राजा के बेटे वर्धन द्वारा किये गये यज्ञ का उल्लेख है।
दूसरे शिलालेख पर यज्ञ की तारीख विक्रम सम्वत् 335 (278 ईसा सन्) लिखी है जिसमें तीन रातो में 5 यज्ञों के दौरान राजा भट्ट द्वारा विष्णु भगवान की आराधना कर 90 गायें मय बछडो के दान करने का वर्णन है।
Inscriptions of Barnala (3rd A.D.)
The two Yuup pillars installed here were discovered by the eminent archaeologist Dayaram Sahani in Barnala village located about 12 Km off the Lalsot- Gangapur road in Rajasthan. They were erected on the occasion of yajnas, which must have been carried out with animal sacrifices forming a part of the rituals. The message on the pillars is engraved in vertical lines in Sanskrit language and Brahmi script.
One of the two pillars bears the date Vikram Samvata 284 (227 A.D.) and refers to the yajna performed by Vardhana, son of a Soharta clan ruler.
The other pillar is dated Vikram Samvata 335 (278 A.D.) and refers to five yajnas performed in three nights by a ruler called Bhatta who gifts 90 cows along with their calves. It also contains a prayer to Lord Vishnu.

**Figure 12: Translation of the Barnala inscription**

*Photo adapted from: https://rootshunt.com/aryans/indiairanandaryans/throneofkings/vikramsamvat.htm*

## References

1. Abhayankar, K. D. and G. M. Ballabh (1996). 'Kaliyuga, Saptarṣi, Yudhiṣṭhira and Laukika Eras.' *Indian Journal of History of Science, Vol.* 31(1), 19–33.

2. Arkasomayaji, Dr. D. (1980). *Siddhānta Śiromaṇi of Bhāskarāchārya: English Exposition and Annotation in the light and language of modern Astronomy (Kendriya Sanskrit Vidyapeetha, Tirupati Series No. 29).* Tirupati: Kendriya Sanskrit Vidyapeetha.

3. Āryabhaṭa (AD 499). 'Kālakriyā or the Reckoning of Time (Ch. III).' in *The Āryabhaṭīya of Āryabhaṭa: An Ancient Indian Work on Mathematics and Astronomy* (Trans. Walter Eugene Clark, 1930). University of Chicago Press.

4. Bailly, Jean-Sylvian (1787). *Traité de L'astronomie Indienne et Orientale* (A Treatise on Indian and Oriental Astronomy). Paris (M.DCC.LXXXVII).

5. Bala, Saroj (2021). *Mahabharata: Retold with Scientific Evidence.* Gurugram: Garuda Prakashan.

6. Balachandra Rao, S. (2000). *Indian Astronomy: An Introduction.* Hyderabad: Universities Press.

7. *Śrīmad Bhāgavata MahāPurāṇa: (Sanskrit) with Hindi translation,* 2 vols. (81st ed., Vikrama Samvat 2071; 1st ed., Samvat 1997). Gorakhpur: Gita Press.

8. Bhandarkar, D. R. (1917). 'Vikrama Era.' in *R. G. Bhandarkar Commemoration Volume (rpt. 1976, No. 19).* Delhi: Bharatiya Publishing House.

9. Björnstjerna, Count (1840). *The British Empire in the East.* London.

10. *The Brahmāṇḍa MahāPurāṇam: (Sanskrit) With English Introduction, Verse-Index and Textual Correction.* Dr. K. V. Sharma (Ed.) Krishnadas Sanskrit Series 41, Madhyama bhāga. Varanasi: Krishnadas Academy.

11. Britannica (1885). *The Encyclopedia Britannica* (9th ed., Vol. 18). Edinburg: Adam and Charlie Black (MDCCCLXXXY).

12. Buchanan, Francis (1807). *A Journey from Madras Through the Countries of Mysore, Canara and Malabar: For the express purpose of investigating the state of Agriculture, Arts and Commerce; The Religion, Manners, and Customs; The History Natural and Civil and Antiquities* (Vol.3, rpt. 1988). New Delhi: Asian Educational Services.

13. Bühler, Dr. G. (1876). 'Sanskrit MSS: Extract from Dr. G. Bühler's

preliminary Report on the results of the search for Sanskrit MSS. in Kaśmīr.' *The Indian Antiquary: A Journal of Oriental Research in Archaeology, History, Literature, Language, Philosophy, Religion, Folklore, etc., Vol. 5,* 27–31. Bombay: Thacker, Vining & Co.

14. Bühler, Dr. G. (1877). 'The Rājatarangiṇi: From Dr. Bühler's Report of a Tour in search of Sanskrit MSS. made in Kaśmīr, Rājputānā, and Central India.' *The Indian Antiquary: A Journal of Oriental Research in Archaeology, History, Literature, Language, Philosophy, Religion, Folklore, etc., Vol. 6,* 264–274. Delhi: Swati Publications (1984).

15. Cunningham, Alexander (1883). *Book of Indian Eras: with Tables for Calculating Indian Dates*. Calcutta: Thacker, Spink and Co.

16. Durgāprasād, Mahāmahopādhyāya Pandit, and Kāshināth Pāṇḍurang Parab (Eds.) (1892). 'Chalukyavaṁśodbhutasya Śrī Pulakeśinaḥ Śilālekhaḥ (16)' in *The Prāchīna-Lekhamālā or A Collection of Ancient Historical Records* (in Sanskrit, Vol. 1, Kāvyamālā 34). Bombay: Nirnaya-Sagara Press.

17. Elphinstone, Mountstuart (1874). *History of India: The Hindu and Mahomedan Periods* (6th ed., Cowell, E. B., Ed.). London.

18. Fleet, J. F. (1876). 'Sanskrit and Old Canarese Inscriptions: No. XIII.' *The Indian Antiquary: A Journal of Oriental Research in Archaeology, History, Literature, Language, Philosophy, Religion, Folklore etc., Vol. 5,* 67–73. Bombay.

19. Fleet, J. F. (1886). 'Sanskrit and Old-Kanarese Inscriptions: No. 163, Mandasar Inscription of Yashodharman and Vishṇuvardhana, The Malava Year 589.' *The Indian Antiquary: A Journal of Oriental Research in Archaeology, History, Literature, Language, Philosophy, Religion, Folklore etc. Vol. 15,* 222–228, 245–258. Bombay.

20. Fleet, J. F. (n.d.). 'Mandasar Stone Pillar Inscription of Yashodharman and Vishṇuvardhana, The Malava year 589 (No. 35, Verse 24).' in *Corpus Inscriptionum Indicarum Vol. III: Inscriptions of the Early Gupta Kings and their Successors, Part I: containing Inscriptions I to XXXVIII*. The Belvedere Press Sanskrit Series No. III.

21. Hultzsch, E. (1889, March). 'Extracts from Kalhana's Rajatarangiṇi.' *Indian Antiquary, A Journal of Oriental Research in Archaeology, Epigraphy, Ethnology, Geography, History, Folklore, Languages, Literature, Numismatic, Philosophy, Religion, etc. Vol. 18* (rpt., 1964), 65–73, 97–105. Delhi: Swati Publications.

22. Hunter, William (1799). 'Some Account of the Astronomical Labours

of Jayasinha, Rajah of Ambhere, Or Jayanagar.' *Asiatic Researches; or Transactions of the Society Instituted in Bengal for inquiring into the History and Antiquities, the Arts, Sciences, and Literature, Vol. 5,* 177–211. London.

23. Hunter, William Wilson (1893). *A Brief History of the Indian Peoples* (20th ed.). Oxford: Clarendon Press.

24. Indraji, Pandit Bhagavānlāl, and Dr. G. Bühler (1884). 'Some Considerations on the History of Nepal.' *The Indian Antiquary: A Journal of Oriental Research in Archaeology, History, Literature, Languages, Philosophy, Religion, Folklore, etc. Vol. 13,* 411–428. Bombay.

25. Jagannadha Rao, Nadimpalli (1931). *The Age of the Mahabharata War.*

26. Jarsha (Yugābda or Kaliyuga 5112, AD 2010). *Panchāṅga Part I* (Hindi Trans. Vasudev Prajāpati). Puṇyabhūmi Bhārata Sanskriti Vācanamālā, Vol. 7(2), Aśāḍha Śukla 15 (July 25). Ahmadabad: Punarutthāna Trust.

27. Jones, William (1807a). 'On the Chronology of the Hindus: written in January 1788 by the President.' in Lord Teignmouth (Ed.), *The Works of Sir William Jones with the Life of the Author* (Vol. 4, 1–47). London.

28. Jones, William (1807b). 'A Supplement to the Essay on the Indian Chronology.' in Lord Teignmouth (Ed.), *The Works of Sir William Jones: with the Life of the Author* (Vol. 4, 48–69). London.

29. Jones, William (1799a). 'On the Chronology of the Hindus, written in January 1788 by the President.' *Asiatic Researches; or Transactions of the Society Instituted in Bengal for inquiring into the History and Antiquities, the Arts, Sciences, and Literature of Asia, Vol. 2,* 111–147. London.

30. Jones, William (1799b). 'The Tenth Anniversary Discourse, delivered on 28 February 1793, by the President, on Asiatic History, Civil and Natural.' *Asiatic Researches; or Transactions of the Society Instituted in Bengal for inquiring into the History and Antiquities, the Arts, Sciences, and Literature, Vol. 4,* 1–18. London.

31. Kalhaṇa (1148). *Rājataraṅgiṇī (Chronicle of the Kings of Kashmir) (Sanskrit text),* Edited with Hindi translation by Shri Ramtej Shastri Pandey (Vikrama Samvat 2017 (AD 1960), rpt. ed. 1985). Delhi & Varanasi: Chaukhamba Sanskrit Pratishthan.

32. Krishnamachariar, M. (1937). *History of Classical Sanskrit Literature: Being an elaborate account of all branches of Classical Sanskrit Literature, with full Epigraphical and Archaeological Notes and References, an Introduction dealing with Languages, Philology and Chronology, and Index of Authors and Works.* Madras.

33. *Mahābhārata: (Sanskrit) with Hindi translation* by Pandit Rāmanārāyaṇadatta Śastri Pāṇdeya, 6 vols. Gorakhpur: Gita Press.

34. *Matsya Purāṇa: (Sanskrit) with Hindi translation*. Gorakhpur: Gita Press.

35. Narahari Achar, B. N. (2003). *Date of the Mahabharata War based on Simulations using Planetarium Software*. https://www.researchgate.net/publication/237283001 (Accessed on February 1 2023).

36. Narahari Achar, B. N. (2012). *Historicity of Mahabharata War*: Astronomical Methods using Planetarium Software [presentation], New Delhi.

37. Narayana Sastry, T. S. (1916). *The Age of Śankara* (2nd ed. 1971, edited by T. N. Kumaraswamy). Madras: B. G. Paul & Co.

38. Parviz Saney (2011). *The Iranians: Their Cultural Heritage, and its Transformation*. California: Createspace Independent Pub.

39. Raghavan, Prof. K. Srinivasa (1969). *The Date of the Maha Bharata War and the Kali Yugadhi*. Srinivasanagar (Saka 1891).

40. Rapson, E. J. (1922). *The Cambridge History of India: Vol I. Ancient India*. Cambridge University Press.

41. Rollin, M. (1850). *The Ancient History: of the Egyptians, Carthaginians, Assyrians, Babylonians, Medes and Persians, Macedonians, and Grecians* (Translated from the French, Vol. II). London.

42. Sachau, Dr. Edward C. (Ed.) (1910). *Alberuni's India: An Account of the Religion, Philosophy, Literature, Geography, Chronology, Astronomy, Customs, Laws and Astrology of India, about A.D. 1030* (English ed., Vol. 2). London: Trübner & Co.

43. Sarada, Har Bilas (1922). *Hindu Superiority: An Attempt to Determine the Position of the Hindu Race in the Scale of Nations* (3rd ed.). Ajmer: Vedic Yantralaya.

44. Satyanarayana, Viswanatha (1953). 'Preface.' in *The Plot in Indian Chronology by* Pandit Kota Venkatachelam (Kali 5054, AD 1953). Arya Vijnana, Publication 17. Vijayawada.

45. Sethna, K. D. (1989). *Ancient India in a New Light: I. The Challenge of India's Traditional Chronology, II. The Momentous Evidence of Megasthenes, III. A Reconstruction of Ancient Indian History: Aśoka – and Before and After*. New Delhi: Aditya Prakashan.

46. Sidharth, B. G. (1999). *The Celestial key to the Vedas: Discovering the Origins*

*of the World's Oldest Civilization*. Rochester: Inner Traditions Bear and Co. http://www.Innertraditions.com

47. Smith, Vincent A. (1910). *The Oxford Student's History of India* (2nd ed.). Oxford: Clarendon Press.
48. Smith, Vincent A. (1914). *Early History of India: From 600 B.C. to the Muhammadan Conquest including the Invasion of Alexander the Great* (3rd ed.). Oxford: Clarendon Press.
49. Smith, Vincent A. (1951). *The Oxford Student's History of India* (15th ed. Revised by H.G. Rawlinson). Oxford University Press.
50. Stein, M. A. (1900). *Kalhaṇa's Rājataraṅgiṇī: A Chronicle of the Kings of Kashmir, English translation with an Introduction, Commentary and Appendices*, Vol. I (MDCCCC). Westminster.
51. *Varahamihira's Brihat Samhita (Sanskrit): with English translation and Notes* (1946) by Panditabhushana Subrahmanya Sastri and Vidwan M. Ramakrishna Bhat. Bangalore.
52. *Varahamihira's Brihat Samhita (Sanskrit): with Hindi translation* by Pandit Śrī Achutānanda Jhā Śarmaṇā, (Vikrama Samvat 2015 (AD 1959)), Adhyay XIII, Shloka 3. Varanasi: Chaukhamba Vidyabhavan (Originally written in the 1st century BC).
53. *Vāyu Purāṇam: (Sanskrit) with Hindi translation by* Rāmapratāpa Tripāthi (2nd ed., Śaka 1909 (AD 1987)). Prayāg: Hindi Sāhitya Sammelan.
54. Venkatachelam, Pandit Kota (1955). *Chronology of Kashmir History Reconstructed*. Arya Vijnana Series, Publication 18. Vijayawada.
55. Venkatachelam, Pandit Kota (Kali 5057, AD 1956a). *Indian Eras*. Arya Vijnana Grandhamala. Vijayawada.
56. Venkatachelam, Pandit Kota (Kali 5058, AD 1957a). *Chronology of Ancient Hindu History Part I*. Arya Vijnana Grandhamala, Publication 23. Vijayawada.
57. Venkatachelam, Pandit Kota (Kali 5058, AD 1957b). *Chronology of Ancient Hindu History Part II*. Arya Vijnana Grandhamala, Publication 24. Vijayawada.
58. Venkatachelam, Pandit Kota (Kali 5092, AD 1991). *Age of The Mahabharata War*. Arya Vijnana Grandhamala, Publication 25. Vijayawada.
59. *Viṣṇu Purāṇa: (Sanskrit) with Hindi translation by* Śrī Munilāl Gupta (6th ed., Samvat 2024; 1st ed., Samvat 1990). Gorakhpur: Gita Press.

# 5

# HASTINĀPURA EMPIRE

## Hastināpura and Magadha Dynasties Before the Mahābhārata War

Hastināpura (हस्तिनापुर) was founded by King Hastī (हस्ती), the 29th king of the Chandra Vaṁśa (dynasty) shown in Appendix I. He was the great-great-great-grandson of Emperor Bharata (भरत), the 24th king in Appendix I. India came to be known as Bhāratavarṣa after this Bharata, the son of Duṣyanta (दुष्यन्त) and Śakuntalā (शकुन्तला). The famous Śākuntala (शाकुन्तल) composed by the great Sanskrit poet Kālidāsa is about this Duṣyanta and Śakuntalā whose story is narrated in detail in the *Mahābhārata* (Vol. 1, Ādi Parva, Adhyay 68–74). See Appendix I for the complete genealogy of the kings of the Chandra Vaṁśa from its beginning to King Kuru (कुरु). Hastināpura is located close to and west of the Ganga, about 120 kilometers northeast of New Delhi. Archaeological evidence for Hastināpura is given at the end of this chapter.

## King Kuru

Ajamīḍha (अजमीढ) was one of the three sons of King Hastī. Ajamīḍha's second son was Ṛkṣa (ऋक्ष), and Ṛkṣa's son was Saṁvaraṇa (संवरण) as shown in the genealogy in Appendix I. Saṁvaraṇa, with his wife Tapati, begot Kuru (कुरु). Kuru left Prayāg (प्रयाग) and made Kurukṣetra, the holy and beautiful land, his capital. The dynasty came to be known as Kuru Vaṁśa after him. Kuru had four sons—Sudhanvā (सुधन्वा), Jahnu (जह्नु), Parīkṣit (परीक्षित्), the brilliant one, and Prajana (प्रजन), known as a destroyer of the foes. Parīkṣit was Kuru's oldest son and had no child. The dynasty split into two after Kuru, one starting from Jahnu and the other starting from Sudhanvā. The kings of the two dynasties are listed in Table 11, starting from Kuru to the time of the Mahābhārata War, as given in the *Matsya Purāṇa* (Adhyay 50), *Viṣṇu Purāṇa* (4th Aṁśa, Adhyay 19–20), and *Śrīmad Bhāgavata Purāṇa* (Skandha 9, Adhyay 22). It must be noted that several kings listed in the Matsya and Viṣṇu Purāṇas are missing from the Bhāgavat Purāṇa.

## Kuru Vaṁśa (Descendants of Kuru's son Jahnu)

The left column in Table 11 shows the genealogy of the branch from Kuru's son Jahnu. The 15th king, Pratīpa, had three sons – Devāpi (देवापि), Śāntanu (शांतनु) and Bāhlīka (बाह्लीक). Bāhlika had seven sons who were all kings of the Bāhlīka (Balkh) Deśa (*Matsya Purāṇa* 50.39). Balkh (बल्ख) is a province in present-day northern Afghanistan. Devāpi was the oldest but of ill health. Therefore, people did not respect him. He gave up the throne, went to a forest, and became a *muni* (monk), and Śāntanu became the king.

Śāntanu was not only very learned but also a great *vaidya* (practitioner of medicine). It was said that whenever Śāntanu touched any sick or old person with his hands, the person became young and healthy. This is why people called him Śāntanu. He married Gangā, the daughter of Jahnu (different from the second king in Table 11), and begat from her a son, named Devavrata (देवव्रत). Devavrata later became famous as Bhīṣma (भीष्म) because of his unprecedented vow to never marry and father a child, and never become a king. He took this vow so that his father Śāntanu might marry Satyavati (सत्यवति) whom Śāntanu so coveted, and to fulfill her condition for the marriage which stated that only her child would inherit the throne.

Śāntanu begot Vicitravīrya (विचित्रवीर्य) and Citrāṅgada (चित्रांगद) from Satyavati. Before her marriage to Śāntanu, Satyavati had given birth to Maharṣi Krishna Dvaipāyana (the great *Ṛṣi* Veda Vyāsa) with sage Parāśara (पराशर). Both Citrāṅgada and Vicitravīrya died without an heir. Hence, Satyavati ordered her son Krishna Dvaipāyana to father heirs to the throne with Vicitravīrya's two widowed wives. Thus, were born Dhṛtrāṣṭra, the father of Kauravas, and Pāṇḍu, the father of Pāṇḍavas.

## Early Cedi and Magadha Kings (Descendants of Kuru's son Sudhanvā)

The right column in Table 11 shows the genealogy of the branch from Kuru's other son, Sudhanvā. Sudhanvā's son Suhotra is missing from Matsya

**Table 11: Kings of Hastināpura, Cedi and Magadha before the Mahābhārata War**

| Hastināpura Kings | Sr. No. | Cedi (चेदि) and Magadha Kings |
|---|---|---|
| Kuru (कुरु) – had 4 sons | 1 | |
| Jahnu (जह्नु) – son of Kuru | 2 | Sudhanvā (सुधन्वा) – son of Kuru |
| Suratha (सुरथ) in all Purāṇas | 3 | Suhotra (सुहोत्र) in Bhāgavata and Viṣṇu Purāṇas, missing from Matsya Purāṇa |
| Vidūratha (विदूरथ) in all Purāṇas | 4 | Cyavana (च्यवन) in all Purāṇas |
| Sārvabhauma (सार्वभौम) in all Purāṇas | 5 | Kṛmi (कृमि) in Matya Purāṇa or Kṛtaka (कृतक) in Viṣṇu Purāṇa or Kṛti (कृति) in Bhāgavata Purāṇa |
| Jayatsena (जयत्सेन) in Viṣṇu and Matsya Purāṇas, Jayasena (जयसेन) in BhāgavataPurāṇa | 6 | Uparicaravasu (ऊपरिचरवसु) in Bhāgavata and Viṣṇu Purāṇas, Caidyoparicara (चैध्योपरिचर) in Matsya Purāṇa |
| Rucira (रुचिर) in Matsya Purāṇa, Ārādhita (आराधित) in Viṣṇu Purāṇa or Rādhika (राधिक) in Bhāgavata Purāṇa | 7 | **Bṛhadratha, 1 (प्रथम बृहद्रथ) – The first king of Magadha** |
| Bhauma (भौम) in Matsya Purāṇa | 8 | Kuśāgra (कुशाग्र) in all Purāṇas |
| Tvaritāyu (त्वरितायु) in Matsya Purāṇa or Ayutāyu (अयुतायु) in Viṣṇu Purāṇa | 9 | Vṛṣabha (वृषभ) in Viṣṇu and Matsya Purāṇas or Ṛṣabha (ऋषभ) in Bhāgavata Purāṇa |
| Akrodhana (अक्रोधन) in Matsya and Viṣṇu Purāṇas, Krodhana (क्रोधन) in Bhāgavata Purāṇa | 10 | Puṇyavān (पुण्यवान्) in Matsya Purāṇa or Puṣpavān (पुष्पवान्) in Viṣṇu and Bhāgavata Purāṇas |
| Devātithi (देवातिथि) in all Purāṇas | 11 | Puṇya (पुण्य) in Matsya Purāṇa |
| Dakṣa (दक्ष) in Matsya Purāṇa, Ṛkṣa (ऋक्ष) in Viṣṇu Purāṇa or Ṛṣya (ऋष्य) in Bhāgavata Purāṇa | 12 | Satyadhṛti (सत्यधृति) in Matsya Purāṇa or Satyahita (सत्यहित) in Viṣṇu Purāṇa |
| Bhīmasena (भीमसेन) in Matsya and Viṣṇu Purāṇas, missing in in Bhāgavata Purāṇa | 13 | Dhanuṣa (धनुष) in Matsya Purāṇa |
| Dilīpa (दिलीप) in all Purāṇas | 14 | Sarva(सर्व) in Matsya Purāṇa |
| Pratīpa (प्रतीप) in all Purāṇas | 15 | Saṁbhava (संभव) in MatsyaPurāṇa |
| Śāntanu (शांतनु) in all Purāṇas | 16 | Bṛhadratha 2 (ध्वितीय बृहद्रथ) in all Purāṇas |
| Vicitravīrya (विचित्रवीर्य) | 17 | **Jarāsandha (जरासंध) in all Purāṇas** |
| **Dhṛtrāṣṭra (धृतराष्ट्र) and Pāṇḍu (पांडु)** | 18 | Sahadeva (सहदेव) – died in the Mahābhārata War in 3139 BC |

Purāṇa. Cyavana (च्यवन), Suhotra's son, was very intelligent and well-versed in the knowledge of *dharma* (righteousness) and *artha* (wealth). Cyavana had a son named Kṛmi from Ṛkṣa. Kṛmi had a valiant son Uparicaravasu, as called in Bhāgavata and Viṣṇu Purāṇas or Caidyoparichara per Matsya Purāṇa. Caidyoparichara literally means *uparicara* (उपरिचर or attendant) of Cedi (चेदि). The *Mahābhārata* (Vol. 1, Ādi Parva 63.1–2) describes King Uparicar as a famous king of the Cedi Deśa, the present-day *Bundelkhand* region in the state of Madhya Pradesh.

Uparicaravasu had seven children with his wife Girikā (गिरिका). The oldest son was the *Mahārathi Magadharāj* (the great king of Magadha) who became famous as Bṛhadratha (*Matsya Purāṇa* 50.27). This is the first time we see Magadha mentioned in the genealogy given in the Purāṇas. Bṛhadratha founded the kingdom of Magadha (Krishnamachariar, p. xliv; Venkatachelam, 1957a, p. 26).

The second son was Pratyaśrava, the third Kuśa, the fourth Harivahana, the fifth Yujush, and the sixth Matsya, who all ruled the Cedi Deśa (*Bhāgavata Purāṇa*, Skandha 9, 22.6). The seventh child was a daughter named Kali. It seems that the kings up to Uparicaravasu were kings of Cedi. Śiśupāla (शिशुपाल) killed by Śrī Krishna was the king of Cedi.

Bṛhadratha the second, the 16th king in Table 11, married two women, beautiful twin daughters of the king of Kashi (*Mahabhārata*, Vol. 1, Sabhā Parva, Adhyay 17) and obtained by the blessings of a *ṛṣi* (sage), a powerful son named Jarāsandha. After installing him on the throne of Magadha, Bṛhadratha retired into the forest with his two wives. Jarāsandha was a very powerful king and won over most kshatriyas (kings). After killing Kaṁsa, Jarāsandha's son-in-law and the king of Mathura, Śrī Krishna incurred Jarāsandha's enmity who then attacked Mathura numerous times (*Mahabhārata*, Vol. 1, Sabhā Parva, Adhyay 17–19).

Jarāsandha's capital was Girivraja (गिरिव्रज), present-day Rājgir in Bihar. The *Mahabhārata* (Vol. 1, Sabhā Parva, 21.2–3) accurately describes the beautiful Girivraja surrounded by five *parvatas* (mountains). The map in Figure 13 shows Rājgir surrounded by five mountains as described in the Mahābhārata!

Jarāsandha was killed by Bhima, the second of the five Pāṇḍavas. He was succeeded by his son Sahadeva who fought on the side of the Kauravas in the Mahābhārata War and was killed. The history of Magadha kings after the Mahābhārata War is described in detail in Chapter 7.

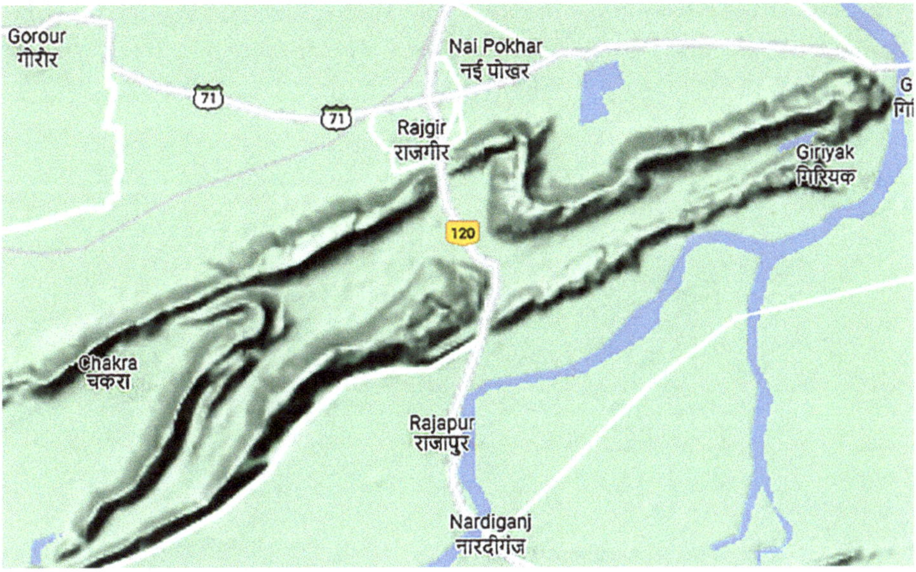


**Figure 13: Google map of Rajgir (ancient Girivraja), Bihar**
*Map courtesy: Google Map Data ©2022*

## Early Pāñcāla Kings and King Drupada

Appendix II shows the genealogy of another branch of the Chandra Vaṁśa, starting from Nīla, the son of Ajamīḍha, the 30th king in Appendix I. The genealogy leads to the Pāñcāla (पांचाल) kingdom, and about ten generations later, king Drupada. Draupadi (literally the daughter of Drupada), the wife of the Pāṇḍavas was also called Pāñcāli (one who hails from Pāñcāla). Kāmpilya (present-day Kampil in Farrukhabad district, Uttar Pradesh), the capital of Pāñcāla, was named after Kāmpilya, one of the five princes of the 36th king as shown in Appendix II.

## Early Eastern Kings

Appendix III shows the genealogy of yet another branch of the Chandra Vaṁśa, starting with Anu, the fourth son of Yayāti. About 13 generations later, the kingdoms of Aṅga, Vaṅga, Kaliṅga, Suha, Puṇḍra, and Āndhra arose in the eastern part of India.

## Emperors of Hastināpura after the Mahābhārata War

As discussed in the preceding chapter, Kaliyuga began in 3102 BC, and the Mahābhārata War was fought at Kurukṣetra towards the end of 3139 BC, 36 years before the beginning of the Kaliyuga. *Matsya Purāṇa* (Adhyay 50) describes that Kurukṣetra was located on the banks of the Drishādvati River. Figure 14 shows some of the major sites and the kingdoms described in the Mahābhārata.

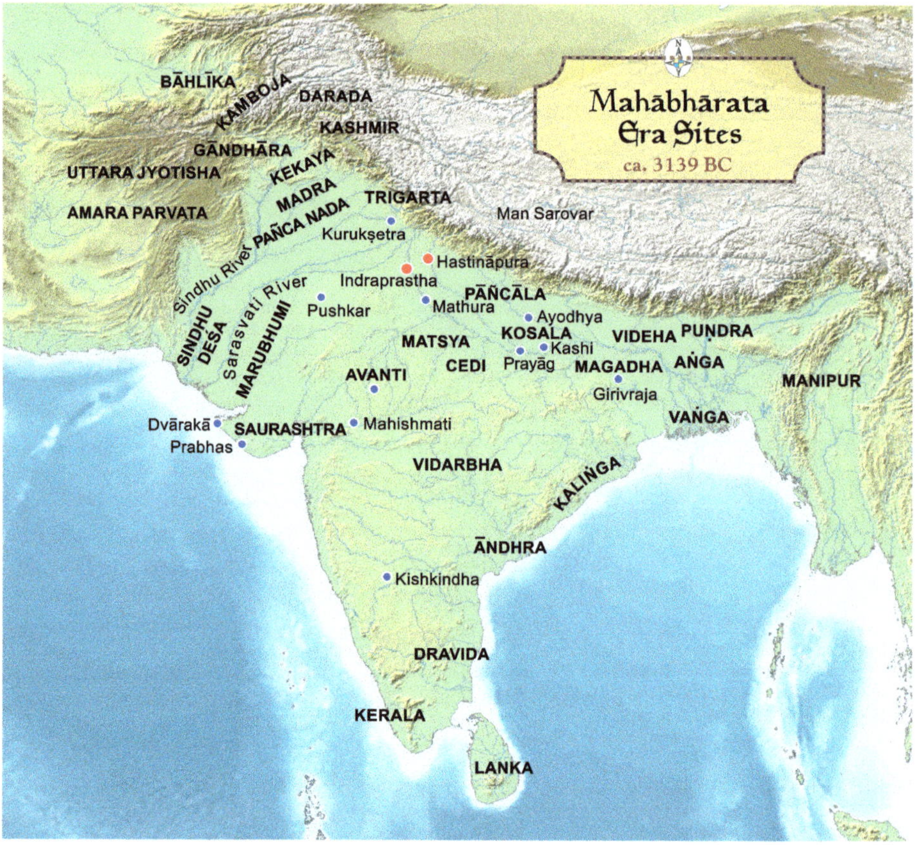


**Figure 14: Some Mahābhārata sites depicted on the map of India**
*Blank map courtesy: DEMIS Mapserver, Wikimedia Commons, CC BY-SA 3.0*

The sites and the kingdoms shown on the map cover essentially the entire Indian subcontinent. The civilization of more than 5,100 years ago wasn't present only in the Sarasvati-Sindhu region of northwestern India but in nearly the entire subcontinent.

The emperors of Hastināpura after the Mahābhārata War, as given in the Purāṇas (*Matsya Purāṇa*, Adhyay 50; *Viṣṇu Purāṇa*, 4th Aṁśa, Adhyay 21; *Bhāgavata Purāṇa*, Skandha 9, Adhyay 22), are shown in Table 12. There are slight differences in the genealogy between the various Purāṇas as noted in the table. Both Viṣṇu Purāṇa and Bhāgavata Purāṇa, list 29 kings, whereas Matsya Purāṇa lists 28 kings. There are also slight differences in some of the names as shown in the table. The Bhāgavata Purāṇa and the Viṣṇu Purāṇa were narrated first during Parīkṣit's time (*Bhāgavata Purāṇa* 9.22.35; *Viṣṇu Purāṇa* 4.20.53).

**Table 12: Emperors of Hastināpura after the Mahābhārata War, 36 BK–Kaliyuga 1468 (3138–1634 BC)**

| Sr. No. | Name of the Emperor |
|---|---|
| 1 | Yudhiṣṭhira (युधिष्ठिर), in all Purāṇas, reigned from 36 years before Kaliyuga to the beginning of the Kaliyuga (3138–3102 BC). |
| 2 | Parīkṣit (परीक्षित्), in all Purāṇas, reigned for 60 years from the beginning of the Kaliyuga (3102–3041 BC). |
| 3 | Janamejaya (जनमेजय), in all Purāṇas, reigned starting from Kaliyuga 61 (3041 BC). **Individual periods of reign are not available from this point onwards.* |
| 4 | Śatānīka 1 (प्रथम शतानीक) in all Purāṇas |
| 5 | Sahasrānīka (सहस्रानीक), given only in Bhāgavata Purāṇa, missing from Viṣṇu and Matsya Purāṇas |
| 6 | Aśvamedhadatta (अश्वमेधदत्त) in Viṣṇu Purāṇa or Aśvamedhaja (अश्वमेधज ) in Bhāgavata Purāṇa, missing in Matsya Purāṇa |
| 7 | Adhisīmakṛṣṇa (अधिसीमकृष्ण) in Viṣṇu and Matsya Purāṇas or Asīmakṛṣṇa (असीमकृष्ण) in Bhāgavata Purāṇa |
| 8 | Nicaknu (निचक्नु) in Viṣṇu Purāṇa or Vivakṣu (विवक्षु) in Matsya Purāṇa or Nemicakra (नेमिचक्र) in Bhāgavata Purāṇa |
| 9 | Uṣṇa (उष्ण) in Viṣṇu Purāṇa or Bhūri (भूरि) in Matsya Purāṇa, missing in Bhāgavata Purāṇa |
| 10 | Vicitraratha (विचित्ररथ) in Viṣṇu Purāṇa or Citraratha (चित्ररथ) in Matsya and Bhāgavata Purāṇas |
| 11 | Śuciratha (शुचिरथ) in Viṣṇu Purāṇa or Śucidrava (शुचिद्रव) in Matsya Purāṇa or Kaviratha (कविरथ) in Bhāgavata Purāṇa |
| 12 | Vṛṣṇimān (वृष्णिमान्) in Viṣṇu and Matsya Purāṇas or Vṛṣtimān (वृष्टिमान्) in Bhāgavata Purāṇa |
| 13 | Suṣeṇa (सुषेण) in all Purāṇas |
| 14 | Sunītha (सुनीथ) in all Purāṇas |
| 15 | Nṛpacakṣu (नृपचक्षु) in Viṣṇu Purāṇa or Nṛcakṣu (नृचक्षु) in Matsya and Bhāgavata Purāṇas |
| 16 | Sukhābala (सुखाबल) in Viṣṇu Purāṇa, Sukhībala (सुखीबल) in Matsya Purāṇa or Sukhīnala (सुखीनल) in Bhāgavata Purāṇa |
| 17 | Pāriplava (पारिप्लव) in Viṣṇu and Bhāgavata Purāṇas or Pariṣṇava (परिष्णव) in Matsya Purāṇa |

*Table Continued...*

| Sr. No. | Name of the Emperor |
|---|---|
| 18 | Sunaya (सुनय) in Viṣṇu and Bhāgavata Purāṇas or Sutapā (सुतपा) in Matsya Purāṇa |
| 19 | Medhāvi (मेधावी) in all Purāṇas |
| 20 | Ripuñjaya (रिपुञ्जय) in Viṣṇu Purāṇa, Puruñjaya (पुरुञ्जय) in Matsya Purāṇa or Nṛpañjaya (नृपञ्जय) in Bhāgavata Purāṇa |
| 21 | Mṛdu (मृदु) in Viṣṇu Purāṇa, Urva (उर्व) in Matsya Purāṇa or Dūrva (दूर्व) in Bhāgavata Purāṇa |
| 22 | Tigma (तिग्म) in Viṣṇu Purāṇa, Tigmātmā (तिग्मात्मा ) in Matsya Purāṇa or Timi (तिमि) in Bhāgavata Purāṇa |
| 23 | Bṛhadradha (बृहद्रथ) in all Purāṇas |
| 24 | Vasudāna (वसुदान) in Viṣṇu Purāṇa, Vasudāmā (वसुदामा) in Matsya Purāṇa or Sudāsa (सुदास) in Bhāgavata Purāṇa |
| 25 | Śatanīka 2 (ध्वितीय शतानीक )in all Purāṇas |
| 26 | Udayana (उदयन) in Matsya Purāṇa or Durdamana (दुर्दमन) in Bhāgavata Purāṇa |
| 27 | Ahīnara (अहीनर) in Viṣṇu Purāṇa or Vahīnara (वहीनर) in Matsya and Bhāgavata Purāṇas |
| 28 | Daṇḍapāṇi (दण्डपाणि) in all Purāṇas |
| 29 | Niramitra (निरमित्र) in Matsya Purāṇa or Nimi (निमि) in Bhāgavata Purāṇa |
| 30 | Kṣemaka (क्षेमक) in all Purāṇas |
| | **The Dynasty ended in Kaliyuga 1468 (1634 BC)** |

## Position of the Saptarṣi at the time of Parīkṣit

The chronology in the Purāṇas has also been described by the Saptarṣi cycle as discussed in **Chapter 4.** According to the *Viṣṇu Purāṇa* (4th Aṁśa, 24.106–107) and *Śrīmad Bhāgavata Purāṇa* (Skandha 12, 2.29–30, 33), the Saptarṣi (Big Dipper) were in *Maghā* (Nakṣatra) at the time of Parīkṣit (ruling), when the Kaliyuga of 1,200 divine years (1 divine year = 360 human years) started, per the following verses.

तेन सप्तर्षयोयुक्तास्तिष्ठन्त्यब्दशतं नृणाम् ।
ते तु पारीक्षिते काले मघास्वासन्द्विजोत्तम ॥१०६॥
तदा प्रवृत्तश्च कलिर्द्वादशाब्दशतात्मकः ॥१०७॥

Tena saptarṣayoyuktās-tiṣthantyabdaśataṁ nṛṇāṁ ।
Te tu Pārīkṣite kāle maghāsvāsan-dvijottama ॥106॥
Tadā pravṛttaśca kalirdvādaśābda-śatātmakaḥ ॥107॥

As discussed in Chapter 4, Yudhiṣṭhira gave up the throne 36 years after the war, upon hearing the news of Śrī Krishna's demise, and crowned Parīkṣit, the grandson of Arjuna, as the next emperor. Parīkṣit ruled for 60 years starting from the first year of Kaliyuga in 3102 BC (*Mahābhārata*, Vol. 1, Ādi Parva 49.17).

Parīkṣit had four sons – Janamejaya (जनमेजय), Śrutasena (श्रुतसेन), Ugrasena (उग्रसेन) and Bhīmasena (भीमसेन). After Parīkṣit died, Janamejaya was crowned as the next emperor. Two inscriptions of Janamejaya on copper plates were found, one of which was published in *The Indian Antiquary* (Fleet, 1875, p. 333–334). The inscriptions are the gift deeds, that refer to a gift of land for the worship of Śrī Sitā and Rāma on the bank of Tungabhadra River (in the Karnataka state), by Janamejaya in the 89th year of Jayābhyudaya Yudhiṣṭhira Śaka, i.e. Kaliyuga 89 (3013 BC). The year *Plavaṅga* mentioned in the inscription tallies with the 89th year of Kaliyuga. Figure 15 shows the initial part of the text of the inscription. See Chapter 14 for the complete text of the inscription. Yes, India had a writing system 5,000 years ago, revealed by the excavations of the Sarasvati-Sindhu valley. See Chapter 14 for details.

"श्रीगणाधिपतये नमः।
श्लो ।। पांतु वो जलदस्यामाः शार्ङ्ग्ज्याघातकर्कशाः।
त्रैलोक्यमंडपस्तंभाश्चत्वारो हरिबाहवः ।। (१)
स्वस्ति श्रीजयाभ्युदये युधिष्ठिरशके प्लवंगाख्ये एकोननवती (89)
वत्सरे सहस्यमासि अमावास्यायां सौम्यवासरे श्रीमन्महाराजाधिराजपरमेश्वरो
वीरप्रताशाली कुरुकुलोद्भावो वैयग्रणीपादगोत्रजः श्रीजनमेजयभूपः किष्किंद्यानगर्या
सिंहासनस्थः सकलवर्णाश्रमधर्मप्रतिपालकः पश्चिमदेशस्थ सीतापुरवृकोदरक्षेत्रे
तत्रत्यमुनिवृन्दमठस्य गरुडवाहनतीर्थ श्रीमच्छिष्यकैकयनाथैराराधितसीतारामस्य पूजार्थं
कृतभूदानसाधनं अस्मत्प्रपितामहयुधिष्ठिराधि स्थितमुनिवृन्दक्षेत्रे स्य
चतुःसीमापरिमितिक्रमः

**Figure 15: Janamejaya's gift deed on a copper plate**

This is the first inscription known that used the Jayābhyudaya Yudhiṣṭhira Śaka. The writing of the Mahābhārata Itihāsa by Veda Vyāsa began in the first year of Kaliyuga. The Itihāsa was first called *Jaya* (victory), hence the Kaliyuga Era was also called the Jayābhyudaya Yudhiṣṭhira Śaka. (Venkatachelam, 1957a, p. 15; 1991, p. 46).

A similar gift by the same Emperor Janamejaya was made on the same day to Śrī Goswami Anandalinga Jangama of Uṣhamath through his disciple Jnanalinga Jangama for the worship of God Kedarnath in Kedara *kṣetra* in the Himalaya. According to Pandit Venkatachelam (1991, p. 49), the copper plate on which the gift deed is inscribed is preserved to this day (as of the 1950s) in the same maṭha. The full text of this second inscription is reproduced in Chapter 14.

Janamejaya (जनमेजय) was succeeded by Śatānīka (शतानीक), the eldest of his five sons. Śatānīka, the fourth king in Table 12, learned Vedas from the famous *Ṛṣi* (sage) Yajñavalkya (याज्ञवल्क्य), learned weapons use from Kṛpāchārya (must be different from Kṛpāchārya of the Mahābhārata time), and attained moksha after obtaining *ātma jñān* (knowledge of the self) from *Ṛṣi* Śaunaka (शौनक) (*Viṣṇu Purāṇa*, 4th Aṁśa, Adhyay 21; *Bhāgavata Purāṇa*, Skandha 9, Adhyay 22).

Sahasrānīka (सहस्रानीक), the fifth king, is only mentioned in Bhāgavata Purāṇa. Aśvamedhadatta (अश्वमेधदत्त), the sixth king, is stated in Viṣṇu and Bhāgavata Purāṇas but is missing from the Matsya Purāṇa. *Matsya Purāṇa* (50.67) was first narrated during the reign of Adhisīmakṛṣṇa (अधिसीमकृष्ण), the seventh king in Table 12. During the reign of Nicaknu (निचक्नु) or Vivakṣu (विवक्षु), the eighth king, Hastināpura was flooded by the Ganga. Then, Nicaknu left Hastināpura and moved to Kauśāmbī (located about 50 kilometers west of Prayāg) according to all the Purāṇas – Matsya, Bhāgavata, and Viṣṇu. The Aśokan pillar currently located in Prayāg was originally located in Kauśāmbī which suggests that Kauśāmbī continued to be an important city till the time of Aśoka.

Thus, 30 emperors of the dynasty reigned for a total of 1,504 years, starting from the coronation of Yudhiṣṭhira in 3138 BC after the Mahābhārata War to the end of the dynasty in Kaliyuga 1468 (1634 BC) with Kṣemaka (क्षेमक) as the last emperor. Thus, ended the dynasty of Puru, Kuru, and Arjuna that produced brahmins and kshatriyas as described in the Purāṇas.

## Archaeological Evidence for Hastināpura and Kauśāmbī

As described in the earlier paragraph, the Purāṇas state that Hastināpura was flooded in the eighth generation from Yudhiṣṭhira, and the capital was then moved to Kauśāmbī. A video of an interview with K. K. Muhammad, the archaeologist and ex-regional director of the Archaeological Survey of India (ASI), has stated that the excavations at Hastināpura, Kurukṣetra (कुरुक्षेत्र), Kauśāmbī (कौशाम्बी), etc. have confirmed what is stated in the Mahābhārata and the Purāṇas.

B. B. Lal (2011, p. 2), the superintending archaeologist of ASI in the 1950s, undertook excavations in western Uttar Pradesh in general and then in Hastināpura specifically. There is a large mound located on the right bank of the Ganga. The excavations revealed that a sizable part of the Painted Grey Ware (PGW) pottery settlement was washed away by heavy flooding of Ganga. The excavations at Kauśāmbī revealed that the lowest levels of Kauśāmbī began with the same kind of material culture as was in existence at Hastināpura when the flood destroyed it.

## References


1. *Śrīmad Bhāgavata MahāPurāṇa: (Sanskrit) with Hindi translation,* 2 vols. (81st ed., Vikrama Samvat 2071; 1st ed., Samvat 1997). Gorakhpur: Gita Press.
2. Fleet, J. F. (1875). 'Sanskrit and Old Canarese Inscriptions: No. VIII (of Janamejaya).' *The Indian Antiquary: A Journal of Oriental Research in Archaeology, History, Literature, Language, Philosophy, Religion, Folklore etc., Vol. 4,* 333–335. Bombay.
3. Krishnamachariar, M. (1937). *History of Classical Sanskrit Literature: Being an elaborate account of all branches of Classical Sanskrit Literature, with full Epigraphical and Archaeological Notes and References, an Introduction dealing with Languages, Philology and Chronology, and Index of Authors and Works.* Madras.
4. Lal, B. B. (2011). *Excavations at Bharadvāja Āśrama 1978–79 & 1982–83 (With a Note on the Exploration at Chitrakūta).* New Delhi: Archaeological Survey of India.
5. *Mahābhārata: (Sanskrit) with Hindi translation* by Pandit Rāmanārāyaṇadatta Śastri Pāṇdeya, 6 vols. Gorakhpur: Gita Press.
6. *Matsya Purāṇa: (Sanskrit) with Hindi translation.* Gorakhpur: Gita Press.
7. Venkatachelam, Pandit Kota (Kali 5058, AD 1957a). *Chronology of Ancient Hindu History Part I.* Arya Vijnana Grandhamala, Publication 23. Vijayawada.
8. Venkatachelam, Pandit Kota (Kali 5092, AD 1991). *Age of The Mahabharata War.* Arya Vijnana Grandhamala, Publication 25. Vijayawada.
9. *Viṣṇu Purāṇa: (Sanskrit) with Hindi translation by* Śrī Munilāl Gupta. (6th ed., Samvat 2024; 1st ed., Samvat 1990). Gorakhpur: Gita Press.

# 6

# THE HISTORICITY OF ŚRĪ KRISHNA

Three principal sources contain accounts of Lord Śrī Krishna* (श्रीकृष्ण). They are the Mahābhārata, the Harivaṁśa (हरिवंश), and the Purāṇas. Harivaṁśa is an appendix to the Mahābhārata. The Mahābhārata is the earliest and contains a great deal of historical information. The Mahābhārata depicts Śrī Krishna more as a human than the other texts (Nayak and Rao, 1992, p. 479).

(*spelled Kṛṣṇa by transliteration rules but Krishna in common parlance)

As discussed in Chapter 4, Śrī Krishna left the earth just before the Kaliyuga began in 3102 BC. He was a virtuous and noble king of the highest caliber, a leader among the kings. He was also the greatest philosopher who, through his upadeśa (sermons) to Arjuna, brought out the essence of the highest philosophy of life which is contained in the Mahābhārata. Separately, it is well known as Śrimad Bhagavadgītā. Over time Śrī Krishna's great deeds immortalized him and he became God in people's hearts.

**Figure 16: Lord Śrī Krishna**
*Illustration by: Pradeep Aeri*

The historicity of the Mahābhārata was well accepted until the rewriting of India's history by the colonial Indologists began in the late 18th century. The list prepared by William Jones in AD 1788 (Chapter 2, Table 3) shows Abhimanyu and Arjun of Mahābhārata as historical persons. See Parasara,

Yudhisthir, Vyasa, and Paricshit in Table 6 (Chapter 2) prepared by Bentley in AD 1796. As the shrinking of ancient India's chronology and rewriting of its history by colonial Indologists progressed over the next hundred years, the Mahābhārata and the Rāmāyaṇa were declared mythical stories. This chapter presents evidence for the historicity of Śrī Krishna whose teachings continue to influence the Indian subcontinent and many parts of the world to the present time.

## Historical Evidence for Śrī Krishna

There is sufficient archaeological, astronomical, geographical, as well as, literary evidence to support the existence of Śri Krishna as a historical figure. Here is some of the evidence:

1. After Śrī Krishna's departure from the earth and the submergence of Dvārakā, Yudhiṣṭhira installed Parīkṣit (परीक्षित्), the son of Abhimanyu and the grandson of Arjuna, on the throne of Hastināpura, and Vrajanābha (व्रजनाभ), the son of Aniruddha (अनिरुध्ध) and the grandson of Śrī Krishna, on the throne of Indraprastha (*Mahābhārata*, Vol. 6, Mahā Prasthānika Parva 1.2,6–9). *Śrīmad Bhāgavata MahāPurāṇa* (Bhāgavata Mahātmya, Adhyay 1) describes that Vrajanābha was installed as the king in Mathura. Perhaps, Vrajanābha later moved from Indraprastha to Mathura.

2. The Bhāgavata MahāPurāṇa further states that Emperor Parīkṣit went from Hastināpura to Mathura to visit Vrajanābha where he was warmly welcomed. Parīkṣit expressed his sincere gratitude for the immense help given to his father and grandfather by Vrajanābha's father, Aniruddha, and grandfather, Śrī Krishna, and assured Vrajanābha of his full support if ever needed.

3. According to the tradition, the original Dwārkādhish Temple in Dvārakā is believed to have been built by Śrī Krishna's grandson, Vrajanābha, over Śrī Krishna's residential place.

4. There are several references to Śrī Krishna in Kalhaṇa's *Rājataraṅgiṇī* (1148/1985, 1.59–71).

    a. Gonanda I, the king of Kashmir, upon invitation by his friend Jarāsandha, joined him with his army in attacking Mathura (Śrī Krishna's capital) and surrounded it. Jarāsandha had become Śrī Krishna's enemy, since he had killed Kaṁsa, his son-in-law. Gonanda-I was killed in this battle by Balarāma, Śrī Krishna's elder brother.

b. Gonanda's son, Dāmodara I, was not at peace because of the death of his father by Balarāma. Upon hearing that Yādavas had been invited to the *svayamvara* of the princess of Gāndhāra, Dāmodara attacked Gāndhāra to disrupt the event and was killed in that battle by Śrī Krishna himself.

c. After Dāmodara's death, Śrī Krishna had Dāmodara's pregnant wife Yaśomati installed on Kashmir's throne even after the hesitation of his ministers. This is perhaps the earliest known incidence of a woman installed on the throne. See Chapter 11 for details.

5. Kautilya in his famous *Arthaśastra* attributes the destruction of Duryodhana to his coveting of another's kingdom (Rao, 2001, p. 46). As discussed in Chapter 7, Kautilya and his contemporary Chandragupta Maurya's time was 1534 BC. Thus, Mahābhārata was well-known even in the 16th century BC, in line with its true date of 3139 BC.

6. Megasthenes, who visited and lived in Pāṭaliputra in around 300 BC, has reported hearing stories of Śrī Krishna. He calls him Hercules or Heracles. Arrian quotes Megasthenes (McCrindle, 1876, p. 16–17):

    > “This Hercules [Krishna] is held in especial honour by the Souraseni [Śūraseni], an Indian tribe possessing two large cities, Methora [Mathura] and Cloisobora, while a navigable river called the Iobares [Yamuna] flows through their country. But the dress which this Hercules wore, Megasthenes tells us, resembled that of the Theban Hercules, as the Indians themselves admit. It is further said that he had a very numerous progeny of male children born to him in India (for, like his Theban namesake, he married many wives).”

7. Jain tradition holds Śrī Krishna to be the contemporary of Neminātha (नेमिनाथ), the 22nd Tirthankara (*Neminātha Caritra*).

8. The Indian historian C. V. Vaidya (1907/1987) has a chapter titled 'The Life and Teaching of Shrikrishna' in his book, *Epic India*.

## Evidence from Genealogy of Yadu Vaṁśa and Śrī Krishna

The vaṁśāvali (genealogy) of Śrī Krishna and Yadu (यदु) Vaṁśa (the Yadu lineage) is preserved in many Purāṇas (*Viṣṇu Purāṇa*, 4th Aṁśa, Adhyay 11–14; *Bhāgavata Purāṇa*, Skandha 9, Adhyay 23–24; *Matsya Purāṇa*, Adhyay 44–46; *Vāyu Purāṇa*, Adhyay 96).

The genealogy shown below starts from Yadu, the oldest of the five sons of Yayāti (the seventh king in Appendix I). Śrī Krishna and his relatives were called Yādava which means 'of Yadu' in Sanskrit. The Yādava community is found in the state of Uttar Pradesh even at present. The genealogy given here is primarily from the Viṣṇu Purāṇa. The names differ slightly between the various Purāṇas. Occasionally a name or two are missing in some Purāṇas. Whenever there are differences between the various Purāṇas, they are noted in parentheses. If there is nothing noted, then the names are the same in all the Purāṇas.

Thus, after the seventh king, Yayāti, come:

8. Yadu (यदु) – had 4 sons – Sahasrajit, Kroṣṭu, Nala, and Nahuṣa
9. Kroṣṭu (क्रोष्टु)
10. Dhvajinīvāna (ध्वजिनीवान) – Vṛjinīvāna in Bhāgavata and Matsya Purāṇas
11. Svāti (स्वाति) – Śvāhi in Bhāgavata, Svāha in Matsya, Svāhi in Vāyu Purāṇa
12. Ruśaṅku (रुशंकु) – Ruśeku in Bhāgavata, Ruśaṅgu in Matsya, Raśādu in Vāyu Purāṇa
13. Citraratha (चित्ररथ)
14. Śaśibindu (शशिबिन्दु) – Śaśabindu in Bhāgavata Purāṇa; was an emperor and had many sons
15. Pṛthuśravā (पृथुश्रवा)
16. Pṛthutama (पृथुतम) – Dharma in Bhāgavata, Suyaṅga in Matsya Purāṇa
17. Uśanā (उशना) – carried out 100 *Aśvamedha yajñas*
18. Śitapu (शितपु) – Rucaka in Bhāgavata, Titikṣu in Matsya Purāṇa

    Maruta – son of Titikṣu per Matsya Purāṇa, Uśana's son per Vāyu Purāṇa, missing in Viṣṇu Purāṇa

    Kambalabarhiśa (कंबलबर्हिश) – son of Maruta per Matsya and Vāyu Purāṇas, missing in Viṣṇu Purāṇa

19. Rukmakavaca (रुक्मकवच) – Rucaka in Bhāgavgata, son of Kambalabarhiśa per Matsya and Vāyu Purāṇas – had five sons (Rukmeśu, Pṛthurukma, Jyāmagha, Parigha, Harita) according to Bhāgavata, Vāyu and Matsya Purāṇas – installed Parigha and Harita as kings in the Videha Deśa

20. Parāvṛt (परावृत्) – Purujit in Bhāgavata Purāṇa

21. Jyāmagha (ज्यामघ) – brother of Parāvṛt, the 20th king

22. Vidarbha (विदर्भ) – had 3 sons – Kratha, Kaiśika, and Romapāda

23. Kratha (क्रथ), Kaiśika (Kuśa in Bhāgavata, Kauśika in Vāyu Purāṇa), and Romapāda (Lomapāda in Matsya Purāṇa). Romapāda's son was Babhṛ, Babhṛ's son was Dhṛti, Dhṛti's son Kaiśika and his son **Cedi (चेदि)**. The descendants of this king were called Caidya kings.

24. Kunti (कुन्ति) – son of Kratha

25. Dhṛṣṭi (धृष्टि) – Druṣta in Matsya and Vāyu Purāṇas

26. Nidhṛti (निधृति) – Nirvṛti in Bhāgavata, Nivṛti in Matsya and Vāyu Purāṇas

27. Daśārha (दशार्ह)

28. Vyomā (व्योमा) – Vyoma in Bhāgavata and Matsya Purāṇas

29. Jīmūta (जीमूत)

30. Vikṛti (विकृति) – Vimala in Matsya Purāṇa

31. Bhīmaratha (भीमरथ)

32. Navaratha (नवरथ)

33. Daśaratha (दशरथ) – Dṛdharatha in Matsya Purāṇa

34. Śakuni (शकुनि)

35. Karambhi (करम्भि) – Karambha in Matsya Purāṇa

36. Devarāta (देवरात)

37. Devakṣatra (देवक्षत्र)

38. Madhu (मधु)

39. Kumārvaṁśa (कुमारवंश) – Kuruvaśa in Bhāgavata Purāṇa, Puravas in Matsya Purāṇa

40. Anu (अनु) – Purudhvān in Matsya and Vāyu Purāṇas

41. Purumitra (पुरुमित्र) – Puruhotra in Bhāgavata, Purudhvaha in Vāyu, missing in Matsya Purāṇa; married a princess from Vidarbha

42. Aṁśu (अंशु) – Āyu in Bhāgavata, Jantu in Matsya, Satva in Vāyu; married Ekṣvāki (daughter of Ikṣavāku Dynasty) per Matsya Purāṇa

43. Satvata (सत्वत) – begot several sons from Kauśalyā (daughter of the Kośal king) – Bhajana (भजन), Bhajamāna (भजमान), Divya, Andhaka (अंधक), Devāvṛdha (देवावृध), Mahābhoja (महाभोज), and Vṛṣṇi (वृष्णि); in some editions of Matsya Purāṇa, Divya is a prefix for Devāvṛdha.

In the genealogy up to Satvata and his sons, there is very good agreement between the various Purāṇas. However, after Satvata, there are significant differences between the various Purāṇas and it is difficult to determine the precise genealogy leading to Śrī Krishna. Four dynasties grew from Satvata according to Matsya and Vāyu Purāṇas.

In the Mahābhārata and the Purāṇas, Śrī Krishna is frequently referred to as hailing from Andhaka and Vṛṣni vaṁśas. Śrī Krishna's lineage is as follows according to the Viṣṇu Purāṇa.

44. Andhaka (अंधक) – Satvata's son
45. Kukura (कुकुर), **Bhajamāna II** (भजमान 2), Śūci (शूचि), Kambalabarhiśa (कंबलबर्हिश)
46. Vidūratha (विदूरथ) – Bhajamāna's son (*Viṣṇu Purāṇa* 4.14.22; *Matsya Purāṇa*, Adhyay 44)
47. Śūra (शूर) – Śūravira *Rajādhideva* in Matsya Purāṇa
48. Śamī (शमी)
49. Pratikṣatra (प्रतिक्षत्र)
50. Svayaṁbhoja (स्वयंभोज) – Bhoja in Matsya Purāṇa
51. Hṛdika (हृदिक) – had several sons viz. Kṛtavarmā, Śatadhanvā, Devārha, Devagarbha, etc.
52. Devagarbha (देवगर्भ)
53. Śūrasena (शूरसेन) – had **ten sons** from wife Māriṣā (मारिषा) – Vasudeva (वसुदेव), Devabhāga (देवभाग), Devaśravā (देवश्रवा), Aṣṭaka (अष्टक), Kakuñcaka (ककुञ्चक), Vatsadhāraka (वत्सधारक), Sṛñjaya (सृञ्जय), Śyāma (श्याम), Śamika (शमिक), and Gaṇḍūṣa (गण्डूष), and **five daughters** – Pṛthā (पृथा), Śrutadevā (श्रुतदेवा), Śrutakīrti (श्रुतकीर्ति), Śrutaśravā (श्रुतश्रवा), and Rājādhidevī (राजाधिदेवी)
54. Vasudeva (वसुदेव) – had seven wives including Devaki (देवकि) and Rohiṇi (रोहिणि), the mother of Balarāma (बलराम)
55. **Śrī Krishna (श्रीकृष्ण) – the eighth child of Devaki**

Śūrasena, the 53rd in the genealogy above, had a friend named Kuntibhoja (कुन्तिभोज) who was childless. Śūrasena gave his daughter Pṛthā (पृथा) to Kuntibhoja in adoption. Hence, Pṛthā became known as Kunti (daughter of Kuntibhoja). Pṛthā married Pāṇḍu, the father of Pāṇḍavas. Arjuna was often called Pārtha ('of Pṛthā' in Sanskrit). Śūrasena's daughter Śrutśravā married Cedirāja (the king of Cedi), Damaghoṣa. Her son was Śiśupāla who was killed by Śrī Krishna. Śiśupāla was thus a paternal cousin of Śrī Krishna.

Vasudeva, Śūrsena's son and Śrī Krishna's father, was a trusted minister of the king of Mathura, Ugrasena, a descendent of Vṛṣni. The oldest son of Ugrasena, Kaṁsa, married the daughter of Jarāsandha on the condition that he immediately be installed on the throne of Mathura. Kaṁsa was installed on the throne and he soon imprisoned his father. Vasudeva served the king faithfully. Therefore, Kaṁsa gave him Devaki in marriage. She was the daughter of Kaṁsa's paternal uncle Devaka (*Mahābhārata*, Vol. 1, Sabhā Parva, Adhyay 22). Devaka had four sons and seven daughters. All seven daughters were married to Vasudeva.

Śrī Krishna's older brother, Balarāma, was born to Rohiṇi, one of the seven wives of Vasudeva. Kaṁsa's father, Ugrasena, had nine sons and four daughters. Names of all his children are given in the Purāṇas. The following is the genealogy of Devaki, Śrī Krishna's mother.

## Genealogy of Devaki

45. Kukura (कुकुर) – Andhaka's son (number 45 in the genealogy of Śrī Krishna)
46. Dhṛṣṭa (धृष्ट) – Vahni (वह्नि) in Bhāgavata Purāṇa, Vṛṣni (वृष्णि) in Matsya Purāṇa) - Kukura's son
47. Kapotaromā (कपोतरोमा)
48. Vilomā (विलोमा)
49. Anu (अनु)
50. Ānakadundubhi (आनकदुन्दुभि)
51. Abhijita (अभिजित)
52. Punarvasu (पुनर्वसु)
53. Āhuka (आहुक) and Āhukī (आहुकी) – twins according to Matsya Purāṇa

54. Devaka (देवक) and Ugrasena (उग्रसेन)

**55. Devaki (देवकि)** and six other daughters of Devaka; **Kaṁsa** (कंस) was the son of Ugrasena.

Vasudeva begot from Devaki – Kirtimāna, Suśeṇa, Udāyu, Bhadrasena, Rujudāsa, and Bhadradeva who were all killed by Kaṁsa.

Finally, Kaṁsa was killed by Śrī Krishna which infuriated Jarāsandha, Kaṁsa's father-in-law. So, he kept attacking Śrī Krishna's city, Mathura. To spare his people from the repeated attacks, Śrī Krishna and his Yādava community migrated from Mathura to Kuśasthali in the west, in Saurashtra (ancient Anarta), the home of their ancestors. Krishna founded a new city near Kuśasthali which was in ruins and named it Dvārakā.

## Archaeological Evidence from Dvārakā

Dvārakā, the capital of Śrī Krishna, as described in the *Mahābhārata* (Vol. 6, Mausal Parva 7.41–42) and the Purāṇas, is located on the westernmost coast of Saurashtra. *Viṣṇu Purāṇa* (5th Aṁśa, 23.13–14) and several other texts describe that the city was built by reclaiming land from the sea. It was a very prosperous city. It was submerged in the sea just after the passing away of Śrī Krishna.

In 1963, Z. D. Ansari and M. S. Mate of the Deccan College in Poona undertook land excavations of the area to the south side and immediately outside the walls encircling the Dwārkādhish Temple complex, under the guidance of H. D. Sankalia. Thereafter, Sankalia (1966, p. 17) wrote:

> “From our observations of the various places in and around Dwarka as also from the evidence of excavation one can definitely say that this is the Dvārakā mentioned in the Musala Parva of the Mhb [Mahābhārata], the Dvārakā-mahātmya of the Skanda Purāṇa, other Purāṇas and the Ghata Jātaka.”

Systematic underwater exploration was carried out at Bet Dwārkā and Dvārakā, by the Marine Archaeological Unit of India's National Institute of Oceanography, under the leadership of the veteran archaeologist S. R. Rao, from 1982–1995. The eroded coastline of Bet Dwārkā revealed remnants of a massive rubble wall at the southern portion of the eastern shore of Bet Dwārkā. The pottery collected from the section was dated 3,520* years before the present, by the thermoluminescence dating method. Dr. S. R. Rao (2001, p. 121) states:

> “The archaeological evidence so far made available from the onshore and offshore excavations at Bet Dwārkā during the years 1983 to 1995

is adequate enough to suggest the identity of the excavated site in Bet Dwārkā island with Kusasthalī where a town was built and named as Dvārakā. Similarly, the port town of Dvārakā on the mainland can be identified with the town built after reclaiming land from the sea when it was found that the narrow strip of land at the foot of the hill in Kusasthali-Dvārakā was not sufficient for the Yadavas.

The topography of Bet Dwārkā reveals that there is a hill 30 to 40 m high, at the foot of which a stretch of 0.5 to 1 km wide flat land was available for human settlement all along the 5 km length of the eastern flank of Bet Dwārkā 3,500 years ago. Bet Dwārkā was then not a complete island. It was connected with the mainland near Gopi talao … where the sea is very shallow even now. The ancient texts including the *Mahābhārata* and *Harivamsa* repeatedly mention that the Yadavas came to Kusasthali, which was well protected by nature itself with a hill on one side and the sea on the other. ”

* The deduction '3,520 years before the present' is based on the dating of the pottery. It does not rule out further exploration leading to much earlier dating of the submerged Dvārakā.

The sea level has risen by about ten meters since 1500 BC (Nayak and Ghosh, 1992, p. xxxi). This would have resulted in the submergence of ancient Dvārakā and many other ancient cities on India's large coastline. More archaeological evidence from the 3000 BC era is discussed in detail in Chapter 14.

## References

1. *Śrīmad Bhāgavata MahāPurāṇa: (Sanskrit) with Hindi translation,* 2 vols. (81st ed., Vikrama Samvat 2071; 1st ed., Samvat 1997). Gorakhpur: Gita Press.

2. Kalhaṇa (1148). *Rājataraṅgiṇī (Chronicle of the Kings of Kashmir) (Sanskrit text),* Edited with Hindi translation by Shri Ramtej Shastri Pandey (Vikrama Samvat 2017 (AD 1960), rpt. ed. 1985). Delhi & Varanasi: Chaukhamba Sanskrit Pratishthan.

3. *Mahābhārata: (Sanskrit) with Hindi translation* by Pandit Rāmanārāyaṇadatta Śastri Pāṇdeya, 6 vols. Gorakhpur: Gita Press.

4. *Matsya Purāṇa: (Sanskrit) with Hindi translation.* Gorakhpur: Gita Press.

5. McCrindle, Watson (1876). *The Indica of Arrian: Translated and Annotated.* Bombay: Education Society's Press.

6. Nayak, B. U., and N. C. Ghosh (Eds.) (1992). 'Life Sketch of Dr. S. R. Rao.' in *New Trends in Indian Art and Archaeology: S.R. Rao's 70th Birthday Felicitation Volume* (Vol. 1). New Delhi: Aditya Prakashan.

7. Nayak, B. U., and S. R. Rao (1992). 'Existence and Location of Dvaraka City of Mahābhārata Era and its Subsequent Submergence: A Reality or a Myth?' in B. U. Nayak and N. C. Ghosh (Eds.), *New Trends in Indian Art and Archaeology: S.R. Rao's 70th Birthday Felicitation Volume* (Vol. 2, Ch. VII.10). New Delhi: Aditya Prakashan.

8. *Neminātha Caritra* (1956). Hindi translation. Kolkata: Ādinātha Hindi-Jain Sāhitya-mālā (Originally written by Guṇavijaya in 1668).

9. Rao, S. R. (2001). *Marine Archaeology in India.* Ministry of Information and Broadcasting, Government of India.

10. Sankalia, H. D. (1966). 'Dwarka in Literature and Archaeology.' in *Excavations at Dwarka (1963):* by Zainuddin Dawood Ansari and Madhukar Shripad Mate. Poona: Deccan College Postgraduate & Research Institute.

11. Vaidya, C. V. (1907). 'The Life and Teaching of ShriKrishna.' in *Epic India: India as Described in the Mahabharata and the Ramayana* (rpt. ed. 1987, Vol. 18 (i), Ch. XVIII). New Delhi: Cosmo Publications.

12. *Vāyu Purāṇam: (Sanskrit) with Hindi translation by* Rāmapratāpa Tripāthi (2nd ed., Śaka 1909 (AD 1987)). Prayāga: Hindi Sāhitya Sammelan.

13. *Viṣṇu Purāṇa: (Sanskrit) with Hindi translation by* Śrī Munilāl Gupta (6th ed., Samvat 2024; 1st ed., Samvat 1990). Gorakhpur: Gita Press.

# 7

# KINGS OF MAGADHA AFTER THE MAHĀBHĀRATA WAR

Starting from the Mahābhārata War near the end of 3139 BC to 82 BC, a total of nine dynasties ruled Magadha as shown in Table 13 and Figure 17. The list of the nine dynasties, the kings, and their years of reign are from *Chronology of the Ancient Hindu History Part I* (Venkatachelam, 1957a), which in turn is based on the information from the Purāṇas. The lists in the *Matsya* (Adhyay 271–273), *Viṣṇu* (4th Aṁśa, Adhyay 23–25), and *Bhāgavata* (Skandah 9, Adhyay 2 (9.2); Skandha 12, Adhyay 1–2 (12.1–2)) *Purāṇas* are similar but with some differences. The *Matsya*,

**Table 13: Magadha Dynasties after the Mahābhārata War in 3139 BC**

| Dynasty Name | Years of Reign | Number of Kings | Years in BC |
|---|---|---|---|
| 1. Bṛhadratha (बृहद्रथ) | 1006 | 22 | 3138–2132 |
| 2. Pradyota (प्रद्योत) | 138 | 5 | 2132–1994 |
| 3. Śiśunāga (शिशुनाग) | 360 | 10 | 1994–1634 |
| 4. Nanda (नन्द) | 100 | 2 | 1634–1534 |
| 5. Maurya (मौर्य) | 316 | 12 | 1534–1218 |
| 6. Śuṅga (शुंग) | 300 | 10 | 1218–918 |
| 7. Kaṇva (कण्व) | 85 | 4 | 918–833 |
| 8. Āndhra (आन्ध्र) | 506 | 32 | 833–327 |
| 9. Gupta (गुप्त) | 245 | 7 | 327–82 |
| **Total** | **3056** | **104** | **3138–82** |

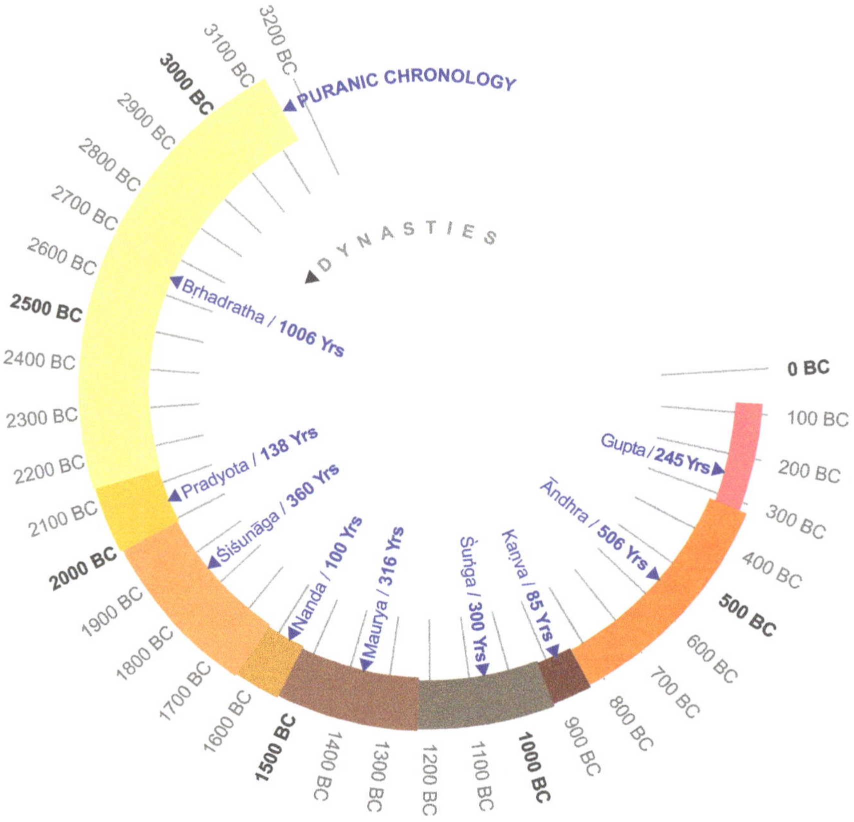


**Figure 17: Magadha Dynasties after the Mahābhārata War in 3139 BC**

*Vāyu* (99.294 onwards) and *Brahmāṇḍa* (74.107 onwards) Purāṇas, and the *Kaliyuga Rājavṛttānta* (1937) give years of reign for each king. The *Viṣṇu* and *Bhāgavata Purāṇas* give only total years of reign for each dynasty.

Each dynasty and its kings are described in varying details in this chapter. Refer to the genius work of Pandit Kota Venkatachelam, *Chronology of Ancient Hindu History Part I*, for additional details. Similar chronology is also available in *The Age of the Mahabharata War* (Jagannadha Rao, 1931) and *History of Classical Sanskrit Literature* (Krishnamachariar, 1937, p. xliv).

## Bṛhadratha Dynasty, Yudhiṣṭhira Śaka 1–1006 (3138–2132 BC)

Bṛhadratha Dynasty, the first dynasty of Magadha, split from the Kuru Dynasty centuries before the Mahābhārata War, as described in Chapter 5 which lists the 12 kings of this dynasty before the war. The chronology of the Bṛhadratha Dynasty after the Mahābhārata War is shown in Table 14.

**Table 14: Chronology of the Bṛhadratha Dynasty, Yudhiṣṭhira Śaka 1–1006 (3138–2132 BC)**

| Sr. No. | Name of the King | Years of Reign | STARTING YEAR IN Yudhiṣṭhira Śaka | Kaliyuga | BC |
|---|---|---|---|---|---|
| 1 | Somādhi (सोमाधि) | 58 | 1 | 36 BK | 3138 |
| 2 | Śrutaśravā (श्रुतश्रवा) | 64 | 58 | 22 | 3080 |
| 3 | Ayutāyu (अयुतायु) | 36 | 122 | 86 | 3016 |
| 4 | Niramitra (निरमित्र) | 40 | 158 | 122 | 2980 |
| 5 | Sukṣatra (सुक्षत्र) | 58 | 198 | 162 | 2940 |
| 6 | Bṛhatkarmā (बृहत्कर्मा) | 23 | 256 | 220 | 2882 |
| 7 | Senājit (सेनाजित्) | 50 | 279 | 243 | 2859 |
| 8 | Śrutañjaya (श्रुतंजय) | 40 | 329 | 293 | 2809 |
| 9 | Mahābala (महाबल) | 35 | 369 | 333 | 2769 |
| 10 | Śuci (शुचि) | 58 | 404 | 368 | 2734 |
| 11 | Kṣema (क्षेम) | 28 | 462 | 426 | 2676 |
| 12 | Suvrata (सुव्रत) | 64 | 490 | 454 | 2648 |
| 13 | Dharmanetra (धर्मनेत्र) | 35 | 554 | 518 | 2584 |
| 14 | Nirvṛti (निवृति) | 58 | 589 | 553 | 2549 |
| 15 | Suvrata (सुव्रत) | 38 | 647 | 611 | 2491 |
| 16 | Dṛḍhasena (दृढसेन) | 58 | 685 | 649 | 2453 |
| 17 | Sumati (सुमति) | 33 | 743 | 707 | 2395 |
| 18 | Sucala (सुचल) | 22 | 776 | 740 | 2362 |
| 19 | Sunetra (सुनेत्र) | 40 | 798 | 762 | 2340 |
| 20 | Satyajit (सत्यजित्) | 83 | 838 | 802 | 2300 |
| 21 | Vīrajita (वीरजित) | 35 | 921 | 885 | 2217 |
| 22 | Ripuñjaya (रिपुंजय) | 50 | 956 | 920 | 2182 |
| | **Total** | **1006** | **1–1006** | **36 BK–970** | **3138–2132** |

1. **Somādhi** (सोमाधि), as called in Matsya and Vāyu Purāṇas, **Somāpi** (सोमापि) in Viṣṇu and Brahmāṇḍa Purāṇas or **Mārjari** (मार्जरि) in Bhāgavata Purāṇa, son of Sahadeva and grandson of Jarāsandha, was the first king of Magadha after the Mahābhārata War. He was enthroned in 3138 BC after his father Sahadeva was killed in the Mahābhārata war. Somādhi's capital was Girivraja (present-day Rajgir) as for his predecessors. He reigned for 58 years according to all the Purāṇas, from Yudhiṣṭhira Śaka 1 to 58 (3138–3080 BC).

2. **Śrutaśravā** (श्रुतश्रवा), as called in all the Purāṇas, son of Somādhi according to Vāyu and Brahmāṇḍa Purāṇas, ruled Magadha for 64 years according to Matsya and Vāyu Purāṇas, from Yudhiṣṭhira Śaka 58 to 122 (3080–3016 BC). Brahmāṇḍa Purāṇa gives him a reign of 67 years.

3. **Ayutāyu** (अयुतायु), as called in all the Purāṇas, reigned for 36 years according to Matsya Purāṇa and Kaliyuga Rājavṛttānta, from Yudhiṣṭhira Śaka 122 to 158 (3016–2980 BC). Vāyu and Brahmāṇḍa Purāṇas give him only 26 years of reign.

4. **Niramitra** (निरमित्र) according to Matsya, Viṣṇu, and Bhāgavata Purāṇas or **Nirāmitra** (निरामित्र) according to Vāyu and Brahmāṇḍa Purāṇas, son of Ayutāyu according to Matsya Purāṇa, reigned for 40 years (Matsya Purāṇa, Kaliyuga Rajavṛttānta) from Yudhiṣṭhira Śaka 158 to 198 (2980–2940 BC). Vāyu Purāṇa and Brahmāṇḍa Purāṇa give him 100 years of reign.

5. **Sukṣatra** (सुक्षत्र) according to Matsya and Brahmāṇḍa Purāṇas, **Sukṛta** (सुकृत) according to Vāyu Purāṇa, **Sunetra** (सुनेत्र) according to Viṣṇu Purāṇa or **Sunakṣatra** (सुनक्षत्र) according to Bhāgavata Purāṇa, reigned for 58 years from Yudhiṣṭhira Śaka 198 to 256 (2940–2882 BC) (Kaliyuga Rājavṛttānta; Venkatachelam, 1957a). Current copies of Matsya, Vāyu, and Brahmāṇḍa Purāṇas give him a reign of 56 years.

6. **Bṛhatkarmā** (बृहत्कर्मा) reigned for 23 years according to all the Purāṇas, from Yudhiṣṭhira Śaka 256 to 279 (2882–2859 BC). The Bhāgavata Purāṇa and Kaliyuga Rājavṛttānta call him **Bṛhatsena** (बृहत्सेन).

7. **Senājit** (सेनाजित्), according to Matsya Purāṇa, reigned for 50 years from Yudhiṣṭhira Śaka 279 to 329 (2859–2809 BC). Viṣṇu Purāṇa calls him **Senajit** (सेनजित्) while Bhāgavata Purāṇa calls him **Karmajit** (कर्मजित्).

8. **Śrutañjaya** (श्रुतंजय), as called in all the Purāṇas, reigned for 40 years from Yudhiṣṭhira Śaka 329 to 369 (2809–2769 BC) according to all the Purāṇas (Kaliyuga Rājavṛttānta, Matsya, Vāyu, and Brahmāṇḍa Purāṇas).

Matsya Purāṇa switches from past tense to future tense for the kings after Senājit. Vāyu and Brahmāṇḍa Purāṇas describe Senājit as the present king which suggests that the Matsya, Vāyu, and Brahmāṇḍa Purāṇas were first narrated during Senājit's reign. It is noted in **Chapter 5** that Matsya Purāṇa was narrated for the first time during the reign of Adhisīmkṛṣṇa, the seventh king of Hastināpura, starting from Yudhiṣṭhira. Thus, Senājit and Adhisīmkṛṣṇa were, likely, contemporaries.

9. **Mahābala** (महाबल), reigned for 35 years, according to Brahmāṇḍa Purāṇa and Kaliyuga Rājavṛttānta, from Yudhiṣṭhira Śaka 369 to 404 (2769–2734 BC). Matsya Purāṇa calls him **Vibhu** (विभु) and gives him a reign of only 28 years. Vāyu Purāṇa calls him **Mahabala** (महबल) and gives him a reign of 33 years. Viṣṇu and Bhāgavata Purāṇas call him **Vipra** (विप्र) but Brahmāṇḍa Purāṇa calls him **Ripuñjaya**.

10. **Śuci** (शुचि), as called in all the Purāṇas, reigned for 58 years (Kaliyuga Rājavṛttānta, Vāyu, and Brahmāṇḍa Purāṇas) from Yudhiṣṭhira Śaka 404 to 462 (2734–2676 BC). Matsya Purāṇa gives him a reign of 64 years.

11. **Kṣema** (क्षेम) reigned for 28 years according to all the Purāṇas (Kaliyuga Rājavṛttānta, Matsya, Vāyu and Brahmāṇḍa Purāṇas) from Yudhiṣṭhira Śaka 462 to 490 (2676–2648 BC). Viṣṇu Purāṇa calls him **Kṣemya** (क्षेम्य).

12. **Suvrata** (सुव्रत), as called in all the Purāṇas except Vāyu Purāṇa, reigned for 64 years according to Kaliyuga Rājavṛttānta, Matsya, Vāyu, and Brahmāṇḍa Purāṇas from Yudhiṣṭhira Śaka 490 to 554 (2648–2584 BC). Vāyu Purāṇa calls him **Bhuvata** (भुवत). Matsya, Vāyu, and Brahmāṇḍa Purāṇas describe him as valiant.

13. **Dharmanetra** (धर्मनेत्र) or **Sunetra** (सुनेत्र) reigned for 35 years (Kaliyuga Rājavṛttānta and Matsya Purāṇa) from Yudhiṣṭhira Śaka 554 to 589 (2584–2549 BC). Viṣṇu Purāṇa calls him **Dharma** and Bhāgavata Purāṇa calls him **Dharmasūtra** (धर्मसूत्र).

14. **Nirvṛti** (निर्वृति) reigned for 58 years according to Matsya, Vāyu, and Brahmāṇḍa Purāṇas, from Yudhiṣṭhira Śaka 589 to 647 (2549–2491 BC). Vāyu and Brahmāṇḍa Purāṇas call him **Nṛpati** (नृपति). Viṣṇu Purāṇa and Bhāgavata Purāṇa miss his name.

15. **Suvrata** (सुव्रत) reigned for 38 years (Kaliyuga Rājavṛttānta, Vāyu, and

Brahmāṇḍa Purāṇas) from Yudhiṣṭhira Śaka 647 to 685 (2491–2453 BC). Matsya Purāṇa calls him **Trinetra** (त्रिनेत्र) and gives him 28 years. Viṣṇu Purāṇa calls him **Suśravā** (सुश्रवा), Brahmāṇḍa Purāṇa calls him **Suśrama** (सुश्रम) and Bhāgavata Purāṇa calls him Śama (शम).

16. **Dṛḍhasena** (दृढसेन), reigned for 58 years (Kaliyuga Rājavṛttānta, Vāyu, and Brahmāṇḍa Purāṇas) from Yudhiṣṭhira Śaka 685 to 743 (2453–2395 BC). Matsya and Bhāgavata Purāṇas call him **Dhyumatsena** (ध्युमत्सेन).

17. **Sumati** (सुमति), as called in Vāyu, Brahmāṇḍa, and Bhāgavata Purāṇas, reigned for 33 years (Matsya, Vāyu, and Brahmāṇḍa Purāṇas) from Yudhiṣṭhira Śaka 743 to 776 (2395–2362 BC). Matsya Purāṇa calls him **Mahīnetra** (महीनेत्र). Viṣṇu Purāṇa omits his name.

18. **Sucala** (सुचल), reigned for 22 years (Vāyu Purāṇa, and Kaliyuga Rājavṛttānta) from Yudhiṣṭhira Śaka 776 to 798 (2362–2340 BC). Matsya Purāṇa calls him **Cancala** (चंचल) and assigns him 32 years of reign. Viṣṇu and Bhāgavata Purāṇas call him **Subala** (सुबल). Brahmāṇḍa Purāṇa omits his name.

19. **Sunetra** (सुनेत्र) reigned for 40 years (Kaliyuga Rājavṛttānta, Vāyu, and Brahmāṇḍa Purāṇas) from Yudhiṣṭhira Śaka 798 to 838 (2340–2300 BC). Viṣṇu Purāṇa calls him **Sunīta** (सुनीत) and Bhāgavata Purāṇa, **Sunītha** (सुनीथ). Matsya Purāṇa omits the names of this and the next two kings.

20. **Satyajit** (सत्यजित्), as called in all the Purāṇas, reigned for 83 years (Kaliyuga Rājavṛttānta, Vāyu, and Brahmāṇḍa Purāṇas) from Yudhiṣṭhira Śaka 838 to 921 (2300–2217 BC).

21. **Vīrajita** (वीरजित) reigned for 35 years (Vāyu Purāṇa and Kaliyuga Rājavṛttānta) from Yudhiṣṭhira Śaka 921 to 956 (2217–2182 BC). Brahmāṇḍa Purāṇa gives him 25 years of reign. Viṣṇu, Brahmāṇḍa, and Bhāgavata Purāṇas call him **Viśvajita** (विश्वजित).

22. **Ripuñjaya** (रिपुंजय) reigned for 50 years according to all the Purāṇas, from Yudhiṣṭhira Śaka 956 to 1006 (2182–2132 BC). Vāyu, and Brahmāṇḍa Purāṇas call him **Ariñjaya** (अरिंजय). He was killed by his minister and, thus, ended the dynasty.

These 22 kings of the Bṛhadratha Dynasty, starting from Somādhi to Ripuñjaya, ruled Magadha after the Mahābhārata War for a total of 1,006 years, from Yudhiṣṭhira Śaka 1 to 1006 (3138–2132 BC). All the Purāṇas give the 22 kings, a total period of a round number of 1,000 years, instead of exactly 1,006 years (Kaliyuga Rājavṛttānta, Vāyu, Matsya, Brahmāṇḍa, and Viṣṇu Purāṇas). See the following verse from the Matsya Purāṇa (Krishnamachariar, 1937, p. xliv).

द्वाविंशतिनृपा ह्येते भवितारो बृहद्रथाः ।
पूर्णं वर्षसहस्त्रं तु तेषां राज्यं भविष्यति ॥

Dvāviṁśatinṛpā hyete bhavitāro Bṛhadrathāḥ ।
Purṇaṁ varṣasahasraṁ tu teṣāṁ rājyaṁ bhaviṣyati ॥

The present copy of the *Matsya Purāṇa* (271.30), published by Gita Press, states 32 kings instead of 22 kings, which is a mistake.

### Distortions by William Jones

As described above, according to the various Purāṇas and Bhāgavatāmrita skandha IX, there were 22 kings in the Bṛhadratha Dynasty, but William Jones reduced the number of the kings to 20 and reduced their total reign period from 1,006 years to 700 years, arbitrarily. As discussed in Chapter 2, Jones simply claimed it to be more likely. Later colonial Indologists discarded this entire dynasty calling it mythical, erasing 1,006 years from India's chronology. For further discussion on distortions, see *Chronology of Ancient Hindu History Part I* (Venkatachelam, 1957a, p. 197–201).

## Pradyota Dynasty, Yudhiṣṭhira Śaka 1006–1144 (2132–1994 BC)

**Pradyota** (प्रद्योत) according to Viṣṇu, Vāyu, Brahmāṇḍa, and Bhāgavata Purāṇas, or **Pradyotana** (प्रद्योतन) according to Kaliyuga Rājavṛttānta, was the son of Munika (Vāyu Purāṇa), Sunika (Viṣṇu Purāṇa), Śunaka (Brahmāṇḍa and Bhāgavata Purāṇas) or Pulaka (Matsya Purāṇa and Kaliyuga Rājavṛttānta), the minister of the last king of the Bṛhadratha Dynasty, Ripuñjaya, whom he treacherously killed. Instead of crowning himself as the king against the wishes of the people, Pulaka got his son Pradyota married to the only daughter of Ripuñjaya and installed him on the throne (Krishnamachariar, 1937, p. xlv). The kings and the chronology of the Pradyota Dynasty are shown in Table 15.

1. **Pradyota** (प्रद्योत), according to all the Purāṇas, reigned for 23 years, from Yudhiṣṭhira Śaka 1006 to 1029 (2132–2109 BC). According to the Purāṇas (Vāyu, Matsya, Brahmāṇḍa, and Bhāgavata), he subjugated the neighboring kings in the very sight of the kshatriyas of his time. The dynasty of Vitihotras of Avanti (present-day Ujjain) ended thereafter.

2. **Pālaka** (पालक), son of Pradyota, reigned for 24 years (Kaliyuga Rājavṛttānta,

**Table 15: Chronology of the Pradyota Dynasty, Yudhiṣṭhira Śaka 1006–1144 (2132–1994 BC)**

| Sr. No. | Name of the King | Years of Reign | STARTING YEAR IN Yudhiṣṭhira Śaka | Kaliyuga | BC |
|---|---|---|---|---|---|
| 1 | Pradyota (प्रद्योत) | 23 | 1006 | 970 | 2132 |
| 2 | Pālaka (पालक) | 24 | 1029 | 993 | 2109 |
| 3 | Viśākhayūpa (विशाखयूप) | 50 | 1053 | 1017 | 2085 |
| 4 | Janaka (जनक) | 21 | 1103 | 1067 | 2035 |
| 5 | Nandivardhana (नन्दिवर्धन) | 20 | 1124 | 1088 | 2014 |
| | **Total** | **138** | **1006–1144** | **970–1108** | **2132–1994** |

Vāyu, Brahmāṇḍa, and Bhāgavata Purāṇas) from Yudhiṣṭhira Śaka 1029 to 1053 (2109–2085 BC). Matsya Purāṇa gives him a reign of 28 years. Viṣṇu Purāṇa calls him **Balāka** (बलाक).

3. **Viśākhayūpa** (विशाखयूप), son of Pālaka, according to all the Purāṇas, reigned for 50 years (Kaliyuga Rājavṛttānta, Vāyu, Brahmāṇḍa, and Matsya Purāṇas) from Yudhiṣṭhira Śaka 1053 to 1103 (2085–2035 BC).

4. **Janaka** (जनक) reigned for 21 years (Kaliyuga Rājavṛttānta, Matsya, Brahmāṇḍa, and Bhāgavata Purāṇas) from Yudhiṣṭhira Śaka 1103 to 1124 (2035–2014 BC). One version of Vāyu Purāṇa gives him a reign of 31 years and calls him **Ajaka** (अजक). Brahmāṇḍa Purāṇa uses the same name. Matsya Purāṇa calls him **Sūryaka** (सूर्यक) and Bhāgavata Purāṇa calls him **Rājaka** (राजक).

5. **Nandivardhana** (नन्दिवर्धन), son of Janaka, reigned for 20 years (Vāyu, and Brahmāṇḍa Purāṇas) from Yudhiṣṭhira Śaka 1124 to 1144 (2014–1994 BC). One version of Matsya Purāṇa and Kaliyuga Rājavṛttānta give him a reign of 30 years. One version of Vāyu Purāṇa calls him **Vartivardhana** (वर्तिवर्धन).

These five kings of the Pradyota Dynasty ruled for a total of 138 years, from Yudhiṣṭhira Śaka 1006 to 1144 (2132–1994 BC) according to all but one Purāṇas. The Matsya Purāṇa gives a total reign of 152 years to the five Pradyota kings.

## Distortions by Colonial Era Indologists

The colonial era European Indologists discarded this entire dynasty as well, calling it mythical, erasing another 138 years from India's chronology in addition to the 1,006 years of the Bṛhadratha Dynasty. Thus, they removed a total of 1,144 years from the Indian chronology by this point.

## Śiśunāga Dynasty, Yudhiṣṭhira Śaka 1144–1504 (1994–1634 BC)

**Śiśunāga** (शिशुनाग) by Kaliyuga Rājavṛttānta, Matsya, Bhāgavata, and Brahmāṇḍa Purāṇas or **Śiśunāka** (शिशुनाक) by Vāyu Purāṇa or **Śiśunābha** (शिशुनाभ) by Viṣṇu Purāṇa, founded this dynasty. He was the king of Varanasi (Kashi) and conquered Magadha. He placed his son as the king of Kashi, while he reigned at Girivraja (present-day Rajgir), the capital of Magadha, according to Matsya, Vāyu, and Brahmāṇḍa Purāṇas. The kings of this dynasty along with their years of reign and the calendar years are given in Table 16.

**Table 16: Chronology of the Śiśunāga Dynasty, Yudhiṣṭhira Śaka 1144–1504 (1994–1634 BC)**

| Sr. No. | Name of the King | Years of Reign | STARTING YEAR IN Yudhiṣṭhira Śaka | Kaliyuga | BC |
|---|---|---|---|---|---|
| 1 | Śiśunāga (शिशुनाग) | 40 | 1144 | 1108 | 1994 |
| 2 | Kākavarṇa (काकवर्ण) | 36 | 1184 | 1148 | 1954 |
| 3 | Kṣemadharmā (क्षेमधर्मा) | 26 | 1220 | 1184 | 1918 |
| 4 | Kṣatraujā (क्षत्रौजा) | 40 | 1246 | 1210 | 1892 |
| 5 | Vidhisāra (विधिसार) | 38 | 1286 | 1250 | 1852 |
| 6 | Ajātaśatru (अजातशत्रु) | 27 | 1324 | 1288 | 1814 |
| 7 | Darbhaka (दर्भक) | 35 | 1351 | 1315 | 1787 |
| 8 | Udayana (उदयन) | 33 | 1386 | 1350 | 1752 |
| 9 | Nandivardhana (नन्दिवर्धन) | 42 | 1419 | 1383 | 1719 |
| 10 | Mahānandī (महानन्दी) | 43 | 1461 | 1425 | 1677 |
| | **Total** | **360** | **1144–1504** | **1108–1468** | **1994–1634** |

1. **Śiśunāga** (शिशुनाग) reigned for 40 years according to all the Purāṇas (Kaliyuga Rājavṛttānta, Matsya, Vāyu, and Brahmāṇḍa Purāṇas), from Yudhiṣṭhira Śaka 1144 to 1184 (1994–1954 BC).
2. **Kākavarṇa** (काकवर्ण) by all Purāṇas except Vāyu Purāṇa which calls him

**Śakavarṇa** (शकवर्ण), son of Śiśunāga, ruled for 36 years, from Yudhiṣṭhira Śaka 1184 to 1220 (1954–1918 BC).

3. **Kṣemadharmā** (क्षेमधर्मा) by all Purāṇas except Kaliyuga Rājavṛttānta which names him as **Kṣemakarmā** (क्षेमकर्मा), or **Kṣemavarmā** (क्षेमवर्मा) by Vāyu Purāṇa, reigned for 26 years according to Kaliyuga Rājavṛttānta and Matsya Purāṇa, from Yudhiṣṭhira Śaka 1220 to 1246 (1918–1892 BC). Vāyu and Brahmāṇḍa Purāṇas give him a reign of 20 years. One version of Matsya Purāṇa gives him a reign of 36 years.

4. **Kṣatraujā** (क्षत्रौजा) by Kaliyuga Rājavṛttānta, Vāyu, and Brahmāṇḍa Purāṇas, **Kṣataujā** (क्षतौजा) by Viṣṇu Purāṇa, **Kṣemajit** (क्षेमजित्) by Matsya Purāṇa or **Kṣetrajña** (क्षेत्रज्ञ) by Bhāgavata Purāṇa, reigned for 40 years from Yudhiṣṭhira Śaka 1246 to 1286 (1892–1852 BC). Matsya Purāṇa gives him a reign of 24 years while all other Purāṇas including the Kaliyuga Rājavṛttānta give him a reign of 40 years. One version of Vāyu Purāṇa (Hindi Sahitya Sammelan, 1987) shows Ajātaśatru, the sixth king of this dynasty, before Kṣatrauja, which is a mistake.

5. **Vidhisāra** (विधिसार) by Kaliyuga Rājavṛttānta, Viṣṇu, Vāyu, Brahmāṇḍa, and Bhāgavata Purāṇas, **Vimbasāra** (विम्बसार) by Matsya Purāṇa or **Bimbisāra** (बिम्बिसार) by Buddhist accounts, reigned for 38 years, from Yudhiṣṭhira Śaka 1286 to 1324 (1852–1814 BC). Matsya Purāṇa and one version of Vāyu Purāṇa give him a reign of 28 years, while all the other authorities give him a reign of 38 years. *Aśokāvadāna* and the Simhalese Buddhist text, *The Mahāvaṁsa* (महावंस), call him Bimbisāra and give him a reign of 52 years.

> All Buddhist and Jain authorities agree in describing Bimbisāra as being five years younger than Gautama Buddha who is said to have attained nirvana at the age of 80, in the eighth year of the reign of his successor, Ajātaśatru. See **Chapter 8** for further details.

6. **Ajātaśatru** (अजातशत्रु) by all Purāṇas, son of Vidhisāra, reigned for 27 years, from Yudhiṣṭhira Śaka 1324 to 1351 (1814–1787 BC). The currently available copy of Matsya Purāṇa gives him a reign of 25 years whereas the copy of the Matsya Purāṇa which Pandit Venkatachelam had, gave him 27 years (Venkatachelam, 1957a, p. 39). Kaliyuga Rājavṛttānta also gives him a reign of 27 years. Vāyu and Brahmāṇḍa Purāṇas give him a reign of 25 years. The Simhalese Buddhist text *The Dīpavaṁsa* (3.51, p. 133), on the

other hand, gives him a reign of 32 years.

7. **Darbhaka** (दर्भक) by Brahmāṇḍa and Bhāgavata Purāṇas, **Darśaka** (दर्शक) by Matsya and Vāyu Purāṇas or **Arbhaka** (अर्भक) by Viṣṇu Purāṇa, son of Ajātaśatru, ruled for 35 years according to Brahmāṇḍa Purāṇa, from Yudhiṣṭhira Śaka 1351 to 1386 (1787–1752 BC). Presently available copies of Matsya and Vāyu Purāṇas give him a reign of 25 years.

8. **Udayana** (उदयन) by Viṣṇu Purāṇa, Kaliyuga Rājavṛttānta, and Brihatkathā, **Udāyī** (उदायी) by Vāyu and Brahmāṇḍa Purāṇas or **Udāsī** (उदासी) by Matsya Purāṇa, reigned for 33 years according to all the Purāṇas, from Yudhiṣṭhira Śaka 1386 to 1419 (1752–1719 BC). The Buddhist text *The Dīpavaṁsa* (4.38, p. 136) mentions prince Udaya.

### Who built Pāṭaliputra?

The Matsya, Vāyu, and Brahmāṇḍa Purāṇas state that Udayana built the city of Kusumpura (later known as Pāṭaliputra) on the southern bank of the Ganga in the fourth year of his reign with which the accounts given in the Brihatkathā, Kathāsaritsāgara, and Kaliyuga RajaVṛttānta completely agree (Venkatachelam, 1957a, p. 41). *Pariśiṣṭaparvan* (Jacobi, canto 6, p. lviii) also states that Udayin founded the new city.

### Distortion by Colonial Era Indologists

Vincent Smith (1914, p. 36) ascribed the building of the fort of Pāṭaliputra to Ajātaśatru, the grandfather of Udayana or Udaya as he calls him, while all the Purāṇas ascribe the foundation of the city of Kusumpura to Udayana.

9. **Nandivardhana** (नन्दिवर्धन) as called by all Purāṇas, ruled for 42 years, from Yudhiṣṭhira Śaka 1419 to 1461 (1719–1677 BC). Vāyu Purāṇa gives him a reign of 42 years whereas Matsya and Brahmāṇḍa Purāṇas give him a reign of 40 years. The Buddhist accounts (Aśokāvadāna, Dīpavaṁsa, Mahāvaṁsa, etc.) make a mess of things between Udayana and Nandivardhana, whom they call **Kālāśoka** (कालाशोक) or **Kākavarṇi** (काकवर्णी).

10. **Mahānandī** (महानन्दी) as called in all the Purāṇas, ruled for 43 years from Yudhiṣṭhira Śaka 1461 to 1504 (1677–1634 BC). All the authorities are

unanimous in ascribing him a reign of 43 years. One version of Brahmāṇḍa Purāṇa gives him a reign of 63 years, which is a mistake.

All the Purāṇas give these ten kings of the Śiśunāga Dynasty, the third dynasty of Magadha, a total reign of 360 years, from Yudhiṣṭhira Śaka 1144 to 1504 (1994–1634 BC), except Viṣṇu and Vāyu Purāṇas which give them a total reign of 362 years.

According to the Matsya, Vāyu and Brahmāṇḍa Purāṇas, starting from the Mahābhārata War near the end of 3139 BC to the end of the Śiśunāga Dynasty, there had been 24 **Ikṣvāku** (इक्ष्वाकु) kings, 27 **Pāñcāla** (पांचाल) kings (25 by Vāyu and Brahmāṇḍa Purāṇas), 24 **Kāśi** (काशी) (Kalaka by Vāyu and Brahmāṇḍa Purāṇas) kings, 28 **Haihaya** (हैहय) kings (24 by Vāyu and Brahmāṇḍa Purāṇas), 32 **Kaliṅga** (कलिंग) kings, 25 **Aśmaka** (अश्मक) kings (Śaka by Vāyu and Brahmāṇḍa Purāṇas, present-day Maharashtra), 26 **Kuru** (कुरु) kings (36 by Vāyu and Brahmāṇḍa Purāṇas), 28 **Mithilā** (मिथिला) kings, 23 **Śūrasena** (शूरसेन) kings (of Mathura), and 20 **Vītihotrā** (वीतिहोत्रा) kings. All these dynasties were contemporary till this time. The Purāṇas describe these dynasties and how King Sagara, the 40th king of the Ikṣvāku Dynasty in **Appendix IV**, had fought against the Haihayas in Northwest India.

## Nanda Dynasty, Yudhiṣṭhira Śaka 1504–1604 (1634–1534 BC)

According to all the Purāṇas, Mahāpadma Nanda (महापद्म नंद), the founder of the Nanda Dynasty, was the son of Mahānandi (the last king of the Śiśunāga Dynasty) from his shudra woman. The Purāṇas give the time interval between the birth of Parīkṣit (at the end of the Mahābhārata War) and the coronation of Mahāpadma Nanda, as 1,500 years. This is shown in the following verse from *Viṣṇu Purāṇa* (4.25.104).

यावत्परीक्षितो जन्म यावन्नन्दभिषेचनम् ।
एतद्वर्षसहस्रं तु ज्ञेयं पञ्चशतोत्तरम् ।। १०४।।

YāvatParīkṣito janma yāvanNandabhiṣecanam ।
Etadvarṣa-sahasraṁ tu jñeyaṁ pañcaśatottaram ।।104 ।।

Translation:

> From the birth of Parīkṣit to the coronation of Nanda, know that period to be fifteen hundred years.

If we add the years of reign of the three preceding dynasties that ruled Magadha from the time of the Mahābhārata War to the start of the Nanda Dynasty, the total of the years is 1,504 as shown in Table 17. This is very close to the 1,500 years stated in the preceding verse. The total given in the Kaliyuga Rājavṛttānta is also 1,500 years as a round figure.

**Table 17: Magadha Dynasties from the Mahābhārata War to the beginning of the Nanda Dynasty**

| Sr. No. | Name of the Dynasty | Number of Kings | Years of Reign |
|---|---|---|---|
| 1 | Bṛhadratha (बृहद्रथ) | 22 | 1006 |
| 2 | Pradyota (प्रद्योत) | 5 | 138 |
| 3 | Śiśunāga (शिशुनाग) | 10 | 360 |
| | **Total** | 37 | **1504** |

## Distortion by Colonial Era Indologists

Some copies of the Matsya Purāṇa and Telugu editions of the same give the time interval as 1,500 years but N. Jagannadha Rao (1931, p.31) has noted in his book that the same verse in the Devanāgarī edition of the *Matsya Purāṇa* (273.36) reads as if this period is one thousand, and fifty (Pañc**ā**śa**du**ttaram or पंचाशदुत्तरम) instead of five hundred (Pañ**ca**śa**to**ttaram or पंचशतोत्तरम) as follows.

Pargiter (1913, p. 58, footnote 21) states in The Dynasties of Kali Age that he found in one manuscript of the Matsya Purāṇa, Pañc**ā**śa**du**ttaram (1,050) and made it the basis of his text, though he admits in the footnote that in the Vāyu and Brahmāṇḍa Purāṇas and a different copy of the Matsya Purāṇa, the verse reads Pañc**a**śa**to**ttaram (1,500). He rejected the majority of the versions which stated 1,500 years and accepted the one manuscript of one Purāṇa which had the smaller number. This makes it abundantly clear that the chief aim of the European Indologists and their Indian followers was to reduce the antiquity of India's history, as far as possible.

महापद्माभिषेकात् तु यावज्जन्म परीक्षितः ।
एवं वर्षसहस्रं तु ज्ञेयं पञ्चाशदुत्तरम् ।। ३६ ।।

Mahāpadmābhiṣekāt tu yāvajjanma Parīkṣitaḥ I
Evaṁ varṣasahasraṁ tu jñeyaṁ pañcāśaduttaram I I 36 I I

As highlighted in bold, it takes a very small change in the letters (changing **'ca (च)'** to **'cā (चा)'** and **'to (तो)'** to **'du (दु)'**) to change the number from 500 to 50. This shows that the original Purāṇa texts have been carelessly or unscrupulously tampered with by later scribes who copied the originals, as stated by Jagannadha Rao.

The chronology of the Nanda Dynasty kings is shown in Table 18.

**Table 18: Chronology of the Nanda Dynasty, Yudhiṣṭhira Śaka 1504–1604 (1634–1534 BC)**

| Sr. No. | Name of the King | Years of Reign | STARTING YEAR IN Yudhiṣṭhira Śaka | Kaliyuga | BC |
|---|---|---|---|---|---|
| 1 | Mahāpadma (महापद्म) | 88 | 1504 | 1468 | 1634 |
| 2 | Sumālya (सुमाल्य) and his seven brothers | 12 | 1592 | 1556 | 1546 |
| | **Total** | **100** | **1504–1604** | **1468–1568** | **1634–1534** |

1. **Mahāpdama** (महापद्म), otherwise known as Nanda, son of the shudra wife of Mahānandi, the last king of the Śiśunāga Dynasty, according to all the Purāṇas, ruled the Magadha Empire for 88 years (Kaliyuga Rājavṛttānta, Matsya, Vāyu, and Brahmāṇḍa Purāṇas), from Yudhiṣṭhira Śaka 1504 to 1592 (1634–1546 BC).

   According to all the Purāṇas, Mahāpadma was a very powerful king, and like Paraśurāma, he subjugated all kshatriyas (kings) of his time, who were ruling in the various parts of India (mainly northern India) after the Mahābhārata War. He became the emperor of northern India, between the Himalayas and the Vindhyās, by putting an end to ancient dynasties such as the Ikṣvākus, Pāñcālas, Kurus, Haihayas, Kalkas, Kaliṅgas, Śūrasenas, Maithilas, etc. who ceased to rule as separate dynasties since that time. The Purāṇas describe him as *"Sarva kṣatrantako nṛpah"* which means the destroyer of all kshatriyas. Figure 18 shows a map of Nanda's empire based on the above description.

   According to the Kaliyuga Rājavṛttānta and the Buddhist accounts,

**Figure 18: Map of Nanda's empire (ca. 1600 BC)**
*Blank map courtesy: DEMIS Mapserver, Wikimedia Commons, CC BY-SA 3.0*

Mahāpadma Nanda was known as Dhana Nanda, due to his habit of hoarding wealth (Venkatachelam, 1957a, p. 44). It is said that he levied taxes on skins, gums, trees, stones, etc., and hoarded money to the extent of 80 *kotis* and buried it in the bed of the Ganga. He did this by diverting the mainstream for a time by an anicut or a dam across the Ganga, and making a large hole in a rock in the bed of the river. He placed his wealth there, sealed it with molten lead, and then restored the river to its original path. Nanda had eight sons according to all the Purāṇas.

2. **Sumālya** (सुमाल्य) or **Sukalpa** (सुकल्प) by Matsya Purāṇa, the eldest, and the rest of the seven sons of Nanda, ruled jointly for a total of 12 years (Matsya and Brahmāṇḍa Purāṇas) from Yudhiṣṭhira Śaka 1592 to 1604 (1546–1534 BC).

According to all the Purāṇas, all eight sons were overthrown by Chāṇakya

(चाणक्य), also known as Kautilya (कौटिल्य) or Viṣṇugupta (विष्णुगुप्त) who then placed Chandragupta* Maurya on the throne of Magadha.

(*spelled **Candragupta** per the transliteration guide but Chandragupta in common parlance)

## Distortion by Colonial Indologists

All the Purāṇas are unanimous in giving these nine Nandas, a total of 100 years of reign. However, Vincent Smith (1914, p. 45–48; Venkatachelam, 1957a, p. 49), the British Colonial Indologist of the early 20th century, chose to give these nine Nandas a total period of only 45–50 years for their reign!

### Tampering of the Vāyu Purāṇa

The Vāyu Purāṇa quoted by Pandit Venkatachelam (1957a, p. 46) gives Mahāpadma Nanda 88 years of reign but all currently available editions of *Vāyu Purāṇa*, one by Ramapratap Tripathi (1987) and one by Ānandāśrama Sanskrit Granthāvaliḥ (1983), both of which are based on the Sanskrit edition by Hari Narayana Apte in AD 1905, give him only 28 years of reign. The verses (99.328–329) about Mahāpadma Nanda in these editions are substantially altered and a mess in the current copies, stating that Mahāpadma had one thousand sons, etc. This is yet another evidence of tampering with the Purāṇas.

# Maurya Dynasty, Yudhiṣṭhira Śaka 1604–1920 (1534–1218 BC)

The Purāṇas clearly state that Chandragupta Maurya was installed on the throne by Chāṇakya and make no statement to the effect that he was a great king or an emperor. This stands in contrast to the declaration by colonial era Indologists who held that he was a great king. The claim, in fact, is based on their wrong identification of *Sandracottus* as Chandragupta Maurya, instead of Chandragupta I of the Gupta Dynasty. Hemachandrāchārya, the 12th century AD Jain scholar, describes in *Pariśiṣṭaparvan* (Jacobi, 1932, Canto 8, 253–278, p. lxxv), how after a certain incident, Chāṇakya gladly inferred that as king, Chandragupta would be an obsequious master to his future minister. Thus, Chandragupta Maurya is not the prodigy destined for royalty as described by Justin when he referred to '*Sandracottus*' (Majumdar, 1960, p. 193). *Sandracottus* of the Greek writers is not Chandragupta of the Maurya Dynasty.

There are varying accounts of the origin of Chandragupta Maurya. The

Purāṇas do not state his parentage. After describing Mahāpadma Nanda as the son of Mahānandi through a shudra woman, they only state that "from this time onwards, there will be kings born from shudra women". *Pariśiṣṭaparvan* (Jacobi, Canto 8, 227–241, p. lxxiv) states that Chandragupta's mother was the daughter of the chief of the village where the feeders of the king's peacocks lived. *Mudra Rakṣasa,* a play written by Viśākhadatta in the 6th or the 11th century AD, 21 or 26 centuries after the time of Chandragupta Maurya, describes Chandragupta as the son of Mura (Venkatachelam, 1953b, p. 99). Maurya in Sanskrit means 'of Mura'.

The chronology of the Maurya Dynasty (Table 19) includes 12 kings who ruled for a total of 316 years, according to the Purāṇas. It is noteworthy that for the previous four dynasties covering over 1,600 years, there are only minor differences between the various Purāṇas in the list of the kings and their reigning periods. However, from the Maurya Dynasty to the beginning of the Gupta Dynasty, we find significant discrepancies in the currently available copies of the Purāṇas. As discussed earlier, the colonial Indologists, after wrongly

**Table 19: Chronology of the Maurya Dynasty, Yudhiṣṭhira Śaka 1604–1920 (1534–1218 BC)**

| Sr. No. | Name of the King | Years of Reign | STARTING YEAR IN | | |
|---|---|---|---|---|---|
| | | | Yudhishtira Śaka | Kaliyuga | BC |
| 1 | Chandragupta (चंद्रगुप्त) | 34 | 1604 | 1568 | 1534 |
| 2 | Bindusāra (बिंदुसार) | 28 | 1638 | 1602 | 1500 |
| 3 | Aśoka (अशोक) | 36 | 1666 | 1630 | 1472 |
| 4 | Supārśva (सुपार्श्व) | 8 | 1702 | 1666 | 1436 |
| 5 | Daśaratha (दशरथ) | 8 | 1710 | 1674 | 1428 |
| 6 | Indrapālita (इंद्रपालित) | 70 | 1718 | 1682 | 1420 |
| 7 | Harṣavardhana (हर्षवर्धन) | 8 | 1788 | 1752 | 1350 |
| 8 | Saṅgata (संगत) | 9 | 1796 | 1760 | 1342 |
| 9 | Śāliśūka (शालिशूक) | 13 | 1805 | 1769 | 1333 |
| 10 | Somaśarmā (सोमशर्मा) | 7 | 1818 | 1782 | 1320 |
| 11 | Śatadhanvā (शतधन्वा) | 8 | 1825 | 1789 | 1313 |
| 12 | Bṛhadradha (बृहद्रथ) | 87 | 1833 | 1797 | 1305 |
| | **Total** | **316** | **1604–1920** | **1568–1884** | **1534–1218** |

concluding Chandragupta Maurya as *Sandracottus* of Alexander's time, focused on the chronology from the Maurya Dynasty to the Gupta Dynasty.

The currently available copies of Viṣṇu Purāṇa omit two kings – Indrapālita and Harṣavardhana, the sixth and the seventh kings, respectively, of this dynasty. Bhāgavata Purāṇa omits the fifth, sixth, and seventh kings of the dynasty. Currently available copies of Vāyu and Brahmāṇḍa Purāṇas omit Harṣavardhana, Saṅgata, and Śāliśuka, the seventh, eighth, and the ninth kings of the dynasty, respectively. The Buddhist accounts, Mahāvaṁsa and Dīpavaṁsa, describe only the first three kings of this dynasty.

The currently available copy of *Matsya Purāṇa* (Gita Press) misses the first three kings of this dynasty and makes a mess of the sequence of the kings and their years of reign. However, a manuscript of the Matsya Purāṇa which Narayana Sastry had in his library, contained a complete list of the Maurya kings with their years of reign as quoted by Pandit Venkatachelam (1957a, p. 89) in his *Chronology of Ancient Hindu History Part I* which is reproduced here as follows:

> “T.S. Narayana Sastry writes:—
>
> "Fortunately in my library I possess a manuscript copy of Matsya Purana in Grantha Character, which gives a complete list of the Maurya kings with years of their individual reigns and I give the same below:–
>
> चतुस्त्रिंशत् समा राजा चन्द्रगुप्तो भविष्यति।
> अष्टाविंशतिवर्षाणि भद्रसारस्तु तत्सुतः ।। २४ ।।
>
> षड्त्रिंशस्तु महाराजो भविताऽशोक एव च।
> तस्य पुत्रः कुनालस्तु वर्षाण्यष्टौ भविष्यति ।। २५।।
>
> कुनालसूनुरष्टौच भोक्ता दशरथ स्ततः।
> सप्तानां दशवर्षाणि तत्सुत श्चेन्द्रपालितः ।। २६ ।।
>
> भविता चाऽष्टवर्षाणि तत्सुतो हर्षवर्धनः।
> भविता नववर्षाणि तस्य पुत्रस्तु सम्मतः ।।२७।।
>
> त्रयोदशहि वर्षाणि शालिशूको भविष्यति ।
> भविता सप्तवर्षाणि सोमशर्मा नराधिपः ।। २८ ।।
>
> भविता शतधन्वातु नववर्षाणि तत्सुतः ।
> बृहद्रथस्तु वर्षाणि तस्य पुत्रोऽथ सप्ततिः ।। २९ ।।
>
> इत्येते दशच द्वेच ये भोक्ष्यन्ति वसुन्धराम् ।
> शतानि त्रीणि वर्षाणि तेभ्यः श्रृङ्गान् गमिष्यति ।। ३० ।।
>
> This version of Matsya Purana tolerably agrees with that given in the

manuscript copy of the Kaliyuga Raja vrittanta, in my library which also I add below for easy reference.

चन्द्रगुप्तस्ततो मौर्यश्चाणक्येनाऽभिरक्षितः।
चतुस्त्रिंशत् समा राज्यं करिष्यति सुधार्मिकः।।

अष्टाविंशतिवर्षाणि बिंदुसारो भविष्यति।
षट्त्रिंशत्तु ततो राजा भविताऽशोकवर्धनः।।

सुपार्श्वस्तत्सुतश्चाऽथ वर्षाण्यष्टौ भविष्यति।
अष्टौ वर्षाणि तत्पुत्रो भोक्ता वै बंधुपालितः।।

बंधुपालितदायादो सप्तर्ति चेन्द्रपालितः।
भविता नव वर्षाणि तस्य पुत्रस्तु संगतः।।

त्रयोदश समा राज्यं शालिशूकः करिष्यति।
भविता सप्तवर्षाणि देवधर्मा नरर्षभः।।

ततः शतधनू राजा भविताऽष्टौ समा भुवि।
बृहद्रथस्तु तत्पुत्रो जरासंध इवाऽपरः।।

क्षत्रियानखिलान् जित्वा महाराजो भविष्यति।
अष्टाशीतिं तु वर्षाणि स राष्ट्रं पालयिष्यति।।

द्वादशैते नृपामौर्याश्चन्द्रगुप्तादयो महीम् ।
शतानि त्रीणि भोक्ष्यन्ति दश षट् च समाः कलौ ।।"

(Bhaga III, Ch. II (vide Age of Sankara, Part I. B, Appendix I. p 56ff) "

The above verses are also found in the *History of Classical Sanskrit Literature* (Krishnamachariar, 1937, p. xlix). Thus, the older version of Matsya Purāṇa and Kaliyuga Rājavṛttānta, list all 12 kings of the Maurya Dynasty. However, there is one point of difference between the two; this version of Matsya Purāṇa assigns 70 years to the last king, instead of 87 years assigned in the Kaliyuga Rājavṛttānta. Accordingly, the former gives the total period for the 12 kings as 300 years instead of 316 years in Kaliyuga Rājavṛttānta. Pandit Venkatachelam (1957a, p. 95) states:

> " The Kaliyugaraja Vrittanta, which appears to be a portion of the Bhavishyottara Purana, and which is still in Manuscripts, enumerates all these 12 kings and gives them a total period of 316 years which perfectly agrees with the total number of years given to individual reign of each of these 12 kings. "

Pandit Venkatachelam states further (1957a):

> “There is however an other version of the Brahmanda Purana which mentions the names of all these 12 kings and the total number of years for which they reigned makes up exactly 316 years, … Miss. C. Mable Duff in her table of the Maurya Dynasty appended to her Chronology of India refers to a version of the Brahmanda Purana in which the names of 11 kings are mentioned, omitting the name of Indrapalita who ruled for 70 years, and the number of years given to each of these kings exactly tallies with this version excepting the fact that Chandragupta is assigned only 24 years instead of 34, and Nandasara [Bindusāra] only 25 years instead of 28, as we have it in this version.” (p. 96)

> “There is however, another version of the Vayu Purana, which enumerates all the names of these twelve kings, and assigns to them a total period of 316 years as given in K. R. V. [Kaliyuga Rājavṛttānta], and this edition is referred to by Mr. Pargiter as ‘e-Va.P.’” (p. 97)

Thus, there is substantial evidence of tampering with the Purāṇas to shorten the chronology. I have not been able to find the versions of Matsya, Brahmāṇḍa, and Vāyu Purāṇas that Pandit Venkatachelam had.

The following is a brief description of each of the 12 kings of the dynasty. For further discussion on the chronology of this dynasty, refer to *The Chronology of Ancient Hindu History Part I* (Venkatachelam, 1957a, p. 88–92).

1. **Chandragupta Maurya** (चंद्रगुप्त मौर्य), according to the copy of Matsya Purāṇa and the Kaliyuga Rājavṛttānta which T. S. Narayana Sastry had, reigned for 34 years, from Yudhiṣṭhira Śaka 1604 to 1638 (1534-1500 BC). Presently available copies of Vāyu and Brahmāṇḍa Purāṇas give him 24 years of reign. See the explanation by Pandit Venkatachelam (1957a, p. 88) on why 24 should be 34 in the Sanskrit verse. Simhalese Buddhist texts, *The Dīpavaṁsa* (5.73, 5.100, p. 146) and *Mahāvaṁsa* (5.18, p. xxiv), also give him a reign of 24 years.

2. **Bindusāra** (बिंदुसार) by Viṣṇu Purāṇa, Kaliyuga Rājavṛttānta, Dīpavaṁsa, Mahāvaṁsa, and Pariśiṣṭaparvan, **Bhadrasāra** (भद्रसार) by Vāyu and Brahmāṇḍa Purāṇas or **Vārisāra** (वारिसार) by Bhāgavata Purāṇa, son of Chandragupta Maurya, reigned for 28 years from Yudhiṣṭhira Śaka 1638 to 1666 (1500–1472 BC). Vāyu and Brahmāṇḍa Purāṇas give him a reign of 25 years. *Mahāvaṁsa* (5.18, p. xxiv) gives him a reign of 28 years.

3. **Aśoka** (अशोक) by Vāyu, Matsya, and Brahmāṇḍa Purāṇas, Dīpavaṁsa, and Pariśiṣṭaparvan or **Aśokavardhana** (अशोकवर्धन) by Kaliyuga Rājavṛttānta,

Viṣṇu, and Bhāgavata Purāṇas, son of Bindusāra, reigned for 36 years (Kaliyuga Rājavṛttānta, Vāyu, Matsya, and Brahmāṇḍa Purāṇas) from Yudhiṣṭhira Śaka 1666 to 1702 (1472–1436 BC). An incomplete version of Matsya Purāṇa calls him Saka (a mistake for Aśoka) and gives him a reign of 36 years. Currently available copies of Vāyu Purāṇa give him a reign of 26 years but the copy of Vāyu Purāṇa, which Pandit Venkatachelam had, gave him a reign of 36 years. Dīpavaṁsa (5.101, p. 146) and Mahāvaṁsa (p. xxiv) give him a reign of 37 years. However, they incorrectly state that Aśoka's consecration happened 218 years after the nirvana of Gautama Buddha (Dīpavaṁsa, 6.1, p. 146; Mahāvaṁsa 5.21, p. 27). As discussed in Chapter 3, the Buddhist accounts are not reliable.

A significant error in the otherwise pioneering work of Pandit Venkatachelam (1957a, p. 91) is equating this Aśoka with Samudragupta. Both, Pandit Venkatachelam and M. Krishnamachariar, (1937, p. lxxxviii, cvi) whom he followed in this aspect, stated:

> "The conquests ascribed to Aśoka in the various Buddhistic accounts are no doubt taken from the conquests of Samudragupta or Aśoka the Great, and the embassy of the Ceylon king is also traceable to the same origin."

M. Krishnamachariar (1937, p. xlix) appears to have been misled by James Talboys Wheeler's (1874) book, *History of India from the Earliest Ages*. Aśoka and Samudragupta, both, ruled over vast empires but in different eras, as evident from their separate inscriptions on the Prayāg pillar. Aśoka's reign is described in further detail following the brief description of the kings of this dynasty.

4. **Suyaśā** (सुयशा) by Viṣṇu Purāṇa, **Suyaśa** (सुयश) by Bhāgavata Purāṇa, **Supārśva** (सुपार्श्व) by Kaliyuga Rājavṛttānta and one version of Viṣṇu Purāṇa, **Kunāla** (कुनाल) by an older copy of Matsya Purāṇa (Venkatachelam's) and Vāyu Purāṇa, or **Kulāla** (कुलाल) by Brahmāṇḍa Purāṇa, son of Aśoka, ruled Magadha, according to all Purāṇas, for eight years from Yudhiṣṭhira Śaka 1702 to 1710 (1436–1428 BC).

5. **Daśaratha** (दशरथ) by Viṣṇu, Bhāgavata, and Matsya Purāṇas, or **Bandhupālita** (बंधुपालित) by Kaliyuga Rājavṛttānta, Vāyu, and Brahmāṇḍa Purāṇas, son of Suyaśā, reigned, according to all the Purāṇas, for eight years, from Yudhiṣṭhira Śaka 1710 to 1718 (1428–1420 BC). One version of

Vāyu Purāṇa gives him a reign of ten years.

6. **Indrapālita** (इंद्रपालित), son of Daśaratha, reigned for a period of 70 years (Kaliyuga Rājavṛttānta, Matsya, and Brahmāṇḍa Purāṇas) from Yudhiṣṭhira Śaka 1718 to 1788 (1420–1350 BC). Pandit Venkatachelam (1957a, p. 93) states in his book that one copy of Vāyu Purāṇa gave him a reign of ten years. Only the tampered copies of the Purāṇas appear to have survived. Currently available copies of Vāyu and Brahmāṇḍa Purāṇas give him a reign of only ten years. The Viṣṇu and Bhāgavata Purāṇas omit this and the next king.

7. **Harṣa** (हर्ष) by Matsya Purāṇa (Pandit Venkatachelam's copy) or **Harṣavardhana** (हर्षवर्धन) by Kaliyuga Rājavṛttānta, son of Indrapālita, reigned for eight years, according to all the Purāṇas, from Yudhiṣṭhira Śaka 1788 to 1796 (1350–1342 BC). Pandit Venkatachelam's copies of Matsya and Brahmānd Purāṇas had this king's name and years of reign but the currently available copies of these Purāṇas miss this king.

8. **Saṅgata** (संगत) by Bhāgavata Purāṇa and Kaliyuga Rājavṛttānta, **Sammati** (सम्मति) by Brahmāṇḍa and Matsya Purāṇas or **Saṁprati** (संप्रति) according to an imperfect version of Matsya Purāṇa and *Pariśiṣṭaparvan* (Jacobi, 1932, p. lxxxii), son of Harṣa, reigned according to all the Purāṇas for nine years from Yudhiṣṭhira Śaka 1796 to 1805 (1342–1333 BC) (Venkatachelam, 1957a, p. 94). Currently available copies of the Matsya, Vāyu, and Brahmāṇḍa Purāṇas are missing this king.

9. **Śāliśūka** (शालिशूक), son of Saṅgata, reigned for 13 years, according to all the Purāṇas, from Yudhiṣṭhira Śaka 1805 to 1818 (1333–1320 BC). Again, the currently available copies of Matsya, Vāyu, and Brahmāṇḍa Purāṇas miss this king.

10. **Somaśarmā** (सोमशर्मा) by Viṣṇu, Bhāgavata, and Matsya (Pandit Venkatachelam's copy) Purāṇas, **Devadharmā** (देवधर्मा) by Kaliyuga Rājavṛttānta or **Devavarmā** (देववर्मा) by currently available versions of Vāyu, and Brahmāṇḍa Purāṇas, son of Śāliśuka, reigned for seven years according to all the Purāṇas, from Yudhiṣṭhira Śaka 1818 to 1825 (1320–1313 BC).

11. **Śatadhanvā** (शतधन्वा) by Viṣṇu, Bhāgavata, and Matsya Purāṇas, Śatadhanu (शतधनु) by Brahmāṇḍa Purāṇa and Kaliyuga Rājavṛttānta, or Śatadhara (शतधर) by Vāyu Purāṇa, reigned for eight years from Yudhiṣṭhira Śaka 1825 to 1833 (1313–1305 BC).

12. **Bṛhadratha** (बृहद्रथ) by Kaliyuga Rājavṛttānta, Viṣṇu, Bhāgavata, Brahmāṇḍa, and Matsya Purāṇas, or **Bṛhadaśva** (बृहदश्व) by Vāyu Purāṇa was the son of Śatadhanvā. He ruled Magadha for a long period of 87 years, according to the copies of the Kaliyuga Rājavṛttānta, Vāyu, and Brahmāṇḍa Purāṇas which Narayana Sastry had, from Yudhiṣṭhira Śaka 1833 to 1920 (1305–1218 BC). The currently available copies of Vāyu and Brahmāṇḍa Purāṇas give him only seven years of reign. Matsya Purāṇa gives him a reign of 70 years.

### Distortion by Colonial Era Indologists

The European Indologists of the colonial era accepted only nine or ten kings of this dynasty and assigned the total reigning period of 137 years to the dynasty. This was the shortest they could find in the tampered versions of the Purāṇas, instead of the total of 316 years for the 12 kings stated in Kaliyuga Rājavṛittānta and the correct versions of the Purāṇas. With 24 years assigned to Chandragupta Maurya, 28 years to Bindusāra and 36 years to Aśoka, the total years assigned for the first three kings are 88 years. This leaves only 49 years, out of the total 137 years assigned to the dynasty, for the next 6–7 kings which is only about 7–8 years per king according to the colonial Indologists!

## Aśoka the Great and his Inscriptions

Emperor Aśoka, the grandson of Chandragupta Maurya, was a contemporary of Aśoka, the king of Kashmir. Aśoka Maurya reigned from 1472 to 1436 BC and Aśoka of Kashmir reigned from 1448 to 1400 BC as discussed in Chapter 11. Figure 19 shows Aśoka Maurya's vast empire based on the inscriptions found throughout the Indian subcontinent.

The empire stretched from Bengal in the east to Kandahar in present-day Afghanistan in the west, and from Shāhbāzgarhi in the Peshawar district and Mānsehara in the northwestern province of Pakistan to southern Karnataka in the south. Besides, he had a significant influence on Sri Lanka where he sent his son and daughter to propagate Buddhism.

Most of the inscriptions are written in Sanskrit, in the Brahmi script. Figure 20 shows the inscription in the Brahmi script on a stone pillar in Sarnath. The major rock edicts contain 13–14 edicts whereas the minor

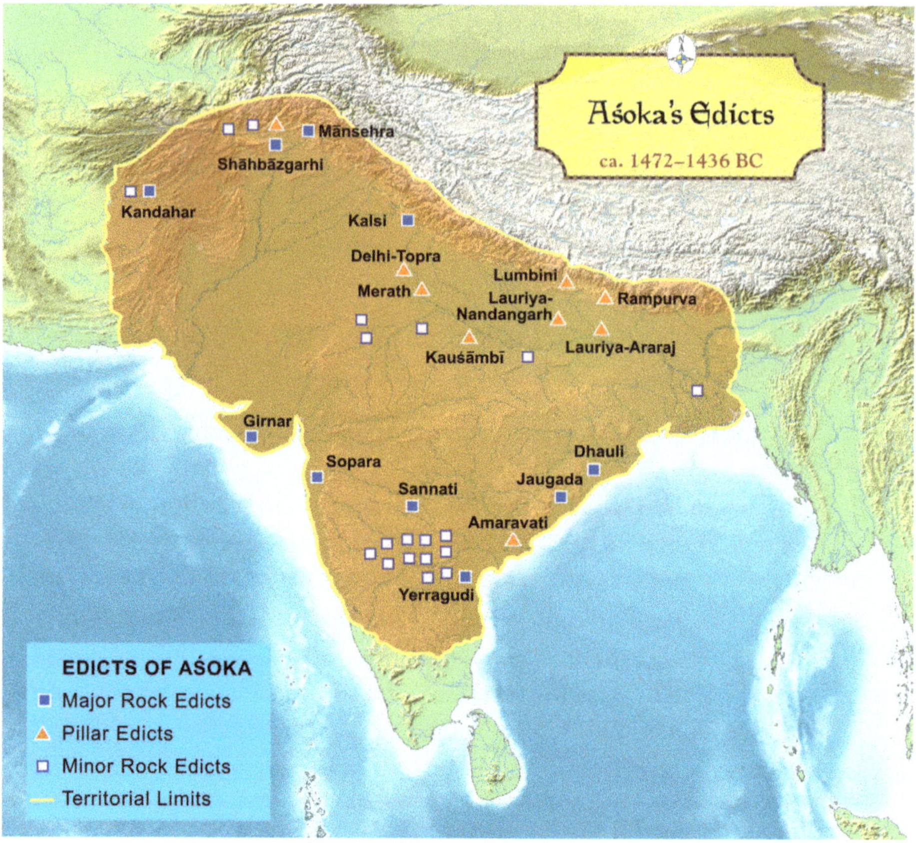


**Figure 19: Aśoka's edicts and empire (ca. 1450 BC)**
*Blank map courtesy: DEMIS Mapserver, Wikimedia Commons, CC BY-SA 3.0*

rock edicts contain only two or three, typically. The inscriptions in the northwest of the subcontinent are in the Kharosthi script. The rock inscription at Kandahar is in Aramaic and Greek. The Greek inscription is of a much later date as explained later in this section. The Brahmi script was deciphered by James Prinsep (1838, p. 219), a British working for the East India Company, and he deserves our gratitude. The text and translation of the second rock edict were published in 1838.

Figure 21 shows the stone pillar inscription of Aśoka at Prayāg (प्रयाग). The pillar was originally installed in Kauśāmbī (45 km southwest from Prayāg) which was the capital of the Hastināpura empire after Hastināpura was flooded by the Ganga as described in Chapter 5. The pillar was moved to Prayāg at a later age. This pillar also contains the inscription from Samudragupta as described in the Gupta Dynasty section of this chapter.

**Figure 20: Pillar inscription in Sarnath**
*Photo courtesy: Wikimedia Commons, CC BY-SA 3.0*

## Key Learning from the Inscriptions

1. The inscriptions are in the name of the King Devānaṁpiye (देवानंपिये) Piyadasina (पियदसिन) or Devānaṁpiyasa (देवानंपियस) Piyadasi (पियदसि) Rāja who ordered them to be written (Sircar, 1979, p. 16). Edict 3, found only in the minor rock inscription from Bairāt, Rajasthan, states 'The Magadha King Priyadarśi'.

2. The minor inscription at Maski, Karnataka, is one of the two in the whole country that mention Aśoka by name—'Devānaṁpiyasa Aśoka' (Sircar, p. 61). The other is the Minor Rock Edict 1 at Gujarra, near Jhansi in Madhya Pradesh, where the name Aśoka is used together with his full title: *Devānaṁpiyasa Piyadasino Asokarājasa* (p. 91). Based on these two and the Bairāt inscription, these and similar inscriptions have been attributed to the King Aśoka of Magadha. The major rock inscriptions, which typically contain 14 edicts, only state King Devānaṁ Piyadasi and do not state Aśoka anywhere.

3. None of the inscriptions states the year of Aśoka himself, but only the year of his reign, e.g. in the 8th year of his reign, or the 13th year of his reign, etc.

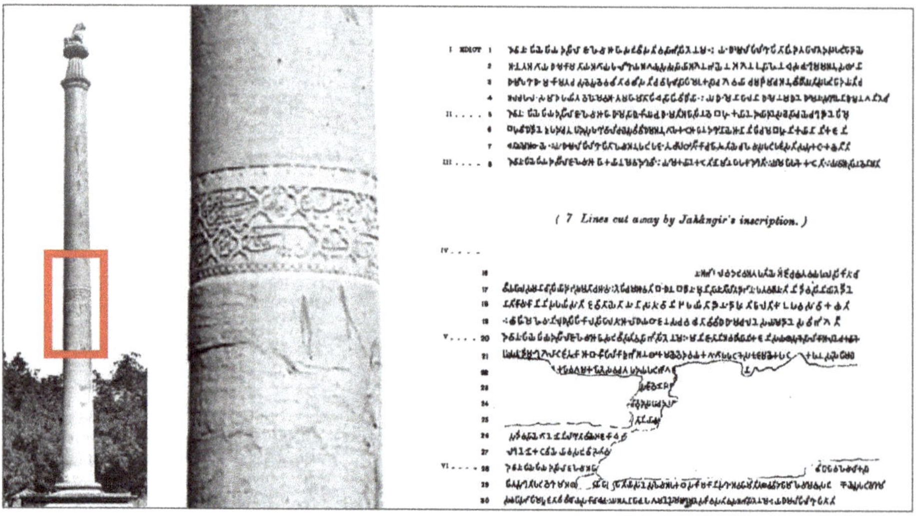


**Figure 21: Prayāg pillar inscription of Aśoka**
*Photo courtesy: Wikimedia Commons, public domain*

4. The Major Rock Edict XIII states that Devānaṁapiya (Aśoka) conquered Kaliṅga when he had been anointed for eight years and expresses his remorse at the pain and sorrow inflicted by the war including the death of over 100,000 people. As described earlier, Mahāpadma Nanda had conquered Kaliṅga and all other ancient dynasties of northern India. Aśoka's conquest of Kaliṅga again implies that Kaliṅga became independent during the reign of one of Aśoka's two predecessors, Chandragupta Maurya or Bindusāra.

5. The Minor Rock inscriptions state that Devānaṁpiyasa became a Buddhist follower.

For the reader's convenience, the following is a translation of the first two parts of the Major Rock Edict II and a small portion of the Major Rock Edict XIII. The latter is a large edict (two pages long), hence, only a small but very important part of the edict is reproduced here.

**The Major Rock Edict II – Translation** (Sircar, 1979, p. 15):

“ (I) Everywhere in the dominions of king Priyadarśin [पियदसि], Beloved of the Gods [देवानंपियस], and likewise (in) the bordering territories such as (those of) the Coḍas [(चो)डा] (and) Pāṇḍyas [पंडिया] (as well as of) the Satīka-putra [सतीक (पुते)] (and in) Tāmraparṇi [तंबपंनि] (and in the territories of) the Yavana king [योन-लाजा] named Antiyoka [(अंतियो)ग] and also (of) the kings who are the neighbours of the said Antiyoka— everywhere king

Priyadarśin, Beloved of the Gods, has arranged two kinds of medical treatment, (viz.), medical treatment for men and medical treatment for animals.*

(II) And, wherever, there were no medicinal herbs beneficial to men and beneficial to animals, everywhere they have been caused to be imported and planted. ”

**The Major Rock Edict XIII** (Sircar, 1979, p. 33, 35):

“ (XVI) So, what is conquest through Dharma is now considered to be the best conquest by the Beloved of the Gods.

(XVII) And such a conquest has been achieved by the Beloved of the Gods not only here (in his own dominions) but also in the territories bordering, as far away as (at the distance of) six hundred Yojanas, (where) the Yavana king [(यो)न-(ला)ज] named Antiyoka [अंतियोक] (is ruling and where), beyond (the kingdom of) the said Antiyoka, four other kings named Tulamāya [(तुल)मय], Antikeni [अं(तिके)नि], Makā [मका] and Alikasudara [अलिक(सुद)ल] (are also ruling), (and) towards the south where the Coḍas [चो(डा)] and Pāṇḍyas [पंडिया] (are living), as far as Tāmraparṇī [(तं)बपनि]. ” *

*Names in Devanāgari within square brackets [ ] have been added from the Devanāgari portion of the cited reference. The text within parentheses ( ) is not present in the inscription but has been added by the author of the cited reference.

## Misinterpretation of the Rock Edicts by Colonial Era Indologists

The 19th century European Indologists placed Aśoka's reign at 268–232 BC as a result of their wrong identification of '*Sandracottous*', of the ancient Greek writers, as Chandragupta Maurya of 1534 BC instead of Chandragupta I Gupta of 327 BC. Then, they misinterpreted the rock inscriptions to support their wrong timeline. First, James Prinsep (1838, p. 221) declared that the fifth edict in the Girnar rock inscription contains the word *Pāṭaliputra*. E. Hultzsch (1925, p. xxx, 9–11) in his translation of the inscriptions also declared that the Fifth Rock Edict of the Girnar inscription, contains the word 'Pāṭaliputra', as shown below:

“ (M) They are occupied everywhere, both in **Pāṭaliputra** and in the outlying ... and whatever other relatives of mine (there are). ” [Emphasis in the original]

Next, Hultzsch (1925, p. xxxviii, 162) argued that the two syllables, *Pāṭa* (पाट) visible at the beginning of the third line of the Sarnath pillar-inscription, are probably the first two letters of *Pāṭaliputra*. However, Hultzsch's translations of the same edict, 5(M) in all other rock inscriptions (Kālsi, Shāhbāzgarhi, Mānsehra, Dhauli) do not contain the word 'Pāṭaliputra' as follows:

> " They are occupied everywhere, here and in all the outlying towns, in the harems of our brothers, of (our) sisters, and (of) whatever other relatives (of ours there are). " (p. 33)

D. C. Sircar's translation (1979, p. 24) of the same edict (Rock Edict V) from the Erragudi Rock inscription also does not find Pāṭaliputra in the inscription as shown below:

> " (XIII) They are engaged everywhere—here and elsewhere in all the towns, in the households of my brothers and sisters and other relatives. "

Thus, contrary to the assertion of the colonial era Indologists, it is doubtful that Emperor Aśoka ruled from Pāṭaliputra.

## Misidentification of the Names from Rock Edict XIII (13)

As shown in the earlier paragraph, the Rock Edict XIII (line XVII) mentions the names – Yona (योन) king Antiyoka (अंतियोक), and his four neighboring kings named, Turamaya (तुरमय) or Tulamaya (तुलमय) as written in a few places, Antikeni (अंतिकेनि), Makā (मका), and Alikasudara (अलिकसुदर) or Alikasudala (अलिकसुदल). The colonial era Indologists wrongly identified Antiyoka as Antiochus (of Seleucid Empire in Syria/Persia), Turamaya as Ptolemy (of Egypt), Antikeni as Antigonus (of Macedonia), Makā as Magas (Greek Macedonian king of Cyrene) and Alikasudara as Alexander (of Epirus/Greece) of the third century BC (Prinsep, 1838. p. 219, 224). These identifications are completely wrong as explained in the following section.

## Why are these Identifications Wrong?

K. D. Sethna (1989, p. 235 onwards), in his book, *Ancient India in New Light*, has meticulously exposed numerous contradictions arising from these wrong identifications and the 268–232 BC date assigned to Aśoka. Sethna has systematically proved that Aśoka's time must be centuries earlier than the presently assigned time. He quotes R.K. Mookerji as follows:

> " There were several kings of Asia Minor of equal and higher status whom Aśoka should have mentioned such as Eumenes of Pergama (262–240 B.C.) or, nearer home, Diodotous of Bactria. " (as cited in Sethna, 1989, p. 236)

Sethna states (p. 237):

> "Our amazement at Aśoka's inconceivable omissions would cease if we refrained from dating him to the post-Alexandrine age. No query could be raised of any kind, were his rājās five border rulers in an age much earlier, ...
>
> Still more strange than Aśoka's blind spot for Diodotous and Eumenes is the absolute ignorance we find about Aśoka in the Classical records concerning the kings in whose domains he is supposed to have propagated his dharma."

Sethna adds (p. 238):

> "With Aśoka put in the time of those five Greek kingdoms, the neglect becomes wholly unintelligible. ... why is there not the slightest hint of Aśoka's activities in the historical passages relating to Ptolemy?"

Further exposing the contradictions, Sethna writes (p. 240):

> "There is also the fact that to the whole Greek world Buddhism in any expressible form was an unknown quantity until we reached the 2nd century A.D. "Greece," says R.C. Majumdar, "knew nothing of Buddhism previous to the rise of Alexandria in the Christian era. Buddha is first mentioned by Clement of Alexandria (A.D. 150–218)." Can we imagine such ignorance if five Greek kingdoms received from Aśoka missionaries who, for all the general humanitarian bearing of their message, were representatives of a great Buddhist emperor?"

Pandit Venkatachelam (1957b, p. 29) writes:

> "The Buddhist historical and religious literature claims missionaries to have been sent by the emperor to the neighbouring countries or the northern border like the Yona Kingdoms on the north-west, Kashmir, Nepal, Bhutan, Sinkiang, Tibet, Khotan, Kucha, Kusthan etc. and never so far as Greece or the Greek kingdoms of those times.
>
> In fact, the words, Greek or Greece are mentioned nowhere in the inscriptions."

K. D. Sethna (1989, p. 245–246) describes yet another contradiction:

> "Another difference between the world of Megasthenes and that of the Mauryas may be thrown into relief. In R.E.V. [Rock Edict V] Aśoka declares: "For a very long time past previously there was no dispatch of business and no reporting at all hours. This, therefore, I have done, namely, that at all hours and in all places ... the Reporters may report people's business to me.

People's business I do at all places." Mookerji, accepting the current equation of Sandrocottus with Chandragupta Maurya, is led to remark: "Aśoka's strictures against his predecessors do not apply even to his grandfather whose devotion to public work is thus described by Megasthenes: 'The king may not sleep during the day-time. He leaves the palace not only in the time of war, but also for the purposes of judging cases. He then remains in the court for the whole day without allowing the business to be interrupted, even though the hour arrives when he must needs attend to his person' (McCrindle, p. 72). Curtius (VIII.9) adds: 'The palace is open to all comers, even when the king is having his hair combed and dressed' ...

Sandrocottus, according to Megasthenes and Curtius, did exactly what Aśoka says his predecessors failed to do. Mookerji is surprised at the discrepancy between the two statements, for he takes Sandrocottus to be Aśoka's grandfather. But both the statements can be correct if Sandrocottus is not Chandragupta Maurya but the founder of the Imperial Guptas. ”

## Yavanas (Yonas) are not Greeks

The *Mahābhārata* (Vol. 1, Sabhā Parva 32.16) describes Yavana (यवन), Barbara (बर्बर), Śaka (शक), etc. people living in northwest India conquered by Nakul. K. D. Sethna (1989, p. 254–255) writes:

“ The *Mahābhārata* (XIII.33.21) and the *Manusaṁhitā* (X.43–44) not only speak of the Yavanas, together with the Kambojas and some other tribes, as being degraded Kshatriyas: they also speak of them as having lost their Aryan status by not consulting Brāhmaṇas. This explanation reminds us at once of Aśoka's own statement in R.E. XIII [Rock Edict 13] singling out the Yonas within the empire as the people who in his days were without the ministrations of Brāhamaṇas and Śramaṇas. The statement, which has been taken as a pointer to the Greek nature of Yona society and culture, is really in tune with India's own tradition and shows that what was true about all north-western border provinces, including Yona, held somehow for just that one province in Aśoka's day. Buddhist literature itself has said of the Kambojas, the close associates of the Yonas, the same thing in essence as the *Mahābhārata* and the *Manusaṁhitā* and, by implication, the *Gaṇapātha*. Law tells us: "In the *Jātakas* we read that the Kambojas were a north-western tribe who were supposed to have lost their original Aryan customs and become barbarous." So Aśoka is merely qualifying in a particular way a common ancient testimony, both Buddhist and non-Buddhist, which is far removed from Greek concerns. Since the condition of his Yona country remains the same as in this testimony and simply the condition of its fellow-provinces changes, no Greek shade requires to be imported into Aśoka's statement. To import such a shade is to realize an entirely false and unnecessary issue. ”

### What about the bilingual inscription near Kandahar?

K. D. Sethna (1989, p. 307–330) concluded after extensive analysis that both versions of the inscription on the same rock near Kandahar are not from the same age. The Aramaic version of the inscription belongs to a much earlier age than the Greek version of the inscription which is from the post-Alexandrine period (275–225 BC). For the detailed analysis of the two inscriptions, see Sethna's *Ancient India in a New Light*.

## Śuṅga Dynasty, Yudhiṣṭhira Śaka 1920–2220 (1218–918 BC)

Bṛhadratha, the last king of the Maurya Dynasty, was a man of low character (fond of women) and neglected the administration of the kingdom (Venkatachelam, 1957a, p. 100). Hordes of Śakas and Yavanas of northwestern India grew bold enough to cross the Sindhu and endanger the lives, property, and honor of the people living east of the river. These marauding hordes had earlier belonged to the kshatriya varṇa but were excommunicated for violation of Vedic rites. So, his general and minister, Puṣyamitra Śuṅga put him to death and proclaimed himself as the emperor and, thus, founded the Śuṅga Dynasty according to all the Purāṇas (Matsya, Vāyu, Brahmāṇḍa, Viṣṇu, and Bhāgavata). He was a Brahmin of the Sāmaveda branch. Table 20 lists all ten kings of the dynasty along with the period of reign for each one.

Pandit Venkatachelam (1957a, p. 102) refers to the complete version of the manuscript copy of Matsya Purāṇa in the possession of T. S. Narayana Sastry from which the verses describing the Śuṅga Dynasty are reproduced as follows, for easy reference:

> “ पुष्पमित्रस्तु सेनानीः समुद्धृत्य बृहद्रधात्।
> कारयिष्यतिवै राज्यं समाः षष्टिं महाबलः ।। (Matsya २७०.३१)
>
> तस्य पुत्रोऽग्निमित्रश्च पंचाशत् भोक्ष्यते महीं।
> वसुमित्रश्च तत्पुत्रः षड्विंशत्तु समा नृपः ।। ३२
>
> वसुमित्रसुतो भाव्यो दशवर्षाणि वै नृपः।
> भविताऽपि वसुज्येष्ठः सप्तवर्षाणि वै पुनः।। ३३

ततोऽन्तकः समास्त्रिंशत् तस्य पुत्रो भविष्यति।
भविष्यति समास्त्रिंशत् त्रीण्येवं स पुलिंदकः ।। ३४

भविता त्रीणि वर्षाणि राजा घोषवसुस्ततः।
वज्रमित्रस्तु तत्पुत्र स्त्वेकोनत्रिंशत समाः ।। ३५

द्वात्रिंशच्च महाभागः समा भागवतो नृपः।
भविष्यति सुतस्तस्य देवभूमिः समा दश ।। ३६

दशैते शुंगराजानो भोक्ष्यंतीमां वसुंधरां ।
शतं पूर्णं शते द्वेच तेभ्यः कण्वान् गमिष्यति ।। ३७ ”

## Corruption of the Matsya Purāṇa

Pandit Venkatachelam (1957a, p. 102) observed that the printed editions of the Matsya Purāṇa (both Nāgari and Telugu) omitted the stanzas referring to Agnimitra and his son Vasumitra, did not give regnal period of Vajramitra, and there were many other errors. Apparently, the same erroneous copies of Matsya Purāṇa are presently available. We need to find the old manuscripts of the Purāṇa.

**Table 20: Chronology of the Śuṅga Dynasty, Yudhiṣṭhira Śaka 1920–2220 (1218–918 BC)**

| Sr. No. | Name of the King | Years of Reign | STARTING YEAR IN Yudhiṣṭhira Śaka | Kaliyuga | BC |
|---|---|---|---|---|---|
| 1 | Puṣyamitra (पुष्यमित्र) | 60 | 1920 | 1884 | 1218 |
| 2 | Agnimitra (अग्निमित्र) | 50 | 1980 | 1944 | 1158 |
| 3 | Vasumitra (वसुमित्र ) | 36 | 2030 | 1994 | 1108 |
| 4 | Sujyeṣṭa (सुज्येष्ट) | 17 | 2066 | 2030 | 1072 |
| 5 | Bhadraka (भद्रक) | 30 | 2083 | 2047 | 1055 |
| 6 | Pulindaka (पुलिंदक) | 33 | 2113 | 2077 | 1025 |
| 7 | Ghoṣavasu (घोषवसु) | 3 | 2146 | 2110 | 992 |
| 8 | Vajramitra (वज्रमित्र) | 29 | 2149 | 2113 | 989 |
| 9 | Bhāgavata (भागवत) | 32 | 2178 | 2142 | 960 |
| 10 | Devahūti (देवहूति) | 10 | 2210 | 2174 | 928 |
| | **Total** | **300** | **1920–2220** | **1884–2184** | **1218–918** |

1. **Puṣyamitra** (पुष्यमित्र) by Kaliyuga Rājavṛttānta, Viṣṇu, and Bhāgavata Purāṇas, and one version of Vāyu and Matsya Purāṇas or **Puṣpamitra** (पुष्पमित्र) by another version of Matsya and Vāyu Purāṇas, was the founder of the dynasty. He reigned for 60 years from Yudhiṣṭhira Śaka 1920 to 1980 (1218–1158 BC). He performed *Ashvamedha yajña* and won great honor. In *Mālvikāgnimitra,* Kālidāsa describes him as the conqueror of the Āryāvarta. The current version of Matsya Purāṇa assigns him a reign of 36 years which is the duration assigned to his grandson, Vasumitra.

2. **Agnimitra** (अग्निमित्र), son of Puṣyamitra, reigned for 50 years according to Kaliyuga Rājavṛttānta and the correct Matsya Purāṇa, from Yudhiṣṭhira Śaka 1980 to 2030 (1158–1108 BC). Current versions of Matsya Purāṇa give him only eight years of reign, and so does Brahmāṇḍa Purāṇa. Vāyu Purāṇa does not give his name and only describes him as the eldest son of Puṣpamitra giving him only seven years of reign.

> *Mālvikāgnimitra,* the play composed by the great Sanskrit poet and dramatist Kālidāsa, is based on the love affair of Mālavikā with King Agnimitra. From this play, we know that Agnimitra was the only son of Puṣyamitra (Venkatachelam, 1957a, p. 103).

3. **Vasumitra** (वसुमित्र), son of Agnimitra, reigned for 36 years, according to Kaliyuga Rājavṛttānta and the correct Matsya Purāṇa, from Yudhiṣṭhira Śaka 2030 to 2066 (1108–1072 BC). Current versions of Matsya, Vāyu, and Brahmāṇḍa Purāṇas give him a reign of only ten years, and Matsya, Brahmāṇḍa, Viṣṇu, and Bhāgavata Purāṇas place Vasumitra after Vasujyeṣṭa, the fourth king of the dynasty.

> According to Kālidāsa's Malavikāgnimitra, Vasumitra is the son of Agnimitra by his wife Dharini. He is said to have conquered the Yavanas (the degraded kshatriyas of Bhārata who inhabited the five Yavana states – Uttara Jyotiṣa, Divya Kataka, Siṁhapura, Urasa, and Abhisara. The first three are in present-day Afghanistan, the fourth in the Khyber Pakhtunkhwa, the northwestern province of Pakistan, and the fifth is in the western part of Kashmir. These Yavanas are not the Greeks as explained earlier. Vasumitra is said to have recovered the sacrificial horse of his grandfather on the banks of the River Sindhu and completed the *Aśvamedha Yajña.*

4. **Sujyeṣṭa** (सुज्येष्ट) by Brahmāṇḍa, Viṣṇu, and Bhāgavata Purāṇas, or Vas**ujyeṣṭa** (वसुज्येष्ट) by Matsya Purāṇa and Kaliyuga Rājavṛttānta, son of Vasumitra, reigned for 17 years according to the correct Matsya Purāṇa and Kaliyuga Rājavṛttānta, from Yudhiṣṭhira Śaka 2066 to 2083 (1072–1055 BC). Brahmāṇḍa Purāṇa and the current version of Matsya Purāṇa give him a reign of only seven years which is a mistake. The current copy of Vāyu Purāṇa misses his name.

5. **Bhadraka** (भद्रक) by Kaliyuga Rājavṛttānta, Brahmāṇḍa, and Bhāgavata Purāṇas, **Antaka** (अंतक) by the correct Matsya Purāṇa, **Andhaka** (अंधक) by the current version of Matsya Purāṇa, **Andhraka** (अंध्रक) by Vāyu Purāṇa or **Udaṅka** (उदंक) by Viṣṇu Purāṇa, son of Sujyeṣṭa reigned for 30 years, from Yudhiṣṭhira Śaka 2083 to 2113 (1055–1025 BC). The copy of Vāyu Purāṇa which Pandit Venkatachelam had, gave him a reign of ten years and the currently available copies of Matsya, Vāyu, and Brahmāṇḍa Purāṇas give him a reign of only two years!

6. **Pulindaka** (पुलिंदक) according to Vāyu, Matsya, and Brahmāṇḍa Purāṇas or **Pulinda** (पुलिंद) by Bhāgavata Purāṇa and Kaliyuga Rājavṛttānta, son of Maru and nephew of Bhadraka, reigned for 33 years (Matsya Purāṇa and Kaliyuga Rājavṛttānta) from Yudhiṣṭhira Śaka 2113 to 2146 (1025–992 BC). Presently available corrupted copies of Matsya, Vāyu, and Brahmāṇḍa Purāṇas give him a reign of only 3 years instead of 33 years.

7. **Ghoṣavasu** (घोषवसु) according to Viṣṇu Purāṇa or **Ghoṣa** (घोष) by Brahmāṇḍa and Bhāgavata Purāṇas, son of Pulindaka, reigned for only three years according to all the Purāṇas, from Yudhiṣṭhira Śaka 2146 to 2149 (992–989 BC). Presently available copy of Matsya Purāṇa misses this king.

8. **Vajramitra** (वज्रमित्र), son of Ghoṣavasu, reigned for 29 years, according to the correct Matsya Purāṇa and Kaliyuga Rājavṛttānta, from Yudhiṣṭhira Śaka 2149 to 2178 (989–960 BC). Presently available copy of Matsya Purāṇa gives him three years of reign; a copy of Brahmāṇḍa Purāṇa gives him seven years. Vāyu Purāṇa calls him **Vikramitra** (विक्रमित्र) and gives him only three years.

9. **Bhāgavata** (भागवत), son of Vajramitra, reigned for 32 years according to all the Purāṇas, from Yudhiṣṭhira Śaka 2178 to 2210 (960–928 BC).

10. **Devahūti** (देवहूति) according to Kaliyuga Rājavṛttānta, **Devabhūti** (देवभूति) according to Viṣṇu, and Brahmāṇḍa Purāṇas, **Devabhūmi** (देवभूमि) by Matsya Purāṇa or **Kṣemabhūmi** (क्षेमभूमि) by Vāyu Purāṇa, son of Bhāgavata, reigned for ten years from Yudhiṣṭhira Śaka 2210 to 2220 (928–918 BC).

These ten kings of the Śuṅga Dynasty ruled for a total of 300 years. Even the existing imperfect copies of the *Matsya Purāṇa* (272.31, 32) state that the ten kings of the dynasty ruled for 300 years; see the following verses.

भविष्यति सुतस्तस्य देवभूमिः समा दश ।
दशैते क्षुद्रराजानो भोक्ष्यन्तीमां वसुन्धराम् ।। ३१ ।।

शतं पूर्णं शते द्वे च ततः शुङ्गान् गमिष्यति ।
अमात्यो वसुदेवस्तु प्रसह्य ह्यवनीं नृपः ।। ३२ ।।

Bhaviṣyati sutastasya Devabhūmiḥ samā daśa ।
Daśaite kṣudrarājāno bhokṣyantīmāṁ vasundharām ।। 31 ।।

Śataṁ pūrṇaṁ śate dve ca tataḥ Śuṅgān gamiṣyati ।
Amātyo Vasudevastu prasahya hyavanīṁ nṛpaḥ ।। 32 ।।

Verse 32 states that the earth then goes to Śuṅgas which is a mistake, as it cannot go from the Śuṅgas to the Śuṅgas. The verses from the old manuscript of the Matsya Purāṇa quoted earlier do not have this mistake.

All the Purāṇas declare that there were ten kings in the Śuṅga Dynasty. Vāyu and Brahmāṇḍa Purāṇas give 112 years of total reign for the ten kings but the sum of the individual reign given for each king is 130 years in the Vāyu Purāṇa (with reign for one king missing) and 142 years in Brahmāṇḍa Purāṇa. Even these totals are smaller than the total Pandit Venkatachelam got (157 and 149 years, respectively) from his copies of those two Purāṇas. The Kaliyuga Rājavṛttānta copy which Narayana Sastry had, and which Pandit Venkatachelam has quoted, gives a complete and correct description of the dynasty.

### Distortion by Colonial Era European Indologists

It is interesting to note that the European scholars picked the shortest total reign period of 112 years, even though it could not be corroborated in any way!

Kaliyuga Rājavṛttānta gives the following interesting account of the last king of the dynasty (Krishnamachariar, 1937, p. lii):

> "Devahuti, the last king of the Śunga dynasty, having been addicted to a life of pleasure and sexual enjoyment from his boyhood, entrusted the kingdom to the care of his Brahman minister Vasudeva, and he himself retired to Vidiśa, noted in those days for its dancing girls, where he began

to lead a most licentious and immoral life with his voluptuary companions, corrupting the fair maidens of the city to satisfy his lust and becoming an object of hatred to his own subjects. On hearing the extraordinary beauty of the daughter of his Brahman minister Vasudeva, who has been living with her husband, he sent for them to come to Vidiśa and live by his side, and on one day, after secretly disposing of her husband, the king seduced her in the disguise of her husband, and the poor girl who was most true and devoted to her husband, coming to know of the treachery practised by the king, at once gave up her life. On hearing the sad news of the fate of his fair daughter and of her innocent husband, Vasudeva contrived to send to the king a dancing woman, fully furnished with poison, dressed as one of the chief queens and had him killed by her hand. People hailed the death of their licentious king with joy, and made Vasudeva his upright minister, to take charge of the kingdom and rule the country henceforth. ”

## Kaṇva Dynasty, Yudhiṣṭhira Śaka 2220–2305 (918–833 BC)

Vasudeva (वसुदेव), the first ruler of the Kaṇva (कण्व) Dynasty, was a descendant of Kaṇvāyana (कण्वायन) Brahmin family. As he was a minister of Devabhūti, the last king of the Śuṅga Dynasty, he is described in some of the Purāṇas as Śuṅgabhṛtyā (शुंगभृत्या), and his dynasty as the Śuṅgabhṛtyā Dynasty (*Matsya Purāṇa* 272.35; Śrīmad *Bhāgavata* 12.1.22). Śuṅgabhṛtyā in Sanskrit means the servants of the Śuṅga. The chronology of this dynasty is given in Table 21.

Pandit Venkatachelam (1957a, p. 113) adds:

“ It appears also from these Puranas that Vasudeva, the Brahmin minister of Devabhuti, had not altogether done away with the family of his master, for there are statements in the Puranas that the Andhra kings who came next, annexed not only the kingdom of the Kanvas but also what yet remained of the once powerful Sunga Dynasty. So it is most likely that Vasudeva ruled the kingdom with Girivraja as his capital, and the descendants of his master ruled a portion of the country with Vidisa, the modern Vilsa, as their capital. ” [There is a city called Vidisha in present-day Madhya Pradesh.]

1. **Vasudeva** (वसुदेव) is said to have ruled the kingdom of Magadha with justice and efficiency for 39 years according to Kaliyuga Rājavṛttānta, and the correct Matsya, and Vāyu Purāṇas, from Yudhiṣṭhira Śaka 2220 to 2259 (918–879 BC). Current copies of Matsya and Vāyu Purāṇas give him

**Table 21: Chronology of the Kaṇva Dynasty, Yudhiṣṭhira Śaka 2220–2305 (918–833 BC)**

| Sr. No. | Name of the King | Years of Reign | STARTING YEAR IN Yudhiṣṭhira Śaka | Kaliyuga | BC |
|---|---|---|---|---|---|
| 1 | Vasudeva (वसुदेव) | 39 | 2220 | 2184 | 918 |
| 2 | Bhūmimitra (भूमिमित्र) | 24 | 2259 | 2223 | 879 |
| 3 | Nārāyaṇa (नारायण) | 12 | 2283 | 2247 | 855 |
| 4 | Suśarmā (सुशर्मा) | 10 | 2295 | 2259 | 843 |
| | **Total** | **85** | **2220–2305** | **2184–2269** | **918–833** |

only nine years and the Brahmāṇḍa Purāṇa gives him only five years of reign. The colonial era Indologists assigned him a reign of nine years.

2. **Bhūmimitra** (भूमिमित्र) according to Matsya and Brahmāṇḍa Purāṇas, **Bhūmitra** (भूमित्र) according to Viṣṇu and Bhāgavata Purāṇas or **Bhūtimitra** (भूतिमित्र) according to one copy of Vāyu Purāṇa, ruled for 24 years (Vāyu and Brahmāṇḍa Purāṇas, the correct copy of Matsya Purāṇa, and Kaliyuga Rājavṛttānta), from Yudhiṣṭhira Śaka 2259 to 2283 (879–855 BC). The present corrupted copy of Matsya Purāṇa gives him a reign of 14 years.

3. **Nārāyaṇa** (नारायण) ruled for 12 years according to all the Purāṇas (Kaliyuga Rājavṛttānta, Matsya, Vāyu, and Brahmāṇḍa Purāṇas), from Yudhiṣṭhira Śaka 2283 to 2295 (855–843 BC).

4. **Suśarmā** (सुशर्मा), son of Nārāyaṇa, the last king of the dynasty, reigned for ten years according to all the Purāṇas (Kaliyuga Rājavṛttānta, Matsya, and Vāyu Purāṇas), from Yudhiṣṭhira Śaka 2295 to 2305 (843–833 BC). A copy of Brahmāṇḍa Purāṇa gives him only four years of reign.

As Pandit Venkatachelam (1957a) has observed, all editions of the *Matsya Purāṇa* (272.36) uniformly state that the four kings of the Kaṇva Dynasty ruled Magadha for a total of 85 years, as follows.

चत्वारिंशद् द्विजा ह्येते काण्वा भोक्ष्यन्ति वै महीम् ।
चत्वारिंशत् पञ्च चैव भोक्ष्यन्तीमां वसुंधराम् ।। ३६ ।।

Catvāriṁśad dvijā hyete Kāṇvā bhokṣyanti vai mahīm ।
Catvāriṁśat pañca caiva bhokṣyantīmāṁ vasundharām ।।36 ।।

The above verse states that these Brahmin kings of the Kaṇva Dynasty will reign for 40 years. They will also reign the earth for another 40 and 5 years.

Some scholars and a Hindi translation (Gita Press) of this Purāṇa interpreted the verse as 40 Kaṇva brahmins will rule the earth for 45 years, which is absurd. As stated by Pandit Venkatachelam, Kaliyuga Rājavṛttānta states in unmistakable terms that these four kings reigned for 85 years, which exactly tallies with the total of the reign of the individual kings. See the detailed analysis of the verses from the various Purāṇas by Pandit Venkatachelam (1957a, p. 113–119).

### Distortion by Colonial Era European Indologists

The colonial era European Indologists ignored the first 40 years stated in the preceding verse and gave these 4 kings a total reign of only 45 years instead of 85 years. Presently available corrupted copies of Brahmāṇḍa, Vāyu, and Viṣṇu Purāṇas give these kings only 45 years of total reign.

## Āndhra Dynasty, Yudhiṣṭhira Śaka 2305–2811 (833–327 BC)

Śimuka ŚrīŚātakarṇi (शिमुक श्रीशातकर्णि) founded the Āndhra Dynasty of the Magadha kings. He traced his origin to the Āndhra Dynasty of kings founded by Śātavāhana (शातवाहन) in the south with Pratishthana as his capital. Śimuka's family name was Balin (बलिन्) by Kaliyuga Rājavṛttānta, Balika (बलिक) by Bhāgavata Purāṇa, or Balipucchaka (बलिपुच्छक) by Viṣṇu Purāṇa.

He is said to have served as a minister under the last two kings of the Kaṇva Dynasty, who appear to have been puppets in his hands. With the aid of the Āndhra forces in his service, he killed Suśarmā, the last king of the Kaṇva Dynasty, and not only usurped the throne of Magadha but also all that remained of the later Śuṅgas who were ruling a small portion of the empire from Vidisha as their capital, simultaneously with Kaṇvas.

All the Purāṇas unanimously state that 836 years elapsed between the coronation of Mahāpadma Nanda and the beginning of the Āndhra kings known as Paulomā as shown in the following verse from *Matsya Purāṇa* (273.37).

पौलोमास्तु तथान्ध्रास्तु महापद्मान्तरे पुनः ।
अनन्तरं शतान्यष्टौ षट्त्रिंशत्तु तु समास्तथा ।। ३७ ।।

Paulomāstu tathĀndhrāstu Mahāpadmāntare punaḥ ।
Anantaraṁ śatānyaṣṭau saṭtriṁśat tu samāstathā ।। 37 ।।

The interval between the dates of the coronation of Mahāpadma (1634 BC) and the beginning of the Āndhra Dynasty (833 BC) is 801 years per the chronology given here. *Kaliyuga Rājavṛttānta* gives 800 years (Krishnamachariar, 1937, p. lxxx; Venkatachelam, 1953b, p. 41). Adding 1,504 years from the Mahābhārata War to the coronation of Mahāpadma Nanda, and then 801 years elapsed from the coronation of Mahāpadma to the beginning of the Āndhra Dynasty, gives a total of 2,305 years from the time of the Mahābhārata War to the beginning of the Āndhra Dynasty. If 836 years are added instead of 801 years, the total years come to 2,340 years. These totals are confirmed by the following verse from *Vāyu Purāṇa* (99.423), referring to the movement of the Saptarṣi (Big Dipper) in the Saptarṣi Era.

सप्तर्षयो मघायुक्ताः काले पारिक्षिते शतम् ।
अन्ध्रांशे सचतुर्विंशे भविष्यन्ति मते मम ।। ४२३ ।।

Saptarṣayo maghāyuktāḥ kāle Pārikṣite śatam ।
Andhrāṁśe sacaturviṁśe bhaviṣyanti mate mama ।। 423 ।।

Translation:

> Saptarṣi (Big Dipper) were in the Maghā (Nakṣatra) for a hundred years (had completed 100 years) at the time of Parīkṣit. At the time of the Āndhrās, they will be in the 24th (nakṣatra).

The Saptarṣi spend one hundred years in each nakṣatra as discussed earlier. Therefore, according to this verse, at the time of the Āndhra Dynasty, 2,300 years were completed from the time of Parīkṣit, and the Saptarṣi were in the 24th nakṣatra. Thus, the chronology given here is amply supported by the Saptarṣi cycle described in the Purāṇas.

## Distortion by Pargiter

To support the shortened chronology, F. E. Pargiter (1913, p. 75) argued that the verses in the Purāṇas had a mistake and suggested altering them. Then, he proceeded to alter them in his book, *The Dynasties of Kali Age*, and base his interpretation on the altered verses! Pandit Venkatachelam (1957a, p. 206–210) has discussed this in detail, calling it high-handed meddling with the text of the Purāṇas.

A complete list of all Āndhra kings of Magadha along with their years of reign is shown in Table 22. The Āndhra Emperors of Magadha claimed to belong to Śātavahana (शातवाहन) lineage and assumed the title of Śātakarṇi (शातकर्णि); they are described with the titles of Śātavāhana and Śātakarṇi in the Purāṇas. The same titles are found in their inscriptions also. Śāta means lion and Śātavāhana means one who uses a lion as his vehicle.

**Table 22: Chronology of the Āndhra Śātavāhana Dynasty, Yudhiṣṭhira Śaka 2305–2811 (833–327 BC)**

| Sr. No. | Name of the King | Years of Reign | STARTING YEAR IN | | |
|---|---|---|---|---|---|
| | | | Yudhiṣṭhira Śaka | Kaliyuga | BC |
| 1 | Siṁhaka ŚrīŚātakarṇi (सिंहक श्रीशातकर्णि) | 23 | 2305 | 2269 | 833 |
| 2 | Kṛṣṇa ŚrīŚātakarṇi (कृष्ण श्रीशातकर्णि) | 18 | 2328 | 2292 | 810 |
| 3 | ŚrīMalla Śātakarṇi (श्रीमल्ल शातकर्णि) | 10 | 2346 | 2310 | 792 |
| 4 | Pūrṇotsaṅga (पूर्णोत्संग) | 18 | 2356 | 2320 | 782 |
| 5 | ŚrīŚātakarṇi (श्रीशातकर्णि) | 56 | 2374 | 2338 | 764 |
| 6 | Skandhastambhi (स्कंधस्तंभि) | 18 | 2430 | 2394 | 708 |
| 7 | Laṁbodara (लंबोदर) | 18 | 2448 | 2412 | 690 |
| 8 | Apītaka (अपीतक) | 12 | 2466 | 2430 | 672 |
| 9 | Meghasvāti (मेघस्वाति) | 18 | 2478 | 2442 | 660 |
| 10 | Śātasvāti (शातस्वाति) | 18 | 2496 | 2460 | 642 |
| 11 | ŚriSkanda Śātakarṇi (श्रीस्कंद शातकर्णि) | 7 | 2514 | 2478 | 624 |
| 12 | Mṛgendra Śātakarṇi (मृगेन्द्र शातकर्णि) | 3 | 2521 | 2485 | 617 |
| 13 | Kuntala Śātakarṇi (कुंतल शातकर्णि) | 8 | 2524 | 2488 | 614 |
| 14 | Saumya Śātakarṇi (सौम्य शातकर्णि) | 12 | 2532 | 2496 | 606 |
| 15 | Śāta Śātakarṇi (शात शातकर्णि) | 1 | 2544 | 2508 | 594 |
| 16 | Puloma Śātakarṇi (पुलोम शातकर्णि) | 36 | 2545 | 2509 | 593 |
| 17 | Megha Śātakarṇi (मेघ शातकर्णि) | 38 | 2581 | 2545 | 557 |

| Sr. No. | Name of the King | Years of Reign | STARTING YEAR IN Yudhiṣṭhira Śaka | Kaliyuga | BC |
|---|---|---|---|---|---|
| 18 | Ariṣṭa Śātakarṇi (अरिष्ट शातकर्णि) | 25 | 2619 | 2583 | 519 |
| 19 | Hāla (हाल) | 5 | 2644 | 2608 | 494 |
| 20 | Maṇḍalaka (मंडलक) | 5 | 2649 | 2613 | 489 |
| 21 | Purīndrasena (पुरीन्द्रसेन) | 21 | 2654 | 2618 | 484 |
| 22 | Sundara Śātakarṇi (सुंदर शातकर्णि) | 1 | 2675 | 2639 | 463 |
| 23a | Cakora Śātakarṇi (चकोर शातकर्णि) | ½ | 2676 | 2640 | 462 |
| 23b | Mahendra Śātakarṇi (महेन्द्र शातकर्णि) | ½ | 2676 | 2640 | 461½ |
| 24 | Śiva Śātakarṇi (शिव शातकर्णि) | 28 | 2677 | 2641 | 461 |
| 25 | Gautamīputra Śātakarṇi (गौतमीपुत्र शातकर्णि) | 25 | 2705 | 2669 | 433 |
| 26 | Pulomā II (पुलोमा २) | 32 | 2730 | 2694 | 408 |
| 27 | ŚivaŚrī Śātakarṇi (शिवश्री शातकर्णि) | 7 | 2762 | 2726 | 376 |
| 28 | Śivaskanda Śātakarṇi (शिवस्कन्द शातकर्णि) | 7 | 2769 | 2733 | 369 |
| 29 | YajñaŚrī Śātakarṇi (यज्ञश्री शातकर्णि) | 19 | 2776 | 2740 | 362 |
| 30 | VijayaŚrī Śātakarṇi (विजयश्री शातकर्णि) | 6 | 2795 | 2759 | 343 |
| 31 | ChandraŚrī Śātakarṇi (चन्द्रश्री शातकर्णि) | 3 | 2801 | 2765 | 337 |
| 32 | Pulomā III (पुलोमा 3) | 7 | 2804 | 2768 | 334 |
| | **Total** | **506** | **2305–2811** | **2269–2775** | **833–327** |

1. **Siṁhaka ŚrīŚātakarṇi** (सिंहक श्रीशातकर्णि) or **Śimuka ŚrīŚātakarṇi** (शिमुक श्रीशातकर्णि) according to Kaliyuga Rājavṛttānta, **Śiśuka** (शिशुक) by Matsya Purāṇa, or **Sindhuka** (सिंधुक) by Vāyu and Brahmāṇḍa Purāṇas founded the Āndhra Dynasty of the Magadha kings. He reigned for 23 years, according to all the Purāṇas, from Yudhiṣṭhira Śaka 2305 to 2328 (833–810 BC).

2. **Kṛṣṇa ŚrīŚātakarṇi** (कृष्ण श्रीशातकर्णि) according to Kaliyuga Rājavṛttānta or **Kṛṣṇa** (कृष्ण) according to all other Purāṇas (Matsya, Brahmāṇḍa, Viṣṇu and Bhāgavata), the younger brother of Śimuka, reigned for 18 years, according to all the Purāṇas, from Yudhiṣṭhira Śaka 2328 to 2346 (810–792 BC). The current copy of Brahmāṇḍa Purāṇa gives him only ten years of reign. This king, colloquially known as Kanha, is said to have extended his kingdom as far as Nasik, near the source of Godavari in the Western Ghats (Venkatachelam, 1957a, p. 178).

3. **ŚrīMalla Śātakarṇi** (श्रीमल्ल शातकर्णि) according to Kaliyuga Rājavṛttānta, **Śrī Śātakarṇi** (श्री शातकर्णि) by Matsya Purāṇa, **Śrī Śāntakarṇi** (श्री शांतकर्णि) by Viṣṇu Purāṇa or **Śrī Śāntakarṇa** (श्री शांतकर्ण) by Bhāgavata Purāṇa, son of Kṛṣṇa, reigned for ten years, according to Matsya Purāṇa and Kaliyuga Rājavṛttānta, from Yudhiṣṭhira Śaka 2346 to 2356 (792–782 BC). Currently available copies of Vāyu and Brahmāṇḍa Purāṇas miss this king.

4. **Pūrṇotsaṅga** (पूर्णोत्संग) by Kaliyuga Rājavṛttānta, Matsya and Viṣṇu Purāṇas or **Paūrṇamāsa** (पौर्णमास) by Bhāgavat Purāṇa, son of ŚriMalla Śātakarṇi, reigned according to all the Purāṇas, for 18 years, from Yudhiṣṭhira Śaka 2356 to 2374 (782–764 BC). Currently available copies of Vāyu and Brahmāṇḍa Purāṇas miss this king.

5. **ŚriŚātkarṇi** (श्रीशातकर्णि) by Kaliyuga Rājavṛttānta and Vāyu Purāṇa, **Śāntakarṇi** (शांतकर्णि) by Matsya and Brahmāṇḍa Purāṇas or **Śātakarṇi** (शातकर्णि) by Viṣṇu Purāṇa, son of Pūrṇotsaṅga, reigned for 56 years from Yudhiṣṭhira Śaka 2374 to 2430 (764–708 BC). Vāyu and Brahmāṇḍa Purāṇas describe him as a great king. While all the Purāṇas assign this king a reign of 56 years, Vincent Smith assigns him a reign of only 40 years arbitrarily! The current version of Matsya Purāṇa has the order of this king and the next reversed.

6. **Skandhastambhi** (स्कंधस्तंभि) according to Kaliyuga Rājavṛttānta and Matsya Purāṇa, son of ŚrīŚātakarṇi, reigned for 18 years from Yudhiṣṭhira Śaka 2430 to 2448 (708–690 BC). The other Purāṇas do not mention this name.

7. **Laṁbodara** (लंबोदर) according to Kaliyuga Rājavṛttānta, Matsya, Viṣṇu and Bhāgavat Purāṇas, son of Skandhastambhi, reigned for 18 years from Yudhiṣṭhira Śaka 2448 to 2466 (690–672 BC). Vāyu and Brahmāṇḍa Purāṇas omit his name.

8. **Apītaka** (अपीतक) by Kaliyuga Rājavṛttānta, **Āpītaka** (आपीतक) by Matsya Purāṇa, **Pilaka** (पिलक) by Viṣṇu Purāṇa, **Cibilaka** (चिबिलक) by Bhāgavata

Purāṇa, **Āpādabaddha** (आपादबद्ध) by Vāyu Purāṇa or **Āpolava** (आपोलव) by Brahmāṇḍa Purāṇa, son of Laṁbodara, reigned for 12 years, according to Kaliyuga Rājavṛttānta, Matsya, Vāyu and Brahmāṇḍa Purāṇas, from Yudhiṣṭhira Śaka 2466 to 2478 (672–660 BC). Present versions of Vāyu Purāṇa give him only ten years.

9. **Meghasvāti** (मेघस्वाति) according to Kaliyuga Rājavṛttānta, Matsya, Viṣṇu, and Bhāgavata Purāṇas, son of Apītaka, reigned for 18 years according to Matsya Purāṇa and Kaliyuga Rājavṛttānta, from Yudhiṣṭhira Śaka 2478 to 2496 (660–642 BC). Brahmāṇḍa and Vāyu Purāṇas omit his name.

10. **Śātsvāti** (शातस्वाति) according to Kaliyuga Rājavṛttānta or **Svāti** (स्वाति) by Matsya Purāṇa, son of Meghasvāti, reigned for 18 years, according to Matsya Purāṇa and Kaliyuga Rājavṛttānta, from Yudhiṣṭhira Śaka 2496 to 2514 (642–624 BC). The other Purāṇas omit his name.

11. **ŚriSkanda Śātakarṇi** (श्रीस्कंद शातकर्णि) by Kaliyuga Rājavṛttānta or **Skandasvāti** (स्कंदस्वाति) by Matsya Purāṇa, son of Śātasvāti, reigned for seven years, according to Matsya Purāṇa and Kaliyuga Rājavṛttānta, from Yudhiṣṭhira Śaka 2514 to 2521 (624–617 BC). Other Purāṇas omit his name.

12. **Mṛgendra Śātakarṇi** (मृगेन्द्र शातकर्णि) by Kaliyuga Rājavṛttānta or **Mṛgendra Svātikarṇa** (मृगेन्द्र स्वातिकर्ण) by Matsya Purāṇa, son of Skandasvāti, reigned according to these Purāṇas for three years from Yudhiṣṭhira Śaka 2521 to 2524 (617–614 BC). The other Purāṇas omit his name.

13. **Kuntala Śātakarṇi** (कुंतल शातकर्णि) by Kaliyuga Rājavṛttānta or **Kuntala Svātikarṇa** (कुंतल स्वातिकर्ण) according to Matsya Purāṇa, son of Mṛgendra Svātikarṇa, reigned for eight years according to these Purāṇas, from Yudhiṣṭhira Śaka 2524 to 2532 (614–606 BC). The other Purāṇas omit his name.

14. **Saumya Śātakarṇi** (सौम्य शातकर्णि) according to Kaliyuga Rājavṛttānta, son of Kuntala Svātikarṇa, reigned for 12 years according to Kaliyuga Rājavṛttānta and one version of Matsya Purāṇa which Pandit Venkatachelam had, from Yudhiṣṭhira Śaka 2532 to 2544 (606–594 BC). The other Purāṇas omit this name.

15. **Śāta Śātakarṇi** (शात शातकर्णि) according to Kaliyuga Rājavṛttānta or **Svātikarṇa** (स्वातिकर्ण) by Matsya Purāṇa, son of Saumya Śātakarṇi, reigned for one year according to these Purāṇas, from Yudhiṣṭhira Śaka 2544 to 2545 (594–593 BC). The other Purāṇas omit his name.

16. **Puloma Śātakarṇi** (पुलोम शातकर्णि) according to Kaliyuga Rājavṛttānta, **Pulomāvi** by (पुलोमावि) by Matsya Purāṇa in Telugu (Venkatachelam 1957a, p. 181), **Patumāna** (पटुमान) by Viṣṇu and Brahmāṇḍa Purāṇas or **Atamāna** (अटमान) by Bhāgavata Purāṇa, son of Śāta Śātakarani, reigned for 36 years according to Kaliyuga Rājavṛttānta and the correct version of Matsya Purāṇa, from Yudhiṣṭhira Śaka 2545 to 2581 (593–557 BC). The verse in the Vāyu and Brahmāṇḍa Purāṇas is corrupted and gives him a reign of 24 years. The present copy of Matsya Purāṇa misses this king. See *Chronology of Ancient Hindu History Part I* (Venkatachelam, 1957a, p. 181) for further details.

17. **Megha Śātakarṇi** (मेघ शातकर्णि) according to Kaliyuga Rājavṛttānta and the correct copy of Matsya Purāṇa), son of Puloma Śātakarṇi, reigned for 38 years according to Kaliyuga Rājavṛttānta, from Yudhiṣṭhira Śaka 2581 to 2619 (557–519 BC). The other Purāṇas omit his name.

18. **Ariṣta Śātakarṇi** (अरिष्ट शातकर्णि) according to Kaliyuga Rājavṛttānta, **Riktavaṇa** (रिक्तवर्ण) by Matsya Purāṇa, **Aniṣtakarmā** (अनिष्टकर्मा) by Brahmāṇḍa and Bhāgavata Purāṇas, **Ariṣtakarmā** (अरिष्टकर्मा) by Viṣṇu Purāṇa or **Nemikṛṣṇa** (नेमिकृष्ण) by Vāyu Purāṇa, son of Megha Śātakarṇi, reigned for 25 years, according to all the Purāṇas, from Yudhiṣṭhira Śaka 2619 to 2644 (519–494 BC).

19. **Hāla** (हाल) according to Kaliyuga Rājavṛttānta, Matsya, Vāyu, and Brahmāṇḍa Purāṇas, **Hālāhala** (हालाहल) by Viṣṇu Purāṇa or **Hāleya** (हालेय) by Bhāgavata Purāṇa, son of Ariṣta Śātakarṇi, reigned for 5 years according to all the Purāṇas, from Yudhiṣṭhira Śaka 2644 to 2649 (494–489 BC). Presently available copies of Vāyu and Brahmāṇḍa Purāṇas, which are corrupted, give him one year of reign.

> “We learn from Chitsukha’s Brihat Sankarvijaya and Sadasivendra’s Jagadguru Ratnamālā that Śrī Ādi Śaṅkarāchārya was a contemporary of King Hāla.” (Venkatachelam, 1957a, p. 182)

Hāla is said to have bestowed special attention to the development of the Prākrut or vernacular literature of the country. The Katantra grammar, arranged with special reference to the needs of the students more familiar with the vernacular speech than with the classical language, is attributed to one of the ministers of this king. Hāla himself is credited with the composition of the anthology of erotic verses, called the *Sapta-Śataka* or *The Seven Centuries* written in the ancient Maharashtri dialect (Venkatachelam, 1957a, p. 182).

20. **Maṇḍalaka** (मंडलक), according to Kaliyuga Rājavṛttānta and correct Matsya Purāṇa, **Mantulaka** (मंतुलक) by currently available Matsya Purāṇa, **Pattalaka** (पत्तलक) by Brahmāṇḍa Purāṇa, **Palalaka** (पललक) by Viṣṇu Purāṇa or **Talaka** (तलक) by Bhāgavata Purāṇa, son of Hāla, reigned for five years according to all the Purāṇas, from Yudhiṣṭhira Śaka 2649 to 2654 (489–484 BC).

21. **Purīndrasena** (पुरीन्द्रसेन) according to Kaliyuga Rājavṛttānta and Matsya Purāṇa, **Putrikaṣeṇa** (पुत्रिकषेण) by Vāyu Purāṇa, **Pulindasena** (पुलिंदसेन) by one version of Viṣṇu Purāṇa or **Purīṣabhīru** (पुरीषभीरु) by Brahmāṇḍa and Bhāgavata Purāṇas, son of Manḍalaka, reigned for 21 years according to all the Purāṇas (Matsya, Vāyu, Brahmāṇḍa) and Kaliyuga Rājavṛttānta, from Yudhiṣṭhira Śaka 2654 to 2675 (484–463 BC). Vincent Smith gives him only five years of reign, arbitrarily.

22. **Sundara Śātakarṇi** (सुंदर शातकर्णि) according to Kaliyuga Rājavṛttānta, **Sundara Śāntikarṇa** (सुंदर शांतिकर्ण) by Matsya Purāṇa, Śātakarṇi (शातकर्णि) by Vāyu and Brahmāṇḍa Purāṇas, **Sundara** (सुंदर) or **Sunandana** (सुनंदन) by Bhāgavata Purāṇa, son of Purīndrasena, reigned according to all the Purāṇas for a year from Yudhiṣṭhira Śaka 2675 to 2676 (463–462 BC).

23a. **Cakora Śātakarṇi** (चकोर शातकर्णि) according to Kaliyuga Rājavṛttānta, **Cakora Svātikarṇa** (चकोर स्वातिकर्ण) by Matsya Purāṇa, **Cakāra Śātakarṇi** (चकार शातकर्णि) by Vāyu Purāṇa or **Śātakarṇi** (शातकर्णि) by Viṣṇu Purāṇa, son of Sundara Śātakarṇi, reigned according to all the Purāṇas for only six months, in Yudhiṣṭhira Śaka 2676 (ca. 462–461 BC). Vincent Smith calls this king Yilivayakura I (Venkatachelam, 1957a, p. 184).

23b. **Mahendra** Śātakarṇi (महेन्द्र शातकर्णि) according to Kaliyuga Rājavṛttānta and one version of Matsya Purāṇa, also the son of Sundara Śātakarṇi, reigned for three months only according to these Purāṇas. We may give these two kings roughly one year for their total reign. The other Purāṇas omit their names.

24. **Śiva Śātakarṇi** (शिव शातकर्णि) according to one version of Matsya Purāṇa, **Śivasvāti** (शिवस्वाति) by Kaliyuga Rājavṛttānta, Matsya, Brahmāṇḍa, Viṣṇu and Bhāgavata Purāṇas or **Śivasvāmi** (शिवस्वामि) by Vāyu Purāṇa, son of Mahendra Śātakarṇi, reigned for 28 years according to all the Purāṇas, from Yudhiṣṭhira Śaka 2677 to 2705 (461–433 BC). Vincent Smith calls him Śivalakura.

25. **Gautamīputra Śātakarṇi** (गौतमीपुत्र शातकर्णि) according to Kaliyuga Rājavṛttānta and Matsya Purāṇa, **Gautamīputra** (गौतमीपुत्र) by Vāyu and Brahmāṇḍa Purāṇas or **Gomatiputra** (गोमतिपुत्र) by Bhāgavata Purāṇa and one version of Viṣṇu Purāṇa, son of Śiva Śātakarṇi, reigned for 25 years per Kaliyuga Rājavṛttānta and correct Matsya Purāṇa, from Yudhiṣṭhira Śaka 2705 to 2730 (433–408 BC). Vāyu and Brahmāṇḍa Purāṇas and the present copy of Matsya Purāṇa give him only 21 years. Vincent Smith calls this king Villivayakura II and gives him a reign of 25 years as determined approximately by inscriptions. He destroyed the Śaka Nahapāna's Kṣaharāta family according to the epigraphic and numismatic evidence (Smith, 1914, p. 210; Sethna, 1989, p. 54).

26. **Pulomā II** (पुलोमा 2) according to Matsya Purāṇa, **PulomaŚrī Śātakarṇi** (पुलोमश्री शातकर्णि) or **Vāśiṣṭīputra** (वाशिष्टीपुत्र) by Kaliyuga Rājavṛttānta, **Alimān** (अलिमान्) by Viṣṇu Purāṇa or **Purīmān** (पुरीमान्) by Bhāgavata Purāṇa, son of Gautamīputra, reigned for 32 years per Kaliyuga Rājavṛttānta and Matsya Purāṇa, from Yudhiṣṭhira Śaka 2730 to 2762 (408–376 BC). A copy of Brahmāṇḍa Purāṇa which Pandit Venkatachelam had, called him **Yantramati** and assigned him a reign of 34 years. Present copies of Vāyu and Brahmāṇḍa Purāṇas omit his name. Vincent Smith (1914, p. 211) calls this king Pulumayi and assigns him 28 years. With the end of this king, the first cycle (of 2,700 years) of the Laukikābda (or Kashmirābda or Saptarṣi) of 3076 BC was completed in 376 BC.

27. **ŚivaŚrī Śātakarṇi** (शिवश्री शातकर्णि) according to Kaliyuga Rājavṛttānta, ŚivaŚrīta Śātakarṇi (शिवश्रीत शातकर्णि) by Viṣṇu Purāṇa, **ŚivaŚrī Pulomā** (शिवश्री पुलोमा) by Matsya Purāṇa or **Medah Śirā** (मेदः शिरा) by Bhāgavata Purāṇa, brother of Pulomā II, reigned according to all the Purāṇas for 7 years, from Yudhiṣṭhira Śaka 2762 to 2769 (376–369 BC). The present copies of the Vāyu and Brahmāṇḍa Purāṇas omit his name.

28. **Śivaskanda Śātakarṇi** (शिवस्कन्द शातकर्णि) according to Kaliyuga Rājavṛttānta, Matsya and Viṣṇu Purāṇas or **Śivaskanda** (शिवस्कन्द) by Bhāgavata Purāṇa reigned according to all the Purāṇas for seven years from Yudhiṣṭhira Śaka 2669 to 2776 (369–362 BC). Present copies of Vāyu, and Brahmāṇḍa Purāṇas omit this king.

29. **YajñaŚrī Śātakarṇi** (यज्ञश्री शातकर्णि) according to Vāyu and Brahmāṇḍa Purāṇas, **YajñaŚrī** (यज्ञश्री) by Viṣṇu and Bhāgavata Purāṇas, YajñaŚrī **Śātakarṇi** or **Gautamīputra** (गौतमीपुत्र) by Kaliyuga Rājavṛttānta or **YajñaŚrī Śantikarṇi** (यज्ञश्री शांतिकर्णि) by Matsya Purāṇa, son of Śivaskanda

Śātakarṇi, reigned for 19 years, according to Kaliyuga Rājavṛttānta, Vāyu and Brahmāṇḍa Purāṇas, from Yudhiṣṭhira Śaka 2776 to 2795 (362–343 BC). The present copy of Matsya Purāṇa and Vincent Smith (1914, p. 211) give him a reign of 29 years.

30. **VijayaŚrī Śātakarṇi** (विजयश्री शातकर्णि) according to Kaliyuga Rājavṛttānta, simply **Vijaya** (विजय) by Matsya, Vāyu, Brahmāṇḍa, a version of Viṣṇu and Bhāgavata Purāṇas or **Dviyajña** (द्वियज्ञ) by Viṣṇu Purāṇa, son of YajñaŚrī Śātakarṇi, reigned according to all the Purāṇas for six years, from Yudhiṣṭhira Śaka 2795 to 2801 (343–337 BC).

31. **ChandraŚrī* Śātakarṇi** (चन्द्रश्री शातकर्णि) according to Kaliyuga Rājavṛttānta and the correct Matsya Purāṇa (which Pandit Venkatachelam had), known as **Vāśiṣṭīputra** (वाशिष्टीपुत्र) by Kaliyuga Rājavṛttānta, **DaṇḍaŚrī Śātakarṇi** (दण्डश्री शातकर्णि) by one version of Vāyu and Brahmāṇḍa Purāṇas, **ChandraŚrī** (चन्द्रश्री) by Viṣṇu Purāṇa or **Chandravijña** (चन्द्रविज्ञ) by Bhāgavat Purāṇa, son of VijayaŚrī Śātakarṇi reigned for three years according to Kaliyuga Rājavṛttānta, Vāyu and Brahmāṇḍa Purāṇas, from Yudhiṣṭhira Śaka 2801 to 2804 (337–334 BC). Presently available copy of Matsya Purāṇa calls him **ChaṇḍaŚrī Śāntikarṇi** (चण्डश्री शान्तिकर्णि) and gives him a reign of ten years.

(*spelled **CandraŚrī** per the transliteration guide)

32. **Pulomā III** (पुलोमा 3) according to Kaliyuga Rājavṛttānta and Matsya Purāṇa, **Pulomāci** (पुलोमाचि) by Viṣṇu Purāṇa, **Pulomāri** (पुलोमारि) by Brahmāṇḍa Purāṇa or **Lomadhi** (लोमधि) by Bhāgavata Purāṇa, son of ChandraŚrī, according to all the Purāṇas reigned for seven years, from Yudhiṣṭhira Śaka 2804 to 2811 (334–327 BC). Vincent Smith calls him Pulumayi IV, with whom the long Āndhra Dynasty ended. Puloma III was murdered by his regent and Commander-in-chief Chandragupta, the founder of the Gupta Dynasty.

Thus, these 32 kings of the Āndhra Dynasty ruled Magadha for a total of 506 years, from Yudhiṣṭhira Śaka 2305 to 2811 (833–327 BC). Various Purāṇas list 16 to 32 kings and all of them give a total reign of 456 to 506 years for the dynasty. Viṣṇu Purāṇa lists 23 kings whereas the Vāyu and Brahmāṇḍa Purāṇas list only 16 kings. Kaliyuga Rājavṛttānta and the correct Matsya Purāṇa which Pandit Venkatachelam had, listed all 32 kings with their individual reigning periods and they closely agreed with each other. See *History of Classical Sanskrit Literature* (Krishnamachariar, 1937, p. liv) or *Chronology of*

*Ancient Hindu History Part I* (Venkatachelam, 1957a, p. 186) for the full set of verses for the Āndhra Dynasty from Kaliyuga Rājavṛttānta.

## Confirmation by the Saptarṣi Cycle

As mentioned in Chapter 5, the Saptarṣi (Big Dipper) were in the Maghā (मघा) Nakṣatra (lunar asterism) at the time of Parīkṣit. As discussed in Chapter 4, it takes 2,700 years for the Saptarṣi to complete one cycle through the 27 nakṣatras. The cycle was completed during the time of the 27th Āndhra king according to the following verses from *Brahmāṇḍa Purāṇa* (74.230–231). This corroborates the 2,700 years elapsed from the time of Parīkṣit to the time of the 27th Āndhra king.

सप्तर्षयस्तदा प्राप्ताः पित्र्ये पारिक्षिते शतम् ।
सप्तविंशैः शतैर्भाव्या अन्ध्राणां तेऽन्वयाः पुनः ।। २३० ।।

सप्तविंशतिपर्यंते कृत्स्ने नक्षत्रमंडले ।
सप्तर्षयस्तु तिष्ठंति पर्यायेण शतंशतम् ।। २३१ ।।

Saptarṣayastadā prāptāḥ pitrye Pārikṣite śatam ।
Saptaviṁśaiḥ śatairbhāvyā Andhrāṇāṁ te'nvayāḥ punaḥ ।। 230 ।।

Saptaviṁśati-paryante kṛtsne nakṣatramaṇdale ।
Saptarṣayastu tiṣthanti paryāyeṇa śataṁ-śatam ।। 231 ।।

Translation:

> The Saptarṣi were in the *Pitrya* (Maghā Nakṣatra), during the time of Parīkṣit, where they had completed a hundred years. There are twenty-seven nakṣatras. The Saptarṣi stay for a hundred years in each nakṣatra. In twenty-seven hundred years, they will start the new cycle again during the time of the (27th king) of the Āndhras (Venkatachelam, 1957a, p. 206).

## Distortion by Colonial Era Indologists

Despite such details given in the Purāṇas, the European Indologists of the 19th and early 20th centuries did not accept the existence of the Āndhra kings for a long time. Afterward, when inscriptions and coins of the Āndhra kings were found, they could not believe the existence of 30 Śātavāhana kings and their titles. The titles of these kings were in the Purāṇas before the inscriptions were found. Similarly, the names of the Gupta emperors and their titles are found in the Kaliyuga Rājavṛttānta (Venkatachelam, 1957b, p. 169–170).

## Pargiter's meddling with the Purāṇas

Colonial Era Indologists did not stop at misinterpreting the Purāṇas. They even proceeded to alter them as they saw fit. Figure 22 shows the changes Pargiter (1913, p. 59, footnote 46) made in the verse 271.39 of *Matsya Purāṇa* and the similar verses in the other Purāṇas.

| | |
|---|---|
| saptarṣayas tadā [40] prāṁśu [41] | saptarṣayas tadā prāhuḥ [42] |
| pradīpten=âgninā [43] samāḥ [44] | Pratīpe rājñi [45] vai śatam [46] |
| sapta[47]-viṁśati-bhāvyānām [48] | sapta-viṁśaiḥ śatair [49] bhāvyā [50] |
| Āndhrāṇ=ânte[51] 'nvagāt[52] punaḥ[53] | Andhrāṇ=ânte[54] 'nvayāḥ[55] punaḥ[56] |
| saptarṣayas tu vartante [57] | sapta-viṁśati[58]-paryante [59] |
| yatra [60] nakṣatra-maṇḍale | kṛtsne nakṣatra-maṇḍale |

**Figure 22: Pargiter's alteration of a verse from Vāyu Purāṇa**

The left-hand side shows the original verse and the right-hand side shows the verse altered by Pargiter. He changed the second line reading *'pradīptena agninā samāḥ* (प्रदीप्तेन अग्निना समाः)' which means 'shining bright like a fire' in the original verse to read *'Pratīpe rājñi vai* śatam (प्रतीपे राज्ञि वै शतम्)' meaning 'while Pratīpa was the king'. What authority did Pargiter have to alter the verses in the Purāṇas? Pratīpa was the father of Śāntanu as shown in Table 11 (Chapter 5). Parīkṣit was the sixth king, descending from Pratīpa. Thus, with this change, Pargiter included five more kings in the same span to justify the shrinking of the chronology.

Unfortunately, currently available copies of *Vāyu Purāṇa* (one in Sanskrit published by Anandāshrama Sanskrit Granthāvali (1983) and the one published with Hindi translation by Rama Pratap Tripathi (1987) contain Pargiter's altered version of the verse (99.418) instead of the original verse as follows.

*सप्तर्षयस्तदा प्राहुः प्रतीपे राज्ञि वै शतम् । सप्तविंशैः शतैर्भाव्या अन्ध्राणां ते त्वया पुनः ॥४१८

Fortunately, the currently available *Matsya Purāṇa* (Gita Press) still has the correct version of the verse (273.39) as shown below.

सप्तर्षयस्तदा प्रांशुप्रदीप्तेनाग्निना समाः ।

सप्तविंशतिभाव्यानामान्ध्राणां तु यदा पुनः ॥ ३९

Saptarṣayastadā prāṁśu-pradīptenāgninā samāḥ |
Saptaviṁśati-bhāvyānām-Āndhrāṇāṁ tu yadā punaḥ || 39

## Gupta Dynasty, Yudhiṣṭhira Śaka 2811–3056 (327–82 BC)

The detailed history of the Gupta Dynasty is given in the Kaliyuga Rājavṛttānta. The verses describing the Gupta Dynasty are found in the *History of Classical Sanskrit Literature* (Krishnamachariar, 1937, p. cii) and the *Chronology of Ancient Hindu History Part I* (Venkatachelam, 1957a, p. 226). Chandragupta I (चन्द्रगुप्त १) who assumed the title Vijayāditya (विजयादित्य) on account of his valor, founded the Gupta Empire. He was the son of Ghaṭoṭkaca (घटोत्कच) Gupta, and the grandson of Śrī Gupta (श्री गुप्त), from whom the dynasty took its name. Śrī Gupta and Ghatotkaca Gupta had entered into the services of ŚivaŚrī Śātakarṇi, the 27th king of the Āndhra Dynasty, as his generals and had won many great victories in the battles for him. They came from Śrī *Parvata* (mountain) in or near Nepal, hence, were known as Śrī *Pārvatiya*.

Chandragupta, by his unsurpassed valor, added greatly to the territories of the Āndhra kings and became the commander-in-chief of a large army of VijayaŚrī Śātkarṇi. Chandragupta married Kumāradevi, the daughter of the king of Nepal, by whom he had a brave and mighty son, Samudragupta. He next married a Licchavi (लिच्छवि) girl, who was the younger sister of the queen of ChandraŚrī Śātakarṇi and thus, became a brother-in-law of the king. By his Licchavi princess, Chandragupta had another son by the name 'Kaca (कच)' in short or Ghaṭoṭkaca (the same name as Chandragupta's father). It is said that the Licchavi connection elevated him from the rank of a general as enjoyed by his father and grandfather to the rank of commander-in-chief, and Chandragupta, seems to have been in charge of the kingdom under his nominal master ChandraŚrī.

It is said that the queen of ChandraŚrī had fallen in love with Chandragupta, her sister's husband. Chandragupta killed ChandraŚrī by some stratagem and then, he was appointed by the queen as regent for her minor prince Pulomā III. Chandragupta then eliminated the young king Pulomā in seven years and proclaimed himself as the king of Magadha in Yudhiṣṭhira Śaka 2811 (327 BC). Chandragupta established an era, known after his name as Gupta Yuga, starting in 327 BC. He then ruled jointly with his son Kaca, born of the Licchavi queen. Table 23 lists the kings of the Gupta Dynasty along with their years of reign.

## Distortion by Colonial Era Indologists

The date of the founding of the Gupta Dynasty was wrongly fixed at AD 320 instead of the true date of 327 BC by Vincent Smith and others because of the grave mistake of the earlier colonial Indologists in identifying Chandragupta Maurya as the contemporary of Alexander. Chandragupta I of the Gupta Dynasty was the contemporary of Alexander as discussed in detail in Chapter 2.

Miss Mable Duff (1899, p. 35) in her Chronology of India gives Śrī Gupta and Ghaṭotkaca Gupta (grandfather and father of Chandragupta I Gupta, respectively), a reign of 15 and 14 years, respectively. Śrī Gupta and Ghaṭotkaca Gupta were never the kings of Pāṭaliputra or a part of Magadha, even though they wielded a great deal of influence as generals under the later Āndhra kings. Since they served the Āndhra kings, they are known as Āndhra bhṛtyā (आन्ध्र भृत्या = servants of Āndhras), and the dynasty founded by their descendent, Chandragupta I, is known in all the Purāṇas under the general name of 'ŚrīParvatīya-Āndhrabhṛtyā (श्रीपर्वतीय आन्ध्रभृत्या) Dynasty.

**Table 23: Chronology of the Gupta Dynasty, Yudhiṣṭhira Śaka 2811–3056 (327–82 BC)**

| Sr. No. | Name of the King | Years of Reign | Starting Year in: Yudhiṣṭhira Śaka | Gupta Yuga | BC |
|---|---|---|---|---|---|
| 1 | Chandragupta I (चन्द्रगुप्त १) | 7 | 2811 | 1 | 327 |
| 2 | Samudragupta (समुद्रगुप्त) | 51 | 2818 | 7 | 320 |
| 3 | Chandragupta II (चन्द्रगुप्त २) | 36 | 2869 | 58 | 269 |
| 4 | Kumāragupta I (कुमारगुप्त १) | 42 | 2905 | 94 | 233 |
| 5 | Skandgupta (स्कन्दगुप्त) | 25 | 2947 | 136 | 191 |
| 6 | Sthiragupta (स्थिरगुप्त) | 5 | 2972 | 161 | 166 |
| 7 | Narasiṁhagupta (नरसिंहगुप्त) | 35 | 2977 | 166 | 161 |
| 8 | Kumāragupta II (कुमारगुप्त २) | 44 | 3012 | 201 | 126 |
| | **Total** | **245** | **2811–3056** | **1–245** | **327–82** |

1. **Chandragupta I** (चन्द्रगुप्त १), designated as the first, to distinguish him from his grandson of the same name, or **Vijayāditya** (विजयादित्य), is described to have extended his dominion along the Ganga valley, as far as the meeting of the Ganga and Yamuna rivers.

   It is said that before his death Chandragupta I selected Kaca, or more fully Ghaṭoṭkaca, his son by his Licchavi queen, as his successor. By then, Samudragupta, his eldest son by Kumārdevi, the daughter of the king of Nepal, had already distinguished himself in many adventures against the Mleccha invaders. When he came to know of the treachery intended by his father in selecting his half-brother, Kaca, as the successor, Samudragupta collected a band of Mlechcha soldiers and marched against his father. After killing his father and his half-brother, Samudragupta succeeded to the throne of Magadha in Pāṭaliputra in Yudhiṣṭhira Śaka 2818 (320 BC).

2. **Samudragupta** (समुद्रगुप्त), who took the title of **Aśokāditya** (अशोकादित्य), son of Chandragupta I, reigned as the emperor of India, with Pāṭaliputra as his capital for a long period of 51 years from Yudhiṣṭhira Śaka 2818 to 2869 (320–269 BC). He was a very ambitious king and went on conquests in North and South India. The account of his achievements, composed by his court poet Harisena (हरिसेन), is engraved on the *Aśoka Stambha* (pillar), currently located at Prayāg, set up in the 15th century BC by Aśoka of the Maurya Dynasty.

## Prayāg Pillar Inscription of Samudragupta

The *Aśoka Stambha* at Prayāg is one of the several stone pillars believed to have been erected by Aśoka of the Maurya Dynasty in many parts of India.

**Figure 23: Samudragupta's inscription on the Prayāg pillar of Aśoka**
*Photo courtesy: Wikimedia Commons, public domain*

The inscription of Samudragupta, also known as Prayāg Praśaśti (प्रयाग प्रशश्ति), is immediately below the inscription of Aśoka. Figure 23 shows the inscription. The inscription is in excellent Sanskrit written in the Brahmi script and is more refined than the earlier inscription attributed to Aśoka.

**Key learnings from the inscription** (Bhandarkar, 1981, p. 216–217):

1. (Verse 7) Samudragupta singly and in a moment uprooted Achyuta, Nāgāsena, and (Gaṇapati) who came together in a battle, thereafter.
2. (Verse 8, lines 17–18) He was skillful in engaging in hundreds of battles of various kinds.
3. (Lines 19–20) Whose magnanimity blended with valor by first capturing, and then releasing all the kings of Dakṣiṇāpatha (South India) such as Mahendra of Kośala, Vyāghrarāja of Mahākāntāra, Mantarāja of Kurāla, Mahendragiri of Pishṭapura, Svāmidatta of Koṭṭūra, Damana of Eraṇḍapalla, Vishṇugopa of Kānchī, Nīlarāja of Avamukta, Hastivarman of Vengi, Ugrasena of Pālakka, Kubera of Devarāshtra, and Dhanañjaya of Kushthalapura.
4. (Line 21) He exterminated many kings of Āryāvarta (North India) such as Rudradeva, Matila, Nāgadatta, Chandravarman, Gaṇapatināga, Nāgasena, Achuta-Nandin, Balavarman, and made all the kings of the forest regions become his servants.
5. (Lines 22–23) His formidable rule was propitiated with payment of all tributes, execution of orders, and visits (to his court) for obeisance by such frontier rulers as those of Samataṭa (present-day Bangladesh), Ḍavāka, Kāmarūpa (Assam), Nepala, Kartripura, the Mālavas, Arjunāyanas, Yaudheyas, Mādrakas (Panjab, Pakistan), Abhīras, Prājunas, Sanakānīkas, Kākas, Kharaparikas and other.
6. He restored many fallen kingdoms and overthrown royal families.
7. (Lines 23–24) He was offered daughters in marriage and administration of their districts and provinces by the **Devaputra-Shāhi-Shāhānushāhi** and the **Śaka** lords who surrendered, and by (rulers) occupying all island countries such as **Siṁhala** and others.
8. Samudragupta was very intelligent. He was a musician as well as a poet.
9. Names of Samudragupta's father, mother, grandfather, and great-grandfather.
10. The inscription was composed by Harisena.

Translation of the regions stated in item 5 above: Ḍavāka is the region between Kāmarūpa and Samataṭa; the Yaudheyas occupied the banks of Satalaj, Mādrakas the central parts of Panjab and Pauravas the northern parts of Panjab (Venkatachelam, 1957a, p. 217).

Figure 24 shows a map of Samudragupta's empire based on the information from his inscription.

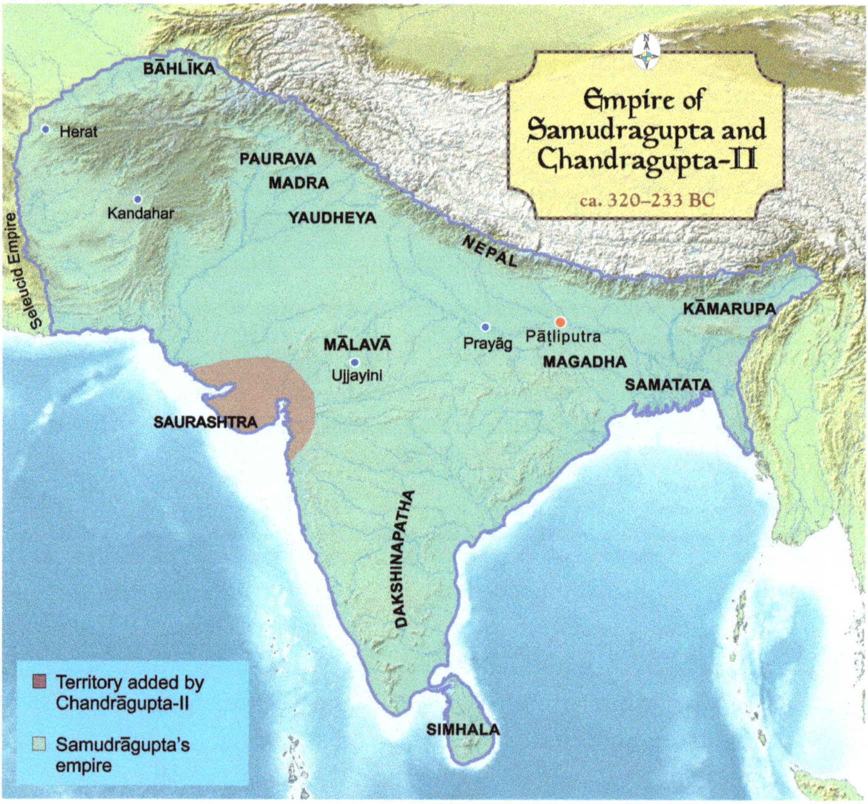


**Figure 24: Map of Samudragupta's empire (ca. 300 BC)**
*Blank map courtesy: DEMIS Mapserver, Wikimedia Commons, CC BY-SA 3.0*

## Accounts of Ancient Greek Writers

See the accounts of Samudragupta by the ancient Greek writers, in Chapter 2 under 'Why is the Identification of *Sandracottus* as Chandragupta Maurya wrong?'. A few points are reiterated in the following.

1. Megasthenes reports:

> " He resided at the court of Sandrakottos, the greatest king in

India. ” (McCrindle, 1877, p. 194)

and *The Geography of Strabo* (Jones, 1917/1949, p. 263, 265) tells us:

> “ They were sent on an ambassadorial mission to Palimbothra (Megasthenes to Sandrocottus, Deimachus to Allitrochades the son of Sandrocottus). ”

The sound of the names *Sandrocottus* and his son *Allitrochades* resembles slightly with the names Chandragupta and his son Samudragupta, respectively, but it doesn't resemble at all that of Chandragupta Maurya and his son Bindusāra, respectively.

2. Megasthenes's writings coming to us through the ancient Greek and Roman writers such as Strabo (*Geography of Strabo*), and Pliny (*Natural History of Pliny*), etc. tell us that Seleucus Nicator gave four satrapies—the Gedrosi (Balochistan), Arachotae (Kandahar, southern Afghanistan), Arri (Herat, western Afghanistan), Paropamisadae (Gāndhāra, and northern Afghanistan), and the present day northwestern province of Pakistan—to *Sandracottus* upon terms of intermarriage and receiving in exchange 500 elephants (Majumdar, 1960, p. 98).

   > “ Not long after, Androkottos, ... with six hundred thousand men attacked and subdued all India. ” (McCrindle, 1877, p. 10)

   This account of *Sandracottus* by the ancient Greek writers matches only with Samudragupta's inscription on the Prayāg pillar. See point number 7 in the key learnings from the inscription. The inscription confirms that it was Samudragupta, and not Chandragupta Maurya, who defeated Devaputra-Shāhi-Shāhānushāhi and the Śaka lords (Seleucus Nicator) and, under a peace treaty, received his daughter in matrimony, and administration of the districts and provinces of Kabul, Herat, Kandahar, and Balochistan.

3. Samudragupta had seen Alexander per 'Plutarch: Ch. LXII' as shown below (Majumdar, 1960, p. 199):

   > “ Androcottus himself, who was then but a youth, saw Alexander himself. ”

4. As discussed in Chapter 2, Megasthenes stated that all the Indians were free, and not one of them was a slave: “ the Indians do not even use aliens as slaves, and much less a countryman of their own. ” (McCrindle, 1876, p. 21)

Vincent Smith (1914, p. 283) called Samudragupta, the 'Indian Napoleon'. *Kaliyuga Rājavṛttānta* states that Samudragupta, after conquering the whole world (Indian subcontinent and beyond) and performing the *Aśvamedha yajña* became the second 'son of Dharma'. Vincent Smith describes that the *Aśvamedha yajña* was duly carried out with appropriate splendor and accompanied by lavish gifts to brahmans, comprising, it is said, millions of coins and gold pieces. Smith (1914, p. 288) adds:

> "Specimens of the gold medals struck for this purpose, bearing a suitable legend and the effigy of the doomed horse standing before the altar, have been found in small numbers."

Speaking of the personal accomplishments of Samudragupta, Vincent Smith states further (p. 288):

> "Although courtly phrases of the official eulogists can not be accepted without a certain amount of reservation, it is clear that Samudragupta was a ruler of exceptional capacity and unusually varied gifts. The laureate's commemoration of his hero's proficiency in song and music is curiously confirmed by the existence of a few rare gold coins depicting his majesty comfortably seated on a high-backed couch, engaged in playing the Indian lyer. The allied art of poetry was also reckoned among the accomplishments of this versatile monarch,"

3. **Chandragupta II** (चन्द्रगुप्त 2), son of the great Samudragupta by his senior queen Dattadevi, who was already a crown prince, came to the throne peacefully under the title of **Vikramāditya** (विक्रमादित्य) in the year 58 of the Gupta Yuga, corresponding to Yudhiṣṭhira Śaka 2869 (269 BC) and ruled the empire from Pāṭaliputra for 36 years. According to the *Kaliyuga*

## Distortion by Colonial Era Indologists

The colonial era Indologists, after erasing from history Vikramāditya of Ujjain of the first century BC, ascribed his legends to this Chandragupta II who also assumed the title of Vikramāditya. Vincent Smith (1914, p. 290) wrote:

> "He also took the title of Vikramāditya ('Sun of Power'), and has a better claim than any other sovereign to be regarded as the original of the mythical king of that name who figures so largely in Indian legends."

*Rājavṛttānta,* he removed Yavanas and Hunas from the country, crossed the *Sapta-Sindhu* (the seven rivers), and conquered Vahlikas (in northern Afghanistan, see Bāhlīka under Kuru Vaṁśa in Chapter 5) and other tribes. He conquered Saurashtra, extending his empire to the Arabian sea. He was surrounded by learned men and was an expert in the Vedas, Purāṇas, history, and poetry.

**Figure 25: The rust-proof Iron Pillar in Delhi (3rd century BC)**

Figure 25 shows a photograph of the rust-proof Iron Pillar constructed by Chandragupta II. The iconic pillar now stands next to the Qutub Minar in Delhi. Based on the true dating of this Chandragupta II, the iron pillar was constructed in the third century BC.

The translation of the inscription is shown in Figure 26. The inscription describes him as follows:

> “When in battle in the Vanga countries (Bengal), he kneaded (and turned) back with (his) breast the enemies who uniting together came against (him), ... he, by whom, having crossed in warfare the seven mouths of the (River) Sindhu, Vahlikas [Bāhlika or Bactria in northern Afghanistan] were conquered.”

4. **Kumārgupta I** (कुमारगुप्त १), son of Chandragupta II by his queen Dhruvadevi, came to the throne under the title of **Mahendrāditya** (महेन्द्रादित्य) in the year 94 of the Gupta Yuga, corresponding to Yudhiṣṭhira Śaka 2905 (233 BC). He ruled the empire from Pāṭaliputra for 42 years (Kaliyuga Rājavṛttānta; Vincent Smith, 1914, p. 299), from Gupta Yuga 94 to 136

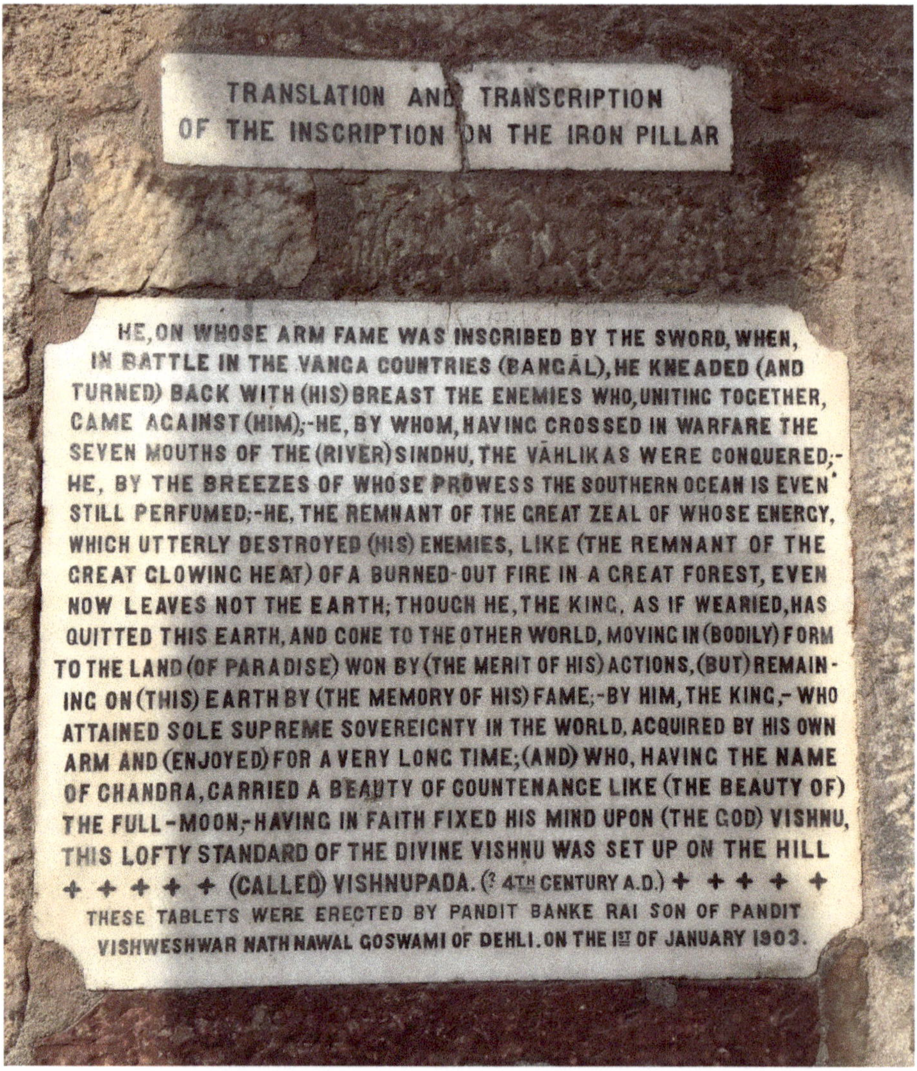
TRANSLATION AND TRANSCRIPTION
OF THE INSCRIPTION ON THE IRON PILLAR
HE, ON WHOSE ARM FAME WAS INSCRIBED BY THE SWORD, WHEN,
IN BATTLE IN THE VANGA COUNTRIES (BANGĀL), HE KNEADED (AND
TURNED) BACK WITH (HIS) BREAST THE ENEMIES WHO, UNITING TOGETHER,
CAME AGAINST (HIM);-HE, BY WHOM, HAVING CROSSED IN WARFARE THE
SEVEN MOUTHS OF THE (RIVER) SINDHU, THE VĀHLIKAS WERE CONQUERED;-
HE, BY THE BREEZES OF WHOSE PROWESS THE SOUTHERN OCEAN IS EVEN
STILL PERFUMED;-HE, THE REMNANT OF THE GREAT ZEAL OF WHOSE ENERGY,
WHICH UTTERLY DESTROYED (HIS) ENEMIES, LIKE (THE REMNANT OF THE
GREAT GLOWING HEAT) OF A BURNED-OUT FIRE IN A GREAT FOREST, EVEN
NOW LEAVES NOT THE EARTH; THOUGH HE, THE KING, AS IF WEARIED, HAS
QUITTED THIS EARTH, AND GONE TO THE OTHER WORLD, MOVING IN (BODILY) FORM
TO THE LAND (OF PARADISE) WON BY (THE MERIT OF HIS) ACTIONS, (BUT) REMAIN-
ING ON (THIS) EARTH BY (THE MEMORY OF HIS) FAME;-BY HIM, THE KING,- WHO
ATTAINED SOLE SUPREME SOVEREIGNTY IN THE WORLD, ACQUIRED BY HIS OWN
ARM AND (ENJOYED) FOR A VERY LONG TIME; (AND) WHO, HAVING THE NAME
OF CHANDRA, CARRIED A BEAUTY OF COUNTENANCE LIKE (THE BEAUTY OF)
THE FULL-MOON;-HAVING IN FAITH FIXED HIS MIND UPON (THE GOD) VISHNU,
THIS LOFTY STANDARD OF THE DIVINE VISHNU WAS SET UP ON THE HILL
+ + + + + (CALLED) VISHNUPADA. (? 4TH CENTURY A.D.) + + + + +
THESE TABLETS WERE ERECTED BY PANDIT BANKE RAI SON OF PANDIT
VISHWESHWAR NATH NAWAL GOSWAMI OF DEHLI. ON THE 1ST OF JANUARY 1903.

**Figure 26: Translation of the inscription on the Iron Pillar**

(233–191 BC). Miss Mabel Duff (1899, p. 31) assigns him a reign of 37 years. Kumārgupta I conquered his foes and, like his grandfather, asserted his sovereignty by celebrating with *Aśvamedha yajña*.

5. **Skandagupta** (स्कन्दगुप्त), son of Kumārgupta I, by his senior queen Anantadevi, came to the throne under the title of **Parākramāditya** (पराक्रमादित्य). He ruled the empire from Pāṭaliputra for 25 years, from Yudhiṣṭhira Śaka 2947 to 2972 or Gupta Yuga 136 to 161 (191–166 BC).

Skanda Gupta fought ferociously with the Hunas who burst into

India through the northwestern passes, humbled their pride, and destroyed Puṣyasena. The people eulogized his conquests in songs and poems during that time. See *Chronology of Ancient Hindu History Part I* (Venkatachelam, 1957a, p. 224) for the songs. The Junāgaḍh inscription records his appointment of Parnadatta as governor of Saurashtra, and Parnadatta's appointment of his own son Chakrapālita as governor of Junāgaḍh, the bursting of the embankment of the Sudarshana Lake in the Gupta Yuga year 136, and its repair by Chakrapālita in the following year (Mabel Duff, 1899, p. 33).

Skandagupta had no heir of his own and appointed Narasiṁha Gupta, son of his half-brother **Sthiragupta** (स्थिरगुप्त), or **Pura Gupta** as Vincent Smith (1914, p. 311) calls him, the son of Kumārgupta I by the junior queen Anandadevi. He passed away in Gupta Yuga 161 (166 BC).

6. **Narasiṁhagupta** (नरसिंहगुप्त), the son of Skandagupta's half-brother Sthiragupta, came to the throne in the Gupta Yuga year 161. As he was a minor at the time of his succession to the throne, his father ruled the empire as a guardian for a brief period of five years under the title of **Prakāśāditya** (प्रकाशादित्य) from Yudhiṣṭhira Śaka 2972 to 2977 or Gupta Yuga 161 to 166 (166–161 BC). He is said to have restored the purity of coinage which suffered a decline in the amount of pure gold during Skanda Gupta's time as a result of the cost of the Huna war.

Narasiṁhagupta came of age in the year 166 of Gupta Yuga, ascended the throne, and reigned from Pāṭaliputra for 35 years from Gupta Yuga 166 to 201 or Yudhiṣṭhira Śaka 2977 to 3012 (161–126 BC) under the title of **Bālāditya** (बालादित्य). Since Sthiragupta reigned only as a guardian to his minor son, the *Kaliyuga Rājavṛttānta* does not count Sthiragupta as a separate king and assigns to Narasiṁhagupta or Bālāditya the total period of 5 + 35 = 40 years for his reign.

Vincent Smith (1914, p. 312) and Mabel Duff (1899, p. 35) treat them as two separate kings in which case there were eight kings in this dynasty instead of the seven kings stated in all the Purāṇas. Narasiṁhagupta is said to have moved his capital to Ayodhya. He built a brick stupa of more than 300 feet for Buddhists at Nalanda, Magadha, which was remarkable for the delicacy of its decorations and inscriptions as well as the lavish use of gold and gems in its furniture. He is said to have rigorously resisted the tyranny of the Hunas and to have successfully put down the pride of the Kalingas who had risen against him (Smith, 1914, p. 312; Venkatachelam, 1957a, p. 222).

7. **Kumārgupta II** (कुमारगुप्त २), son of Narasiṁhagupta by his queen Mahādevi or Śrīmati Devi came to the throne under the title of **Kramāditya** (क्रमादित्य) and reigned for 44 years, from Yudhiṣṭhira Śaka 3012 to 3056 or Gupta Yuga 201 to 245 (126–82 BC) (*Kaliyuga Rājavṛttānta*). He went to war with the Hunas and defeated Isānavarman. His commander Bhattārka loyally served him. Thus, the Gupta Empire lasted for 245 years and disintegrated after Kumārgupta.

## End of the Gupta Empire and Rise of Vikramāditya in Ujjain

The fall of the Gupta Empire was followed by the ascendance of Vikramāditya to the throne of Ujjain in 82 BC who went on to become one of the greatest emperors of India. With this, the center of power in India moved from Pāṭaliputra in eastern India to Ujjain in central India after more than 1,500 years.

## References


1. *The Aśokāvadāna: Sanskrit Text compared with Chinese Versions* (Edited and partly translated by Sujitkumar Mukhopadhyaya, 1960). New Delhi: Sahitya Akademi.

2. *Śrīmad Bhāgavata MahāPurāṇa: (Sanskrit) with Hindi translation*, 2 vols. (81st ed., Vikrama Samvat 2071; 1st ed., Samvat 1997). Gorakhpur: Gita Press.

3. Bhandarkar, Devadatta Ramkrishna (Rev.) (1981). *Corpus Inscriptionum Indicarum Vol. III: Inscriptions of the Early Gupta Kings* (Bahadurchand Chhabra & Govind Swamirao Gai., Eds.). New Delhi: Archaeological Survey of India.

4. Bhattacharya, Dr. B. (1944, March). 'New Light on the History of the Imperial Gupta Dynasty.' *The Journal of the Bihar Research Society, Vol.30, Article I.*

5. *The Brahmāṇḍa MahāPurāṇam: (Sanskrit) With English Introduction, Verse-Index and Textual Correction.* Dr. K. V. Sharma (Ed.) Krishnadas Sanskrit Series 41, Madhyama bhāga. Varanasi: Krishnadas Academy.

6. *The Dīpavaṁsa: An Ancient Buddhist Historical Record* (English translation by Herman Oldenberg, 2006). New Delhi (First published: Berlin, 1879).

7. Hultzsch, E. (1925). *Corpus Inscriptionum Indicarum Vol. I: Inscriptions of Asoka (New ed.).* Oxford: Clarendon Press.

8. Jacobi, Hermann (Ed.) (1932). *Sthavirāvalicarita or Pariśiṣṭaparvan: an Appendix of the Triśaśti-Śalākāpuruṣacarita by Hemacandra* (Bibliotheca Indica Work No. 96, 2nd ed.). Calcutta: Asiatic Society of Bengal.

9. Jagannadha Rao, Nadimpalli (1931). *The Age of the Mahabharata War.*

10. Jones, Horace Leonard (Trans.) (1917). *The Geography of Strabo: With an English Translation* (rpt. MCMXLIX (1949), Vol. I, Book II, Ch. I.9). Cambridge: Harvard University Press.

11. *Kaliyuga Rājavṛttānta*, segments quoted by M. Krishnamachariar in *History of Classical Sanskrit Literature* (1937, p. xlviii–lvi, cii–civ).

12. Krishnamachariar, M. (1937). *History of Classical Sanskrit Literature: Being an elaborate account of all branches of Classical Sanskrit Literature, with full Epigraphical and Archaeological Notes and References, an Introduction dealing with Languages, Philology and Chronology, and Index of Authors and Works.* Madras.

13. Mabel Duff, C. (1899). *The Chronology of India: from the earliest times to the beginning of the sixteenth century*. Westminster.

14. *Mahābhārata: (Sanskrit) with Hindi translation* by Pandit Rāmanārāyaṇadatta Śastri Pāṇdeya, 6 vols. Gorakhpur: Gita Press.

15. *The Mahāvaṁsa:* or *The Great Chronicle of Ceylon* (English translation by Wilhelm Geiger, 1912). The Pali text Society, Oxford University Press.

16. Majumdar, Dr. R. C. (1960). *The Classical Accounts of India, Being a compilation of the English translations of the accounts left by Herodotus, Megasthenes, Arrian, Strabo, Quintus, Diodorus Siculus, Justin, Plutarch, Frontinus, Nearchus, Apollonius, Pliny, Ptolemy, Aelian and others with Maps, editorial notes, comments, analysis and Introduction*. Calcutta: Firma K. L. Mukhopadhyay.

17. *Matsya Purāṇa: (Sanskrit) with Hindi translation*. Gorakhpur: Gita Press.

18. McCrindle, J. W. (1877). *Ancient India as Described by Megasthenes and Arrian: a translation of the Fragments of the Indika of Megasthenes collected by Dr. Schwanbeck, and of the First part of the Indika of Arrian*. London: Trübner & Co.

19. McCrindle, Watson (1876). *The Indica of Arrian: Translated and Annotated*. Bombay: Education Society's Press.

20. Narayana Sastry, T. S. (1916). *The Age of Śankara* (2nd ed. 1971, edited by T. N. Kumaraswamy). Madras: B. G. Paul & Co.

21. Pargiter, F. E. (1910). 'Ancient Indian Genealogies and Chronology.' *The Journal of the Royal Asiatic Society of Great Britain and Ireland*, January 1910, Article I. London.

22. Pargiter, F. E. (1913). *The Purāṇa Text of the Dynasties of The Kali Age: with Introduction and Notes*. Oxford: University Press.

23. Prinsep, James (1838). 'VII.—On the Edicts of PIYADASI, or Asoka, the Buddhist monarch of India, preserved on the Girnar rock in the Gujerat peninsula, and on the Dhauli rock in Cuttack; with the discovery of PTOLEMY's name therein [Read at the Meeting of the 4th April 1838].' *Journal of the Asiatic Society*, No. 75, March, 219–282.

24. Sethna, K. D. (1989). *Ancient India in a New Light: I. The Challenge of India's Traditional Chronology, II. The Momentous Evidence of Megasthenes, III. A Reconstruction of Ancient Indian History: Aśoka – and Before and After*. New Delhi: Aditya Prakashan.

25. Sircar, D. C. (1979). *Aśokan Studies*. Calcutta: Indian Museum.

26. Smith, Vincent A. (1914). *Early History of India: From 600 B.C. to the Muhammadan Conquest including the Invasion of Alexander the Great* (3rd ed.). Oxford: Clarendon Press.

27. Wheeler, James Talboys (1874). *The History of India: From the Earliest Ages* (Vol. III). London: Trübner & Co. (MDCCCLXXIV).

28. *Vāyu Purāṇam: (Sanskrit)* (Śālivāhana Śaka 1905, AD 1983). Ānandāśrama Sanskrit Granthāvaliḥ, No. 49.

29. *Vāyu Purāṇam: (Sanskrit) with Hindi translation by* Rāmapratāpa Tripāthi (2nd ed., Śaka 1909 (AD 1987)). Prayāga: Hindi Sāhitya Sammelan.

30. Venkatachelam, Pandit Kota (Kali 5054, AD 1953b). *The Plot in Indian Chronology*. Arya Vijnana, Publication 17. Vijayawada.

31. Venkatachelam, Pandit Kota (Kali 5058, AD 1957a). *Chronology of Ancient Hindu History Part I*. Arya Vijnana Grandhamala, Publication 23. Vijayawada.

32. Venkatachelam, Pandit Kota (Kali 5058, AD 1957b). *Chronology of Ancient Hindu History Part II*. Arya Vijnana Grandhamala, Publication 24. Vijayawada.

33. *Viṣṇu Purāṇa: (Sanskrit) with Hindi translation by* Śrī Munilāl Gupta (6th ed., Samvat 2024; 1st ed., Samvat 1990). Gorakhpur: Gita Press.

# 8

# THE AGE OF GAUTAMA BUDDHA

## The Ikṣvāku Dynasty of Kośala

Gautama Buddha, shown in Figure 27, was born in the Ikṣavāku (इक्ष्वाकु) Dynasty of Kośala (कोशल), one of the many branches of the Ikṣavāku Dynasty (or the Sūrya Vaṁśa) of Ayodhya (अयोध्या) in which Lord Śrī Rāma was born. Appendix IV shows the genealogy of the Ikṣavāku Dynasty consisting of 96 kings. Starting from King Ikṣavāku, Śrī Rāma was the 65th king in descent. Some of the famous kings of the dynasty such as Māndhātā, Hariśchandra, Sagara, Bhagīratha, Raghu, and Daśaratha, etc. are highlighted in bold.

**Figure 27: Statue of Buddha at Sarnath Museum**

Bṛhadbala (बृहद्बल), the 96th king in descent, was killed by Abhimanyu (अभिमन्यु) in the Mahābhārata War (*Viṣṇu Purāṇa* 4.4.112) in 3139 BC. His son Bṛhatkṣaya (बृहत्क्षय) was crowned as the king of Ayodhya after the war. Table 24 lists the kings of this dynasty, starting from the Mahābhārata War to the end of the

**Table 24: Kings of the Ikṣvāku Dynasty of Kośala, 36 BK– Kaliyuga 1468 (3138–1634 BC)**

| Sr. No. | Name of the Kings |
|---|---|
| 1 | Bṛhatkṣaya (बृहत्क्षय) – valorous, crowned in 36 BK (3138 BC) |
| 2 | Urukṣaya (उरुक्षय) |
| 3 | Vatsavyūha (वत्सव्यूह) |
| 4 | Prativyoma (प्रतिव्योम) |
| 5 | Divākara (दिवाकर) – his capital was the beautiful city of Ayodhya |
| 6 | Sahadeva (सहदेव) – called *mahāyaśasvi* (महायशस्वी = of great fame) |
| 7 | Bṛhadaśva (बृहदश्व) |
| 8 | Bhānuratha (भानुरथ) |
| 9 | Pratīpāśva (प्रतीपाश्व) |
| 10 | Supratīka (सुप्रतीक) |
| 11 | Marudeva (मरुदेव) |
| 12 | Sunakṣatra (सुनक्षत्र) |
| 13 | Kinnarāśva (किन्नराश्व) – destroyer of the enemies |
| 14 | Antarikṣa (अंतरिक्ष) |
| 15 | Suṣeṇa (सुषेण) |
| 16 | Sumitra (सुमित्र) 1 |
| 17 | Bṛhadrāja (बृहद्राज) |
| 18 | Dharmi (धर्मि) |
| 19 | Kṛtañjaya (कृतंजय) |
| 20 | Raṇañjaya (रणंजय) – *vidvān (established in knowledge)* |
| 21 | Sañjaya (संजय) – brave king |
| 22 | Śākya (शाक्य) |
| 23 | **Śuddhodana** (शुध्धोदन) |
| 24 | **Siddhārtha** (सिध्धार्थ) **– Became Gautama Buddha** |
| 25 | **Rāhula** (राहुल) |
| 26 | Prasenajit (प्रसेनजित्) |
| 27 | Kṣudraka (क्षुद्रक) |
| 28 | Kulaka (कुलक) |
| 29 | Suratha (सुरथ) |
| 30 | Sumitra (सुमित्र) 2 – the last king, the dynasty ended in Kaliyuga 1468 (1634 BC) |

dynasty, from *Matsya Purāṇa* (Adhyay 271). The list in the *Viṣṇu Purāṇa* (4th Aṁśa, Adhyay 22) is very similar except it has one less king because it does not include Prince Siddhārtha (सिध्दार्थ) who gave up royal life and became Gautama Buddha. *Śrīmad Bhāgavata Purāṇa* (Skandha 9, Adhyay 12) also lists 30 kings with differences in some of the names.

These 30 kings (more accurately, 29 kings, not counting Siddhārtha) reigned for 1,504 years after the Mahābhārata War. The dynasty ended with the 30th king Sumitra in the year Kaliyuga 1468 (1634 BC) (Venkatachelam, 1955, p. 135).

The old Kośala kingdom of the Ikṣvāku Dynasty gradually disintegrated, with the kingdom getting divided and subdivided among the descendants, with each faction founding a new sub-dynasty. Thus, several capitals formed, Ayodhya not being the capital of anyone. Among these sub-dynasties, there were Pava Malla Kshatriyas, the Kusinara Malla Kshatriyas, the Vaideha (Licchavi) Kshatriyas, bearing the gotra name of Vaśiṣta, Śākya, Śākya Licchavi, etc.

While there were so many kings of the Ikṣvāku dynasties ruling over so many kingdoms, Śākya (शाक्य) was considered to be particularly important because he descended from a succession of the eldest sons of the dynasty. Therefore, he was mentioned in the Purāṇas in the list of Ikṣvākus. Śākya, the 22nd king of the Ikṣvāku Dynasty after the Mahābhārata War became the ruler of the northwestern province of the Kośala kingdom, lying at the foot of the Himalayas, with Kapilvastu as its capital.

Śuddhodana (शुध्धोदन) was the son of this Śākya, the 22nd king in Table 24. He had queens named Māyā (माया) and Prajāpati (प्रजापति). Siddhārtha was his son from Queen Māyā. Siddhārtha renounced worldly life in his 29th year and, after a continued penance of six years, attained enlightenment while in meditation sitting under a tree. Henceforth, this tree became famous as the Bodhi tree. His son Rāhula was the 25th king as shown in Table 24. Buddhist scriptures confirm that Buddha was the son of Śuddhodana.

According to the Buddhist tradition, Gautama Buddha was born in Lumbini, in the present-day Nepal, when the Queen mother, Maya, was on her way from Kapilvastu to her father's place to give birth. Kapilvastu is near the border of India and Nepal. Its exact location is unknown. It may have been either Piprahwa, Uttar Pradesh, in the present-day India or Tilaurakot, in the present-day Nepal. See Figure 28.

**Figure 28: Gautam Buddha's birthplace depicted on a map**
*Map courtesy: Unknown*

# The Current Date of Gautama Buddha

In the currently accepted history of India, constructed by colonial era European historians and their Indian followers, the birth of Buddha is assigned to 563 BC and his death to 483 BC. This is based on their greatly erroneous assumption that Chandragupta Maurya was a contemporary of Alexander and making that the basis for redating the entire history of India forward and backward.

## How was the Currently Accepted Date Arrived at?

Buddha's nirvana date of 483 BC was arrived at by using the information in the Simhalese Buddhist text, *The Mahāvaṁsa* (1912, p. xxiv). It states that Chandragupta Maurya reigned for 24 years; then Bindusāra reigned for 28 years, and then Aśoka's *abhisheka* (coronation) was performed when he had reigned for 4 years and it had been 218 years after the nirvana of Buddha. Chandragupta Maurya's starting year of reign was assumed to be 321 BC based on the false identification of *Sandracottous* of the ancient Greek writers as Chandragupta Maurya instead of Chandragupta I of the Gupta Dynasty. The date 321 BC – 24 – 28 – 4 + 218 = 483 BC was then arrived at for Buddha's nirvana. Since Buddha lived for 80 years, his birth date was fixed at 563 BC.

Thus, the colonial Indologists, having started with the wrong basis for redating India's history, ended up with a very wrong date for Buddha.

E.J. Rapson (1922, p. 171) admitted in his book, *The Cambridge History of India*:

> " Unfortunately, even after all that has been written on the subject of the early Buddhist chronology, we are still uncertain as to the exact date of the Buddha's birth. **The date 483 B.C. which is adopted in this History must still be regarded as provisional.** The causes of this uncertainty which were explained by the present writer in 1877 still remain the same: " [Emphasis added]

Sadly, the provisional date 563–483 BC became a widely accepted date without any further investigation when a case for greater antiquity of Buddha's existence can be made.

## The Case for Greater Antiquity of Buddha

1. A. P. Sinnett (1883/1907, p. 175), an English author and theosophist, in his book, *Esoteric Buddhism*, assigns 643 BC for Buddha's date.
2. According to Max Müller (1859/1926, p. 141–143), the Chinese accounts assign 850 BC for Aśoka. The interval between Buddha's nirvana and Aśoka's coming to the throne is at least 214 years even by the current dating (335 years by the true dating). Therefore, Buddha's nirvana year would be at least before 850 BC + 214 = 1064 BC per the Chinese account.
3. Chinese pilgrim Fa-hsien, who visited India from AD 399 to 414, when asked by the monks if he knew when Buddhism first went to the east, replied:

   > " When I enquired of the people of those parts, they all said that according to an old tradition, Shamans from India began to bring after the Sūtras and Disciplines across this river from the date of setting up the image of Maitreya Bodhisattva [Buddha]. " (Giles, 1923, p. 10; similar statement in Legge, 1886, p. 27)

   The image was put up about 300 years after Buddha's nirvana which occurred during the reign of King Ping of the Chau Dynasty (770–719 BC). This would place Buddha's nirvana in the 11th century BC (Venkatachelam, 1956b, p. 19).
4. Somayajulu writes in his *Dates in Ancient History of India* (p. 112–114):

   > " All Jains and Hindus agreed that in 528 B.C. Vardhamana Mahavira died and that Kumarila Bhatta (557–493 B.C.) was vehemently attacking the Jains all over India and was followed by Sankaracharya

(509–477 B.C.). The interval of time between Sankara and Buddha was about 1400 or 1500 years. Hence no Buddha lived in the sixth century B.C. The scanty accounts kept by the inhabitants of Ceylon are no authorities for fixing the date of Buddha and for calculating all dates in Indian history on that basis. The Japanese acquired Buddhism in seventh century A.D. Hence the Japanese calendar is no genuine authority for fixing the date of Buddha as it is only a second hand information. The western scholars piled conjecture upon conjecture according to their whims and fancies. The history now taught in Indian schools is simply a heap of such misrepresentations and baseless conjectures. ” (as cited in Pandit Venkatachelam, 1956b, p. 46)

5. Ādi Śaṅkarāchārya lived from 509 to 477 BC as discussed in depth in Chapter 9. Pandit Venkatachelam (1956b, p. 29) states:

 “ By the time of Sankara the religion of Buddha had reached a decadent stage. So the Buddha must have lived long before the time of Sankara. Neither in the writings of Sri Sankara nor those of any contemporary of his, do we find, any evidence to support the view that Buddha was alive in 563–483 B.C., the period assigned to his life by the modern European historians of Ancient India. Their view in this matter is based upon their original erroneous hypothesis of the contemporaneity of Alexander of Greece and Chandragupta of the Maurya dynasty of Magadha. The view as well as the underlying hypothesis is quite contradictory to the dates mentioned in the sacred books of Hindus, Jains and Buddhists of ancient times. ”

6. Aśoka Maurya's true date is 1472–1436 BC as discussed in Chapter 7. According to the Simhalese Buddhist text, *The Dīpavaṁsa* (2006, 3.58), Buddha's nirvana date is 214 years before Aśoka's coming to the throne in 1472 BC which gives us 1686 BC for Buddha's nirvana. In truth, Buddha's nirvana was more than 214 years before the beginning of Aśoka's reign.

## Evidence for Greater Antiquity of Gautama Buddha

1. Inscriptional Evidence (Venkatachelam, 1955, p. 169):

 “ Mr. A.V. Thyagaraja Aiyar in his 'Indian Architecture' states that the tomb in Athens discovered recently contains an inscription which reads as follows:—

 "Here lies Indian Sramanacharya from Bodha Gaya a Sakya monk taken to Greece by his Greek pupils and the tomb marks his death at about 1000 B.C." If Buddhist monks have gone to Greece in 1000 B.C., the date of Kanishka must be at least 1100 B.C. and that of Aśoka 1250 B.C. and that of Chandragupta Maurya 1300 B.C. (Vide A. Somayajulu's 'Dates in Ancient History of India', pp.112, 113) ”

2. In the paper he presented in 1788, William Jones (1799a, p. 42–46) guessed Buddha's date to be 1027 BC (Chapter 2, Table 3), as he had begun to shrink India's chronology.

3. The Nepal Rāja Vaṁśāvali states that soon after the reign of Vrishadevavarman (in the fifth century BC), Śaṅkarāchārya came from the south and destroyed the Buddha faith (Wright, 1877/1990, p. 120). Hence, the Buddhist faith must have started well before the fifth century BC.

4. In Kalhaṇa's (1148/1985) *Rājataraṅgiṇī* (राजतरंगिणी), the history of the kings of Kashmir:

   i. The shloka 1.171 states that Buddhists were powerful during the time of Hushka, Jushka, and Kaniṣka, the three kings who ruled jointly.

   ii. The shloka 1.172 states that 150 years had passed since the nirvana of *Bhagavān* Śākyasiṁha (Buddha).

   iii. The shloka 1.173, describing the reign of Kaniṣka, states that Nāgārjuna, a Bodhisatva, was considered the lord of the land.

   iv. The shloka 1.177 states that at that time (during the reign of Abhimanyu, the successor of Kaniṣka), Buddhists, protected by Nāgārjuna, were very strong in the land.

Therefore, Buddha must have lived before the time of Abhimanyu (1234–1182 BC) and Kaniṣka. As discussed in detail in Chapter 11 of this book, Gonanda the third was the 53rd king of Kashmir. He came to the throne after Abhimanyu and began his reign in 1182 BC. Kaniṣka reigned from 1298 to 1234 BC before Abhimanyu. According to point ii. above, if at the time of Kaniṣka, 150 years had passed since the nirvana of Buddha, Buddha's time must be at least before 1400 BC.

If Kaniṣka flourished in AD 78 according to the colonial era Indologists, Buddha's date would be (AD 78 – 150 =) 72 BC, but it could not be 483 BC, which is currently widely accepted. Thus, on a critical examination, the chronology given by the colonial era European Indologists is full of contradictions.

5. Abul Fazal Allami, the writer of Ain-I-Akbari, in giving an account of the Buddhists and their philosophy, stated in AD 1595 that 2,962 years had passed from the date of Buddha's death. This places Buddha's nirvana in AD 1595 – 2,962 = 1367 BC (Triveda, 1947, p. 227).

6. Dr. D. S. Triveda (1947, p. 220–238) determined the date of Lord Buddha as 1793 BC after analyzing all available dates in his paper titled *The Date of Lord Buddha, 1793 B. C.*

   The 1793 BC date determined by Dr. Triveda is only 14 years apart from the 1807 BC date arrived at by Pandit Venkatachelam and discussed below.

## The True Date of Gautama Buddha (1887–1807 BC)

According to all the Purāṇas, and as discussed in Chapter 7, by the time of the coronation of Mahāpadma Nanda in Magadha, 1,500 (more precisely 1,504) years had elapsed from the Mahābhārata War at the end of 3139 BC. During these 1,504 years, 37 kings ruled in succession in Girivraja, the capital of Magadha, and 30 kings in Kośala. Śuddhodana, Buddha's father, was the 23rd Kośala king as shown in Table 24. The Kośala Dynasty ended in 1634 BC with Sumitra, the 30th and the last king, when Mahāpadma Nanda became the ruler of Magadha and destroyed the ancient kingdoms of North India. Hence, Buddha's time must be well within the 1,504 years after the Mahābhārata War i.e. well before 1634 BC (Venkatachelam, 1957a, p. 19).

All the Buddhist and Jain authorities such as *The Dīpavaṁsa* (3.58), *Mahāvaṁsa, Aśokāvadāna,* and *Pariśiṣṭaparvan* agree in describing Bimbisāra, the fifth king of the Śiśunāga Dynasty, as being five years younger than Gautama Buddha. Since Bimbisāra reigned from 1852 to 1814 BC as shown in Table 17 in Chapter 7, Gautam Buddha must have been born before 1852 BC. These works also describe Buddha having become an ascetic in his 29th year and achieving enlightenment when he was 35 years old. Gautama Buddha is said to have attained nirvana at the age of 80 years, in the eighth year of the reign of Ajātaśatru. Since Ajātaśatru reigned from 1814 to 1787 BC as shown in Table 17 (Chapter 7), Gautam Buddha must have died in 1807 BC and his birth year would be 1887 BC. Buddha's 29th year in which he became an ascetic, must be 1858 BC which is during the time of Bimbisāra. See *The Age of Buddha, Milinda & Amtiyoka and Yugapuraṇa* (Venkatachelam, 1956b, p. 55–60) for further proof of the true date of Gautama Buddha.

## References


1. *The Aśokāvadāna: Sanskrit Text compared with Chinese Versions* (Edited and partly translated by Sujitkumar Mukhopadhyaya, 1960). New Delhi: Sahitya Akademi.
2. *Śrīmad Bhāgavata MahāPurāṇa: (Sanskrit) with Hindi translation*, 2 vols. (81st ed., Vikrama Samvat 2071; 1st ed., Samvat 1997). Gorakhpur: Gita Press.
3. *The Dīpavaṁsa: An Ancient Buddhist Historical Record* (English translation by Herman Oldenberg, 2006). New Delhi (First published: Berlin, 1879).
4. Giles, Herbert A. (Re-trans.) (1923). *The Travels of Fa-hsien (399–414 A.D.), or Record of the Buddhistic Kingdoms*. Cambridge University Press.
5. Jones, William (1799a). 'On the Chronology of the Hindus, written in January 1788 by the President.' *Asiatic Researches; or Transactions of the Society Instituted in Bengal for inquiring into the History and Antiquities, the Arts, Sciences, and Literature of Asia, Vol. 2,* 111–147. London.
6. Jones, William (1807a). 'On the Chronology of the Hindus: written in January 1788 by the President.' in Lord Teignmouth (Ed.), *The Works of Sir William Jones with the Life of the Author* (Vol. 4, 1–47). London.
7. Kalhaṇa (1148). *Rājataraṅgiṇī (Chronicle of the Kings of Kashmir) (Sanskrit text),* Edited with Hindi translation by Shri Ramtej Shastri Pandey (Vikrama Samvat 2017 (AD 1960), rpt. Ed. 1985). Delhi & Varanasi: Chaukhamba Sanskrit Pratishthan.
8. Legge, James (1886). A *Record of Buddhist Kingdoms: Being an account by the Chinese monk Fâ-hien of his travels in India and Ceylon (A.D. 399–414) in search of the Buddhist books of discipline, Translated and annotated with a Corean recension of the Chinese text*. Oxford: Clarendon Press.
9. *The Mahāvaṁsa:* or *The Great Chronicle of Ceylon* (English translation by Wilhelm Geiger, 1912). The Pali text Society, Oxford University Press.
10. *Matsya Purāṇa: (Sanskrit) with Hindi translation*. Gorakhpur: Gita Press.
11. Max Müller (1859). *A History of Ancient Sanskrit Literature: So far as it illustrates the Primitive Religion of the Brahmans* (Allahabad ed. 1926). London: Williams and Norgate.
12. Rapson, E. J. (1922). *The Cambridge History of India: Vol I. Ancient India*. Cambridge University Press.
13. Sinnett, A. P. (1883). *Esoteric Buddhism* (8th ed., rpt. 1907). London: Trübner.

14. Smith, Vincent A. (1914). *Early History of India: From 600 B.C. to the Muhammadan Conquest including the Invasion of Alexander the Great* (3rd ed.). Oxford: Clarendon Press.

15. Triveda, Dr. D. S. (1947). 'The Date of Lord Buddha, 1793 B.C.' *Bhāratīya Vidyā: A Monthly Research Organ of the Bhavan on all subjects connected with Indology* Vol. 8(8, 9 & 10, Aug–Sept–Oct), 220–238. Bombay: Bharatiya Vidya Bhavan.

16. Venkatachelam, Pandit Kota (1955). *Chronology of Kashmir History Reconstructed*. Arya Vijnana Series, Publication 18. Vijayawada.

17. Venkatachelam, Pandit Kota (Kali 5057, AD 1956b). *The Age of Buddha, Milinda & Amtiyoka and Yugapurana*. Arya Vijnana Series, Publication 20. Vijayawada.

18. Venkatachelam, Pandit Kota (Kali 5058, AD 1957a). *Chronology of Ancient Hindu History Part I*. Arya Vijnana Grandhamala, Publication 23. Vijayawada.

19. *Viṣṇu Purāṇa: (Sanskrit) with Hindi translation by* Śrī Munilāl Gupta (6th ed., Samvat 2024; 1st ed., Samvat 1990). Gorakhpur: Gita Press.

# 9

# THE AGE OF ĀDI ŚAṄKARĀCHĀRYA

**Figure 29 Ādi Śaṅkarāchārya**
*Image courtesy: Sri Sharada Peetham, Sringeri (https://sringeri.net/history/sri-adi- shankaracharya)*

Śrī Ādi **Śaṅkarāchārya*** (आदि शंकराचार्य) holds an extremely important place in the history of India. He was responsible for reviving the essence of Hinduism after the influence of Buddhism had spread far and wide in India. Colonial era European Indologists fixed Ādi Śaṅkarāchārya's time wrongly at AD 788–820 and this became the accepted date. This date is grossly wrong, post-dated by about 1300 years!

(*spelled **Śaṅkarācārya** by transliteration guide and **Shankaracharya** in common parlance)

## How was the AD 788–820 Date Arrived at?

As discussed in Chapter 2, the European Indologists of the colonial era, with their strong belief in biblical history, threw away the long-existing history tradition of India and wrongly identified '*Sandracottus*' of the ancient Greek writers with Chandragupta Maurya instead of Chandragupta I of the Gupta Dynasty and made it the basis for rewriting ancient India's entire history. This new but wrong basis resulted in shrinking ancient India's chronology by over 1,200 years and created much confusion in the study of ancient India's history, as nothing from ancient India's history traditions and records matched with the new basis.

The new compressed chronology of India could not accommodate Ādi Śaṅkarāchārya's true date. The pre-existing true chronology for him was thrown away and all effort was focused on finding a more recent date. Adding to the confusion was the European historian's superficial knowledge of Śaṅkarāchāryas of the five *maṭhas* established by Ādi Śaṅkarāchārya, and their traditions.

T. S. Narayana Sastry (1916/1971, p. 31) who devoted his life to researching the time of Ādi Śaṅkarāchārya, writes in his book, *The Age of Śankara*:

> " There have been many Śaṅkarāchāryas all over the Advaitic Maths in India and many of them have been famous writers on the Advaita [non-duality] Philosophy and Religion. In the Kāmkoti-Piṭha alone, one of the five Maṭhs established by Ādi Śaṅkarāchārya and originally located at Kānchi (Conjeeveram), but subsequently removed to Kumbhakonam, there have been up to this time [AD 1916] 68 Āchāryas, who all bore the title of Śrī Śaṅkarāchārya, and among whom there have been no less than eight Āchāryas, who also actually bore the name of Śaṅkara. Of these latter again, the 38th Āchārya was, in addition considered, like the First Śaṅkarāchārya, an incarnation of Śiva, possessed of a genius and personality in no way inferior to those of his illustrious predecessors, so much so that he has been by later writers identified with the First Śaṅkarāchārya himself, the greatest of the Expounders of the Advaita Philosophy and Religion. This identity in name, in title, in function, in status and in views has given room to no small confusion between the Ādi Śaṅkarāchārya and his successors. There are innumerable works, large and small, which go under the name of Śaṅkarāchārya, and it is really impossible at this distant period of time to determine with certainty which of them were the handworks of Ādi Śaṅkarāchārya, and which were written by his successors. But it is really fortunate that all scholars should uniformly agree in ascribing the Bhāshyas on the Prasthāna-Traya to the First Śaṅkarāchārya or to Śankara as we shall call him hereafter. It is also a matter of great satisfaction to us to find that we have sufficient materials for determining the main incidents of his remarkable life. "

Regarding how the currently accepted date was arrived at, Natalia Isayeva (1993, p. 83–84) writes in *Shankara and Indian Philosophy*:

> " In 1877 a German scholar, Prof. K.P. Tiele, in his essays on ancient

religions suggested as a probable date of Śaṅkara's life an interval between 788 and 820. He based his estimate on the evidence of a later Vedantin, Yajneśvara Śāstri, who cites in his treatise *Aryavidyā-Sudhākar* (The moon of noble knowledge) an earlier work by Bhaṭṭa Nīlakaṇṭha, entitled *Śaṅkara-mandāra-saurabha* (The fragrance of Śaṅkara's paradise tree). Somewhat later, an Indian scholar, K. Pathak, found corroboration for these data in a treatise by an anonymous mediaeval author. One must note that in principle the reliability of these sources is not much higher than that of the hagiographical materials. Still, the date 788–820 was accepted as a serious working hypothesis by such prominent Indologists as F. Max Müller, A. Macdonell, A.B. Keith, M. Winternitz. Later this dating became generally accepted by their followers. ”

## The Fallacy of the Currently Accepted Date

Now, let us look at the quality of the source of K. B. Pathak which formed the basis for the currently accepted date. Pandit N. Bhashya Charya (1889, p. 102) writes in *The Theosophist*:

> “ The authority on which Mr. Pathak bases his conclusion is a Sanskrit MS. [manuscript] of three pages written in Bālabodh characters, and containing about 24 lines in all? It says, as we stated before, that Sri Sankarāchārya was born in the year Vibhava (Kali 3889) on the full moon day in Visākha month (May–June). This corresponds to 788 A.C. But it carries a fiction along with it, *viz.*, that Sri Madhavāchārya was the son of a demon called Madhu! This clearly shows that the MS. in question was written in the 12th century A.C., and that the writer was an enemy of Dwaitees, the followers of Sri Madhavāchārya. ”

Swami Tapasyananda (1986, p. XV), a senior monk of the Ramakrishna Mission and an erudite scholar in Indian and western philosophy, states in the introduction to his translation of the book, *Sankara-Dig-Vijaya by Madhava-Vidyaranya*:

> “ Every date in ancient Indian history, except that of the invasion of Alexander (326 B.C.), is controversial, and Sankara's date is no exception. Max Muller and other orientalists have somehow fixed it as 788 to 820 A.D., and Das Gupta and Radhakrishnan, the well-known writers on the history of Indian Philosophy, have accepted and repeated it in their books. To do so is not in itself wrong, but to do it in such a way as to make the layman believe it to be conclusive is, to say the least, an injustice to him. It is held by

the critics of this date that the Sankara of 788–820 A.D. is not the Adi-Sankara (the original Sankara), but Abhinava Sankara ... of later times (788–839). ”

Many other scholars, too, opposed the AD 788–820 date as stated by Natalia Isayeva (1993, p. 84). She writes in *Shankara and Indian Philosophy*:

> “ Nevertheless, after some time many serious scholars agreed that the dating of Śaṅkara's life needed closer definition, and that its limits should be set farther back in the past. Similar views were advocated by Indian scholars K. Telang, T. Chitamani and S. Kuppuswami Sastri. Also inclined to an earlier dating is a well-known Japanese Indologist, Hajime Nakamura. ”

## Ādi Śaṅkarāchārya's True Date (509–477 BC)

T. S. Narayana Sastry carried out thorough research in ascertaining the true date of Ādi Śaṅkarāchārya as well as the chronology of ancient India and published his work in the book, *The Age of Śankara*, in 1916. I was not able to obtain the first edition of his book but found the second edition edited and published by his son in 1971. Sastry (1916/1971, p. 36) writes in his book:

> “ In the ancient *agrāhara* of Kālati ... on the northern bank of the Chūrṇi (Alavoi) river, in the enchanted country of Kerala, in the sacred land of Paraśurāma, there lived a pious Brāhmaṇa pair by name Śivaguru and Āryambā, of the family of Vidyādhirāja, famous for their great learning and wealth. The husband and wife, though possessed of all other blessings, had no issue for a long time. By the grace of the God Vṛishādrinātha, in the all-auspicious Nandana Saṁvatsara of the year 2593 of the Kali Yuga (corresponding to 509 B.C.), on a Sunday (Bhānu Vāsara) when the Sun was on its Northern Path (Uttarāyaṇa), on the 5th day (Pañchami Tithi) of the Bright Half (Śukla Paksha) of the month of Vaiśākha (May-June), in the asterism Punarvasu under the sign Sagittarius of the Zodiac (Dhnaur Lagna), was born, in a miraculous manner, a wonderful male child from the sacred womb of Āryambā, the dutiful wife of Śivaguru. ”

The birth date of Ādi Śaṅkarāchārya according to the *Śaṅkara Vijaya* and the accounts kept by the Dvārakā and Puri Maṭhas is 2593rd year of Kaliyuga as given by the following verse (Venkatachelam, 1953a, p. 61):

“तिष्ये प्रयात्यनलसेवधि बाण नेत्रे ।
योनंदने दिनमणा ऊदगध्वभाजि ।

राधेदितेरुडु विनिर्गत मंगलग्नेप्या।
हूतवान् शिवगुरुः सचशंकरेति ।।

Tiṣye prayātyanalasevadhi bāṇa netre ।
Yonandane dinamaṇā udagadhvabhāji ।
Rādhediteruḍu vinirgata maṅgalagnepyā ।
Hūtavān Śivaguruḥ sacaŚaṅkareti ।।

Meaning:

Anala=3, Sevadhi=9, Bāna=5, Netra=2, which comes to the year 2593rd year of Kaliyuga (read in reverse as was the practice in the old Sanskrit tradition) (509 BC).

Translation:

On Sunday, Vaiśākha Śukla Panchami in the constellation of Punarvasu, and in the lagna of Dhanus in the (Cycle) Year Nandana a son was born to Sivaguru and he was named "Sankara" by his father in 2593 Kali. This year corresponds to 509 B.C., (Vide "Epochs of the History of Bharata Varsha" by Jagadguru Sri Kalyanananda Bharati Māntachārya Swāmiji Maharaj, p. 130, Ed. 1931).

### Corroboration of the True Date

The corroboration of the true date of Ādi Śaṅkarāchārya can be found in certain works.

1. Dr. W. R. Antarkar in his doctoral study examined exhaustively, about 15 biographies of Ādi Śaṅkarāchārya and wrote a thesis titled *Śaṅkara Vijayas: A Comparative and a Critical Study* in 1960 which was accepted by the Poona University. Dr. Antarkar concluded that there is sufficient evidence to show that Śaṅkara was born in 509 BC and passed away in 477 BC.

2. A. Nataraja Aiyer and S. Lakshminarasimha Sastri (1962) also concluded in their book, *The Traditional Age of Sri Sankaracharya and the Maths* that Ādi Śaṅkarāchārya lived from 509 to 477 BC.

## Evidence for the True Date

### Evidence from the Age of Kumārila Bhatta and Mandana Misra

The *Jina Vijaya* says that Kumārila Bhattāchārya, the advocate of *karmakāṇḍa* (rituals), was born in the year 2077 of the Yudhiṣṭhira Śaka (of Jains). Jains' Yudhiṣṭhira Śaka started in 2634 BC (See Chapter 4), which means that the year

2077 of the Jain Yudhiṣṭhira Śaka is (2634 – 2077 =) 557 BC. Kumārila was born in the sacred village, Jayamangala, on the bank of the River Mahanadi, at the meeting place of the Āndhra and Utkala countries. He was an Āndhraite by birth and belonged to the *Taittiriya* Vedic school (Krishna Yajurveda Śākhā). His mother was Chandraguṇa, the pious, and his father was Yajneswara. He was a great debater and a staunch adherent of the Vedas (Venkatachelam, 1953a, p. 57–58; 1956b, p. 30).

He lived among the Jains as their student and committed the heinous sin of attacking the religion of his Jain gurus and was, therefore, hated by them. Two years after the death of Mahāvira, Kumārila was pushed down from the terrace, in the year 2109 of Yudhiṣṭhira Śaka (of Jains) which is 525 BC (=2634–2109). Fortunately, he did not die but did lose an eye. Chitsukhāchārya says in his Bṛhat Śankara Vijaya that Kumārila was older than Śaṅkara by 48 years. This matches with the birthdate of Śaṅkarāchārya being 509 BC since Kumārila Bhatta was born in 557 BC.

Years later, Kumārila Bhatta, feeling guilty for betraying his guru (*gurudroha*) wanted to expiate for his sin by burning himself in a slow fire of grain husk. However, he had heard of Śaṅkarāchārya and wanted to meet him before his death with the satisfaction that his great mission would be continued by a worthier agent. The news of Kumārila's self-immolation reached Śaṅkara at Prayāg and he hurried to Ruddhapura (near Prayāg) to avert the gruesome end of Bhatta. He reached in time to see the great exponent of *karma mārga* (rituals) alive amidst the flames and vainly tried to dissuade him from the suicidal act. In the end, the adamant Bhatta directed Śaṅkara to meet his famous pupil and advocate of Mimāṁsā doctrine, Mandana Misra (Narayana Sastry, 1916/1971, p. 170).

Referring to the extraordinary meeting of Śaṅkara with Kumārila Bhatta on his funeral pyre, the *Jina Vijaya* declares (Narayana Sastry, 1916/1971, p. 152):

> "Thereupon when 15 years had elapsed from his birth, Śaṅkara met Bhattāchārya for the first and the last time."

Thus, Śaṅkara met Kumārila Bhatta in his 16th year, that is about 493 BC.

## Debate with Mandana Misra

Leaving Ruddhapura, Śaṅkara journeyed to Mahishmati (See the map in Figure 30) where Mandana was living. Mandana Misra, the great *Mimaṁsaka*, was a faithful student of Bhatta. It is said that his devoted spouse was a very learned lady. Mandana Misra was the chief of Mahishmati and had great

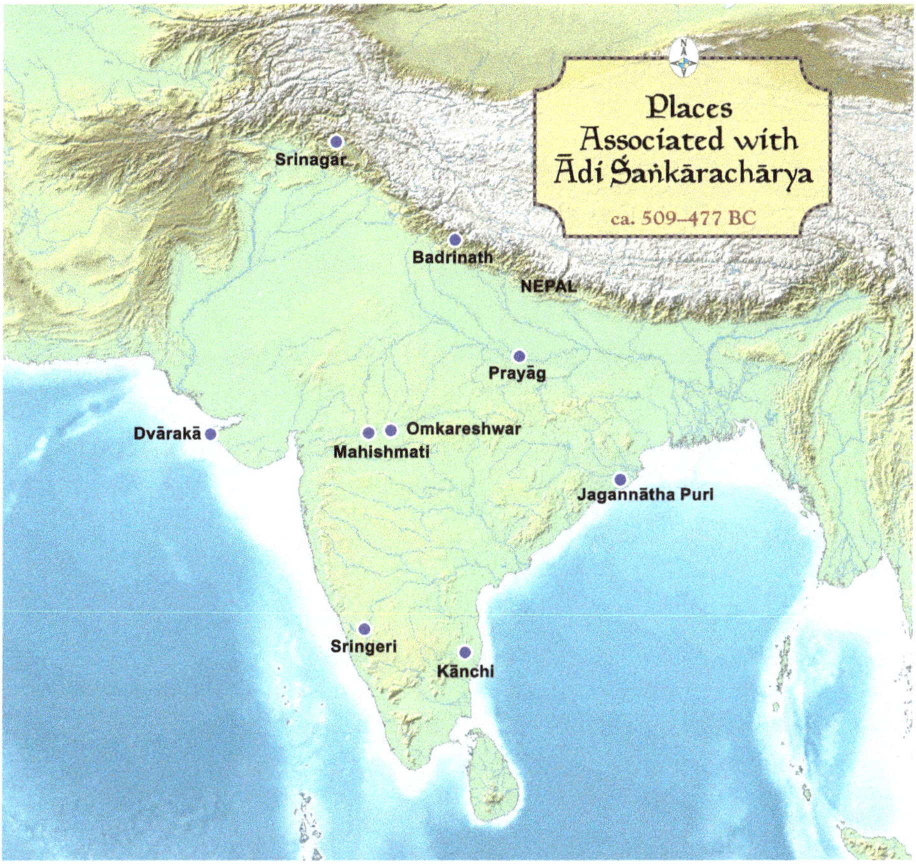


**Figure 30: Places associated with Ādi Śaṅkarāchārya depicted on a map**
*Blank map courtesy: DEMIS Mapserver, Wikimedia Commons, CC BY-SA 3.0*

influence. He lived grandly in a fine mansion. He was performing a śrāddha ceremony when Śaṅkara arrived in front of him and desired to have a debate with him (Narayana Sastry, 1916/1971, p. 173).

It was stipulated that the party defeated in the debate would become an adherent of the victor. After the great debate lasting days, Mandana Misra accepted defeat and became Śaṅkarāchārya's disciple and a sannyāsī, leaving his *gruhasthāshrama* (family life). His sannyāsa name was Sureswarāchārya. He is the author of numerous works on Vedanta and Mimāṁsā.

## Evidence from the History of Govindabhagavatpāda (Śaṅkarā's Guru)

Śrī Govindabhagavatpāda was the guru of Śrī Ādi Śaṅkarāchārya, as discussed in Chapter 10. His prior name was Chandra Sharma before he took sannyāsa (renouncing worldly life) in his later age. Chandra Sharma was the father of Bhartruhari and Śrī Harśa Vikramāditya, the illustrious kings of Ujjain in the fifth century BC.

## Contemporary of King Hāla of the Āndhra Dynasty of Magadha

While describing King Hāla Śātavāhana of the Āndhra Dynasty of Magadha, Pandit Venkatachelam (1957a, p. 182) writes:

> "We learn from Chitsukha's Brihat Sankarvijaya and Sadasivendra's Jagadguru Ratnamala that Sri Adi Sankaracharya, the author of the famous Bhashyas on the Prasthanatrya, was a contemporary of this king."

Table 22 (Chapter 7) shows that the 19th Āndhra King Hāla Śātavāhana's reigning period was 494–489 BC, matching with Ādi Śaṅkarāchārya's time of 509–477 BC.

## Copper Plate Inscription of Sudhanva

King Sudhanva, who ruled over Gujarat from Dvārakā in the fifth century BC, has been mentioned in the biography of Ādi Śaṅkara by Swami Vidyāranya. King Sudhanva presented a memorandum inscribed on a copper plate to Ādi Śaṅkarāchārya after the religious debate which he won. T. S. Narayana Sastry (1916/1971, p. 152) writes:

> "The Jina Vijaya refers to King Sudhanvan, as a contemporary of Kumārila and Śaṅkara, and speaks of him, in unmistakable terms, as a wicked king and as a persecutor of the pious Jains."

The inscription was originally published by His Holiness, the late Śrī Śaṅkarāchārya of the Dvārakā Maṭha on page 29 of his book, *Vimarsa*. T. S. Narayana Sastry (1916/1971, p. 154) adds:

> "There cannot be any doubt after perusing the Tāmrapatrānanusāsana [copper plate inscription] issued by King Sudhanvan addressed to Śaṅkara Bhagavatpāda himself on the 15th day of the bright half of the month of Aśvina in the year 2663 of the Yudhishṭhira Śaka, corresponding to 478 B.C., and after duly considering the adverse account given in the Jina Vijaya, that the story of Kumārila Bhaṭṭa is mainly based on the historical facts."

See the text of the inscription in *The Age of Śankara* (Narayana Sastry, 1916/1971, p. 220). The inscription contains a brief and authentic account of the life of Śrī Ādi Śaṅkarāchārya.

## Evidence of Guru Vaṁśāvali from the Dvārakā Maṭha

The Guru Vaṁśāvali published in the *Vimarsa* by the Acharya of the Dvārakā Maṭha contains dates of the main events of Ādi Śaṅkrarāchārya's life. All the dates are stated in the Yudhiṣṭhira Śaka. According to this chronology, Ādi Śaṅkarāchārya was born in the Yudhiṣṭhira Śaka 2631 (507 BC) and established the Śāradā Pīṭha at Dvārakā in the Yudhiṣṭhira Śaka 2649 (489 BC) (Narayana Sastry, 1916/1971, p. 217). Thus, according to the Dvārakā Maṭha records, the time of Śaṅkarāchārya is two years later and it tallies with the date of Yudhiṣṭhira Śaka 2663 (475-476 BC) of King Sudhanva's inscription which was issued in the last year of Śaṅkarāchārya's life of 32 years.

## Evidence from Nepal Rāja Vaṁśāvali

The Nepal Rāja Vaṁśāvali (Wright, 1877/1990, p. 120; Indraji and Bühler, 1884, p. 411) states that Śaṅkarāchārya came from the south and destroyed the Buddha faith. In the Sūryavaṁśi Dynasty of Nepal, the 18th king was Vrishadevavarman. He reigned from Kaliyuga 2554 to 2615 (547–486 BC). (See Table 41, Chapter 12.) When Ādi Śaṅkarāchārya came to Nepal, the king had already died, leaving the queen pregnant. The prince was born in the due course of time and was named Śaṅkaradeva after Śaṅkarāchārya. Thus, Ādi Śaṅkarāchārya's visit to Nepal in about Kaliyuga 2615 (486 BC) tallies with the account in the Nepal Rāja Vaṁśāvali.

## The Temple of Śaṅkarāchārya in Kashmir

As described in Rājataraṅgiṇī and shown in Table 32 in Chapter 11, Gopāditya was the great king of Kashmir from 418 to 358 BC. P. Gwasha Lal (1932, p. 27) states in his book, *A Short History of Kashmir,* that Gopāditya the Good was a great builder. He built *agraharas,* and the temples of Jyeṣṭheshvara (ज्येष्ठेश्वर) and Śaṅkarāchārya. Pandit Venkatachelam (1956b, p. 28) quotes the following from the article published in the newspaper Hindu:

> “ "Sankaracharya"—"This shrine is situated in the city of Srinagar. Sankaracharya is an ancient temple crowning the Takht-i-Sulaiman hill and standing 1000 ft. above the valley. The temple and the hill on which it stands take their name from Sankaracharya— the great South Indian Teacher of Monism who came to Kashmir from Travancore. This temple was built by king Gopaditya, who reigned in Kashmir from 368 to 308 B.C. It was repaired later by the liberal-minded Muslim king Zainul Abdin." (Vide The Hindu dated 17-7-1949 p: 15, 2nd column, and Kali Saka Vijnanam by K. Venkatachelam part III. p. 66). ”

**Figure 31: Śaṅkarāchārya Temple on Śaṅkarāchārya Hill, Srinagar, Kashmir**
*Photo courtesy: John Burke, AD 1868, Wikimedia Commons, public domain*

Since Gopāditya's real time is 418–358 BC as discussed in Chapter 11, Ādi Śaṅkarāchārya must have lived before that time. Figure 31 shows a photograph of this temple.

## Evidence from Esoteric Buddhism

A. P. Sinnett (1883/1907, p. 182–183) in his book, *Esoteric Buddhism,* assigns about 503 BC or so for Ādi Śaṅkarāchārya by stating that Śaṅkarāchārya appeared in India about 60 years after the death of Buddha. Sinnett (1883/1907, p. 175) thinks that Buddha lived from 643 to 563 BC. The approximate date of 503 BC for Śaṅkarāchārya is very close to the date 509 BC given in *Bṛhat Sankara Vijaya* and *Jina Vijaya* (Venkatachelam, 1956b, p. 29).

## Evidence from Maṭhāmnāya (मठाम्नाय) Setu or Mahānushāsanam

Parameshwar Nath Mishra (2001, p. 15), an advocate of the High Court at Kolkata and a visiting advocate at the Supreme Court of India, in his commentary on Ādi Śaṅkarāchārya's *Maṭhāmnāya Setu* has shown the time of Ādi Śaṅkarāchārya to be 507–475 BC. This time is two years later than the 509–477 BC time accepted by many scholars. The two-year difference is insignificant compared to the dating by the colonial Indologists which is wrong by about 1,300 years.

## Evidence from the Chronology of the Maṭhas established by Ādi Śaṅkarāchārya

Ādi Śaṅkarāchārya established five great maṭhas (monastic institutions) in the four corners of India as follows (Narayana Sastry, 1916/1971, p. 198).

(1) The Śāradā Pīṭha at Dvārakā on *Māgha Śukla Saptami* in the year *Sādhārana* in Kaliyuga 2611 (491 BC) with Śrī Brahma Svarupāchārya (Viśvarupa), the brother of the famous Sureśvarāchārya (formerly Mandana Misra) as its first Āchārya. According to the Dvārakā Maṭha records (Narayana Sastry, p. 218), the Maṭha was established in Yudhiṣṭhira Śaka 2649 which corresponds to Kaliyuga 2613 (489 BC). Thus, there is a discrepancy of two years in the dates.

(2) The Jyotir Maṭha at Badrikāshrama in the Himalayas on *Pauṣa (Puṣya) Purṇimā* of the year *Rākṣasa* in Kaliyuga 2616 (486 BC) with Śrī Totakāchārya (formerly Anandagiri) as its first Āchārya. Again, according to the Dvārakā Maṭha records, the Jyotir Maṭha was established in Yudhiṣṭhira Śaka 2654 which corresponds to Kaliyuga 2618 (484 BC) and thus, there is a discrepancy of two years here also.

(3) The Govardhana Maṭha at Jagannātha Puri on *Vaiśakha Śukla Daśami* of the year *Nala* in Kaliyuga 2617 (484 BC) with Śrī Padmapādāchārya (formerly Sanandana) as its first Āchārya. Again, according to the Dvārakā Maṭha records, the Maṭha was established in Yudhiṣṭhira Śaka 2655 which corresponds to Kaliyuga 2619 (482 BC) and thus, there is a discrepancy of two years.

(4) The Śāradā Pīṭha at Sringeri on *Pauṣa Purṇimā* of the year *Piṅgala* in Kaliyuga 2618 (484 BC) with Hastāmalakāchārya (formerly Prithvidhara) as its first Āchārya.

(5) Kāmakoti Pīṭha at Kānchi on *Vaiśakha Purṇimā* of the year *Siddhārthi* in Kaliyuga 2620 (481 BC) with himself as its first Āchārya.

The Kānchi Kāmakoṭi, Dvārakā, and Jagannātha Puri maṭhas have maintained a complete chronology of their Pīṭhādhipatis (head of the Pīṭha) from their beginning to the present time.

## Chronology of Pīṭhādhipatis of the Kānchi Kāmakoṭi Maṭha

The chronology of the āchāryas of the Kāmakoṭi Pīṭha from its beginning to the present time is shown in Table 25 (Venkatachelam, 1956b, p. 23; Narayana Sastry, 1916/1971, Appendix III). There are a few differences between the two sources cited here. The names are spelled as given in the cited references. The website of the pīṭha has a similar list and provides more details on each of the āchāryas. (http://www.kamakoti.org/peeth/origin.html#appendix2)

**Table 25: Chronology of Pīṭhādhipatis of the Kānchi Kāmakoṭi Pīṭha, Kaliyuga 2620 (481 BC)–present**

| Sr. No. | Name of the Āchārya | Years as Āchārya | Date of Demise | | |
|---|---|---|---|---|---|
| | | | Cyclic Year | Month, Pakṣa, and Tithi (day) | Christian Year |
| | Pīṭha established in | | | Vaiśākha O | 481 BC |
| 1 | Ādi Śaṅkarāchārya | 4 | Raktākṣī | Vaiśākha S11 | 477 BC |
| 2 | Suresvarāchārya | 70 | Bhāva | Jyeṣṭha S12 | 407 BC |
| 3 | Sarvajnatman | 43 | Nala | Vaiśākha K14 | 364 BC |
| 4 | Satyabodha | 96 | Nandana | Mārgas K8 | 268 BC |
| 5 | Jnanananda | 63 | Manmatha | Mārgas S7 | 205 BC |
| 6 | Suddhananda | 81 | Nala | Jyeṣṭha S6 | 124 BC |
| 7 | Anandajnana | 69 | Krodhana | Vaiśākha K9 | 55 BC |
| 8 | Kaivalyananda | 83 | Sarvadhāri | Makara 1 | 28 AD |
| 9 | Kripa Sankara (II) | 41 | Vibhava | Kārtika K3 | 69 AD |
| 10 | Suresvara | 58 | Akṣaya | Aṣāḍha O | 127 AD |
| 11 | Chidghana | 45 | Virodhikṛt | Jyeṣṭha K10 | 172 AD |
| 12 | Chandrashekhara I | 63 | Ānanda | Aṣāḍha S9 | 235 AD |
| 13 | Sachchidghana | 37 | Khara | Mārgas S1 | 272 AD |
| 14 | Vidyaghana I (Śaka 239) | 45 | Dhātṛ | Mārgas N | 317 AD |
| 15 | Gangadhara I | 12 | Sarvadhāri | Chaitra S1 | 329 AD |
| 16 | Ujjvala Sankara (III) | 38 | Akṣaya | Vrishabha S8 | 367 AD |
| 17 | Sadasiva | 8 | Bhāva | Jyeṣṭha S10 | 375 AD |
| 18 | Surendra (Kali 3486) | 10 | Tāraṇa | Mārgas S1 | 385 AD |
| 19 | Vidyaghana II | 13 | Hevilambi | Bhādra K9 | 398 AD |
| 20 | Muka Sankara (IV) (Śaka 359) | 39 | Dhātṛ | Śrāvaṇa O | 437 AD |
| 21 | Chandrachuda I | 10 | Vyaya | Śrāvaṇa K8 | 447 AD |

| Sr. No. | Name of the Āchārya | Years as Āchārya | Date of Demise: Cyclic Year | Month, Pakṣa, and Tithi (day) | Christian Year |
|---|---|---|---|---|---|
| 22 | Paripurna Bodha | 34 | Raudri | Kārtika S9 | 481 AD |
| 23 | Sachchitsukha | 31 | Khara | Vaiśākha S7 | 512 AD |
| 24 | Chitsukha I | 15 | Prabhava | Śrāvaṇa K9 | 527 AD |
| 25 | Sachchidanandaghana (Śaka 470) | 21 | Prabhava | Aṣāḍha S1 | 548 AD |
| 26 | Prajnaghana | 16 | Svabhānu | Vaiśākha S8 | 564 AD |
| 27 | Chidvilasa | 13 | Durmukhi | New Year - Day S1 | 577 AD |
| 28 | Mahadeva I | 24 | Raudri | Kārtika K10 | 601 AD |
| 29 | Purnabodha | 17 | Iśvara | Śrāvaṇa S10 | 618 AD |
| 30 | Bodha I | 37 | Ānanda | Vaiśākha K4 | 655 AD |
| 31 | Brahmanandaghana I | 13 | Prabhava | Jyeṣṭha S12 | 668 AD |
| 32 | Chidanandaghana | 4 | Prajotpati | Mārgas S6 | 672 AD |
| 33 | Sachchidananda II | 20 | Khara | Bhādra K6 | 692 AD |
| 34 | Chandrasekhara II | 18 | Saumya | Mārgas N | 710 AD |
| 35 | Chitsukha II | 27 | Dhātṛ | Aṣāḍha S6 | 737 AD |
| 36 | Chitsukhananda | 21 | Hevilambi | Aśvina O | 758 AD |
| 37 | Vidyaghana III | 30 | Prabhava | Puṣya S2 | 788 AD |
| 38 | Abhinava Sankara (V) (Kaliyuga 3941) | 52 | Siddhārthi | Aṣāḍha N | 840 AD |
| 39 | Sachchidvilasa | 33 | Nandana | Vaiśākha O | 873 AD |
| 40 | Mahadeva II | 42 | Bhāva | Vaiśākha S6 | 915 AD |
| 41 | Gangadhara II | 35 | Saumya | Śrāvaṇa S1 | 950 AD |
| 42 | Brahmanandaghana II | 28 | Iśvara | Kārtika S8 | 978 AD |
| 43 | Anandaghana | 36 | Pramādi | Chaitra S9 | 1014 AD |
| 44 | Purnabodha II | 26 | Pramāthi | Bhādra K13 | 1040 AD |
| 45 | Paramasiva I | 21 | Śārvari | Aśvina S7 | 1061 AD |
| 46 | Bodha II | 37 | Iśvara | Aṣāḍha N | 1098 AD |
| 47 | Chandrasekhara III | 68 | Pārthiva | Chaitra N | 1166 AD |
| 48 | Advaitananda Bodha | 34 | Siddhārthi | Jyeṣṭha S10 | 1200 AD |
| 49 | Mahadeva III | 47 | Parābhava | Kārtika K8 | 1247 AD |
| 50 | Chandrachuda II | 50 | Durmukhi | Jyeṣṭha S6 | 1297 AD |
| 51 | Vidyatirtha | 88 | Raktākṣī | Māgha K1 | 1385 AD |

*Table Continued...*

| Sr. No. | Name of the Āchārya | Years as Āchārya | Date of Demise | | |
|---|---|---|---|---|---|
| | | | Cyclic Year | Month, Pakṣa, and Tithi (day) | Christian Year |
| 52 | Sankarananda | 32 | Durmukhi | Vaiśākha S1* | 1417 AD* |
| 53 | Purnananda Sadasiva | 81 | Piṅgala | Jyeṣṭha S10 | 1498 AD |
| 54 | Mahadeva IV | 9 | Akṣaya | Aṣāḍha K1 | 1507 AD |
| 55 | Chandrachuda III | 17 | Svabhānu | Mina S11 | 1524 AD |
| 56 | Sarvajna Sadasivabodha | 15 | Vilambi | Chaitra S8 | 1539 AD |
| 57 | Paramasiva II | 47 | Pārthiva | Śrāvaṇa S10 | 1586 AD |
| 58 | Atmabodha | 52 | Iśvara | Tula K8 | 1638 AD |
| 59 | Bodha III | 54 | Prajotpati | Bhādra O | 1692 AD |
| 60 | Advayatma Prakasha | 12 | Svabhānu | Chaitra K2 | 1704 AD |
| 61 | Mahadeva V | 42 | Krodhana | Jyeṣṭha S9 | 1746 AD |
| 62 | Chandrasekhara IV | 37 | Subhakṛt | Puṣya K2 | 1783 AD |
| 63 | Mahadeva VI | 31 | Śrīmukha | Aṣāḍha S12 | 1814 AD |
| 64 | Chandrasekhara V | 37 | Sādhāraṇa | Kārtika K2 | 1851 AD |
| 65 | Mahadeva VII | 40 | Virodhi | Phālguna N | 1891 AD |
| 66 | Chandrasekhara VI | 17 | Parābhava | Māgha K8 | 1907 AD* |
| 67 | Mahadeva VIII | 7 days | Parābhava | Phālguna S1 | 1907 AD* |
| 68 | Chandrasekharendra Saraswati VII* | 87 | | Dhanur K12* | 1994 AD* |
| 69 | Jayendra Saraswati* | 24 | | February 28* | 2018 AD* |
| 70 | Sankara Vijayendra Saraswati – the present Āchārya* | | | | |
| | Śaka = Śālivāhana Śaka<br>* from the website www.kamakoti.org | | | S = Śukla Pakṣa<br>K = Kṛṣṇa Pakṣa<br>O = Full moon<br>N = New moon | |

## Chronology of Pīṭhādhipatis of the Śāradā Pīṭhā at Dvārakā

Dvārakā Maṭha's Jagadguru *paramparā* (tradition) has maintained the complete chronology of its Pīṭhādhipatis from its beginning to the present time and is available at the pīṭha and in its Hindi publication *Divya-Dwarka* (2018). The chronology was maintained in the Yudhiṣṭhira Śaka (YS) until the Vikrama Samvat (VS) started in 57 BC. The complete chronology of the Pīṭhādhipatis is given in Table 26 (Mishra, 2000, p. 60–64). Pandit Venkatachelam (1956b, p. 26) has also provided a similar chronology with a few differences.

**Table 26: Chronology of Pīṭhādhipatis of the Dvārakā Pīṭha, Yudhiṣṭhira Śaka 2649 (489 BC)–present**

| Sr. No. | Name of the Āchārya | Years as Āchārya | End Date: Samvat YS or VS | End Date: Month, Pakṣa, and Tithi (day) | End Date: Christian Year |
|---|---|---|---|---|---|
| | Pīṭha established in | | YS 2649 | Māgha S7 | 489 BC |
| 1 | Brahmaswarupāchārya (Sureśvarāchārya) | 42 | YS 2691 | Chaitra K8 | 447 BC |
| 2 | Citsukhāchārya | 24 | YS2715 | Puṣya S3 | 423 BC |
| 3 | Sarvajñānāchārya | 59 | YS 2774 | Śrāvaṇa S11 | 364 BC |
| 4 | Brahmānandatirtha | 49 | YS 2823 | Śrāvaṇa S1 | 315 BC |
| 5 | Svarupābhijñānāchārya | 67 | YS 2890 | Jyeṣṭha K15 | 248 BC |
| 6 | Mangalamūrtyāchārya | 52 | YS 2942 | Puṣya S14 | 196 BC |
| 7 | Bhāskarāchārya | 23 | YS 2965 | Puṣya S12 | 173 BC |
| 8 | Prajñānāchārya | 43 | YS 3008 | Aṣāḍha S7 | 130 BC |
| 9 | Brahmajyotsnāchārya | 32 | YS 3040 | Chaitra K4 | 98 BC |
| 10 | Anandāvirbhāvāchārya | 51 | VS 9 | Phālguna S9 | 47 BC |
| 11 | Kalānidhitirtha | 73 | VS 82 | Puṣya S6 | 26 AD |
| 12 | Cidvilāsāchārya | 37 | VS 119 | Mārgas S13 | 63 AD |
| 13 | Vibhūtyānandāchārya | 35 | VS 154 | Śrāvaṇa K11 | 98 AD |
| 14 | Sphurtinilayapāda | 49 | VS 203 | Aṣāḍha S6 | 147 AD |
| 15 | Varatantupāda | 56 | VS 259 | Aṣāḍha K3 | 203 AD |
| 16 | Yogāruḍhāchārya | 101 | VS 360 | Mārgas K11 | 304 AD |
| 17 | Vijayaḍiṇḍimāchārya | 34 | VS 394 | Puṣya K8 | 338 AD |
| 18 | Vidyātirtha | 43 | VS 437 | Chaitra S1 | 381 AD |
| 19 | Cicchaktideśika | 1 | VS 438 | Aṣāḍha S12 | 382 AD |
| 20 | Vijñāneśvara Tirtha | 73 | VS 511 | Aśvina S15 | 455 AD |
| 21 | Rutambharāchārya | 61 | VS 572 | Māgha S10 | 516 AD |
| 22 | Amareśvara Guru | 36 | VS 608 | Bhādra K6 | 552 AD |
| 23 | Sarvatomukha Tirtha | 61 | VS 669 | Puṣya S4 | 613 AD |
| 24 | Ānandadeśika | 52 | VS 721 | Vaiśākha K5 | 665 AD |
| 25 | Samādhirarasika | 78 | VS 799 | Phālguna S12 | 743 AD |
| 26 | Nārāyanāśrama | 37 | VS 836 | Chaitra S14 | 780 AD |
| 27 | Vaikunthāśrama | 49 | VS 885 | Aṣāḍha K6 | 829 AD |
| 28 | Trivikramāśrama | 26 | VS 911 | Aṣāḍha S3 | 855 AD |

*Table Continued...*

| Sr. No. | Name of the Āchārya | Years as Āchārya | End Date | | |
|---|---|---|---|---|---|
| | | | Samvat YS or VS | Month, Pakṣa, and Tithi (day) | Christian Year |
| 29 | Nṛsiṁhāśrama | 49 | VS 960 | Jyeṣṭha K14 | 904 AD |
| 30 | Tryambakāśrama | 5 | VS 965 | Vaiśākha K15 | 909 AD |
| 31 | Viṣṇavāśrama | 36 | VS 1001 | Jyeṣṭha S1 | 945 AD |
| 32 | Kesavāśrama | 59 | VS 1060 | Māgha K5 | 1004 AD |
| 33 | Cidambarāśrama | 23 | VS 1083 | Mārgas K9 | 1027 AD |
| 34 | Padmanābhāśrama | 26 | VS 1109 | Jyeṣṭha S15 | 1053 AD |
| 35 | Mahādevāśrama | 39 | VS 1148 | Śrāvaṇa K9 | 1092 AD |
| 36 | Saccidānandāśrama | 59 | VS 1207 | Aśvina K5 | 1151 AD |
| 37 | Vidyāśankarāśrama | 58 | VS 1265 | Aśvina K4 | 1209 AD |
| 38 | Abhinava Saccidānandāśrama | 28 | VS 1293 | Vaiśākha S6 | 1237 AD |
| 39 | Śaśiśekharāśrama | 33 | VS 1326 | Vaiśākha S1 | 1270 AD |
| 40 | Vāsudevāśrama | 36 | VS 1362 | Phālguna K10 | 1306 AD |
| 41 | Puruṣottamāśrama | 32 | VS 1394 | Māgha K5 | 1338 AD |
| 42 | Janāradanāśrama | 14 | VS 1408 | Bhādra S15 | 1352 AD |
| 43 | Hariharāśrama | 3 | VS 1411 | Śrāvaṇa S11 | 1355 AD |
| 44 | Bhavāśrama | 10 | VS 1421 | Vaiśākha K5 | 1365 AD |
| 45 | Brahmāśrama | 15 | VS 1436 | Aṣāḍha S9 | 1380 AD |
| 46 | Vāmanāśrama | 17 | VS 1453 | Chaitra K12 | 1397 AD |
| 47 | Sarvajñāśrama | 36 | VS 1489 | Chaitra K8 | 1433 AD |
| 48 | Pradyumnāśrama | 6 | VS 1495 | Chaitra S7 | 1439 AD |
| 49 | Govindāśrama | 28 | VS 1523 | Jyeṣṭha K4 | 1467 AD |
| 50 | Cidāśrama | 53 | VS 1576 | Phālguna S2 | 1520 AD |
| 51 | Viśveśvarāśrama | 32 | VS 1608 | Mārgas S1 | 1552 AD |
| 52 | Dāmodarāśrama | 7 | VS 1615 | Chaitra K5 | 1559 AD |
| 53 | Mahādevāśrama | 1 | VS 1616 | Chaitra S1 | 1560 AD |
| 54 | Aniruddhāśrama | 9 | VS 1625 | Māgha K4 | 1569 AD |
| 55 | Acyutāśrama | 4 | VS 1629 | Śrāvaṇa K6 | 1573 AD |
| 56 | Mādhavāśrama | 36 | VS 1665 | Māgha K4 | 1609 AD |
| 57 | Anantāśrama | 51 | VS 1716 | Chaitra S12 | 1660 AD |
| 58 | Viśvarūpāśrama | 5 | VS 1721 | Śrāvaṇa K2 | 1665 AD |
| 59 | Cidghanāśrama | 5 | VS 1726 | Māgha S6 | 1670 AD |

| Sr. No. | Name of the Āchārya | Years as Āchārya | End Date Samvat YS or VS | Month, Pakṣa, and Tithi (day) | Christian Year |
|---|---|---|---|---|---|
| 60 | Nṛsiṁhāshrama | 9 | VS 1735 | Vaiśākha S4 | 1679 AD |
| 61 | Manoharāśrama | 26 | VS 1761 | Bhādra S9 | 1705 AD |
| 62 | Prakāśānanda Sarasvati | 34 | VS 1795 | Aśvina K6 | 1739 AD |
| 63 | Viśuddhānandāśrama | 4 | VS 1799 | Vaiśākha K15 | 1743 AD |
| 64 | Vāmanedrāśrama | 32 | VS 1831 | Śrāvaṇa S6 | 1775 AD |
| 65 | Kesavāśrama | 7 | VS 1838 | Kārtika K9 | 1782 AD |
| 66 | Madhusūdanāśrama | 10 | VS 1848 | Māgha S5 | 1792 AD |
| 67 | Hayagrivāśrama | 14 | VS 1862 | | 1806 AD |
| 68 | Prakāśāśrama | 1 | VS 1863 | | 1807 AD |
| 69 | Hayagrivānanda Sarasvati | 11 | VS 1874 | | 1818 AD |
| 70 | Śrīdharāśrama | 40 | VS 1914 | | 1858 AD |
| 71 | Dāmodarāśrama | 14 | VS 1928 | | 1872 AD |
| 72 | Keśavāśrama | 7 | VS 1935 | Aśvina K7 | 1879 AD |
| 73 | Rājarājeśvara Śankarāśrama | 22 | VS 1957 | Aṣāḍha S5 | 1901 AD |
| 74 | Mādhavatirtha | 14 | VS 1972 | Bhādra K15 | 1916 AD |
| 75 | Śātyānanda Sarasvati | 10 | VS 1982 | | 1926 AD |
| 76 | Candraśekharāśrama | 19 | VS 2001 | | 1945 AD |
| 77 | Abhinava Saccidānanda | 37 | VS 2038 | | 1982 AD |
| 78 | Svarūpānand Sarasvati – the present Āchārya | | | | |
| YS = Yudhisthira Śaka, VS = Vikrama Samvat, S = Śukla Pakṣa, K = Kṛṣṇa Pakṣa | | | | | |

*Note: The Christian year lags the Vikrama Samvat by 56–57 years, but in the table above, 56 years have been subtracted uniformly from the Vikrama Samvat year to obtain the Christian year. Therefore, the years given in the Christian year may be off by one year in some cases.*

## Chronology of Pīṭhādhipatis of the Govardhana Maṭha at Jagannātha Puri

The Govardhana Maṭha has a complete list of the Pīṭhādhipatis, a total of 145 from its beginning to the present time along with the dates as shown in Table 27. The names are spelled as given on their website. (https://www.govardhanpeeth.org/en/about-us-en/adi-Shankaracharya-successor)

**Table 27: Chronology of Pīṭhādhipatis of the Jagannātha Puri Maṭha, Kaliyuga 2617 (484 BC)–present**

| Sr. No. | Name of the Āchārya | Years as Āchārya | End Year | |
|---|---|---|---|---|
| | | | Kaliyuga Year | Christian Year |
| | Pīṭha established in | | 2617 | 484 BC |
| 1 | Anantashri Padmapad | 25 | 2642 | 459 BC |
| 2 | Anantashri Shoolapani | 20 | 2662 | 439 BC |
| 3 | Anantashri Narayan | 17 | 2679 | 422 BC |
| 4 | Anantashri Vidyaranya | 18 | 2697 | 404 BC |
| 5 | Anantashri Vamdev | 16 | 2713 | 388 BC |
| 6 | Anantashri Padmanabh | 15 | 2728 | 373 BC |
| 7 | Anantashri Jagannatha | 14 | 2742 | 359 BC |
| 8 | Anantashri Madhureshwar | 10 | 2752 | 349 BC |
| 9 | Anantashri Govind | 21 | 2773 | 328 BC |
| 10 | Anantashri Shridhar | 18 | 2791 | 310 BC |
| 11 | Anantashri Madhavanand | 17 | 2808 | 293 BC |
| 12 | Anantashri Krishnabrahmanand | 18 | 2826 | 275 BC |
| 13 | Anantashri Ramanandteertha | 16 | 2842 | 259 BC |
| 14 | Anantashri Vagishwarteertha | 15 | 2857 | 244 BC |
| 15 | Anantashri Parameshwarteertha | 14 | 2871 | 230 BC |
| 16 | Anantashri Gopalteertha | 12 | 2883 | 218 BC |
| 17 | Anantashri Janardanteertha | 14 | 2897 | 204 BC |
| 18 | Anantashri Jnanandateertha | 20 | 2917 | 184 BC |
| 19 | Anantashri Brihadaranya | 19 | 2936 | 165 BC |
| 20 | Anantashri Mahadevteertha | 18 | 2954 | 147 BC |
| 21 | Anantashri Brahmanandateertha | 16 | 2970 | 131 BC |
| 22 | Anantashri Ramanandteertha | 15 | 2985 | 116 BC |
| 23 | Anantashri Sadashivateertha | 14 | 2999 | 102 BC |
| 24 | Anantashri Harishwaranandteertha | 12 | 3011 | 90 BC |
| 25 | Anantashri Bodhanandteertha | 14 | 3025 | 76 BC |
| 26 | Anantashri Ramakrishnateertha | 20 | 3045 | 56 BC |
| 27 | Anantashri Chidbodhatmateertha | 10 | 3055 | 46 BC |
| 28 | Anantashri Tattvaksharteertha | 18 | 3073 | 28 BC |
| 29 | Anantashri Shankarteertha | 16 | 3089 | 12 BC |
| 30 | Anantashri Vasudevteertha | 20 | 3109 | 8 AD |
| 31 | Anantashri Hayagrivateertha | 17 | 3126 | 25 AD |

| Sr. No. | Name of the Āchārya | Years as Āchārya | End Year | |
|---|---|---|---|---|
| | | | Kaliyuga Year | Christian Year |
| 32 | Anantashri Shrutishwarateertha | 14 | 3140 | 39 AD |
| 33 | Anantashri Vidyanandateertha | 20 | 3160 | 59 AD |
| 34 | Anantashri Mukundanandateertha | 18 | 3178 | 77 AD |
| 35 | Anantashri Hiranyagarbhateertha | 19 | 3197 | 96 AD |
| 36 | Anantashri Nityanandateertha | 18 | 3215 | 114 AD |
| 37 | Anantashri Shivananda | 16 | 3231 | 130 AD |
| 38 | Anantashri Yogishwarteertha | 18 | 3249 | 148 AD |
| 39 | Anantashri Sudarshan | 15 | 3264 | 163 AD |
| 40 | Anantashri Vyomkesh | 17 | 3281 | 180 AD |
| 41 | Anantashri Damodarteertha | 21 | 3302 | 201 AD |
| 42 | Anantashri Yoganandateertha | 20 | 3322 | 221 AD |
| 43 | Anantashri Golokesh | 21 | 3343 | 242 AD |
| 44 | Anantashri Shrikrishnandateertha | 18 | 3361 | 260 AD |
| 45 | Anantashri Devanandateertha | 23 | 3384 | 283 AD |
| 46 | Anantashri Chandrachudteertha | 15 | 3399 | 298 AD |
| 47 | Anantashri Halayudhateertha | 14 | 3413 | 312 AD |
| 48 | Anantashri Siddhasevyateertha | 15 | 3428 | 327 AD |
| 49 | Anantashri Tarakatmateertha | 20 | 3448 | 347 AD |
| 50 | Anantashri Bodhayanteertha | 21 | 3469 | 368 AD |
| 51 | Anantashri Shreedharteertha | 19 | 3488 | 387 AD |
| 52 | Anantashri Narayanteertha | 18 | 3506 | 405 AD |
| 53 | Anantashri Sadashivateertha | 15 | 3521 | 420 AD |
| 54 | Anantashri JayaKrishna | 13 | 3534 | 433 AD |
| 55 | Anantashri Virupaksha | 11 | 3545 | 444 AD |
| 56 | Anantashri Vidyaranya | 7 | 3552 | 451 AD |
| 57 | Anantashri Vishveshwarteertha | 20 | 3572 | 471 AD |
| 58 | Anantashri Vivudheshwarteertha | 23 | 3595 | 494 AD |
| 59 | Anantashri Maheshwarteertha | 21 | 3616 | 515 AD |
| 60 | Anantashri Madhusudan | 19 | 3635 | 534 AD |
| 61 | Anantashri Raghuttama | 15 | 3650 | 549 AD |
| 62 | Anantashri Ramachandrateertha | 13 | 3663 | 562 AD |
| 63 | Anantashri Yogindra | 11 | 3674 | 573 AD |
| 64 | Anantashri Maheshwarteertha | 7 | 3681 | 580 AD |

*Table Continued...*

| Sr. No. | Name of the Āchārya | Years as Āchārya | End Year | |
|---|---|---|---|---|
| | | | Kaliyuga Year | Christian Year |
| 65 | Anantashri Omkarateertha | 27 | 3708 | 607 AD |
| 66 | Anantashri Narayanteertha | 22 | 3730 | 629 AD |
| 67 | Anantashri Jagannathateertha | 21 | 3751 | 650 AD |
| 68 | Anantashri Shridharteertha | 19 | 3770 | 669 AD |
| 69 | Anantashri Ramachandrateertha | 13 | 3783 | 682 AD |
| 70 | Anantashri Tamraksha | 12 | 3795 | 694 AD |
| 71 | Anantashri Ugreshwarteertha | 15 | 3810 | 709 AD |
| 72 | Anantashri Uddandateertha | 18 | 3828 | 727 AD |
| 73 | Anantashri Sankarshateertha | 22 | 3850 | 749 AD |
| 74 | Anantashri Janardana | 21 | 3871 | 770 AD |
| 75 | Anantashri Akhandatmateertha | 13 | 3884 | 783 AD |
| 76 | Anantashri Damodarteertha | 12 | 3896 | 795 AD |
| 77 | Anantashri Shivanandateertha | 15 | 3911 | 810 AD |
| 78 | Anantashri Gadadharateertha | 18 | 3929 | 828 AD |
| 79 | Anantashri Vidyadharateertha | 22 | 3951 | 850 AD |
| 80 | Anantashri Vamanteertha | 21 | 3972 | 871 AD |
| 81 | Anantashri Shankarteertha | 14 | 3986 | 885 AD |
| 82 | Anantashri Neelkanthateertha | 11 | 3997 | 896 AD |
| 83 | Anantashri Ramakrishnateertha | 20 | 4017 | 916 AD |
| 84 | Anantashri Raghuttamateertha | 20 | 4037 | 936 AD |
| 85 | Anantashri Damodarteertha | 10 | 4047 | 946 AD |
| 86 | Anantashri Gopal | 13 | 4060 | 959 AD |
| 87 | Anantashri Mrityunjayteertha | 21 | 4081 | 980 AD |
| 88 | Anantashri Govindateertha | 22 | 4103 | 1002 AD |
| 89 | Anantashri Vasudevteertha | 12 | 4115 | 1014 AD |
| 90 | Anantashri Gangadharateertha | 12 | 4127 | 1026 AD |
| 91 | Anantashri Sadashivateertha | 21 | 4148 | 1047 AD |
| 92 | Anantashri Vamdevteertha | 22 | 4170 | 1069 AD |
| 93 | Anantashri Upamanyuteertha | 15 | 4185 | 1084 AD |
| 94 | Anantashri Hayagriva | 16 | 4201 | 1100 AD |
| 95 | Anantashri Hariteertha | 18 | 4219 | 1118 AD |
| 96 | Anantashri Raghuttamateertha | 19 | 4238 | 1137 AD |
| 97 | Anantashri Pundarikakshateertha | 7 | 4245 | 1144 AD |
| 98 | Anantashri Parashankarteertha | 16 | 4261 | 1160 AD |

| Sr. No. | Name of the Āchārya | Years as Āchārya | End Year | |
|---|---|---|---|---|
| | | | Kaliyuga Year | Christian Year |
| 99 | Anantashri Vedgarbhateertha | 18 | 4279 | 1178 AD |
| 100 | Anantashri Vedantabhaskarteertha | 20 | 4299 | 1198 AD |
| 101 | Anantashri Vigyanatma | 20 | 4319 | 1218 AD |
| 102 | Anantashri Shivanandateertha | 21 | 4340 | 1239 AD |
| 103 | Anantashri Maheshwarteertha | 20 | 4360 | 1259 AD |
| 104 | Anantashri Ramkrishnateertha | 19 | 4379 | 1278 AD |
| 105 | Anantashri Vrishabhadhwajateertha | 14 | 4393 | 1292 AD |
| 106 | Anantashri Shuddabodhateertha | 13 | 4406 | 1305 AD |
| 107 | Anantashri Someshwarteertha | 20 | 4426 | 1325 AD |
| 108 | Anantashri Vopdevateertha | 21 | 4447 | 1346 AD |
| 109 | Anantashri Shambhuteertha | 20 | 4467 | 1366 AD |
| 110 | Anantashri Bhriguteertha | 13 | 4480 | 1379 AD |
| 111 | Anantashri Keshavanandateertha | 12 | 4492 | 1391 AD |
| 112 | Anantashri Vidyananda | 14 | 4506 | 1405 AD |
| 113 | Anantashri Vedanandateertha | 16 | 4522 | 1421 AD |
| 114 | Anantashri Yoganandateertha | 15 | 4537 | 1436 AD |
| 115 | Anantashri Sutapanandateertha | 24 | 4561 | 1460 AD |
| 116 | Anantashri Shridharateertha | 11 | 4572 | 1471 AD |
| 117 | Anantashri Janardanateertha | 21 | 4593 | 1492 AD |
| 118 | Anantashri Kamnashanandteertha | 12 | 4605 | 1504 AD |
| 119 | Anantashri Hariharanand | 16 | 4621 | 1520 AD |
| 120 | Anantashri Gopalteertha | 15 | 4636 | 1535 AD |
| 121 | Anantashri Krishnanandateertha | 16 | 4652 | 1551 AD |
| 122 | Anantashri Madhavanand | 21 | 4673 | 1572 AD |
| 123 | Anantashri Madhusudanteertha | 13 | 4686 | 1585 AD |
| 124 | Anantashri Govindateertha | 16 | 4702 | 1601 AD |
| 125 | Anantashri Raghuttamateertha | 20 | 4722 | 1621 AD |
| 126 | Anantashri Vamdevteertha | 15 | 4737 | 1636 AD |
| 127 | Anantashri Shikeshteertha | 13 | 4750 | 1649 AD |
| 128 | Anantashri Damodarateertha | 25 | 4775 | 1674 AD |
| 129 | Anantashri Gopalanandateertha | 12 | 4787 | 1686 AD |
| 130 | Anantashri Govindateertha | 14 | 4801 | 1700 AD |
| 131 | Anantashri Raghuttamateertha | 19 | 4820 | 1719 AD |

*Table Continued...*

| Sr. No. | Name of the Āchārya | Years as Āchārya | End Year | |
|---|---|---|---|---|
| | | | Kaliyuga Year | Christian Year |
| 132 | Anantashri Ramchandrateertha | 21 | 4841 | 1740 AD |
| 133 | Anantashri Govindateertha | 15 | 4856 | 1755 AD |
| 134 | Anantashri Raghunathateertha | 15 | 4871 | 1770 AD |
| 135 | Anantashri Ramakrishnateertha | 21 | 4892 | 1791 AD |
| 136 | Anantashri Madhusudanteertha | 13 | 4905 | 1804 AD |
| 137 | Anantashri Damodarteertha | 23 | 4928 | 1827 AD |
| 138 | Anantashri Raghuttamateertha | 22 | 4950 | 1849 AD |
| 139 | Anantashri Shiv | 21 | 4971 | 1870 AD |
| 140 | Anantashri Loknath | 13 | 4984 | 1883 AD |
| 141 | Anantashri Damodarteertha | 15 | 4999 | 1898 AD |
| 142 | Anantashri Madhusudanteertha | 27 | 5027 | 1925 AD |
| 143 | Anantashri BharatiKrishnateertha | 34 | 5061 | 1959 AD |
| 144 | Anantashri Niranjanadevteertha | 28 | 5093 | 1992 AD |
| 145 | Anantashri Nishchalananda Saraswati – the present Āchārya | | | |

Thus, we have complete chronologies for the Kānchi Kāmakoṭi, Dvārakā, and Jagannātha Puri maṭhas established by Śrī Ādi Śaṅkarāchārya which provide ample evidence that Ādi Śaṅkarāchārya lived either from 509 to 477 BC or from 507 to 475 BC.

### Chronology of Pīṭhādhipatis of the Śāradā Pīṭhā at Sringeri

The list of the first two and the last 32 (starting in around AD 800) Pīṭhādhipatis of the Sringeri Maṭha is available in *The Age of Śankara* (Narayana Sastry, 1916/1971, p. 200). Narayana Sastry did thorough research and has discussed at length the chronology of the Sringeri Maṭha and the discrepancies in it. The records of the āchāryas before AD 800 have been lost.

## Life of Ādi Śaṅkarāchārya in Brief

The most authentic account of Ādi Śaṅkarāchārya's life is found in the Sankara Vijaya of Chitshukhāchārya, also known as *Bṛhat Sankara Vijaya*. It is believed to have been written during or immediately after the time of Śaṅkarāchārya. Chitsukhāchārya's original name was Viṣṇu Sharma. He was five years older than Śaṅkara and was associated with him since Śaṅkara was five years old, during his studies in the gurukul. When Śaṅkara himself became a sannyāsī in his tenth year, he followed him, receiving his initiation from Śaṅkara. He was always with him after that throughout his wandering all over the country. T. S. Narayana Sastry (1916/1971, p. 63) writes in his book, *The Age of Śankara*:

“ In his Bṛihat Śaṅkara Vijaya, Chitsukha informs us that Śaṅkara took the permission of his mother to become a Sannyasin on the 11th day of the bright-half of the month of Kartika of the year 2639 of the Yudhishthira Śaka (corresponding to 500 B.C.), and was ordained as a regular Sannyasin by Govinda Bhagavatpada on the 2nd day of the bright half of the month of Phālguna of the year 2640 of the Yudhishthira Śaka (corresponding to 499 B.C.). So Śaṅkara became a full Sannyasin in his tenth year, and under the guidance of Govinda Bhagavatpada and his worthy son Bhartṛihari, he became master of all the Śastras before he completed his twelfth year. It is said that Śaṅkara had very great reverence for Bhartṛihari or Bhartṛiprapancha as he calls him and it was in emulation of him and at his inducement that Śaṅkara wrote many of his minor works and commentaries.

The following oft-quoted stanza :

अष्टवर्षे चतुर्वेदी द्वादशे सर्वशास्त्रवित् ।
षोडशे कृतवान्भाष्यं द्वात्रिंशे मुनि रम्यगात् ।।

[Aṣtavarṣe caturvedī dvādaśe sarvaśāstravit ।
Ṣodaśe kṛtavān-bhāṣyaṁ dvātriṁśe muni ramyagāt ।।]

clearly shows how extraordinarily intelligent and active Śaṅkara was throughout his life. According to this, Śankara learned all the Vedas by the eighth year of his age and completed his study of the Śastras in the house and under the guidance of his teacher before he completed his twelfth year. There will be nothing strange in this when we remember how remarkable the life of some of the modern English poets had been even in these degenerate days. ”

Regarding the biographies written on Śaṅkarāchārya, Pandit Venkatachelam (1953a, p. 63–65) writes:

“ On the life of Sankara, we have no less than ten Sankara-Vijayas or biographies of Sankarāchārya, purporting to have been written by the followers of his school of philosophy ; …

Besides these various Sankara-Vijayās, we have a number of Puṇyaśloka-Manjarīes and Guru-Paramparas preserved by the various Adhvaitic Maṭhs in which we have a brief account of the chief incidents of Sankara’s life recorded by his own immediate disciples. … There are also hostile references to the life of Sankara in works of the Jainas, Maddhvās and Vaiṣhṇavās such as Jina-Vijaya, Maddhva-Vijaya, Mani-Manjari etc.”

Dr. W. R. Antarkar (1960, p. 120) summarized the results of his research on the authenticity of *Bṛhat Sankara Vijaya* as follows:

> “It, therefore, can be concluded that there did exist till recently two such works as Br. S.V. [Bṛhat Śaṅkara Vijaya] of Citsukhāchārya and Pr. S.V. [Prācīna Śaṅkara Vijaya] of Ānandajñāna a/s Ānandagiri though none of them is available to us today and that they are not mere names, as believed by some.”

Śaṅkara, after wandering for nearly a year in search of a guru, arrived with his friend and disciple, Viṣṇu Sharma, on the bank of Narmada. There he met Śrī Govinda Yogi in his hermitage by coincidence, surrounded by his illustrious son, Bhartruhari (also a sannyāsī), and his disciples. Śaṅkara gladly chose Govinda Yogi as his guru, and the guru was most happy to accept Śaṅkara as his worthy student (see Chapter 10). Table 28 provides a brief chronicle of Śrī Ādi Śaṅkarāchārya's life (Narayana Sastry, 1916/1971, p. 181). Some of the dates in the table have been adjusted by one year.

**Table 28: Brief chronology of Śrī Ādi Śaṅkarāchārya's life, Kaliyuga 2593–2625 (509–477 BC)**

| Sr. No. | Event | Kaliyuga Year | Year in BC |
|---|---|---|---|
| 1 | Birth of Śaṅkara at Kālati on Vaiśākha Śukla Pañchami (Cyclic year Nandana) | 2593 | 509 |
| 2 | Upanayana of Śaṅkara | 2598 | 504 |
| 3 | Lost father Śivaguru at the beginning of his eighth year | 2601 | 501 |
| 4 | Completed study of the four Vedas and Vedāngas | 2601 | 501 |
| 5 | Obtained mother's permission to enter the holy order of sannyāsa (Kārtika Śukla Ekādaśi, cyclic year Plava) | 2602 | 500 |
| 6 | Initiated by Govinda Bhagavatpādāchārya into Karma Sannyāsa at Amarkantak on the banks of the Narmada (Phālguna Śukla Dvitiya of the cyclic year Śubhakṛt | 2603 | 499 |
| 7 | Studied philosophical systems under Govinda Bhagavatpādāchārya | 2603–2605 | 499–497 |
| 8 | Visited Paramaguru Gaudapādāchārya, who was aged 120 years at that time, at Badarikāshrama on the Himalayas and stayed there for four years to study further, directly under the paramaguru | 2605–2609 | 497–493 |

| Sr. No. | Event | Kaliyuga Year | Year in BC |
|---|---|---|---|
| 9 | By the order of his paramaguru, Śaṅkara wrote a Bhāshya (commentary) on Gaudapāda Karikās and sixteen Bhāshyās on Prasthāna traya, etc. in this period of four years | 2605–2609 | 497–493 |
| 10 | Initiation of Viṣṇu Sharma into sannyāsa by Śaṅkara He was his co-student at Kālati and followed him in all his activities. His sannyāsa name is Chitsukhāchārya, author of Bṛhat Sankara Vijaya, the first biography of Sankara (now lost). | 2609 | 493 |
| 11 | Death of Śaṅkara's mother Āryambā (cyclic year Plavaṅga) | 2609 | 492 |
| 12 | Nirvana of the Guru Govinda Bhagavatpāda (Kārtika Purṇimā, cyclic year Plavaṅga) | 2609 | 492 |
| 13 | Initiation of Sanandana into sannyāsa (sannyāsa name is Padmapādāchārya) | 2609 | 492 |
| 14 | Śaṅkara went to Prayāg to propagate the Advaita Philosophy (Māgha, Bahula Amāvasya). | 2609 | 492 |
| 15 | The Brahmin who was suffering from leprosy and was cured by Śaṅkara at Prayāg was his third disciple. His name is Udanka. | 2609 | 492 |
| 16 | The fourth disciple, the dumb man, was the son of Prabhākaradhavarin by the name Prithvidhara. His sannyāsa name given by Śaṅkarāchārya was Hastāmalakāchārya. | 2609 | 492 |
| 17 | Śaṅkara in his 16th year met Kumārila Bhatta for the first and the last time in Ruddhapura near Prayāg in the act of self-immolation. | 2609 | 492 |
| 18 | The Great Pandit Mandana Misra, the disciple of Kumārila Bhatta and a staunch adherent of Karmakāṇḍa of the Vedas became the disciple of Śaṅkarāchārya and a sannyāsī leaving his gruhasthāshrama (family life) after a great debate. His sannyāsa name was Sureśvarāchārya. (Cyclic year Sādhāraṇa) | 2611 | 491 |
| 19 | Founded the Dvārakā Maṭha (on Māgha Śukla Saptami of the cyclic year Sādhāraṇa) with Hastāmalaka as its first Āchārya. | 2611 | 491 |
| 20 | Śaṅkarāchārya visited Nepal and refuted the Buddhists (Indraji and Bühler, 1884, p. 412). | 2614–2615 | 488–487 |

*Table Continued...*

| Sr. No. | Event | Kaliyuga Year | Year in BC |
|---|---|---|---|
| 21 | Founded Jyotir Maṭha in the Himalayas (on Puṣya Purṇimā of the cyclic year Rākṣasa) with Totakāchārya as its first Āchārya | 2616 | 486 |
| 22 | Founded the Govardhana Maṭha at Jagannātha Puri (on Vaiśākha Śukla Daśami, of the cyclic year Nala) with Padmapādācharya as its first Āchārya | 2617 | 484 |
| 23 | Founded the Śāradā Pīṭha at Sringeri (on Puṣya Purṇimā of the year Piṅgala) with Sureśvarāchārya as its first Āchārya | 2618 | 484 |
| 24 | Founded the Kāmakoṭi Pīṭha at Kānchi (on Vaiśākha Purṇimā of the year Siddhārthi) with Ādi Śaṅkara himself as its first Āchārya | 2620 | 481 |
| 25 | Brahmibhāva of Sri Śaṅkarāchārya in his 32nd year, at Kānchi (on Vaiśākha Śukla Ekādaśi in the cycle year Raktākṣi) | 2625 | 477 |

Śrī Ādi Śaṅkarāchārya, after propagating the Advaita (non-duality) philosophy throughout the whole of India, attained heavenly abode at Kānchi in the Kaliyuga 2625 (477 BC).

## References

1. Antarkar, Dr. W. R. (1960, September). 'Bṛhat-Śaṅkara-Vijaya of Citsukhācārya and Prācīna-Śankara-Vijaya of Ānanadagiri A/S Ānanda-Jñāna.' *Journal of the University of Bombay, Arts No. 35, Vol. 29* (New Series), 113–121.

2. Antarkar, Dr. W. R. (1960/2003). Śaṅkara *Vijayas: A Comparative and a Critical Study* (Ph. D. Thesis submitted to the University of Poona, 1960). Mumbai: Veda Sastra Pandita Raksha Sabha (1st ed. 2003).

3. Bhashya Charya, Pandit N. (1889). 'The Age of Srī Sankarāchārya.' *The Theosophist: A Magazine of Oriental Philosophy, Art, Literature and Occultism, Vol. 11(122– November)*, 98–107. Madras: Adyar.

4. *Divya-Dwarka* (8th ed., Samvat 2075 (Guru Purnima), AD 2018). Mahamahopadhyay Prof. Jaiprakash Narayan Dwivedi (Ed.). Dandi Swami Śrī Sadananda Saraswati, Shri Dwārkādhish Sanskrit Academy & Indological Research Institute, Devbhumi Dwarka, Gujarat.

5. Govardhana Maṭha at Jagannātha Puri website: https://www.govardhanpeeth.org/en/about-us-en/adi-Shankaracharya-successor (Accessed February 3, 2023).

6. Gwasha Lal, P. (1932). *A Short History of Kashmir: From the Earliest Times to the Present Day* (3rd ed.). Kashmir Research Institute.

7. Indraji, Pandit Bhagavānlāl, and Dr. G. Bühler (1884). 'Some Considerations on the History of Nepal.' *The Indian Antiquary: A Journal of Oriental Research in Archaeology, History, Literature, Languages, Philosophy, Religion, Folklore, etc. Vol. 13*, 411–428. Bombay.

8. Isayeva, Natalia (1993). *Shankara and Indian Philosophy*. Albany: State University of New York Press.

9. Kalhaṇa (1148). *Rājataraṅgiṇī (Chronicle of the Kings of Kashmir) (Sanskrit text)*, Edited with Hindi translation by Shri Ramtej Shastri Pandey (Vikrama Samvat 2017 (AD 1960), rpt. ed. 1985). Delhi & Varanasi: Chaukhamba Sanskrit Pratishthan.

10. Kānchi Kāmakoṭi Maṭha website: http://www.kamakoti.org/peeth/origin.html#appendix2 (Accessed February 3, 2023).

11. Mishra, Parameshwarnath (VS 2057, AD 2000). *Amita Kālarekhā: 2500 years of Śankarāchārya (Arvācīna Mata Khaṇdana)* (in Hindi, rpt. VS 2058, AD 2001). Patna: Akhīl Bhāratiya Pīthpariśad Bihar Pradesh.

12. Mishra, Parameshwarnath (2001). *Mathāmnāya Setu or Mahānushāsanam (Sharada Bhashyam)*. Dwarka: Shankaracharya Memorial Trust.

13. Narayana Sastry, T. S. (1916). *The Age of Śankara* (2nd ed. 1971, edited by T. N. Kumaraswamy). Madras: B. G. Paul & Co.

14. Nataraja Aiyer, A., and S. Lakshminarasimha Sastri (1962). *The Traditional Age of Sri Shankaracharya and the Maths*. Madras.

15. Sinnett, A. P. (1883). *Esoteric Buddhism* (8th ed., rpt. 1907). London: Trübner.

16. Tapasyananda, Swami (Trans.) (1986). *Sankara-Dig-Vijaya: The Traditional Life of Sri Sankaracharya: by Madhava-Vidyaranya* (3rd ed.). Madras: Sri Ramakrishna Math.

17. Venkatachelam, Pandit Kota (Kali 5054, AD 1953a). *Chronology of Nepal History Reconstructed (Nepalraja Vamsavali)*. Arya Vijnana, Publication 16. Vijayawada.

18. Venkatachelam, Pandit Kota (Kali 5057, AD 1956b). *The Age of Buddha, Milinda & Amtiyoka and Yugapurana*. Arya Vijnana Series, Publication 20. Vijayawada.

19. Venkatachelam, Pandit Kota (Kali 5058, AD 1957a). *Chronology of Ancient Hindu History Part I*. Arya Vijnana Grandhamala, Publication 23. Vijayawada.

20. Wright, Daniel (1877). *History of Nepal: with an Introductory Sketch of the Country and People of Nepal* (Translated from Parbatiya by Munshi Shew Shunker Singh & Pandit Śhrī Gunanand, rpt. 1990). New Delhi: Asian Educational Services.

# 10

# UJJAIN, AGNI VAṀŚAS, VIKRAMĀDITYA, AND ŚĀLIVĀHANA

## History of Ancient Mālavā

Mālavā was an independent kingdom before the Mahābhārata War. After the war, it was incorporated into the Hastināpura Empire as its vassal state (Venkatachelam, 1955, p. 125). As discussed in Chapter 7, Mahāpadma Nanda came to the throne of Magadha in Kaliyuga 1468 (1634 BC), soon conquered all ancient dynasties of northern India, and became the emperor.

The Buddhist texts, *Dīpavaṁsa* (6.15) and *Mahāvaṁsa* (5.39), state that Emperor Aśoka, when he was a prince, was the governor of Ujjayini (Ujjain) charged with collecting the revenue. During that time, he came to Vidisha and met Devi, the mother of his son, Mahendra, who was later sent to Sri Lanka. As discussed in Chapter 7, Emperor Aśoka reigned from 1472 to 1436 BC.

In 850 BC, a brahmin by the name of Dhunji united the Mālava people and became their king, however, he was obliged to be the vassal king of the Magadha Empire. In 730 BC, a descendant of the Dhunji family declared Mālavā an independent state (Malcolm, 1824, p. 22; Venkatachelam, 1955, p. 125–126). When Mālavā asserted its independence, there was a quarrel with Śātavāhana Emperor Sri Śātakarṇi of Magadha, the fifth king in the list of the Āndhra kings shown in Table 22 (Chapter 7). By 725 BC, Mālavā had its independence recognized and entered a friendly alliance with the rulers of the Magadha Empire. Mālava-gaṇa Śaka was started in memory of this event.

# Ujjain, Harṣa Vikramāditya, and Ādi Śaṅkarāchārya's Guru

Ujjain was a great center of learning from at least Kaliyuga 2450 (652 BC) (Venkatachelam, 1953a, p. 112–118). The literary greatness of Ujjain can be realized from the history of Śrī Harṣa Vikramāditya who started a new era in Kaliyuga 2646 (457 BC). Since ancient times, Ujjain was the center of Indian astronomy and the Indian standard time with the 0° longitude assigned to it (Smith, 1914, p. 292) until the British colonial rulers of India switched to the Greenwich Mean Time. Ujjain is also the seat of one of the 12 Jyotirlingas, Mahākāla.

## Chandra Sharma and his Four Illustrious Sons

Before Harṣa Vikramāditya, Ujjain was ruled by his maternal grandfather. The mother of Śrī Harṣa was the daughter of the king of Ujjain. Śrī Harṣa's father was the well-known scholar, Chandra Sharma. Chandra Sharma studied *Mahābhāṣya* of Patanjali, from Gaudapāda and propagated it throughout the length and breadth of India, during his *gruhasthāshrama* (family life). He took *sannyāsa* (renounced the world) in his later age, received *Brahma-vidyā* (spiritual knowledge) from the same Gaudapāda and taught it to Śrī Ādi Śaṅkarāchārya. Thus, Chandra Sharma was Govinda Yogi or Govinda Bhagavatpāda, the holy guru of Śrī Ādi Śaṅkarāchārya. He was the renowned grammarian who is said to have had the special fortune of preserving for the world, Patanjali's Mahābhāsya on Pāṇini's Aṣṭādhyāyī, amplified by Katyāyani's *Vartaka* as we possess it presently (Venkatachelam, 1953a, p. 112–118).

Chandra Sharma had settled in Ujjain and married Śeelavati, the only daughter of the Brahmin king of Ujjain, a descendent of the Brahmin Dynasty of Dhunji who had established the kingdom in Ujjain in the ninth century BC.

**Bhartruhari or Bhartru-prapañca (भर्तृ प्रपंच)** as he was generally known in his later āshrama, was the eldest son of Govinda Bhagavatpāda (गोविंद भगवतपाद) by his royal brahmin wife Śeelavati (daughter of the king of Ujjain). He is said to have ruled the kingdom of Ujjain for some time, being the eldest son of his royal mother and Chandra Sharma; but being disgusted with the unchastity of his beloved queen, he soon abdicated the throne in favour of his valorous younger brother Śrī Harṣa Vikramāditya (श्री हर्ष विक्रमादित्य) and took sannyāsa. He lived with his aged father as one of his followers. His proper name was Hari and Bhartru was a title like his Majesty.

It is written that he also married two other women (Sumati and Mananarekha) from the Vaishya and Shudra communities and had four sons who all became renowned in Indian literature under the names of Bhartruhari (भर्तृहरि), Harṣa Vikramāditya (हर्ष विक्रमादित्य), Bhatti (भट्टी) and Vararuchi (वररुचि). This Vararuchi is different from the Vararuchi of 57 BC, one of the nine gems in the court of Emperor Vikramāditya of the first century BC.

## Govinda Bhagavatpāda – the Guru of Ādi Śaṅkarāchārya

Śrī Govinda Bhagavatpāda, formerly Chandra Sharma, lived partly at Badrikāshrama in the Himalayas, where his guru, Gaudapāda (गौडपाद), *Paramaguru* (guru's guru) Sukha Yogindra (सुख योगिन्द्र), and Paramaguru's guru Bādarāyaṇa (बादरायण) lived, learning Vedanta. He also partly lived at Amarkantak on the bank of the Narmada, teaching Vedanta to his disciples in turn. Govinda Bhagavatpāda, like his Paramaguru (Sukha Yogindra), was a born *siddha* (achiever) and a great yogi. Besides the Mahābhāsya, three other works – Yoga Tārāvali, Advaitānubhūti (अध्वैतानुभूति), and Brahmamrita are ascribed to him (Venkatachelam, 1953a, p. 112–118).

While Śrī Ādi Śaṅkarāchārya was in Kālati attending his mother's funeral, a young brahmin by the name of Sanandana (सनंदन) arrived at Kālati and informed him that his revered guru Śrī Govinda Bhagavatpāda, whom he had left at Badrikāshrama, had returned to his hermitage at Amarkantak. Guru Govinda Bhagavatpāda had returned due to a serious illness. He was very anxious to see Śaṅkarāchārya before quitting his body. After inquiring about the young man and his objective in coming to him, Śaṅkarāchārya accepted Sanandana as his disciple and started at once for Amarkantak with his two disciples Chitsukha (चित्सुख) and Sanandana and arrived at his Guru's hermitage in a month.

There on the island of Māndhātā (मांधाता) formed on the Vaiduryamani Parvata in the middle of Narmada, Śaṅkarāchārya found his aged and revered guru, Govinda Bhagavatpāda, lying on his death-bed surrounded by his devoted son Bhartruhari and his other loving disciples anxiously watching the last moments of his earthly existence as a Yogi. Śaṅkarāchārya was deeply moved by the pitiable sight of his guru who had already lost consciousness. It was in the cycle year *Plavaṅga*, the *Purṇimā* (full moon) day of the month of Kārtika of the year 2646 of the Yudhiṣṭhira Śaka (of 3138 BC). On hearing the sweet voice of Śaṅkarāchārya crying by his side, Govinda Bhagavatpāda suddenly recovered his senses, rose like a strong healthy man from his bed, and embraced Śaṅkara. He exhorted Śaṅkara to undertake a *Digvijaya* (victory tour) throughout India to establish his *Advaita* (Non-duality) philosophy in the world and ordered his pupils to follow Śaṅkara as their master. He imparted to them his last lesson on the duties of a sannyāsī called *Turiyāshrama Dharmopadesha*. After blessing Śaṅkara once more, Guru Govinda Bhagavatpāda passed away uttering the sacred sound 'Om' as his last word in 493 BC.

Chitsukhāchārya has stated in his *Bṛhat Sankara Vijaya* (Venkatachelam, 1953a, p. 117) that when the wonderful news of the *Samādhi* (demise) of Govinda Bhagavatpāda reached Śrī Harṣa Vikramāditya, the Emperor of Ujjain, he proceeded to the island of Māndhāta in Amreshvara on the bank of the Narmada where the sacred body of his revered father lay by his disciples. Śrī Harṣa Vikramāditya commissioned the great temple of Omkāranātha to be erected over his father's *samādhi* in his memory whose last word was Om. This great shrine at Omkareshwar is considered by Hindus one of the most sacred places of pilgrimage even at present. A grand festival is celebrated every year in this shrine on Kārtika Purnimā in memory of the great day on which Śrī Govinda Bhagavatpāda attained his *Brahmibhāva (moksha)*.

Omkareshwar is located in Madhya Pradesh and has one of the 12 Jyotirlingas of Lord Shiva. The cave where Ādi Śaṅkarāchārya met his guru for the first time can still be seen below the Omkareshwar temple.

## The Four Agni Vaṁśas

The history of the kings of the Agni Vaṁśas (dynasties) is fully described in the *Bhaviṣya MahāPurāṇa*. The Bhaviṣya MahāPurāṇa is divided into four *parvas* (sections), namely – (1) Brahma Parva, (2) Madhyama Parva, (3) Pratisarga Parva, and (4) Uttara Parva. The Pratisarga Parva describes the history and genealogy of the kings of *Bhārata* (India). In this Parva, 72 out of the total 100 chapters describe the kings of Agni Vaṁśas which were established in Kaliyuga 2711 (391 BC). Of the 72 chapters, 44 are devoted exclusively to describing the great deeds of the two great emperors of the Agni Vaṁśas, Vikramāditya and Śālivāhana (शालिवाहन) (Venkatachelam, 1957a, p. 230).

There were four Agni dynasties, also known as the Brahma-kshatra dynasties. The ancestors of these four dynasties were (1) Pramara (प्रमर), (2) Chapahāni (चपहानि), (3) Śukla (शुक्ल), and (4) Parihāra (परिहार). The Bhaviṣya MahāPurāṇa states that when the country was invaded by Mlecchas (uncultured people) and was in a state of chaos, a learned brahmin, named Kashyapa, of Kānyakubja (Kannauj) went with these four to the Arbudā Parvata (Mount Ābu) in Rajaputānā and invoked Goddess Agni (the fire deity) with prayers and oblations to endow these four brave persons with martial valor and peerless prowess for defense and protection of the land (Venkatachelam, 1957a, p. 246). Pramara belonged to the Sāmaveda sect, Chapahāni to the Yajurveda, Śukla to the Ṛgveda, and Pratihāra to the Atharvaveda sect per the following verses (*Bhaviṣya MahāPurāṇa* 3.1.6.46–47).

वेदमन्त्रप्रभावाच्च जाताश्चत्वारि क्षत्रियाः ।
प्रमरस्सामवेदी च चपहानिर्यजुर्विदः ।। ४६

त्रिवेदी च तथा शुक्लोथर्वा स परिहारकः ।
ऐरावतकूले जातान्गजानारुह्यते पृथक् ।। ४७

Vedamantraprabhāvācca jātāścatvāri kṣatriyāḥ ।
Pramaras-Sāmavedi ca ChapahānirYajurvidaḥ ।। 46

Trivedī ca tathā Śuklo'tharvā sa Parihārakaḥ ।
Airāvatakūle jātān-gajānāruhyate pṛthak ।। 47

Emperor Pramara made Ambāvati (Ujjain), a city of four yojanas in the Avanti Deśa, his capital and lived happily there per the verse below (*Bhaviṣya MahāPurāṇa* 3.1.6.49).

अवन्ते प्रमरो भूपश्चतुर्योजनविस्तृताम् ।
अम्बावतीं नाम पुरीमध्यास्य सुखितोऽभवत् ।। ४९

Avante Pramaro bhupaścaturyojana-vistṛtām ।
Ambāvatīṁ nāma purīmadhyāsya sukhito'bhavat ।। 49

Mahīpati (Mahārāj) Parihāra lived in the Kalinjarapuram located in the Chitrakut mountain region (near the border of Madhya Pradesh and Uttar Pradesh) per the following verse (*Bhaviṣya MahāPurāṇa* 3.1.7.1).

चित्रकूटगिरेर्देशे परिहारो महीपतिः ।
कलिञ्जरपुरं रम्यमक्रोशायतनं स्मृतम् ।। १

Citrakutagirerdeśe Parihāro mahīpatiḥ ।
Kaliñjarapuraṁ ramyamakrośāyatanaṁ smṛtam ।। 1

Mahīpati Chapahāni ruled the four *varṇas* at Ajamer in Rajaputra Deśa (Rajasthan) per the verse below (*Bhaviṣya MahāPurāṇa* 3.1.7.2,3).

राजपुत्राख्य देशे च चपहानिर्महीपतिः ।। २

अजमेरपुरं रम्यं विधिशोभासमन्वितम् ।
चातुर्वर्ण्ययुतं दिव्यमध्यास्य सुखितोऽभवत् ।। ३

Rājaputrākhya deśe ca Capahānirmahīpatiḥ ।। 2

Ajamerapuraṁ ramyaṁ vidhiśobhāsamanvitam ।
Cāturvarṇyayutaṁ divyamadhyāsya sukhito'bhavat ।। 3

Mahīpala Śukla, having rebuilt Dvārakā in Ānarta Mandala (the ancient name of Gujarat), ruled in peace and prosperity per the verse below. Śukla was the son of the brahmin Kashyapa (*Bhaviṣya MahāPurāṇa* 3.1.7.4).

शुक्लोनाम महीपालो गत आनर्तऽमण्डले ।
द्वारकां नाम नगरीमध्यास्य सुखितोऽभवत् ।। ४

Śuklonāma mahīpālo gata Ānartamaṇḍale ।
Dvārakāṁ nāma nagarīmadhyāsya sukhito'bhavat ।। 4

## Pramara or Paramāra or Panvara Vaṁśa

The Pramara (प्रमर) or Paramāra (परमार) or Panvara (पन्वर) Vaṁśa (Dynasty) in which Vikramāditya and Śālivāhana were born, is the most important of the four Agni Vaṁśas. After the completion of 2,710 years of Kaliyuga (in 391 BC), Pramara reigned as emperor for six years per the following verse from Bhaviṣya MahāPurāṇa (Venkatachelam, 1957a, p. 248).

"सप्तविंशतिशते वर्षे दशाब्दे चाधिकेकलौ ।
प्रमरोनाम भूपालः कृतंराज्यं च षट्समाः " ॥
Bhavishya 3—1—7—7, 8.)

Saptaviṁśati-śate varṣe daśābde cādhikekalau ।
Pramaronāma bhūpālaḥ kṛtaṁ-rājyaṁ ca ṣatsamāḥ ।।

### Tampering of the Bhaviṣya MahāPurāṇa

In the currently available copy of the *Bhaviṣya MahāPurāṇa* (3.1.7.7–8), this verse is written as 'Sapta**triṁśa**-śate varṣe' which means 'after completion of 3,710 years of Kaliyuga' as shown in the following (in bold), instead of 'Sapta**viṁśati**-śate varṣe' which means 'after completion of 2,710 years of Kaliyuga' as cited above.

पूर्णे द्वे च सहस्रान्ते सूतो वचनमब्रवीत् ।
सप्तत्रिंशशते वर्षे दशाब्दे चाधिके कलौ ।। ७
प्रमरो नाम भूपालः कृतं राज्यं षड्समाः । ८ – 1st half

It is shocking to see that the priceless historical information in the Bhaviṣya MahāPurāṇa has been tampered with. All tampering was likely towards shrinking the chronology of India and making the information in the Purāṇas less credible.

Table 29 lists the genealogy of the Pramara Vaṁśa (Dynasty) beginning with the first king, Pramara, to the last king, Gangāsiṁha, based on the description in the *Bhaviṣya MahāPurāṇa* (3.1.7, 3.3.2–4, 3.4.1) and the *Chronology of Ancient Hindu History Part I* (Venkatachelam, 1957a, p. 267).

According to the Bhaviṣya MahāPurāṇa, Pramara's son Mahāmara reigned for three years and died. His son Devāpi was the king for three years and then, his son Devadūta reigned for three years too. It is unlikely that these four kings were from more than two successive generations. They all waged wars with Śakas and died in battle.

The kings of the Pramara Dynasty, at first established their kingdom, Avanti Rāshtra, with Ujjain as their capital, and later extended their rule over the whole of Mālavā to Āndhra Deśa in the south. It appears that the Śakas conquered and ruled Mālavā from Kaliyuga 2726 to 2782 (376–320 BC) and the Pramara kings moved to Śrī Sailam in the south (Āndhra Pradesh) and ruled there during that time. Names of these kings are not given in the Purāṇa.

**Table 29: Kings of the Pramara Dynasty, Kaliyuga 2711–4294 (391 BC–AD 1192)**

| Sr. No. | Name of the King | Years of Reign | Starting Year in | |
|---|---|---|---|---|
| | | | Kaliyuga | BC/AD |
| 1 | Pramara (प्रमर) | 6 | 2711 | 391 BC |
| 2 | Mahāmara (महामर) | 3 | 2717 | 385 BC |
| 3 | Devāpi (देवापि) | 3 | 2720 | 382 BC |
| 4 | Devadūta (देवदूत) | 3 | 2723 | 379 BC |
| 5 | Kings defeated by Śakas left Ujjain, migrated to Sri Sailam, and ruled from there. Their names are not available in the Purāṇas | 194 | 2726 | 376 BC |

Table Continued...

| Sr. No. | Name of the King | Years of Reign | Starting Year in Kaliyuga | Starting Year in BC/AD |
|---|---|---|---|---|
| 6 | Gandharvasena (गन्धर्वसेन) (First time) | 50 | 2920 | 182 BC |
| 7 | Śaṅkharāja (शंखराज) | 30 | 2970 | 132 BC |
| | Śaṅkharāja (शंखराज) (No. 7) died without a child, Gandharvasena returned from the forest and took up the reign again. | 20 | 3000 | 102 BC |
| 8 | **Vikramāditya (विक्रमादित्य)** – 2nd son of Gandharvasena | 100 | 3020 | 82 BC |
| 9 | Devabhakta (देवभक्त) | 10 | 3120 | 18 AD |
| 10 | Name(s) not given in the Purāṇa | 50 | 3130 | 28 AD |
| 11 | **Śālivāhana (शालिवाहन)** | 60 | 3180 | 78 AD |
| 12 | Śālihotra (शालिहोत्र) | 500 for No. 12–20 | 3240 | 138 AD |
| 13 | Śālivardhana (शालिवर्धन) | | | |
| 14 | Suhotra (सुहोत्र) | | | |
| 15 | Havirhotra (हविर्होत्र) | | | |
| 16 | Indrapāla (इन्द्रपाल) | | | |
| 17 | Mālyavāna (माल्यवान) | | | |
| 18 | Śambhudatta (शंभुदत्त) | | | |
| 19 | Bhaumarāja (भौमराज) | | | |
| 20 | Vatsarāja (वत्सराज) | | | |
| 21 | **Bhojarāja (भोजराज)** | 54 | | 638 AD |
| 22 | Śambhudatta (शंभुदत्त) | 300 for No. 22–28 | | 692 AD |
| 23 | Bindupāla (बिन्दुपाल) | | | |
| 24 | Rajapāla (राजपाल) | | | |
| 25 | Mahīnara (महीनर) | | | |
| 26 | Somavarmā (सोमवर्मा) | | | |
| 27 | Kāmavarmā (कामवर्मा) | | | |
| 28 | Bhūmipāla (भूमिपाल) or Vīrasiṁha (वीरसिंह) | | | |
| 29 | Raṅgapāla (रंगपाल) | 200 for No. 29–31 | | 992 AD |
| 30 | Kalpasiṁha (कल्पसिंह) | | | |
| 31 | Gangāsiṁha (गंगासिंह) – without a child | | | |

Samudragupta, soon after coming to the throne of Magadha in Kaliyuga 2782 (320 BC), conquered Mālavā (ruled by Śakas) and made them pay tribute and execute his orders according to the inscription on the Prayāg pillar summarized in Chapter 7. Again, Chandragupta II (of the Gupta Dynasty) conquered Mālavā from the Śakas in the Kaliyuga 2845 (257 BC) and added the territory to his empire. During the reign of Skandagupta (191–166 BC), in Kaliyuga 2920 (182 BC), the Agnivaṃśi king of the Pramara Dynasty, Gandharvasena, the father of Vikramāditya, obtained Ujjain and made it his capital (*Bhaviṣya MahāPurāṇa* 3.4.1; Venkatachelam, 1957a, p. 266).

After ruling for 50 years, Gandharvasena crowned his son, Śankha, and retired to the forest to do penance. Śankha reigned for 30 years and died without a child. Gandharvasena then returned from the forest. He was blessed with a son from Veeramati in Kaliyuga 3001 (101 BC) and named him Vikramāditya (*Bhaviṣya MahāPurāṇa* 3.1.7.11–12). Vikramāditya ruled for 100 years; he is described in detail in the following section. After Vikramāditya, his son Devabhakta ruled for ten years and was killed in a battle with the Śakas, per the following verse from *Bhaviṣya MahāPurāṇa* (3.4.1.22).

शिवाज्ञया च नृपतिर्विक्रमस्तनयस्ततः ।
शतवर्षं कृतं राज्यं देवभक्तस्ततोऽभवत् ।
दशवर्षं कृतं राज्यं शकैर्दुष्टैर्लयं गतः ।। २२

Śivājñayā ca nṛpatir-Vikramastanayastataḥ ।
Śatavarṣaṁ kṛtaṁ rājyaṁ Devabhaktastato'bhavat ।
Daśa varṣaṁ kṛtaṁ rājyaṁ Śakairduṣṭairlayaṁ gataḥ ।।

The name(s) of the king(s) after Devabhakta is not known. Kalhaṇa's (1148/1985) *Rājataraṅgiṇī* (3.330) states that King Pravarsena of Kashmir helped Emperor Vikramāditya's son Śīlāditya, known as Pratāpaśīla, get back Ujjain from the enemies and restored him to the throne; see Pravarsena II in Table 34 (Chapter 11).

Śālivāhana who next reigned for 60 years (AD 78–138), is described in detail in the following section. The *Bhaviṣya MahāPurāṇa* (3.3.3.1) states that after Śālivāhana, ten kings in this dynasty ruled for a total of 500 years. This would bring the last year of the tenth King Bhojarāja's reign to AD 638. The 500 years total is likely a round number. Since Harṣa Śiladitya (Harṣavardhana) ruled over the entire North India from AD 606 to 647 with Kānyakubja (present-day Kannauj) as his capital, Bhojarāja's time was likely soon after AD 647. The first nine kings after Śālivāhana were weak and during their rule, *Vedic dharma* (virtues) had declined.

After Bhojarāja, seven weak kings ruled for 300 years according to the *Bhaviṣya MahāPurāṇa* (3.3.4.1). During this period, the Gurjara Pratihāra Dynasty became very powerful from the time of Nāgbhata I (AD 730–756) and dominated most of North India for the next three centuries. In the Pramara Dynasty, the seventh king after Bhojarāja, Vīrasiṁha was an able monarch. After Vīrasiṁha, three kings reigned for 200 years according to *Bhaviṣya MahāPurāṇa* (3.3.4.3). This dynasty ended when Gangāsiṁha, the last king of the dynasty, fought along with Prithvirāj Chauhan in the battle against Mohammad Ghori in AD 1192 at Kurukṣetra (Thaneshvar). Gangāsiṁha was 90 years old then and died like a hero.

It appears that there might have been more kings in this dynasty who may be missing from this list, for example, King Bhoja of the 11th century was different from Bhoja of the 7th century, as discussed in the following section.

## Emperors of the Pramara Vaṁśa

Among the kings of the Pramara Dynasty which lasted from Kaliyuga 2711 to 4294 (391 BC–AD 1192), there were three illustrious Emperors: 1. Vikramāditya, 2. Śālivāhana, and 3. Bhoja. Vikramāditya was the 8th, Śālivāhana the 11th, and Bhoja was the 21st king of the dynasty as shown in Table 29. Of these, Vikramāditya and Śālivāhana conquered all of India from the Himalayas to the Setu (Rāmasetu), reigned as emperors, and established eras in their names, which are still widely used in India and Nepal.

### Vikramāditya (विक्रमादित्य)

As described by Raj Bali Pandey (1951, p. iii), Vikramāditya is one of the most renowned and popular figures of ancient India. Except for Śrī Rāma and Śrī Krishna, no other person is so universally remembered and admired as Vikramāditya. His defense of the freedom of the country against foreign invasion, his military and political achievements, his ideal administration, his sense of justice, and his large-hearted patronage of literature and art have rendered his name immortal.

Vikramāditya was born after 3,000 years of Kaliyuga were completed, i.e. in Kaliyuga 3001, per the following verses from *Bhaviṣya MahāPurāṇa* (3.1.7.14–16).

पूर्णे त्रिंशच्छते वर्षे कलौ प्राप्ते भयङ्करे ।। १४ – 2nd half

शकानां च विनाशार्थमार्यधर्म विवृद्धये ।
जातश्शिवाज्ञया सोऽपि कैलासाद् गुह्यकालयात् ।। १५

विक्रमादित्यनामानं पिता कृत्वा मुमोद ह ।
स बालोऽपि महाप्राज्ञः पितृमातृप्रियङ्करः ।। १६

Pūrṇe triṁśacchate varṣe kalau prāpte bhayaṅkare ।। 14

Śakānāṁ ca vināśārtham-Āryadharma vivṛddhaye ।
JātaśŚivājñayā so'pi Kailāsād guhyakālayāt ।। 15

Vikramādityanāmānaṁ pitā kṛtvā mumoda ha ।
Sa bālo'pi mahāprājñaḥ pitṛmātṛ-priyaṅkaraḥ ।। 16

Translation:

After completion of 3,000 years of the terrible Kaliyuga (in 101 BC), a person descended from the abode of Guhyaka in Kailās, at the command of Śiva, to destroy the Śakas and uplift the *Ārya-dharma* (righteousness). The father rejoiced at the birth of the son and named him Vikramāditya. Even as a child, he was very wise and a source of joy to his parents.

Vikrama went to the forest when he was five years old and did penance for 12 years. After enriching his greatness by penance, he arrived at the city of Ambāvati (Ujjain), his ancestral city (*Bhaviṣya MahāPurāṇa* 3.1.7.17–18).

### Vikramāditya and Vetāla

Stories of Vikaramāditya and Vetāla are popular in India. The following paragraph gives historical background for these stories.

On the eve of his coronation to the throne adorned with 32 golden dolls, there came a learned brahmin named Vetāla who praised and blessed the king. Then, he spoke: "Oh! King! If you would like to listen, I will narrate to you a great tale full of history" (*Bhaviṣya MahāPurāṇa* 3.1.7.19–26). So bidding, he told 32 tales which are narrated in the 32 chapters of *Bhaviṣya MahāPurāṇa* (3.2.1–32). After that, Vikramāditya was crowned in Kaliyuga 3020 (82 BC). Figure 32 shows a photo of his statue in Ujjain.

Vikramāditya expelled the Śakas and conquered the subcontinent from the Setu (Rāmasetu) to the Himalayas. Kalhaṇa's (1148/1985) *Rājataraṅgiṇī* (3.125-128) states that Vikramāditya of Ujjain destroyed the Śakas. He was called Śakāri. The word 'Śakāri' is a combination of the two Sanskrit words 'Śaka' (Śaka people) and 'Ari' (enemy). Śakāri means the enemy of the Śaka. In the year Kaliyuga 3046 (57 BC), Vikramāditya went to Nepal, paid off their debt, made King Aṁśuvarman (अंशुवर्मन) of Nepal his feudatory and founded the Vikrama Samvat (Era). The following paragraphs provide evidence of Emperor Vikramāditya's historicity (Venkatachelam, 1951, p. 12; 1957a, p. 251–252) and shed more light on him.

**Figure 32: 30-feet statue of Emperor Vikramāditya, Ujjain**
*Photo courtesy: NehalDaveND, Wikimedia Commons, CC BY-SA 4.0*

## Evidence for Vikramāditya's Historicity

1. The great Sanskrit poet and dramatist, Kālidāsa (the author of *Raghuvaṁśa, Kumārasambhava, Meghadūta, Śākuntala, Ṛtu-saṁhāra,* and more) describes in his book *Jyotirvidābharaṇa* that Vikramāditya conquered the Śaka king and retrieved the capital of Ujjain of his father's time (Venkatachelam, 1957a, p. 251). Kālidāsa writes:

   यो रुम्मकेशाधिपतिं शकेश्वरं जित्वा ग्रहीतोज्जयिनीं महाहवे।
   आनीय संभ्राम्य मुमोच तं त्वहो श्रीविक्रमार्कसमसह्यविक्रमः।।
   (Jyotirvidābharaṇa 22.17)

   Translation:

   > Vikrama of irresistible valor defeated the Śaka king of the province of Rummaka, brought him to Ujjain, took him around the city as a captive, and released him.

2. Kālidāsa states that he began the composition of *Jyotirvidābharaṇa* (22nd Aswasa) which he dedicated to Emperor Vikramāditya in the Vaiśākha month after 3,068 years of Kaliyuga had passed (in 33 BC), per the following verse.

   वर्षे सिंधुरदर्शनांबरगुणैर्याते (3068) कलेस्सम्मिते।
   मासे माधवसंज्ञिके च विहितो ग्रंथक्रियोपक्रमः।।

3. Kālidāsa (*Jyotirvidābharaṇa* 22.19) says: " In the court of Vikramārka, Kālidāsa was the friend of the king, while there were many poets and scholars like Śanku and astronomers like Varāhamihira. "

4. Kālidāsa states further in *Jyotirvidābharaṇa* (22.10):

## Vikramāditya's Navaratna (Nine Jewels)

" Nine gems adorned the court of Vikrama: 1. Dhanvantari (धन्वन्तरि), 2. Kṣapaṇaka (क्षपणक), 3. Amarsiṁha (अमरसिंह), 4. Śaṅku (शंकु), 5. Vetālabhatta (वेतालभट्ट), 6. Ghaṭakharpara (घटखर्पर), 7. Kālidāsa (कालिदास), 8. The late Varāhamihira (वराहमिहिर) (had died in 41 BC, Kālidāsa wrote the book in 33 BC), and 9. Vararuchi (वररुचि) "

5. Krishnamishra, one of the poets adorning the court of Vikramāditya, gives benediction to his emperor in the very first chapter of his book *Jyotiṣhphala Ratnamālā* (p. 363), the astronomical treatise, as follows:

" श्रीविक्रमार्को जगतीतलेऽस्मिन जीयान् मनुप्रख्ययशा नरेन्द्रः।
पुपोष यः कोटिसुवर्णतो मां सबान्धवं सप्तति वत्सराणि।।

ŚrīVikramārko jagatītale'smina jīyān manuprakhyayaśā narendraḥ ।
puposa yaḥ koṭisuvarṇato māṁ sabāndhavaṁ saptati vatsarāṇi ।।

Translation:

I have lived with my brothers for 70 years, well supported with one crore gold coins received from Śrī Vikramāditya, the famous king among human beings. "

From the above statement of the contemporary poet, it is clear that Vikramāditya reigned for more than 70 years. He reigned for 100 years according to the *Bhaviṣya MahāPurāṇa* (3.2.23.16).

6. As discussed in Chapter 12, Nepal Rāja Vaṁśāvali states that around the time when the king of Nepal, Viṣvadevavarman, had died, Vikramāditya, a very powerful monarch from India came to Nepal, liquidated Nepal's all debt and introduced his new era, Vikrama Samvat, there (Wright, 1877/1990, p. 131; Indraji and Bühler, 1884, p. 413).

7. As discussed in Chapter 11, when the King Hiraṇya of Kashmir died without a child, the ministers from Kashmir reported the matter to their Emperor Vikramāditya in Ujjain requesting him to nominate

a successor. Kalhaṇa's (1148/1985) Rājataraṅgiṇī (Taranga 3) narrates in detail the course of the procedure followed by the emperor in deciding whom to appoint as the next king of Kashmir. See the following highlighted text. The use of the name Śrī Harṣa in front of the name Vikramāditya is likely a corruption of the *Rājataraṅgiṇī* (3.125).

### Who will be the next king of Kashmir?

The emperor contemplated a whole night on who should be the proper person to sit on the throne of Kashmir and decided upon Mātrugupta, the learned poet and administrator as the right candidate. However, without disclosing his decision to Mātrugupta, he dispatched messengers to the ministers of Kashmir and at the same time, gave a sealed order to Mātrugupta, addressed to the ministers of Kashmir, anointing him to deliver the sealed order to the ministers without breaking it open. Mātrugupta fulfilled the emperor's orders. The ministers after opening the order, questioned Mātrugupta whether the person named in the order is himself. Mātrugupta replied in affirmative and he was then acclaimed with jubilations as the king of Kashmir and crowned forthwith. See the 83rd king in **Table 34 in Chapter 11.**

8. William Jones (1799, p. 136–146), the founder of the Asiatic Society and the pioneer of the colonial rewriting of India's history, never doubted the historicity of Vikramāditya. He considered his date (57 BC) a well-established milestone in India's history. See Table 3 and Table 4 in Chapter 2. John Bentley (1799, p. 318), a member of the Asiatic Society, also listed Vikramāditya in his table (see Table 7).

Vikramāditya was one of the greatest-ever emperors of India. During his reign, people enjoyed peace and prosperity and observed the religious duties and rites prevalent in the Dvāparayuga. As stated in the following verse from *Bhaviṣya MahāPurāṇa* (3.2.23.16), by the grace and command of Śiva, Vikramāditya reigned for 100 years without trouble and passed away.

विक्रमादित्य एवास्य भुक्त्वा राज्यमकण्टकम्।
शतवर्षं मुदा युक्तो जगाम मरणे दिवम् ।। १६

Vikramāditya evāsya bhuktvā rājyam-akaṇṭakam I
Śatavarṣaṁ mudā yukto jagāma maraṇe divam II 16

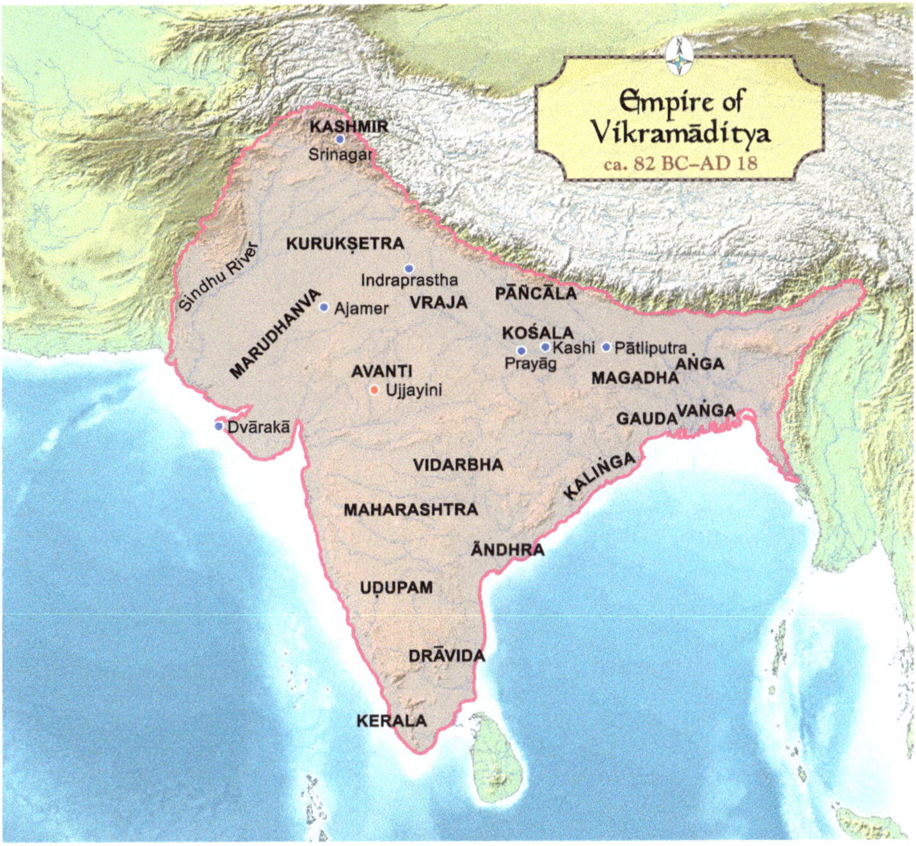


**Figure 33: Map of Vikramāditya's empire (ca. 82 BC–AD 18)**
*Blank map courtesy: DEMIS Mapserver, Wikimedia Commons, CC BY-SA 3.0*

Figure 33 shows a map of Emperor Vikramāditya's empire which encompassed the entirety of India. A summary of the key events of this great emperor's life is given in Table 30.

**Table 30: Important dates in Emperor Vikramāditya's life, Kaliyuga 3001–3120 (101 BC–AD 18)**

| Sr. No. | Event | Kaliyuga Year | Christian Year |
|---|---|---|---|
| 1 | Birth of Vikramāditya | 3001 | 101 BC |
| 2 | Coronation | 3020 | 82 BC |
| 3 | Starting of Vikrama Samvat | 3046 | 57 BC |
| 4 | Dedication of *Jyotirvidābharaṇa* by Kālidāsa | 3069 | 33 BC |
| 5 | Appointed Mātrugupta as the king of Kashmir | 3115 | 13 AD |
| 6 | Death of Vikramāditya | 3120 | 18 AD |

After Vikramāditya left the earth, the empire from beyond Sindhu in the west to Kāpila (Assam) in the east, and from Badaristhāna in the north to Setubandha in the south, split up into 18 separate states listed as follows (*Bhaviṣya MahāPurāṇa* 3.3.2.9–14).

1. Indraprastha (इन्द्रप्रस्थ)
2. Pāñcāla (पांचाल)
3. Kurukṣetra (कुरुक्षेत्र)
4. Kāpila (कापिल)
5. Antarvedī (अन्तर्वेदी)
6. Vraja (व्रज)
7. Ajamer (अजमेर्)
8. Marudhanva (मरुधन्व) (Māravād)
9. Gaurjjara (गौर्ज्जर)
10. Mahārāṣṭra (महाराष्ट्र) (spelled Maharashtra in common parlance)
11. Drāviḍa (द्राविड)
12. Kaliṅga (कलिंग) – included Āndhra Deśa
13. Avanti (अवन्ति) (Ujjain)
14. Uḍupam (उडुपम्)
15. Vaṅgadeśa (वंगदेश) (present-day Bangladesh)
16. Gaudadeśa (गौडदेश) (present-day West Bengal)
17. Magadha (मगध)
18. Kośala (कोशल)

Having heard of the decline of *Āryadharma* (life of virtues), the Śaka, and Mleccha people, crossed the Sindhu and Himalaya in large hoards, invaded the Ārya territory, plundered the country, killed the old, infants, and women and abducted many women (*Bhaviṣya MahāPurāṇa* 3.3.2.15–17).

## Śālivāhana (शालिवाहन)

Under these circumstances, Śālivāhana, the grandson (more likely great-grandson) of Vikramāditya, recovered his father's kingdom. Śālivāhana defeated and captured the kings of the difficult Śakas, Chīnas, Tatars,

Bāhlikas, Kāmarūpās, Romās, and Khurās, and recovered the treasures plundered by them. He demarcated the River Sindhu as the dividing line between the Āryas and the Mlecchas. The land east of the Sindhu where Āryas lived was called Sindhusthāna (सिन्धुस्थान) and the land west of the Sindhu was called Mlecchasthāna (म्लेच्छस्थान) as described by the following verses (*Bhaviṣya MahāPurāṇa* 3.3.2.17–21).

एतस्मिन्नतरे तत्र शालिवाहनभूपतिः ।। १७ – 2nd half

विक्रमादित्यपौत्रश्च पितृराज्यं गृहीतवान् ।
जित्वा शकान्दुराधर्षाश्चीनतैत्तिरिदेशजान् ।। १८

बाह्लीकान् कामरूपांश्च रोमजान् खुरजाञ्छठान् ।
तेषां कोशान् गृहीत्वा च दण्डयोग्यानकारयत् ।। १९

स्थापिता तेन मर्यादा म्लेच्छार्याणां पृथक्पृथक् ।
सिन्धुस्थानमिति ज्ञेयं राष्ट्रमार्यस्य चोत्तमम् ।। २०

म्लेच्छस्थानं परं सिन्धोः कृतं तेन महात्मना । २१ – 1st half

Etasminnantare tatra Śālivāhana-bhupatiḥ | 17

Vikramāditya pautrasca pitṛrājyaṁ gṛhītavān
Jitvā Śakān-durāgharṣāsCīna Taittiridesajān || 18

Bāhlikān Kāmarūpānśca Romajān Khurajāñchathān
Teṣām kośān gṛhitvā ca daṇḍayogyānakārayāt || 19

Sthāpitā tena maryādā Mlecchāryāṇāṁ pṛthak-pṛthak
Sindhusthānam-iti jñeyam rāṣṭram-Āryasya cottamam || 20

Mlecchasthānaṁ paraṁ Sindhoḥ kṛtaṁ tena mahātmanā | 21

This is the first historical reference to the word **Sindhusthāna** from which the name **Hindustān** is derived. After completing the conquests, Śālivāhana performed *Aśvamedha yajña*. In Kaliyuga 3181 (AD 79), he started a new era, Śālivāhana Śaka, which is still used in most parts of India. It is one of the two official calendars of the Government of India and is found in all Panchāngas every year (See Figure 8). See the Śālivāhana Śaka also mentioned in the Nepal Rāja Vaṁśāvali (Chapter 12, Table 42, 4th king). Śālivāhana ruled for 60 years (AD 78–138).

## Distortion by Colonial Era European Indologists

The colonial era Indologists confused Śālivāhana with the Magadha Emperor

Hāla-Śātavāhana (हाल-शातवाहन) of the Āndhra Śātavāhana Dynasty who ruled in the fifth century BC but placed him in the first century. This was needed because they used the wrong basis—Chandragupta Maurya instead of Chandragupta I of the Gupta Dynasty as the contemporary of Alexander, and thus erased over 1,200 years from the chronology of ancient India.

## Bhojarāja (भोजराज)

Bhojarāja was the 21st king of the Pramara Dynasty shown in Table 29. *Bhaviṣya MahāPurāṇa* (3.3.3) states that after seeing the decline of law and order, Bhoja marched with his army to conquer the country and restore order. With an army of ten thousand men, accompanied by Kālidāsa (must be different from Kālidāsa in the court of Vikramāditya in the first century BC) and learned people, he crossed the Sindhu, defeated the Mlecchas of Gāndhāra, Kashmirās, and Aravāns (may be Ariya) and took their treasures as a punishment to them (*Bhaviṣya MahāPurāṇa* 3.3.3.2–4). Bhoja ruled for 50 years according to *Bhaviṣya MahāPurāṇa* (3.3.3.29). His reigning period is estimated to be from AD 638 to 692, as shown in Table 29, which overlaps a little with the reign of Harṣa Śiladitya (Harṣavardhana). Either Bhoja's time of reign is a little different or, initially, he may have been a vassal king of Harṣavardhana. Col. James Tod (1829/1920, p. 109) mentions an inscription dated Vikrama Samvat 770 (AD 714) in the name of Bhoj as follows:

> “The era[2] of Bhoj, the son of Munja, has been satisfactorily settled; and an [92] inscription[3] in the nail-headed character, carries it back a step further[4], and elicits an historical fact of infinite value, giving the date of the last prince of the Pramars of Chitor, …
>
> Note [2]: See *Transactions of the Royal Asiatic Society*, vol. i. p. 227. [Rāja Munja of Mālwa reigned A.D. 974-975. The famous Bhoja, his nephew, not his son, 1018-60 (Smith, *EHI*, 395).]
>
> Note [3]: Which will be given in the *Transactions of the Royal Asiatic Society.*
>
> Note [4]: S. 770 (Vikrama Samvat), or A.D. 714.”

The inscription date of AD 714 in Note [4] above is not too far from the date of AD 638–692 reigning period estimated by Pandit Venkatachelam (1957a, p. 261).

### More than One Bhoja Rāja

As alluded to earlier, there were more than one Bhoja Rājas. Col. Tod (1829/1920, p. 110) states in his *Annals and Antiquities of Rajasthan*:

> “While Hindu literature survives the name of Bhoj Pramara and ‘ the nine gems ’ of his court can not perish ; though it is difficult to say which of the three[2] princes of this name is particularly alluded to, as they all appear to have been patrons of science.”

> “Note [2]: The inscription gives S. 1100 (A.D. 1044) for the third Bhoj : and this date agrees with the period assigned to this prince in an ancient Chronogrammatic Catalogue of reigns embracing all the Princes of the name of Bhoj, which may therefore be considered authentic. This authority assigns S. 631 and 721 (or A.D. 575 and 665) to the first and second Bhoj.”

The year of AD 665, in Note [2], assigned to the second Bhoj tallies very well with AD 638–692 estimated for Bhojarāja. An ancient text titled, *Prabandha Cintāmaṇi*, narrates stories and chronology of the Chālukya Dynasty of Gujarat as well as stories from the time of the contemporary kings Munja and Bhoja of Mālavā.

## Distortions by Colonial Era European Indologists

As stated by Pandit Venkatachelam, the 19th and early 20th century European Indologists certainly read the detailed history of the Agnivaṃśis in the Bhaviṣya MahāPurāṇa and took from it short accounts of a few kings such as Bhojarāja, Prithvirāj, Jayachandra, etc. and incorporated them in their histories but left out the two great Emperors, Vikramāditya and Śālivāhana, completely as they could not fit them in their severely compressed timeline. These historians then asserted that Vikramāditya and Śālivāhana were not historical persons at all and attributed the eras started by them to other kings as discussed in Chapter 4. Vincent Smith (1910, p. 50–51) assigned the Śālivāhana Śaka (era) to Kaniṣka stating:

> “The Saka era dating from 78 A.D., called in later ages the era of Sālivāhana, certainly was introduced by foreigners, and perhaps the most probable theory is that it marks the accession of Kanishka. Indian authors use the term Saka in a vague way for all sorts of foreigners from the other side of the passes, and would have felt no difficulty in describing a Kushān king as a Saka. Certain reasons, however, support the opinion that Kanishka's accession took place about 120 or 125 A.D., and some scholars are inclined to believe that the Saka Satraps of Saurāshtra originated the Saka era. Further discoveries are likely to settle the dispute before long.”

The truth is that Kaniṣka never started an era and, as shown in Chapter

11, he lived more than a millennium earlier than the time assigned to him. In response to the disparaging of the Bhavișhya MahāPurāṇa, Pandit Venkatachelam (1957a, p. 230) states:

> "Besides this denial [of the existence of Vikramāditya and Śālivāhana], they proclaimed that the Bhavishya Purana was not at all an authority, as it contained the history of the Muhammadan and Christian rulers. Further, they pronounced that the Bhavishya Purana in its early form, was the source for all the Puranas and as it consisted of modern history, could not be accepted as authority. We request the readers to consider who might have inserted the fables of Adam and Eve, in Bhavishya Purana ! The Indian Sanskrit scholars, nowhere have added the histories of other countries in their holy works; but they made only slight references to the history of Mlechcha sects (who were excommunicated Hindu Kshatriya sub-sects) as far as they had a connection with our country's history. In this case, it is neither plausible nor probable that they inserted the history of countries like Arabia and Particularly of the Hebrew race, in their sacred Puranas."

> If the colonial era historians had accepted the existence of Vikramāditya and Śālivāhana, their entire fabricated chronology would have fallen apart.

## Chapahāni or Chayahāni or Vayahāni or Chauhāna Vaṁśa

Maharaja Chapahāni (चपहानि) or Chayahāni (चयहानि) or Vayahāni (वयहानि) ruled from Ajamer, Rajasthan. He had two sons, Tomara and Sāmaladeva. According to the *Bhavișya MahāPurāṇa* (3.4.2.4–5), the elder son, Tomara, ruled from Ajamer for ten years and then, having conquered Indraprastha, ruled from there while the younger son, Sāmaladev, ruled at Ajamer. The dynasty of Sāmaladeva, till it was destroyed in the battle against Ghori in AD 1192, remained Brahma-kshatriya. The dynasty of Tomara, having gradually given up the religious rites of the brahmins, became kshatriya. The following is the genealogy of the dynasty (*Bhavișya MahāPurāṇa* 3.4.2).

### Vaṁśavali (genealogy) of Chayahāni Vaṁśa (Dynasty)

1. Chayahāni (चयहानि) or Vayahāni (वयहानि)
2. Tomara (तोमर) – went to Indraprastha (इन्द्रप्रस्थ), began the Tomara Dynasty

3. Sāmaladeva (सामलदेव) – brother of Tomara
4. Mahādeva (महादेव)
5. Ajaya (अजय)
6. Vīrasiṁha (वीरसिंह) – reigned for 50 years
7. Bindusura (बिन्दुसुर) – had twins – daughter Vīrā and son Vīra Vihāttaka
8. Vīra Vihāttaka (वीर विहात्तक)
9. Māṇikya (माणिक्य) – ruled for 50 years
10. Mahāsiṁha (महासिंह)
11. Chandragupta (चंद्रगुप्त)
12. Pratāpa (प्रताप)
13. Mohana (मोहन) – ruled for 3 years
14. Śvetarāya (श्वेतराय)
15. Nāgavāha (नागवाह)
16. Lohadhāra (लोहधार)
17. Vīrasiṁha (वीरसिंह)
18. Vibudha (विबुध) – ruled for 50 years
19. Chandrarāya (चंद्रराय)
20. Harihara (हरिहर)
21. Vasanta (वसंत)
22. Balāṅga (बलांग)
23. Pramatha (प्रमथ)
24. Aṅgarāya (अंगराय)
25. Viśāla (विशाल)
26. Śārṅgadeva (शार्ङ्गदेव)
27. Mantradeva (मंत्रदेव)
28. Jayasiṁha (जयसिंह) – conquered Āryāvarta – ruled for 50 years
29. Ānandadeva (आनंददेव) – ruled for 50 years

30. Someśvara (सोमेश्वर) – valorous, married Kīrtimālini, daughter of King Anangapal of Indraprastha
31. Dundhukāra (धुंधुकार), Kumāra (कुमार), and Pṛthvirāja* (पृथ्वीराज) (*spelled Pruthvirāj or Prithvirāj in common parlance)

Thirty-one kings ruled in this dynasty as shown above. Someśvara, the 30th king, married Kīrtimālinī (कीर्तिमालिनी), the older daughter of Anangapāl (अनंगपाल) of Indraprastha and had three sons – Dundhukāra, Kumāra, and Prithvirāj. The eldest son, Dhundhukāra, ruled Mathura, and the second son, Kumāra, ruled Ajamer. Anangapāl, having no son of his own, gave the Indraprastha throne to his grandson through his daughter, Prithvirāj, who went on to be an illustrious and powerful king.

Prithvirāj built a new fort with a *dehali* (tunnel) around it and got it populated. The new city came to be known as *Dehalī* (देहली). (*Bhaviṣya MahāPurāṇa* 3.3.5-6, 3.4.2).

Prithvirāj defeated Mohammad Shahabuddin Ghori in his first expedition to Dehali in AD 1191. Ghori was badly wounded but recovered, attacked again in AD 1192 and defeated Prithvirāj.

## Śukla or Chālukya Vaṁśa

Śukla, the first king of the vaṁśa (dynasty), rebuilt Dvārakā, spent his time in meditation and worship of Śrī Krishna, and reigned over western India for ten years. Viṣvaksena, his son, was the next king who ruled for 20 years. The following is the genealogy of the dynasty (*Bhaviṣya MahāPurāṇa* 3.4.3).

### Vaṁśavali (genealogy) of Śukla or Chālukya Dynasty

1. Śukla (शुक्ल) or Chālukya (चालुक्य) – 10 years
2. Viṣvaksena (विष्वक्सेन) – 20 years
3. Jayasena (जयसेन) – 30 years
4. Viśena (विशेन) – 50 years – gave his daughter to Vikrama
5. Pramoda (प्रमोद) and Madasiṁha (मदसिंह) - twins
6. Sindhuvarma (सिंधुवर्म) – left his father's throne and founded a kingdom on the banks of the Sindhu which came to be known as Sindhu Deśa

7. Sindhudvīpa (सिंधुद्वीप)
8. Śrīpati (श्रीपति) – married Kācchapi (काच्छपी) from Gautama Dynasty, moved to Kaccha Deśa (कच्छ देश) and founded a kingdom on the banks of the Sindhu after defeating Pulinda and Yavanas; the kingdom was known as Śrīpati.
9. Bhujavarma (भुजवर्म) – founded the Bhuja Deśa kingdom – Bhuj is the capital of the Kaccha district in Gujarat.
10. Raṇavarma (रणवर्म)
11. Citravarma (चित्रवर्म) – built Citranagari
12. Dharmavarma (धर्मवर्म)
13. Kṛṣṇavarma (कृष्णवर्म)
14. Udaya (उदय)
15. Vāpyakarmā (वाप्यकर्मा) – built many *vāvs* (step wells) and lakes, and defeated the Mleccha king Balada (बलद) who attacked with an army of one lakh.
16. Guhila (गुहिल)
17. **Kālabhoja (कालभोज) – famous as Bappā Rāval** (ca. AD 728–753)
18. Rāṣṭrapāla (राष्ट्रपाल) – gave up his father's throne, founded Puri; had twin sons, Vijaya and Prajaya; Prajaya left his parents and went to **Kānyakubja (Kannauj)**
19. Jayapāla (जयपाल)
20. Veṇuka (वेणुक)
21. Yaśovigraha (यशोविग्रह) – strong and righteous and ruled for 20 years
22. Mahīchandra (महीचंद्र)
23. Chandradeva (चंद्रदेव)
24. Mandapāla (मन्दपाल)
25. Kumbhapāla (कुम्भपाल) or Vaiśyapāla (वैश्यपाल) – tactfully turned back Muhammad
26. Devapāla (देवपाल) – married Chandrakānti, daughter of Anangapāla of Indraprastha
27. Jayachandra (जयचंद्र) and Ratnabhānu (रत्नभानु)

It appears that there should be more kings on the list. Perhaps, some names have been lost. The Chālukya kings of South India were descendants of the Chālukya Dynasty. According to the Bhaviṣya MahāPurāṇa, the descendants of the 16th king, Guhila (गुहिल) Mahārāja, became a kshatriya sect called Guhilas. In the genealogy of the kings of Mewad described later, Guhila is the first king of the dynasty.

Rāṣṭrapālas, descendants of Rāṣṭrapāla (राष्ट्रपाल), the 18th king, remained Brahma-kshatriyas. These may be the Raṣtrakutas who ruled South India. The descendants of the Kumbhapāla (Vaiśyapāla) flourished into many branches; they were called Vaiśyapālas and remained Brahma-kshatriyas.

The 26th king, Devapāla (देवपाल), born in the family line of Raṣtrapāla, married Chandrakānti (चन्द्रकान्ति), the second daughter of Anangapāla of Indraprastha and obtained two sons, Jayachandra and Ratnabhānu. Prithvirāj was the son of the first daughter of Anangapāla. Thus, Prithvirāj and Jayachandra were maternal cousins. Ratnabhānu, the younger prince, was brave and valorous. He defeated the kings of Gauda, Vanga, Maru, etc. kingdoms. *Bhaviṣya MahāPurāṇa* (3.3.4–7) narrates in detail how Prithvirāj and Jayachandra became enemies of each other.

Dr. Rajendra Singh Kushwaha (2003, p. 207) states in his book, *Glimpses of Bhāratiya History,* that the story of relation and enmity between Prithvirāj Chauhan and Jaychandra Rathod is false and is a result of three different Prithvirājas, almost being at the same time, namely Prithvirāj Tomar, Prithvirāj II and Prithivrāj III (Chauhan), and Vigraharāja IV (Bisaldev) who was married to the daughter of Anangapāla. Dr. Kushwaha (2003, p. 214) states further that the story of Jayachandra having invited Muhammad Ghori is false and that Jayachandra was a great ruler of his time as follows:

> “Jaya Chand … has been the worst sufferer of distortion of Bhāratiya history. He was a great ruler of his time and extended his empire upto Bengal and Assam and gave a crushing defeat to the Muslim rulers of Punjab from where he forcibly married a Hindu princess from the hilly tract called Sahiba. She not only betrayed him but planned his murder and conspired the invasion of Muhammad Ghori just to get her son Dhirshaha on the throne of Kannauj.”

## Arab Invasions of India – Fall of Sindh and its Recovery

William Hunter (1893, p. 111) states in his book, *A Brief History of Indian Peoples,* that about 15 years after the death of Prophet Muhammad in AD 632, Usman sent a naval expedition to Thane, Maharashtra, and Bharuch, Gujarat. Raids towards Sindh took place in AD 662 and 664 without any lasting results. In AD 712, Mir Kasim conquered Sindh after defeating Dāhar, the king of Sindh. However, this conquest didn't last long.

As described in the following paragraph, Rajputs expelled the Mohammedan governor from Sindh during the Mewad king, Bappā Rāval's reign (ca. AD 728–753) and completely regained possession of the province. For the next four centuries, the invaders were able to capture only a small portion of Panjab between AD 977 and 1176.

## Kings of Mewad

According to the genealogy and chronology preserved in the Mahārānā Pratāp Museum in Udaipur, Rajasthan, shown in Figure 6 (Chapter 3), Guhila (Guhadutta) founded this dynasty in Vikrama Samvat 623 (AD 566). Guhila was succeeded by Bhoja, Mahendra, Nāgaditya, Śilāditya, Aparājita, Mahendra II, and Kālabhoja, in that order. See Guhila and Kālabhoja at numbers 16 and 17 in the genealogy of the Chalukya Dynasty shown earlier. Kālabhoja's reigning date is Vikrama Samvat 791 (AD 734). He was more popularly known as Bappā Rāval. He, together with Nāgabhata I (AD 730–756), a Pratihāra king, organized the neighboring rulers and gave a crushing defeat to the Arab invaders. Bappā Rāval pursued the invaders and conquered Gajani, Afghanistan (Tod, 1829, p. 247).

During the reign of Khumana II, the 13th king of Mewad in Figure 6, (AD 812–836), Khalifa Alamamu invaded Chittod with a great force to avenge the defeat of Arabs at the hands of Bappā Rāval, but Khumana II gave him a crushing defeat between AD 813 and 833 and pushed back the Arabs beyond the Sindhu (Kushwaha, 2003).

## Gurjara-Pratihāra Empire

After successfully resisting the Arab invasions, starting with Nāgabhata I, the Gurjara-Pratihāra rulers dominated North India from about the mid-8th to the 11th century. The empire reached its zenith under Mihir Bhoj who reigned from AD 836 to 885. K. M. Munshi (1959, p. xiii) states in *The Age of Imperial Kanauj* that at the time of Bhoja's death in AD 888, his empire comprised North India from the Himalayas to a little beyond Narmada, from East Panjab and Sindh to Bengal. The Arabs on the northwest frontier were kept at bay and Sindh had been wrested from them.

## Parihāra or Pratihāra Vaṁśa

Parihāra (परिहार) or Pratihāra (प्रतिहार), a scholar of Atharvaveda, won over the Buddhists and worshipped Goddess Śakti (Durga). He founded Kalinirjara (कलिनिर्जर) or Kalinjara (कलिन्जर) near the Chitrakuta hills and ruled from there. Thirty-five kings ruled in this dynasty as follows (*Bhaviṣya MahāPurāṇa* 3.4.4).

### Vaṁśavali (genealogy) of the Parihāra Dynasty

1. Parihāra (परिहार)
2. Gauravarmā (गौरवर्मा) – put his younger brother on the throne of Kalinirjara, went to Gauda Deśa (present-day West Bengal), and founded a kingdom there.
3. Suparṇa (सुपर्ण) – son of Gauravarmā (number 2)
4. Rūpaṇa (रुपण)
5. Kāyavarmā (कायवर्मा)
6. Bhogavarmā (भोगवर्मा)
7. Kalivarmā (कलिवर्मा) – devotee of Kāli, founded Kalikātā (present-day **Kolkata**)
8. Kauśika (कौशिक)
9. Kātyāyana (कात्यायन)
10. Hemavata (हेमवत)
11. Śivavarmā (शिववर्मा)
12. Bhavavarmā (भववर्मा)
13. Rudravarmā (रुद्रवर्मा)
14. Bhojavarmā (भोजवर्मा)– founded a kingdom called Bhojarāṣṭra
15. Gavavarmā (गववर्मा)
16. Vindhyavarmā (विन्ध्यवर्मा) – gave the throne to his younger brother and went to the Vanga Deśa (present-day Bangladesh)
17. Sukhasena (सुखसेन)

18. Balāka (बलाक)
19. Lakṣamaṇa (लक्ष्मण)
20. Mādhava (माधव)
21. Keśava (केशव)
22. Sūrasena (सूरसेन)
23. Nārāyaṇa (नारायण)
24. Śāntivarmā (शान्तिवर्मा) – founded Śantipura on the banks of Ganga (present-day Shantipur in Nadia district, West Bengal)
25. Nadīvarmā (नदीवर्मा)
26. Gaṅgādatta (गंगादत्त) – the dynasty came to be known as Ganga Vaṁśa after him (Bhaviṣya MahāPurāṇa 3.4.4.27).
27. Śārṅgadeva (शार्ङ्गदेव)
28. Gaṅgādeva (गंगादेव)
29. Anaṅga Bhūpati (अनंग भूपति)
30. Rājeśvara (राजेश्वर)
31. Nṛsiṁha (नृसिंह)
32. Kalivarmā (कलिवर्मा) – conquered the Rāṣṭra Deśa (Maharashtra) and moved to Mahāvatī (महावती) city
33. Dhṛtivarmā (धृतिवर्मा)
34. Mahīpati (महीपति)

The 24th king, Śāntivarmā, built Śāntipura on the banks of the Ganga. From Gaṅgadatta, the 26th king, this dynasty became famous as the Gangā Dynasty (*Bhaviṣya MahāPurāṇa* 3.4.4.27). In this dynasty, the 32nd king, Kalivarmā conquered Maharashtra. The last king of the dynasty, Mahīpati, fought against Mohammad Shahabuddin Ghori in the war at Kurukṣetra (Thaneshvar) and died as a hero.

The descendants of the Agnivaṁśa's branches who took upon martial duties besides the brahmana duties are still found in the regions of Rajasthan, Panjab, Gujarat, and southern India. They call themselves Brahma-kshatras even today. The kings of the Chālukya Dynasty reigned over Āndhra for a long time.

## References

1. *Bhaviṣya MahāPurāṇa: (Sanskrit) with Hindi translation* by Pandit Baburam Upadhyay, 3 vols. (2006). Prayāg: Hindi Sahitya Sammelan.

2. *The Dīpavaṁsa: An Ancient Buddhist Historical Record* (English translation by Herman Oldenberg, 2006). New Delhi (First published: Berlin, 1879).

3. Hunter, William Wilson (1893). *A Brief History of the Indian Peoples* (20th ed.). Oxford: Clarendon Press.

4. Indraji, Pandit Bhagavānlāl, and Dr. G. Bühler (1884). 'Some Considerations on the History of Nepal.' *The Indian Antiquary: A Journal of Oriental Research in Archaeology, History, Literature, Languages, Philosophy, Religion, Folklore, etc. Vol. 13,* 411–428. Bombay.

5. Jones, William (1799a). 'On the Chronology of the Hindus, written in January 1788 by the President.' *Asiatic Researches; or Transactions of the Society Instituted in Bengal for inquiring into the History and Antiquities, the Arts, Sciences, and Literature of Asia, Vol. 2,* 111–147. London.

6. *Jyotishphala Ratnamala of Krishnamishra.* Chandrashekhar Sharma (Trans., n.d.).

7. Kalhaṇa (1148). *Rājataraṅgiṇī (Chronicle of the Kings of Kashmir) (Sanskrit text),* Edited with Hindi translation by Shri Ramtej Shastri Pandey (Vikrama Samvat 2017 (AD 1960), rpt. ed. 1985). Delhi & Varanasi: Chaukhamba Sanskrit Pratishthan.

8. Kushwaha, Dr. Rajendra Singh (2003). *Glimpses of Bhāratiya History.* New Delhi: Ocean Books.

9. *The Mahāvaṁsa:* or *The Great Chronicle of Ceylon* (English translation by Wilhelm Geiger, 1912). The Pali text Society, Oxford University Press.

10. Malcolm, Maj. Gen. John (1824). *Memoir of Central India, including Malwa and Adjoining Provinces* (Vol. 1, 2nd ed.). London.

11. Munshi, Dr. K. M. (Foreword) (1959). *The Age of Imperial Kanauj (Bharatiya Vidya Bhavan's History and Culture of the Indian People, Vol. IV).* Bombay: Bharatiya Vidya Bhavan.

12. Pandey, Raj Bali (1951). *Vikramāditya of Ujjayinī [The Founder of the Vikrama Era].* Banaras: Shatadala Prakashana.

13. *Prabandha Cintāmaṇi of Śrī Merutungāchārya* (ca. 1304), Hindi translation by Pandit Hajāriprasādjī Dvivedī (1940). Ahmedabad & Kolkata: Singhi

Jain Granthamālā.

14. Smith, Vincent A. (1910). *The Oxford Student's History of India* (2nd ed.). Oxford: Clarendon Press.

15. Tod, Lt. Col. James (1829). *Annals and Antiquities of Rajasthan or the Central and Western Rajpoot States of India* (Vol. 1). London.

16. Tod, Lt. Col. James (1829/1920). *Annals and Antiquities of Rajasthan or the Central and Western Rajpoot States of India,* Edited with an Introduction and Notes by William Crooke (Vol. 1) (1920). Oxford: University Press.

17. Venkatachelam, Pandit Kota (1955). *Chronology of Kashmir History Reconstructed.* Arya Vijnana Series, Publication 18. Vijayawada.

18. Venkatachelam, Pandit Kota (Kali 5052, AD 1951). *The Historicity of Vikramāditya & Sālivāhana [A Great Research work].* Arya Vijnanam 10, Publication 15. Vijayawada.

19. Venkatachelam, Pandit Kota (Kali 5054, AD 1953a). *Chronology of Nepal History Reconstructed (Nepalraja Vamsavali).* Arya Vijnana, Publication 16. Vijayawada.

20. Venkatachelam, Pandit Kota (Kali 5058, AD 1957a). *Chronology of Ancient Hindu History Part I.* Arya Vijnana Grandhamala, Publication 23. Vijayawada.

21. Wright, Daniel (1877). *History of Nepal: with an Introductory Sketch of the Country and People of Nepal* (Translated from Parbatiya by Munshi Shew Shunker Singh & Pandit Śhrī Gunanand, rpt. 1990). New Delhi: Asian Educational Services.

# 11

# THE KINGS OF KASHMIR

The greatest source of ancient Kashmir history is Pandit Kalhaṇa's (1148/1985) *Rājataraṅgiṇī* (राजतरंगिणी) (1.52) written in Laukikābda 4224 or Śaka 1070 (AD 1148). Pandit Kalhaṇa (कल्हण) was a great Sanskrit scholar. His father was the prime minister to the king of Kashmir. Kalhaṇa states in *Rājataraṅgiṇī* (1.8–20) that he started writing a critical systematic history of the kings after scrutinizing records of 11 ancient chroniclers, including the works of Suvrata, Kṣemendra, Helārāja, Pūrvamihira, and Śrīcchavillakara and the Purāṇa of Nīlamuni. He also examined the edicts and inscriptions of the ancient kings together with their recorded praises and eulogies, and other *śāstras* (books of knowledge), clearing all his doubts. See the comments of various historians admiring Rājataraṅgiṇī in Chapter 3.

The beautiful valley of Kashmir was originally a great lake called Satīsara (सतीसर). Maharṣi Kashyapa (कश्यप) got the lake drained and founded the Kashmir Mandala (*Rājataraṅgiṇī* 1.26–27).

## Five Milestones of the Chronology of Kashmir

The reigning periods of the kings of Kashmir from the time of the Mahābhārata War at the end of 3139 BC to Kashmirābda (also called Laukikābda or Saptarṣi Kāla) 4224 (AD 1148), when Rājataraṅgiṇī was written, are demarcated into five landmarks or milestones as stated by Pandit Venkatachelam (1955, p. 42). With the help of these landmark events, we can get the true chronology of the kings of Kashmir. The five milestone events are as follows:

1. Date of Kalhaṇa's Rājataraṅgiṇī: Laukikābda 4224 or Śālivāhana Śaka 1070 (AD 1148) (*Rājataraṅgiṇī* 1.52).

2. The starting date of the reign of Gonanda III, the 53rd ruler in the list of the Kashmir kings, is 2,330 years before Kalhaṇa's time (*Rājataraṅgiṇī* 1.53). This equals to (AD 1148 – 2,330 =) 1182 BC.
3. The date of Gonanda II corresponds to the date of the Mahābhārata War (end of 3139 BC).
4. The date of Mātrugupta, the 83rd king in the list of the Kashmir kings, who ruled from AD 13 to 18 and was appointed as the king by Emperor Vikramāditya of Ujjain, the emperor of India at that time.
5. Saṅgrāmarāja, the 127th king in the list of the Kashmir kings, was the contemporary of Trilochana-Pāla, the eighth king of the Hindu Shahi Dynasty, who ruled Panjab and Afghanistan. Trilochana was killed by Muhammad Ghazani in a battle in AD 1021. Rājataraṅgiṇī describes that Saṅgrāmarāja sent his army to assist Trilochana in that fight.

Thus, there are five epochs in the history of Kashmir: the first – 3139 BC, the second – 1182 BC, the third – AD 13–18, the fourth – AD 1021, and the fifth – AD 1148.

### Distortion by Colonial Era Indologists

M. A. Stein (1900) who translated Rājataraṅgiṇī into English, accused Kalhaṇa of independently imagining the 2,330 years and wrote that he could not accept it. He decreased the period arbitrarily from 2,330 years to 1,070 years!

## Kings of Kashmir (in Taranga 1), 374 BL–Laukikābda 1894 (3450–1182 BC)

The kings of Kashmir from 374 BL–Laukikābda 1894 (3450–1182 BC) are listed in Table 31. The dates in the table are first shown in Laukikābda, also known as Kashmirābda or Saptarṣi Kāla, which started in 3076 BC and has been the most popular calendar in Kashmir since ancient times. The calendar is still used there by the Hindus as discussed in Chapter 4. Before 3138 BC, eight kings ruled Kashmir. Of these, the names of the first five kings are not known and the kings sixth, seventh, and eighth are shown as the first, second, and third in the table. The first five kings whose names are not known ruled for 212 years total, from 3450 to 3238 BC (Venkatachelam, 1955, p. 92).

Kalhaṇa (1148/1985, 1.44, 48) has written that there was a tradition of 52 kings starting from Gonanda, the contemporary of Kauravas and Pāṇḍavas, and they ruled for 2,268 years in Kaliyuga before Gonanda III of 1182 BC.

**Table 31: Chronology of the kings of Kashmir, 374 BL–Laukikābda 1894 (3450–1182 BC)**

| King No. | Name of the King | Years of Reign | Starting Year in | |
|---|---|---|---|---|
| | | | Laukikābda (Saptarṣi) | BC |
| 1-5 | Names not known | 212 | 374 BL* | 3450 |
| 1 | Gonanda I (गोनन्द १) | 50 | 162 BL | 3238 |
| 2 | Dāmodara I (दामोदर १) | 48 | 112 BL | 3188 |
| 3 | Yaśovatī (यशोवती) – wife of Dāmodara I (No. 2) and mother of Gonanda II (No. 4) | ½ | 64 BL | 3140 |
| 4 | Gonanda (गोनन्द) II – 1 ½ years before to 55 years after the Mahābhārata War | 56 ½ | 63 ½ BL | 3139 ½ |
| | Parīkṣit (परीक्षित्) | 42 | 7 BL | 3083 |
| 5 | Harṇadeva | | | |
| 6 | Rāmadeva | | | |
| 7 | Vyāsadeva | | | |
| 8 | Dronadeva | | | |
| 9 | Siṁhadeva | | | |
| 10 | Gopāladeva | | | |
| 11 | Vijayananda | | | |
| 12 | Sukhadeva | | | |
| 13 | Ramanana | | | |
| 14 | Sandhimān | | | |
| 15 | Marahaṇdeva | | | |
| 16 | Kamaṇdeva | | | |
| 17 | Chandradeva | | | |
| 18 | Ānandadeva | | | |
| 19 | Drupadadeva | | | |
| 20 | Harṇamdeva | | | |
| 21 | Sulkandeva | | | |
| 22 | Sinaditya | | | |
| 23 | Mangaladitya | | | |
| 24 | Kshemendra | | | |
| 25 | Bhimasena | | | |
| 26 | Indrasena | | | |

*Table Contd.*

**BL = Before Laukikābda*

| King No. | Name of the King | Years of Reign | Starting Year in | |
|---|---|---|---|---|
| | | | Laukikābda (Saptarṣi) | BC |
| 27 | Sundarasena | | | |
| 28 | Gagendra | | | |
| 29 | Baladeva | | | |
| 30 | Nalasena | | | |
| 31 | Gokarṇa | | | |
| 32 | Prahlāda | | | |
| 33 | Bambru | | | |
| 34 | Pratāpaśīla | | | |
| 35 | Saṅgrāmachandra | | | |
| 36 | Larikchandra | | | |
| 37 | Biramchandra | | | |
| 38 | Babighaṇa | | | |
| 39 | Bhagavanta | | | |
| | Kings numbered 5th to 39th ruled from Laukikābda 35 to 1324 (3041–1752 BC), i.e. 1,289 years. | | | |
| 40 | Lava (लव) | | 1324 | 1752 |
| 41 | Kuśeśayākṣa (कुशेशयाक्ष) or Kuśa (कुश) | | | |
| 42 | Khagendra (खगेन्द्र) | | | |
| 43 | Surendra (सुरेन्द्र) – childless | | | |
| 44 | Godhara (गोधर) – from another kshatriya family | | | |
| 45 | Suvarṇa (सुवर्ण) | | | |
| 46 | Janaka (जनक) | | | |
| 47 | Śacīnara (शचीनर) | 31 | 1597 | 1479 |
| 48 | **Aśoka** (अशोक) | 48 | 1628 | 1448 |
| 49 | Jalauka (जलौक) | 56 | 1676 | 1400 |
| 50 | Dāmodara II (दामोदर २) | 50 | 1732 | 1344 |
| 51 | Huṣka, Juṣka, **Kaniṣka** (कनिष्क) | 60 | 1782 | 1294 |
| 52 | Abhimanyu (अभिमन्यु) | 52 | 1842 | 1234 |
| | **Total years** | **2,268** | **374 BL–1894** | **3450–1182** |

**BL = Before Laukikābda*

The historians before Kalhaṇa mentioned the same chronology. Thus, the beginning of the Kashmir chronology can be calculated: 1182 BC – 2,268 = 3450 BC. Gonanda I was the first king whose name is known. He was a contemporary and a friend of Jarāsandha, the king of Magadha. He was killed by Balarāma when he and Jarāsandha surrounded and attacked Śrī Krishna's Mathura (*Rājataraṅgiṇī* 1.58–63). Dāmodara I, the son of Gonanda I, was the second king, who was killed by Śrī Krishna in the fight that took place on the banks of the Sindhu. In vengeance for the death of his father, Dāmodara I had attempted to spoil the *svayamvara* (ceremony for choosing a husband by a princess) of the daughter of the king of Gāndhāra to which the Yādavas had been invited. Then, Śrī Krishna had Yaśovatī, the pregnant queen of Dāmodara I, enthroned as the third ruler (*Rājataraṅgiṇī* 1.70). A few months later, she gave birth to a son who was named after his grandfather, Gonanda. The 12-day-old son was crowned as the fourth king under the name Gonanda II.

The history of these four monarchs was written by Nīlamuni. When the fourth king, Gonanda II, was one and a half years old, the Mahābhārata War took place at the end of 3139 BC, 36 years before the starting of the Kaliyuga in 3102 BC. *Rājataraṅgiṇī* (1.82) states that as Gonanda II was a child then, the Kauravas and the Pāṇḍavas did not seek his support for the war. Emperor Janamejaya, the son of Parīkṣit, had asked *Ṛṣi* Vaiśampāyana (*Nīlamat Purāṇa*, Shlokas 3–10) that all kings of the Bharatavarṣa took part in the Mahābhārata War; why didn't the king of Kashmir participate in the war. *Ṛṣi* Vaiśampāyana had then explained to him the reason for the absence of the Kashmir King in the war.

Pandit Venkatachelam (1955, p. 92) states that Gonanda II (the fourth king) was killed in the battle with Parīkṣit, the emperor of Hastināpura in 3083 BC. As Gonanda II left no heir, Parīkṣit incorporated Kashmir into his empire. He ruled it from Hastināpura for 42 years and at the time of his death in 3041 BC, gave Kashmir to Harṇadeva (हर्णदेव). Twenty-three kings of the Pāṇḍava Dynasty and 12 other kings ruled Kashmir for 1,331 years, from 3083 to 1752 BC.

Kalhaṇa (1148/1985, 1.45) has stated that the successors of the fourth king Gonanda II, the 5th–39th king, 35 kings, did not follow their duties, hence they failed to attract the poets who would write their history, and thus, their histories were not recorded. According to Kalhaṇa, the names of these kings are lost. Mulla Ahmed's *History of Kashmir* written in Persian gives the names of the lost 35 kings, as stated by Pandit Venkatachelam (1955, p. 92). However, he has given in his book 34 names instead of 35 names, missing the

## Mulla Ahmad's History of Kashmir

Here is a story I found on the internet about Mulla Ahmad's writing of the history of Kashmir. A portion of this story is also found in the book *Tarikh-i-Hassan* (Hassan, 1954). "During the reign of Zain-ul-Abidin (AD 1418–1470), a search was launched to look for old Sanskrit works so that an updated version of the history of Kashmir could be brought out in the Persian language. The job was entrusted to the court poet, Mulla Ahmad Malik. It was a difficult job because the foolish and barbaric rulers of the Shah Mir Dynasty had destroyed all old books of Hindus in the 14th century AD. At that time, Mulla Ahmad had the names of 15 different Rājataraṅgiṇīs but only those of Kalhana, Kṣemendra, Wachulakar, and Padmamihira could be traced.

A few years later, some birch bark leaves of a Rājataraṅgiṇī, written by Pandit Ratnakar, were found by Mulla Ahmad through Praja Pandit. The work of Ratnakara contained a list of 35 lost kings and seven unknown kings who ruled over Kashmir. Mulla Ahmad had translated the Ratnakara's work into Persian, a copy of which was found by Maulvi Hassan Shah in Rawalpindi. Maulvi Hassan Shah (AD 1832–1898), the compiler of *Tarikh-i-Hassan Kashmir*, was a distinguished scholar in Persian and Arabic. His seventh ancestor was a Kashmiri Brahman, named Ganesh Kaul. He once went to Rawalpindi and there he found a copy of Tarikh-i-Hassan Kashmir written by Mulla Ahmad of the 15th century AD." This led me to search for *Tarikh-i-Hassan Kashmir* and I was fortunate to find one.

16th king. The list in Table 31 contains all 35 names. The missing name was obtained from the book *Tarikh-i-Hassan* (Hassan, 1954).

The aforementioned copy of the *Tarikh-i-Hassan* shows a complete list of the 35 lost kings and the years of reign for each. Some of the years of reign are a little difficult to read accurately but their total still comes close to 1,289 years as stated in Table 31.

The 40th king was Lava, the 41st Kuśa, 42nd Khagendra, 43rd Surendra, 44th Godhara, 45th Suvarṇa, 46th Janaka, and 47th Śacīnara. The history of these eight kings, from the 40th to 47th, was originally written by Pūrvāmihira, based on the chronicles of Helārāja (हेलाराज). The history of the 48th to 52nd kings was written by Śrīcchavillakara (श्रीच्छविल्लाकर), a great scholar.

## Aśoka

Śacīnara (शचीनर), the 47th king, had no son. Therefore, his great-grandfather's brother, Śakuni's, great-grandson, Aśoka, reigned as the 48th king from 1448 to 1400 BC. This Aśoka was the contemporary of Emperor Aśoka of Magadha, the grandson of Chandragupta Maurya. Aśoka Maurya ruled from 1472 to 1436 BC as stated in Chapter 7. Kalhaṇa states that the Kashmir Aśoka was a very noble and virtuous king. He embraced Buddhism, erected many stupas, built many temples, and the city of Srinagar (श्रीनगर) full of beautiful buildings. He prayed to Lord Śiva, too.

### Distortion by J. F. Fleet

J. F. Fleet (1901, p. 12), a colonial era Indologist, while disparaging Rājataraṅgiṇī, wrote the following, mistaking this Aśoka for Aśoka Maurya of Magadha who, according to the false chronology of the colonial era Indologists, reigned in the third century BC:

> "It [Rājatarangiṇi] places the great Maurya king Aśoka a thousand years before his real time."

Kashmir Aśoka's son Jalauka (जलौक) was the 49th king as shown in Table 31. Although he worshiped Lord Śiva, he built *vihāras* for Buddhists. Jalauka was a king of great prowess and conquered many regions including Kānyakubja (कान्यकुब्ज), the present-day Kannauj, from where he had experts from all *varṇas* (occupations) settled into Kashmir. His fame spread far and wide. He reformed the administration by establishing 18 departments instead of the 7 in the past. Dāmodara II was next, the 50th king.

## Huṣka, Juṣka, and Kaniṣka

Huṣka, Juṣka, and Kaniṣka, the three Turuṣka brothers (likely, descendants of Turvasu, one of the sons of the 7th king in Appendix I), ruled jointly as the 51st king and founded three towns named Huṣkapur, Juṣkapur, and Kaniṣkapur. The three brothers reigned for 60 years, from Laukikābda 1782 to 1842 (1294–1234 BC). Kaniṣka was the most prominent of the three. Buddhism was in prominence in Kashmir during this time and Nāgārjuna was a well-known Bodhisatva.

The next ruler was Abhimanyu who reigned as the 52nd king. Upon Abhimanyu's asking, Chandrāchārya and other great pandits revived

Sanskrit grammar and wrote a *mahābhāṣya* (great commentary) on grammar, called Chāndra.

## Distortion by Colonial Era Indologists

To fit with their fancy of the compressed chronology, the colonial era Indologists declared Kaniṣka to be the Kushan king and brought him down to AD 78. They opined that the Śālivāhana Śaka of AD 79 was started probably by Kaniṣka, thus, wiping out about 1,300 years from the chronology given in Rājataraṅgiṇī, similar to the 1,200 years erased from the chronology of Magadha as discussed in Chapter 2. See the 'Distortions' section in Chapter 10 and at the end of this chapter for the quotes from Vincent Smith for further details.

Colonial era Indologists routinely misinterpreted the inscriptions to fit their conjectures. T. S. Narayana Sastry (1916/1971, p.7) cites an example as follows:

> " For instance, from the inscription on a coin bearing the figure of a standing king in Greek costume, and some modified Greek characters and figures deciphered as ' Kanerki, ' the conclusion has been drawn by Dr. Fleet and implicitly accepted by many an other Orientalist, that the ' Kanerki ' of the said coin must be the ' Kanishka ' of Kalhaṇa's Rāja-Taraṅgiṇi, ... The fact, however, is that these orientalists have been "simply indulging in their fancy and piling conjecture upon conjecture to construct their cloud-land." They accept the authority of the Itihāsas and Purāṇas and works like Rāja-Taraṅgiṇi so far as those works support them in their theories, but tear them mercilessly to pieces ... whatever portions thereof conflict with their preconceived notions. "

# Dynasty of Gonanda III (Kings in Taranga 1), Laukikābda 1894–2803 (1182–273 BC)

The chronology of the kings of Kashmir from 1182 to 273 BC is shown in Table 32, starting with Gonanda III, the 53rd king. Gonanda III's time was 2,330 years before the time of Kalhaṇa's writing of Rājataraṅgiṇī in AD 1148 as stated by Kalhaṇa. Hence, the date of Gonanda III is AD 1148 – 2,330 = 1182 BC.

According to the currently available Rājataraṅgiṇī, these 21 kings, the 53rd to 73rd, reigned for a total of 1,014 years as stated at the end of Taranga 1. Rājataraṅgiṇī states the reigning period for each of the kings except for

**Table 32: Chronology of the dynasty of Gonanda III, Laukikābda 1894–2803 (1182–273 BC)**

| King No. | Name of the King | Years of Reign | Starting Year in | |
|---|---|---|---|---|
| | | | Laukikābda (Saptarṣi) | BC |
| 53 | Gonanda (गोनन्द) III | 35 | 1894 | 1182 |
| 54 | Vibhīṣaṇa (विभीषण) | 53 ½ | 1929 | 1147 |
| 55 | Indrajīta (इन्द्रजीत) | 35 | 1982 ½ | 1093 ½ |
| 56 | Rāvaṇa (रावण) | 30 | 2017 ½ | 1058 ½ |
| 57 | Vibhīṣaṇa (विभीषण) II | 35 ½ | 2047 ½ | 1028 ½ |
| 58 | Kinnara (किन्नर) or Nara (नर) | 39 ¾ | 2083 | 993 |
| 59 | Siddha (सिध्ध) | 60 | 2123 | 953 |
| 60 | Utpalākṣa (उत्पलाक्ष) | 30 ½ | 2183 | 893 |
| 61 | Hiraṇyākṣa (हिरण्याक्ष) | 37 ½ | 2213 ½ | 862 ½ |
| 62 | Hiraṇyakula (हिरण्यकुल) | 60 | 2251 | 825 |
| 63 | Vasukula (वसुकुल) | 60 | 2311 | 765 |
| 64 | **Mihirkula** (मिहिरकुल) | 70 | 2371 | 705 |
| 65 | Baka (बक) | 40* | 2441 | 635 |
| 66 | Kṣitinanda (क्षितिनन्द) | 30 | 2481 | 595 |
| 67 | Vasunanda (वसुनन्द) – poet, author of *Smara Śāstra* | 52 | 2511 | 565 |
| 68 | Nara (नर) | 35* | 2563 | 513 |
| 69 | Akṣa (अक्ष) | 60 | 2598 | 478 |
| 70 | **Gopāditya** (गोपादित्य) | 60 | 2658 | 418 |
| 71 | Gokarṇa (गोकर्ण) | 35* | 2718 | 358 |
| 72 | Khiṅkhilānya (खिंखिलान्य) or Narendrāditya | 31** | 2753 | 323 |
| 73 | Andha Yudhiṣṭhira (युधिष्ठिर) | 19* | 2784 | 292 |
| | **Total years** | **909** | **1894–2803** | **1182–273** |

* *Years of reign decreased.* ** *per the manuscript quoted by Wilson (1825); the current version of Rājataraṅgiṇī states 36 years.*

the last king, Andha Yudhiṣṭhira. He was called 'Andha' because of his small eyes. The years of reign shown in Table 32 contain a few adjustments to the years given in the Rājataraṅgiṇī, similar to the adjustments done by Pandit Venkatachelam (1955, p. 87–89). The reigning periods of the kings marked with an asterisk (*) have been decreased to bring the total reigning period of the 21 kings from 1,014 years to 909 years. This is to ensure that one of the five key milestones of the chronology stated at the beginning of this chapter, the date of the 83rd king Mātrugupta's reign from AD 13–18 is adhered to. Mātrugupta abdicated the throne when he heard of the passing away of Emperor Vikramāditya of Ujjain in AD 18 as discussed later in this chapter.

As discussed in detail by Pandit Venkatachelam (1955, p. 45, 87) and as mentioned at the end of this chapter, it appears that some of the reigning periods of the kings in the presently available copies of Rājataraṅgiṇī might have been tampered with by the colonial era European Indologists (Bühler, 1877/1984, p. 264–267).

## Mihirkula

*Rājataraṅgiṇī* (1.309) describes that Mihirkula, the 64th king in Table 32, reigned for 70 years. He was a tyrant; he was compared to *Yama*. He conquered Siṁhala and replaced the king there. On his return journey, he dethroned the kings of Chola, Karṇāta, and Lāta countries and imprisoned many enemy rulers in his fortress.

### Distortion

European historians of the colonial era turned this Mihirkula of 705 BC into a Huna king of AD 532 as elaborated at the end of this chapter.

## Gopāditya

Gopāditya, the 70th king, who reigned from 418 to 358 BC, was a virtuous king. His rule made his subjects feel that they were living in *Satyayuga* (Golden Age). Gopāditya had the temple of Ādi Śaṅkarāchārya built in 367–366 BC on a hill, now known as the Śaṅkarāchārya Hill near Srinagar, as discussed in the 'Evidence ...' section of Chapter 9.

## Dynasty of Pratāpāditya (Kings in Taranga 2), Laukikābda 2803–2995 (273–81 BC)

Andha Yudhiṣṭhira, the last king of the preceding dynasty, was attacked by enemies and ran away. Later, his ministers brought Pratāpāditya, a descendant of king Vikramāditya, from another state and placed him on the throne of Kashmir. Vikramāditya referred to here is Harṣa Vikramāditya of Ujjain of 457 BC as discussed in Chapter 9. Kalhaṇa (1148/1985, 2.5–7) has clearly stated that this Vikramāditya was not the Śakāri (शकारि) Vikramāditya (of 57 BC) who destroyed the Śaka people. Śakāri means the enemy of the Śaka. Kalhaṇa states that Kashmir was under the sovereignty of Harṣa and his successors for some time.

In Table 33, the chronology of the dynasty of Pratāpāditya is given. A total of six kings in this dynasty ruled for a total of 192 years, from 273 to 81 BC. The reigning periods of the kings are from Rājataraṅgiṇī without any change. During the reign of Tuñjīna, a dramatist named Chandak, believed to be a descendant of Dvaipāyana Vyāsa muni, was around.

**Table 33: Chronology of the dynasty of Pratāpāditya, Laukikābda 2803–2995 (273–81 BC)**

| King No. | Name of the King | Years of Reign | Starting Year in | |
|---|---|---|---|---|
| | | | Laukikābda (Saptarṣi) | BC |
| 74 | Pratāpāditya (प्रतापादित्य) | 32 | 2803 | 273 |
| 75 | Jalauka (जलौक) | 32 | 2835 | 241 |
| 76 | Tuñjīna (तुंजीन) – did not have a child | 36 | 2867 | 209 |
| 77 | Vijaya (विजय) – from another kshatriya family | 8 | 2903 | 173 |
| 78 | Jayendra (जयेन्द्र) | 37 | 2911 | 165 |
| 79 | Sandhimati (संधिमति) | 47 | 2948 | 128 |
| | **Total years** | **192** | **2803–2995** | **273–81** |

## Gonanda Dynasty (Kings in Taranga 3), Laukikābda 2995–3669 (81 BC–AD 593)

The king of Gāndhāra had raised Gopāditya (different from Gopāditya, the 70th king), the great-grandson of Andha Yudhiṣṭhira, to win Kashmir. This

Gopāditya obtained a son named Meghavāhana. Sandhimati, the 79th king, wanted to give up the throne. Upon hearing Meghavāhana's desire to regain the throne of his ancestors, he happily installed Meghavāhana on the throne despite the people's desire for him to continue as their beloved king. Thus, the Kashmir throne returned to the Gonanda Dynasty (Kalhaṇa, 1148/1985, 2.143–155). According to the current version of the Rājataraṅgiṇī, a total of ten kings ruled in his dynasty as shown in Table 34.

The Taranga in the current version does not state the total years of reign for this dynasty, unlike the other Tarangas. The reigning periods for each of

**Table 34: Chronology of the Gonanda Dynasty, Laukikābda 2995–3669 (81 BC–AD 593)**

| King No. | Name of the King | Years of Reign | Starting Year in | |
|---|---|---|---|---|
| | | | Laukikābda (Saptarṣi) | BC/AD |
| 80 | Meghavāhana (मेघवाहन) | 34 | 2995 | 81 BC |
| 81 | Śreṣṭhasena (श्रेष्ठसेन), Pravarasena (प्रवरसेन) I or Tuñjīna (तुंजीन) II | 30 | 3029 | 47 BC |
| 82 | Hiraṇya (हिरण्य) – older brother of Toramāṇa (तोरमाण) | 30 | 3059 | 17 BC |
| 83 | Mātrugupta (मातृगुप्त) | 5 | 3089 | 13 AD |
| 84 | Pravarasena (प्रवरसेन) II – Toramāṇa's son | 63 | 3094 | 18 AD |
| 85 | Yudhiṣṭhira II (युधिष्ठिर) – contemporary of Śālivāhana of Ujjain | 39 | 3157 | 81 AD |
| 86 | Narendrāditya (नरेन्द्रादित्य) or Lakhaṇa (लखण) | 13 | 3196 | 120 AD |
| 87 | Raṇāditya (रणादित्य) or Tuñjīna (तुंजीन) - younger brother of Narendrāditya<br>**Kings missing?** | | **3209–3590** | **133–514 AD** |
| 88 | Vikramāditya (विक्रमादित्य) | 42 | 3590 | 514 AD |
| 89 | Bālāditya (बालादित्य) – younger brother of Vikramāditya | 37 | 3632 | 556 AD |
| | **Total years** | **674** | **2995–3669** | **81 BC–593 AD** |

the kings except for the 87th king, Raṇāditya, are from the Rājataraṅgiṇī. *Rājataraṅgiṇī* (3.470) states an impossible reigning period of 300 years for Raṇāditya. It is unlikely that Pandit Kalhaṇa would have given such an impossible number for one king unless this number was meant to indicate an unaccounted gap in the chronology. We do not know when this number got corrupted or tampered with. Kalhaṇa has mentioned the 87th king Raṇāditya as the younger brother of the 86th king but has not mentioned any relation between Raṇāditya and the king succeeding him.

Since, Durlabhavardhana, the first king of the next dynasty, was the son-in-law of the 89th king Bālāditya, the last king of this dynasty, the dates for the last two kings of this dynasty, must be immediately before the next dynasty, the Kārkota Dynasty. There were likely additional kings between the 87th king, Raṇāditya, and the 88th king, Vikramāditya, and their names and information have been lost. This conclusion is significantly different from the conclusion of Pandit Venkatachelam (1955, p. 90) in which he assigns the missing years to the Kārkota Dynasty.

Not long after I had arrived at the above conclusion, I found the book, *Tarikh-i-Hassan* (Hassan, 1954), which listed not only the 35 missing kings discussed earlier but also additional seven kings, six before Raṇāditya and one after Raṇāditya along with the dates of their reign for each, from AD 191 to 521, covering 330 years as shown in Table 35. This was an incredible finding.

Adding to my very pleasant surprise, the dates of these seven kings fall almost exactly in the gap in the chronology, from AD 133 to 514, shown in Table 34. With these seven 'lost and found' kings, there is a slight overlap of seven years at the end of the reign of the missing kings, and a gap of 58 years at the beginning, resulting in an overall gap of 51 years in the chronology for this dynasty.

Returning to the kings of the dynasty in Table 34, while the 82nd king Hiraṇya was ruling, Toramāṇa, his younger brother, was the crown prince. When Toramāṇa got new coins minted, Hiraṇya felt insulted. He was angry and imprisoned Toramāṇa suspecting that he was trying to overthrow him. Hiraṇya later released Toramāṇa but the latter soon died. When Hiraṇya died without a child, the ministers reported the matter to their Emperor Vikramāditya in Ujjain, according to the Rājataraṅgiṇī.

**Table 35: The lost and found kings of the last Gonanda Dynasty**

| Sr. No. | Name of the King | Years of Reign | Christian Year |
|---|---|---|---|
| 1 | Tuñjīna | 43 | 191–234 AD |
| 2 | Sarabsena | 48 | 234–282 AD |
| 3 | Gandharvsena | 37 | 282–319 AD |
| 4 | Lachhman | 33 | 319–352 AD |
| 5 | Surak | 51 | 352–403 AD |
| 6 | Vajraditya | 11 | 403–414 AD |
| 7 | **Raṇāditya** | 60 | 414–474 AD |
| 8 | Vainyaditya | 47 | 474–521 AD |
| | **Total years** | **330** | **191–521 AD** |

## Mātrugupta Appointed by Vikramāditya

Rājataraṅgiṇī (Kalhana, 1148/1985, 3.125 onwards) narrates the greatness of Emperor Vikramāditya whose fame had reached faraway lands. Good people could approach him without any difficulty and thus, a poet named Mātrugupta was in his court. Vikramāditya appointed Mātrugupta (मातृगुप्त) as the next king of Kashmir. The section on Vikramāditya (Evidence 8) in Chapter 10 describes at length the course of the procedure followed by the emperor in selecting the next king of Kashmir. Mātrugupta, the 83rd king of Kashmir, reigned for five years. *Rājataraṅgiṇī* (3.290 onwards) describes in detail Mātrugupta's life after he abdicated the throne as follows:

> "On hearing the death of Emperor Vikramāditya, Mātrugupta abdicated the throne of Kashmir and went to Kashi to lead the life of a sannyāsī. Then Toramāṇa (तोरमाण)'s son Pravarsena II administered the kingdom and remitted the surplus income of Kashmir to Mātrugupta, despite the latter's refusal to accept the amount. Mātrugupta gave it away as gifts to the poor and lived on *bhikṣa*."

As stated in Chapter 10, Kaliyuga 3120 (AD 18) was the last year of Emperor Vikramāditya. Therefore, the same must be the year of abdication of the throne by Mātrugupta.

Pravarasena II, the next king and Toramāṇa's son, was a victorious king. He conquered Saurashtra and helped Emperor Vikramāditya's son,

### Corruption in the Current Version of Rājataraṅgiṇī?

Presently available *Rājataraṅgiṇi* (3.125) calls this Vikramāditya as Harṣa Vikramāditya which is not correct. Kalhaṇa has already described the 74th king Pratāpāditya as a descendant of Harṣa Vikramāditya of the earlier era in Taranga 2, shlokas 5–7.

Śīlāditya (also known as Pratāpaśīla), regain Ujjain from the enemies and restored him to the throne (*Rājataraṅgiṇī* 3.330). Although the present copy of the Rājataraṅgiṇī states 60 years of reign for Pravarasena, the older manuscript of the Rājataraṅgiṇī, summarized by Prof. H. H. Wilson (1825, p. 60), stated 63 years for Pravarsena's reign. After a long reign, Pravarasena gave up the throne and went to Kailash.

Bālāditya, the 89th (not including the seven lost and now found kings) and the last king of the dynasty, conquered Bengal and constructed victory pillars on the shores of the eastern sea (*Rājataraṅgiṇī* 3.480). Thus, he was the dominant king of India during his time (AD 556–593). Bālāditya did not have a son, but a daughter, and thus he was the last king of the great Gonanda Dynasty of Kashmir which ruled Kashmir for about 4,000 years.

## Kārkota Dynasty (Kings in Taranga 4), Laukikābda 3669–3931 (AD 593–855)

Durlabhavardhana, the first king of this dynasty was the son-in-law of Bālāditya, the last king of the preceding dynasty. He was a son of the Kārkota Nāg (कार्कोट नाग) family; hence, this dynasty is known as the Kārkota Dynasty. The chronology of this dynasty is shown in Table 36. A total of 17 kings ruled in this dynasty. Rājataraṅgiṇī (4.703) states that the 103rd king, Cippaṭa-Jayāpiḍa who was a minor and a nominal king under the care of his five maternal uncles, was killed in Saptarṣi (Laukika) Samvat 3889 (AD 813). This is the first mention of the precise year in the Rājataraṅgiṇī. Ajitāpiḍa, the 104th king, ruled for 26 years (or 36 years in Wilson's manuscript). The next king ruled for three years and the reign of the last king of the dynasty, Utpalāpiḍa, ended in Saptarṣi Samvat 3931 (AD 855) (*Rājataraṅgiṇī* 4.716). The years of the reign of each king add up to a total of 261.5 years, rounded to 262 years. With the end year of the dynasty known to be AD 855, the starting year of the dynasty works out to AD 593.

The Chinese pilgrim Hiuen Tsiang visited Kashmir during the reign of

**Table 36: Chronology of the Kārkota Dynasty, Laukikābda 3669–3931 (AD 593–855)**

| King No. | Name of the King | Years of Reign | Starting Year in Laukikābda (Saptarṣi) | Starting Year in AD |
|---|---|---|---|---|
| 90 | Durlabhavardhana (दुर्लभवर्धन) or Prajñāditya | 36 | 3669 | 593 |
| 91 | Durlabhaka (दुर्लभक) or Pratāpāditya | 50 | 3705 | 629 |
| 92 | Chandrāpiḍa (चंद्रापीड) or Vajrāditya (वज्रादित्य) | 9 | 3755 | 679 |
| 93 | Tārāpiḍa (तारापीड) or Udayāditya – younger brother of Chandrāpiḍa (No. 92) | 4 | 3764 | 688 |
| 94 | Muktāpiḍa (मुक्तापीड) or **Lalitāditya** (ललितादित्य) – younger brother of Tārāpiḍa (No. 93) | 37 | 3768 | 692 |
| 95 | Kuvalayāpiḍa (कुवलयापीड) – older son of Lalitāditya | 1 | 3805 | 729 |
| 96 | Vajrāditya (वज्रादित्य) or Bappiyaka (बप्पियक) or Lalitāditya – step brother of Kuvalyāpiḍa (No. 95) | 7 | 3806 | 730 |
| 97 | Pṛthivyāpiḍa (पृथिव्यापीड) I – elder son of Vajrāditya (No. 96) | 4 | 3813 | 737 |
| 98 | Saṅgrāmāpiḍa (संग्रामापीड) I – younger son of Bappiyaka (No. 96) | 7 | 3817 | 741 |
| 99 | Jajja (जज्ज) – the brother-in-law of Jayāpiḍa while the latter was away on a conquest march | 3 | 3824 | 748 |
| 100 | **Jayāpiḍa** (जयापीड) or Vinayāditya (विनयादित्य) – youngest son of Bappiyaka (No. 96), grandson of the great Lalitāditya | 31 | 3827 | 751 |
| 101 | Lalitāpiḍa (ललितापीड) – son of Jayāpiḍa | 12 | 3858 | 782 |
| 102 | Saṅgrāmāpiḍa (संग्रामापीड) II or Pṛthivyāpiḍa (पृथिव्यापीड) II - younger son of Jayāpiḍa | 7* | 3870 | 794 |
| 103 | Cippaṭa-Jayāpiḍa (चिप्पट-जयापीड) or Bṛhaspati – son of Lalitāpiḍa, 101 | 12 | 3877 | 801 |

| King No. | Name of the King | Years of Reign | Starting Year in | |
|---|---|---|---|---|
| | | | Laukikābda (Saptarṣi) | AD |
| 104 | Ajitāpiḍa (अजितापीड) – son of Tribhuvanapiḍa – older step brother of Cippaṭa (No. 103) | 26** | 3889 | 813 |
| 105 | Anangāpiḍa (अनंगापीड) – son of Sangrāmāpiḍa II (No. 102) | 3 | 3915 | 839 |
| 106 | Utpalāpiḍa (उत्पलापीड) – son of Ajitāpiḍa (No. 104) | 13 | 3918 | 842 |
| | **Total years** | **262** | **3669–3931** | **593–855** |

**Abul Fazal's Persian translation has 37 years (Wilson, 1825, p. 59).*
***Wilson's manuscript (1825, p. 60) stated 36 years. In that case, the years of reign for Utpalāpiḍa, the last king, will be 3 instead of 13 years because the last calendar year of his reign is fixed.*

this dynasty when he visited India from AD 630 to 646 (Beal, 1906). He has not mentioned the name of the king ruling Kashmir at that time. He recorded that the regions around Kashmir such as Takshashila, Simhapura, Urasa, etc. were either under the direct rule of Kashmir or were its tributaries.

## Rājataraṅgiṇī Tampered?

The presently available copy of Rājataraṅgiṇī gives this dynasty a total reign of 260 years, 6 months, and 10 days at the end of Taranga 4. It gives seven days of reign for Saṅgrāmāpiḍa, the 98th king, and 26 years of reign for Ajitāpiḍa, the 104th king. Whereas, the summary of Rājataraṅgiṇī given by H. H. Wilson (1825, Ch. 1) states seven years of reign for Saṅgrāmāpiḍa, three years of reign for Jajja (brother-in-law of Jayāpiḍa who usurped the throne while Jayāpiḍa was on a conquest march), and 36 years of reign for Ajitāpiḍa. Thus, the presently available copy of Rājataraṅgiṇī has shorter reigning periods for these three kings. It has a shorter reigning period also for Pravarsena of the earlier dynasty as pointed out earlier. The three changes made in Rājataraṅgiṇī after AD 1825, have the net effect of shortening the total years of reign for this dynasty by ten years. Thus, the chronology in the original Rājataraṅgiṇī may have been tampered with to shorten it. Dr. G Bühler states (1877/1984, p. 265):

> “Some years later Mr. A. Troyer began a critical edition of the text, and in 1840 issued the first six cantos together with a translation of the whole eight cantos, which was completed in 1852. ... It may seem scarcely credible that a book which has engaged the attention of so

many Sanskṛitists, and of some of the first rank, is, after all the labour expended, not in a satisfactory condition, and its explanation leaves a great deal to desire. ”

Thus, the 19th century European Indologists made a case for editing the Purāṇas as they saw fit to justify their shortened chronology. Changes in the Rājataraṅgiṇī might have been made even before AD 1825. Abul Fazal in his Persian translation of Rājataraṅgiṇī states 37 years of reign instead of seven years for Saṅgrāmāpiḍa II, the 102nd king. If his reign was indeed 37 years, the chronology of the 88th to 101st kings, preceding Saṅgrāmāpiḍa will move up by 30 years.

## Lalitāditya and his Empire

Lalitāditya, the 94th king in Table 36, was the greatest king of the Kārkota Dynasty. Rājataraṅgiṇī narrates in detail Lalitāditya's *digvijay*, the conquest march through the whole Indian subcontinent and beyond. He started his campaign by defeating King Yashovarma (a patron of Vākpatirāj, Bhavabhuti, etc. famous Sanskrit poets) of Kānyakubja and reached the eastern sea. While in Kaliṅga, he received elephants from Gauda Deśa (West Bengal). He then marched south through the coastal forests, conquered Karnataka and Dakshinapatha (ruled by Ratta Devi), reached the River Kaveri, and conquered the islands. He then turned west, conquered the seven Kramuk Deśas, Koṅkaṇa, and Dvārakā, and then entered Ujjayini. Thus, having conquered all, he marched to Uttarapatha (northwest regions) where he conquered Kamboja (west of Kashmir), Darada (north of Kashmir), and the Tukhkhara people i.e. present-day Afghanistan and Turkmenistan. Lalitāditya defeated Mummuni, the king of Tukhāras, thrice. Figure 34 shows a map of Lalitāditya's march through the Indian subcontinent and beyond.

Lalitāditya returned to Kashmir with immense wealth and rewarded his key helpers by making them kings of the Jalandhar and Lohar (present-day Lahore), etc. provinces. There was not a town or a village in the country where he did not have a temple constructed. Thus, Lalitāditya established his supremacy over the subcontinent and beyond up to Turkmenistan in the west. C.V. Vaidya (1921, p. 208) narrates in his book, *History of Mediaeval Hindu India*, the confirmation of Lalitāditya's conquests found in *The ChachNamah* (1900, p. 83), a contemporary foreign account of the conquest of Sindh by Arabs in AD 712:

“ In a letter addressed by Dāhar [the king of Sindh] to Mahomed Kasim

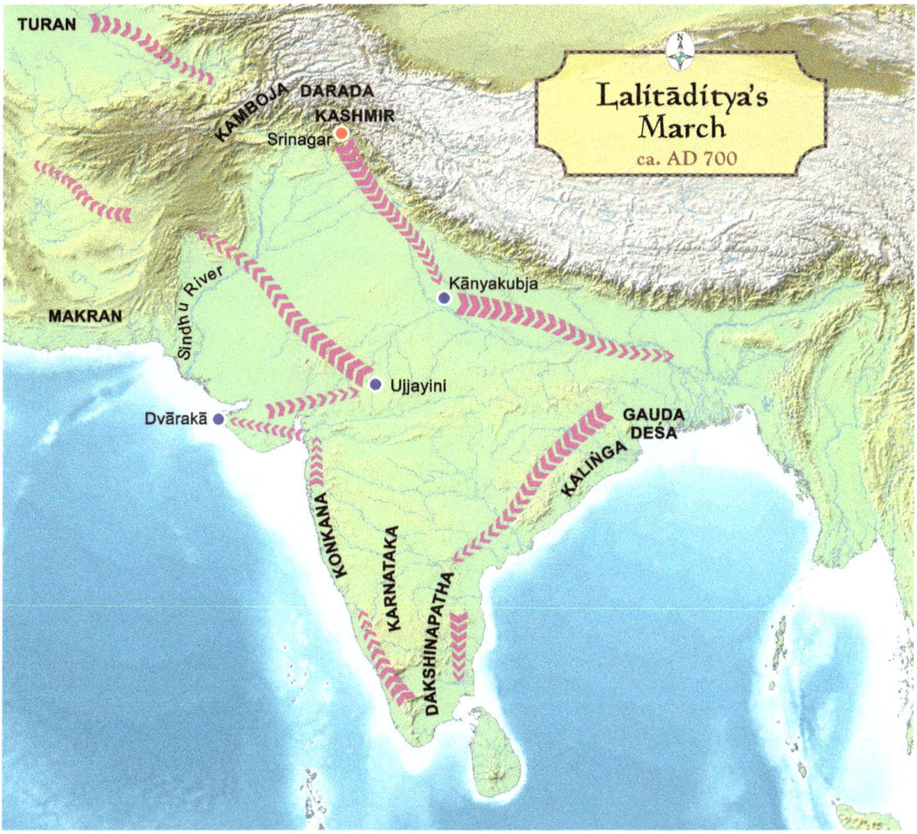


**Figure 34: Map of Laitāditya's march (ca. AD 700)**
*Blank map courtesy: DEMIS Mapserver, Wikimedia Commons, CC BY-SA 3.0*

(p. 87) occurs the following passage: "If I had sent against you the king of Kashmir, on whose royal threshold the other rulers of Hind had placed their heads, who sways the whole of Hind, even the countries of Makran [Baluchistan] and Turan [Turkmenistan], whose chains a great many noblemen and grandees have willingly placed on their knees, and against whom no human being can stand etc. …

The above quoted passage occurs in the Chach-nāma in a letter written in 712 A.D. The conquests of Lalitāditya must therefore be placed a few years only before this, as they appear to be fresh in Dāhar's mind. ”

Regarding Lalitāditya's conquest of Turan, C. V. Vaidya (1921, p. 211) states:

“ But there is no doubt of the truth of this conquest or rather success in battle. For we have not only the mention of Mummuni their king but the extract above given from the Chacha-nāma also states that the king of

Kashmir had conquered *Mekran* (Baluchistan) and *Turan* (Turkestan). ”

Lalitāditya also accomplished many great works for his people.

## Jayāpiḍa

Jayāpiḍa, Lalitāditya's grandson, also, was a great conqueror and emperor. Mummuni, who had been defeated thrice by his grandfather, Laitāditya, was at his service. Jayāpiḍa invited the best people from various branches of knowledge to Kashmir, patronized them, and made Kashmir again the center of learning in India. He revived the study of *Mahābhāsya* (the great work of grammar) and appointed Kṣirasvāmi, a famous grammarian as the Pandit of grammar and himself learned from him. Bhattodbhatta, the well-known author of *Udbhattalankāra* on poetics, Manoratha, Śankhadanta, Chaṭanka, Sandhimān, etc. were some of the famous poets in his court.

**Table 37: Chronology of the Utpalā Dynasty, Laukikābda 3931–4015 (AD 855–939)**

| King No. | Name of the King | Years of Reign | Starting Year in Laukikābda (Saptarṣi) | Starting Year in AD |
|---|---|---|---|---|
| 107 | Avantivarmā (अवंतिवर्मा) | 28 | 3931 | 855 |
| 108 | Śaṅkaravarmā (शंकरवर्मा) | 18 | 3959 | 883 |
| 109 | Gopālavarmā (गोपालवर्मा) – minor, reign by mother Sugandhā | 2 | 3977 | 901 |
| 110 | Saṅkaṭa (संकट) – minor, brother of Gopālavarmā | 10 days | 3979 | 903 |
| 111 | Sugandhā (सुगंधा) – widow of Śaṅkaravarmā (No.108) | 2 | 3979 | 903 |
| 112 | Pārtha (पार्थ) – minor son of No. 113 | 16 | 3981 | 905 |
| 113 | Nirjitavarmā (निर्जितवर्मा) – relative of Sugandhā | 1 | 3997 | 921 |
| 114 | Cakravarmā (चक्रवर्मा) – second minor son of Nirjitvarmā | 11 | 3998 | 922 |
| 115 | Śūravarmā (शूरवर्मा) son of Nirjitvarmā (No.113), followed by Cakravarmā (No 114) again | 4 | 4009 | 933 |
| 116 | Unmatta Avanti (उन्मत्त अवंति) | 2 | 4013 | 937 |
| | **Total years** | **84** | **3931–4015** | **855–939** |

## Utpalā Dynasty (Kings in Taranga 5), Laukikābda 3931–4015 (AD 855–939)

The chronology of the kings of the Utpalā Dynasty is shown in Table 37. From this dynasty onwards, Rājataraṅgiṇī states precise calendar dates including the month and the day for each king's crowning and other noteworthy events.

Avantivarmā, the first king of the dynasty, was a very virtuous king. Many poets like Ānandavardhana, Ratnākara, etc. flourished in his court. Śrī Bhatt-Kallat was present during his time. Śankaravarmā, the next king, after securing his position, set out on a victorious campaign with an army of nine lakhs (9,00,000) foot soldiers, one lakh horses, and 300 elephants to conquer Gurjara. He subdued King Prithvichandra of Trigarta (Kangra, Himachal Pradesh) and defeated Alakhāna of Gurjara (probably of the Gurjara-Pratihāra Dynasty which ruled much of North India from the mid-8th to the 11th century). He also helped one of the kings get his kingdom back from the powerful Bhoja (Wilson, 1825, p. 66). He conquered many kings in the northwest. Eventually, Śankarvarmā got spoiled by his wealth.

## Brahmin Kings (Kings in Taranga 6), Laukikābda 4015–4079 (AD 939–1003)

Upon the death of Unmatta Avanti, the last king of the Utpalā Dynasty, a learned brahmin called Yaśaskara was chosen to be the next king. The chronology of the Brahmin kings from Taranga 6 is shown in Table 38.

Kṣemagupta, the 121st king, married Diddā, the daughter of Siṁharāja of Lohar (present-day Lahore). Siṁharāja was the son-in-law of Bhima Shahi, the ruler of Kabul at that time.

**Table 38: Chronology of the Brahmin kings, Laukikābda 4015–4079 (AD 939–1003)**

| King No. | Name of the King | Years of Reign | Starting Year in | |
|---|---|---|---|---|
| | | | Laukikābda (Saptarṣi) | AD |
| 117 | Yaśaskara (यशस्कर) | 9 ½ | 4015 | 939 |
| 118 | Varṇaṭa (वर्णट) | 1 month | 4024 | 948 |
| 119 | Saṅgrāmadeva (संग्रामदेव) – minor son of Yaśaskara | 1/2 | 4024 | 948 |
| 120 | Parvagupta (पर्वगुप्त) – minister of the previous king | 2 | 4024 (RT* 6.129) | 948 |

| King No. | Name of the King | Years of Reign | Starting Year in | |
|---|---|---|---|---|
| | | | Laukikābda (Saptarṣi) | AD |
| 121 | Kṣemagupta (क्षेमगुप्त) – son of Parvagupta | 8 | 4026 | 950 |
| 122 | Abhimanyu (अभिमन्यु) – a minor under his mother, Diddā | 14 | 4034 | 958 |
| 123 | Nandigupta (नन्दिगुप्त) – second minor son under Diddā | 1 | 4048 | 972 |
| 124 | Tribhuvanagupta (त्रिभुवनगुप्त) – minor grandson of Diddā | 2 | 4049 | 973 |
| 125 | Bhīmagupta (भीमगुप्त) – second minor grandson of Diddā | 5 | 4051 | 975 |
| 126 | Diddā (दिद्दा), wife of Kṣemagupta (No. 121) | 23 | 4056 | 980 |
| | **Total years** | **65** | **4015–4079** | **939–1003** |

* *Rājataraṅgiṇī*

## Dynasty of Saṅgrāmarāja (Kings in Taranga 7), Laukikābda 4079–4177 (AD 1003–1101)

Saṅgrāmarāja, the son of Udayarāja who was a brother of Diddā, became the 127th king of Kashmir after the death of Queen Diddā. Saṅgrāmarāja was a contemporary of Trilochana Pāl, the eighth king of the Shahi Dynasty that ruled Panjab and Afghanistan. Trilochana Pāl was killed by Muhammad Ghazani in a battle in AD 1021. Rājataraṅgiṇī describes how Trilochana Pāl had sought help from Saṅgrāmarāja who had promptly sent his army to help the former in that fight. The chronology of this dynasty is given in Table 39.

Mālavā King Bhoja of Dharanagar was a contemporary of Anantadeva, the 129th king. He had a *kunda* (pool) built at Kapateśvar in Kashmir.

## Kings in Taranga 8, Laukikābda 4177–4224 (AD 1101–1148)

The chronology of the kings in Taranga 8 is given in Table 40. Like Harṣa, the last king of the preceding dynasty, Uccala, the first king of this dynasty, was a descendant of the Siṁharāja of Lohar, the father of Diddā. One of the other brothers of Diddā was Kāntirāja. Kāntirāja's son was Jassarāja whose son was Gunga; Gunga's son was Mallarāja and his sons were Uccala and Sussala.

**Table 39: Chronology of the dynasty of Saṅgrāmarāja, Laukikābda 4079–4177 (AD 1003–1101)**

| King No. | Name of the King | Years of Reign | Starting Year in | |
|---|---|---|---|---|
| | | | Laukikābda (Saptarṣi) | AD |
| 127 | Saṅgrāmarāja (संग्रामराज) – son of Diddā's brother Udayarāja | 25 | 4079 | 1003 |
| 128 | Harirāja (हरिराज) – son of Saṅgrāmarāja | 22 days | 4104 | 1028 |
| 129 | Anantadeva (अनंतदेव) – son of Saṅgrāmarāja | 35 | 4104 | 1028 |
| | Kalaśa/ Anantadeva | 16 | 4139 | 1063 |
| 130 | Kalaśa (कलश) | 10 | 4155 | 1079 |
| 131 | Utkarṣa (उत्कर्ष) – son of Kalaśa | 22 days | 4165 | 1089 |
| 132 | Harṣa (हर्ष) – son of Kalaśa | 12 | 4165 | 1089 |
| | **Total years** | **98** | **4079–4177** | **1003–1101** |

**Table 40: Chronology of the kings in Taranga 8, Laukikābda 4177–4224 (AD 1101–1148)**

| King No. | Name of the King | Years of Reign | Starting Year in | |
|---|---|---|---|---|
| | | | Laukikābda (Saptarṣi) | AD |
| 133 | Uccala (उच्चल) | 10 | 4177 | 1101 |
| 134 | Salhaṇa (सल्हण) | 4 months | 4187 | 1111 |
| 135 | Sussala (सुस्सल) – younger brother of Uccala | 14 | 4188 | 1112 |
| 136 | Jayasiṁha (जयसिंह) – son of Sussala | 22 | 4202 | 1126 |
| | **Total years** | **47** | **4177–4224** | **1101–1148** |

Kalhaṇa started writing Rājataraṅgiṇī in the Śaka 1070 when Jayasiṁha was the ruler. Since the Śālivāhana Śaka started in AD 79, Śaka 1070 is AD 1148. Sussala's son, Jayasiṁha, was a powerful king. He destroyed the killers of his father and regained the throne. He was ruling Kashmir well when Kalhaṇa was writing *Rājataraṅgiṇī* as stated in the following shloka (8.3448).

सुतः सुस्सलभूभर्तुः संप्रत्यप्रतिमक्षमः ।
नन्दयन्मेदिनीमास्ते जयसिंहो महीपतिः ।।

Sutaḥ Sussala-bhūbhartuḥ saṁpratyapratimakṣamaḥ ।
Nandayan-medinīmāste Jayasiṁho mahīpatiḥ ।।

Translation:

> Sussala's son, king Jayasiṁha, of incomparable strength, now delights the earth.

The chronology of the kings of Kashmir from AD 1148 to 1948 is available in *Chronology of Kashmir History Reconstructed* (Venkatachelam, 1955).

## Distortions by Colonial Era European Indologists

The 19th century European Indologists started rewriting ancient India's history with the wrong basis of synchronizing Alexander of 326 BC with Chandragupta Maurya of 1534 BC instead of Chandragupta I of the Gupta Dynasty of 327 BC and thereby shrank India's history by more than 1,200 years. They then continued on the wrong path and found nothing from India's historical traditions including Rājataraṅgiṇī matching their new basis. They rejected nearly the entire history of the kings of Kashmir given in detail in Rājataraṅgiṇī, notwithstanding the praise they had for Rājataraṅgiṇī. Even though Kalhaṇa has described in detail the sources he used in Rājataraṅgiṇī, M. A. Stein (1900, p. 69) who translated it into English, accused Kalhaṇa of fixing the imaginary date of a legendary event (Mahābhārata War) as the starting-point of his chronology and added:

> “ the chronological system of the first three Books of the Rājataraṅgiṇī cannot be accepted as the basis of any critical account of the periods of the Kaśmir history preceding the seventh century of our era. ”

The period of Gonanda III as 2,330 years before Kalhaṇa's time (AD 1148 – 2,330 = 1182 BC) was accepted by M. A. Troyer (1840) in his French translation of the Rājataraṅgiṇī but the writers of the volumes of the *Indian Antiquary* suppressed the findings of M. Troyer and gave prominence to the writing of persons like Dr. Bühler and Stein who misrepresented the facts.

Bühler (1877, p. 267) ignored most of the kings of Kashmir described in Rājataraṅgiṇī, professedly on the ground that their historicity was not otherwise corroborated by coins, buildings, and inscriptions, as shown below in his words:

> “I would not fill the intervals between the historically certain dates of Aśoka, Kanishka, and Durlabhaka by cutting down the years of the kings placed between them by Kalhana. But I would altogether ignore all Kaśmirian kings for whose existence we have no evidence from other sources, be it through Indian or foreign writers, or through coins, buildings, and inscriptions.”

In response to Dr. Bühler's statements, Pandit Venkatachelam writes (1955, p. 104):

> “As regards Kalhana and his Rajatarangini, ... We are not able to reconcile, how Buhler could accept the authenticity of 'Saptarshi Era' made use of by Kalhana and recognize the last three books of his chronicle, while at the same time he rejects the authority of the first three Tarangas, (i.e. the whole history of the Gonanda dynasty consisting of 89 kings, covering a period of 3702 years, from 3450 B.C. to 252 A.D.)
>
> "The first inclination of European thinkers is to deny the existence of that which they so much dislike." (Page 2, Ed VIII, Esoteric Buddhism by A. P. Sinnet, 1903 first Edition being printed in 1883.)”

## Kaniṣka and Mihirkula

The 19th century European Indologists kept only Kaniṣka and Mihirkula from the long list of Kashmir kings detailed in the Rājataraṅgiṇī and ignored the rest. They even ignored the great King Aśoka of Kashmir, saying that this Aśoka was probably the Aśoka Maurya of Magadha. Then, they moved Kaniṣka from the 13th century BC to AD 78, denied the existence of Śālivāhana, the great king of Ujjain and the Emperor of India, who started the Śālivāhana Śaka in AD 79, and declared that the Śālivāhana Śaka was probably started by Kaniṣka. The history of India written by the colonial Indologists is based on conjectures upon conjectures!

The colonial Indologists moved King Mihirkula from 705 BC to the sixth century AD as described below in the words of E. Hultzsch (1889/1964, p. 65, 97) in his comment on Rājataragini:

> “His [Mihirkula's] initial date, as deduced from the *Rājataraṅgiṇi* itself, is Kaliyuga-Saṁvat 2397 expired, or B.C. 704 ; and the end of his reign, seventy years later. Prof. H. H. Wilson brought him down to B.C. 200, (*loc. Cit.* p. 81). And Gen. Sir A. Cunningham arrived at the conclusion that he should be placed in A.D. 163 (*loc. Cit.* p. 18). <u>With the help, however, of newly discovered inscriptions,</u> which are the only really safe guide, **Mr. Fleet** (ante, Vol. XV. P. 252) has now shown that **his true date was in**

> **the beginning of the sixth century A.D.** ; ... and that A.D. 530, or very soon after, was the year in which his power was overthrown, after which he proceeded to Kaśmir and established himself there. This illustrates very pointedly the extent of the adjustments that will have to be made in Kalhaṇa's earlier details ; and furnishes us with a **definite point from which the chronology may be regulated** backwards and forwards for a considerable time. **A similar earlier point** is provided by Kalhana's mention, in Taranga i, verse 168, of the Turushka king **Kanishka**, who, according to his account, was anterior by two reigns to B.C. 1182,—the date of the accession of Gonanda III.,—but who is undoubtedly the king Kanishka from the commencement of whose reign in all probability runs the Śaka era, commencing in A.D. 77. And **a still earlier point** is furnished by the mention of king **Aśoka** in Taraṅga i. verse 101. According to Kalhaṇa, he stood five reigns before B. C. 1182. But it can hardly be doubted that he is intended for the great Buddhist king Aśoka [Maurya], whose accession has now been shewn by Gen. Sir A. Cunningham to have been in B.C. 260 (*Corp. Inscr. Indic.* Vol. I Preface, p. vii.) ” [Emphasis in bold in the original, Emphasis in underline added]

Thus, E. Hultzsch mistook Aśoka of Kashmir for Emperor Aśoka Maurya of Magadha, erasing Aśoka of Kashmir from history. Hultzsch moved Mihirkula from 704 BC to about AD 530, erasing 1,200 years from the history of Kashmir.

Regarding the statement by E. Hultzsch citing the newly discovered inscriptions, (underlined in the preceding paragraph), Pandit Venkatachelam writes (1955, p. 71):

> “ A scrutiny of that inscription shows that it was an invention and many inscriptions published in the Indian Antiquary are fabrications. ... As they could not find the date of that inscription mentioned in it, they borrowed the date of Mandasor No. 3 inscription and decided that Mihirkula existed in the 6th century A.D. Then they adjusted the kings and altered their dates, forwards and backwards, from Mihikula's forged date of 532 A.D.; and manufactured a modern history of Kashmir. ”

The aforementioned Mandasar No. 3 inscription (Fleet, 1886) is dated Mālava-gaṇa Samvat 589 which converts to 725 BC – 589 = 136 BC. However, the colonial Indologists used the year 589 of Vikrama Samvat which gives 589 – 57 BC = AD 532. Thus, their so-called evidence for Mihirkula's existence in the sixth century AD does not stand scrutiny.

## Tampering of Rājataraṅgiṇī

The writing below by E. Hultzsch (1889/1964, p. 105), calling a couple of verses (which they didn't like) spurious, shows evidence of tampering with Rājataraṅgiṇī:

> “In the Calcutta and Paris editions, the first Taraṅga contains 375 verses. Deducting the two spurious verses 308 and 309, which are omitted by P, there remain 373 verses. This actual number differs only by one from the colophon of P, according to which the first Taraṅga consists of 372 verses.”

Pandit Venkatachelam (1955, p. 26–27) states that the four verses Verse 49, 50, 51, and 54 in the first Taranga which state that the Bhārata war occurred after 653 years of Kaliyuga had elapsed are not the original authored by Kalhaṇa but are much later insertions because these verses run counter to all Purāṇas and popular tradition. However, K. D. Sethna (1989, p. 47) has expressed a different view on these in his book, *Ancient India in a New Light*, as follows:

> “He [Kalhaṇa] calculated backwards from the Śaka Era of 78 A.D. and interpreted Varāhamihira to mean that Yudhishthira's period was 2526 years before 78 A.D. – i.e., 2448 B.C., which is 654 years after the advent of the Kaliyuga in 3102 B.C.”

Thus, K. D. Sethna has explained that Kalhaṇa used the (Śālivāhana) Śaka of AD 78 instead of the Śaka Kāla of 550 BC (See Chapter 4) while adding 2,526 years to arrive at Yudhiṣṭhira's time.

## References


1. Beal, Samuel (1906). *Si-Yu-Ki Buddhist Records of The Western World: Translated from the Chinese of Hiuen Tsiang (A.D. 629)* (Vol. 1). London.

2. Bühler, Dr. G. (1877). 'The Rājatarangiṇi: From Dr. Bühler's Report of a Tour in search of Sanskrit MSS. made in Kaśmīr, Rājputānā, and Central India.' *The Indian Antiquary: A Journal of Oriental Research in Archaeology, History, Literature, Language, Philosophy, Religion, Folklore, etc., Vol. 6,* 264–274. Delhi: Swati Publications (1984).

3. *The ChachNamah: An Ancient History of Sind; Giving the Hindu period down to the Arab Conquest,* Translated from Persian by Mirza Kalichbeg Fredunbeg (1900), pdf format (2008). Karachi: The Commissioner's Press.

4. Fleet, J. F. (1886). 'Sanskrit and Old-Kanarese Inscriptions: No. 163, Mandasar Inscription of Yashodharman and Vishṇuvardhana, The Malava Year 589.' *The Indian Antiquary: A Journal of Oriental Research in Archaeology, History, Literature, Language, Philosophy, Religion, Folklore etc. Vol. 15,* 222–228, 245–258. Bombay.

5. Fleet, J. F. (1901). 'The Present Position of Indian Historical Research.' *The Indian Antiquary: A Journal of Oriental Research in Archaeology, History, Literature, Language, Philosophy, Religion, Folklore, etc. Vol. 30,* 1–27. Bombay.

6. Hassan, Pir Gulam (1954). *The Kashmir Series of Texts and Studies No. 82: Tarikh-i-Hassan Vol. I: Geography of Kashmir.* Srinagar: Research and Publication Department, Jammu & Kashmir Government.

7. Hultzsch, E. (1889). 'Extracts from Kalhana's Rajatarangiṇi.' *Indian Antiquary, A Journal of Oriental Research in Archaeology, Epigraphy, Ethnology, Geography, History, Folklore, Languages, Literature, Numismatic, Philosophy, Religion, etc. Vol. 18* (rpt., 1964), 65–73, 97–105. Delhi: Swati Publications.

8. Kalhaṇa (1148). *Rājataraṅgiṇī (Chronicle of the Kings of Kashmir) (Sanskrit text),* Edited with Hindi translation by Shri Ramtej Shastri Pandey (Vikrama Samvat 2017 (AD 1960), rpt. Ed. 1985). Delhi & Varanasi: Chaukhamba Sanskrit Pratishthan.

9. Narayana Sastry, T. S. (1916). *The Age of Śankara* (2nd ed. 1971, edited by T. N. Kumaraswamy). Madras: B. G. Paul & Co.

10. *Nīlamat Purāṇam (in Sanskrit) With Introduction, Appendices, Notes etc. in English* (1924) Ram Lal Kanjilal and Pt. Jagaddhar Zadoo (Eds). Lahore: Moti Lal Banarasi Das.

11. *NīlamatPurāṇa (in Sanskrit) with Hindi translation* (2016) Prof. Vedkumarī Ghai (Trans.). Jammu: J&K Academy of Art, Culture and Languages.

12. Sethna, K. D. (1989). *Ancient India in a New Light: I. The Challenge of India's Traditional Chronology, II. The Momentous Evidence of Megasthenes, III. A Reconstruction of Ancient Indian History: Aśoka – and Before and After.* New Delhi: Aditya Prakashan.

13. Sinnett, A. P. (1883). *Esoteric Buddhism* (8th ed., rpt. 1907). London: Trübner.

14. Stein, M. A. (1900). *Kalhaṇa's Rājataraṅgiṇī: A Chronicle of the Kings of Kashmir, English translation with an Introduction, Commentary and Appendices,* Vol. I (MDCCCC). Westminster.

15. Troyer, M. A. (1840). *Rādjataranginī: Histoire Des Rois Du Kachmīr.* Paris: L'Impremerie Nationale (MDCCCXL).

16. Vaidya, C. V. (1907). 'The Life and Teaching of ShriKrishna.' in *Epic India: India as Described in the Mahabharata and the Ramayana* (rpt. Ed. 1987, Vol. 18 (i), Ch. XVIII). New Delhi: Cosmo Publications.

17. Venkatachelam, Pandit Kota (1955). *Chronology of Kashmir History Reconstructed.* Arya Vijnana Series, Publication 18. Vijayawada.

18. Wilson, Horace Hayman (1825). 'An Essay on the Hindu History of Cashmir.' *Asiatic Researches; or Transactions of the Society Instituted in Bengal for inquiring into the History and Antiquities, the Arts, Sciences, and Literature of Asia, Vol. 15,* 1–119.

# 12

# THE KINGS OF NEPAL

The Nepal Rāja Vaṁśāvali (Genealogy of the kings of Nepal) describes in detail the dynasties of Nepal, the kings, and their reigning periods. The chronology is mainly given in the Kaliyuga Era. The text of the Nepal Rāja Vaṁśāvali is inscribed on lengthy sheets of rolled-up paper and the names of the kings are written in a sequence. When any important historical event is noted, it is added under the name of the corresponding king. The dates of only the very important events are clearly and unequivocally specified in the Kaliyuga Era. Several Vaṁśāvalis exist in the libraries of the country (Indraji and Bühler, 1884, p. 411). *History of Nepal* by Daniel Wright (1877/1990) is a translation of one such Vaṁśāvali manuscript written in the Parbatiya language. Daniel Wright (Preface) mentions that he procured several manuscripts for the university library of Cambridge. Regarding Daniel Wright's book, Pandit Bhagavānlāl Indraji (1884, p. 411) states:

> “A careful comparison of my MS. of the Pārvatiya *Vaṁśāvali* with Dr. Wright's extracts has shown that his data are, on the whole, trustworthy.”

Nepal derives its name from Ne Muni (sage) who installed the son of a *gopāla* (cowherd), whose cow was dropping milk on a particular spot at a certain time every day, as king. The following is a list of the kings of Nepal from the Parbatiya Vaṁśāvali.

## Gopāla Dynasty, before the Mahābhārata War in 37 BK (3139 BC)

1. Bhuktamāna – 88 years

2. Jaya Gupta – 72 years
3. Parama Gupta – 80 years
4. Harṣa Gupta – 93 years
5. Bhīma Gupta – 38 years
6. Maṇi Gupta – 37 years
7. Vishṇu Gupta – 42 years
8. Yaksha Gupta – 71 years

The gopālas (cowherds) thus reigned for 521 years. The last king, Yaksha Gupta, was childless. Thereafter, Vara Siṁha, an Ahir from the plains (India), came and ruled Nepal, starting the Ahir Dynasty.

## Ahir Dynasty, before the Mahābhārata War

1. Vara Siṁha
2. Jayamati Siṁha
3. Bhuvana Siṁha – conquered by the Kirātas who came from the east.

## Kirāta Dynasty, before and after the Mahābhārata War

1. Yalambara – reigned 13 years
2. Pavi
3. Skandhara
4. Valamba
5. Hriti
6. Humati – went into the forest with Pāṇḍavas

> Descriptions for the 6th–8th kings of the Kirāta Dynasty in the Nepal Rāja Vaṁśāvali provide an independent confirmation of the historicity of the Mahābhārata War.

7. Jitedāsti – went to Kurukṣetra to fight along with Pāṇḍavas in the Mahābhārata War (3139 BC) and was killed

8. Gali, son of Jitedāsti – crowned in 3138 BC after the war
9. Pushka
10. Suyarma
11. Parba
12. Bunka
13. Svananda
14. Sthunko
15. Gighri
16. Nane
17. Luk
18. Thor
19. Thoko
20. Varma
21. Guja
22. Pushkara or Pushka
23. Kesu
24. Sunsa or Suga
25. Sammu or Sansa
26. Guṇana
27. Khimbu
28. Patuka
29. Gasti

According to the Vaṁśāvali, these 29 kings (an unbroken family line) resided at Gokarṇa and ruled for a total of 1,118 years. Jitedāsti, the seventh king of the dynasty, went to Kurukṣetra and fought along with Pāṇḍavas in the Mahābhārata War at the end of 3139 BC where he was killed. His son, Gali, was crowned the king of Nepal in 3138 BC. Thus, the first seven kings reigned before the Mahābhārata War and the next twenty-two kings, 8th to 29th, reigned after the war. The Vaṁśāvali states that in the time of Sthunko, the 14th king, Aśoka of Pāṭaliputra came to Nepal. Since this dynasty lasted for a total of 1,118 years including the years before the Mahābhārata War in 3139 BC, Sthunko must have reigned well before the time of Aśoka (1472–1436 BC, see Chapter 7). Aśoka's visit to Nepal would have happened centuries after Sthunko's time. Aśoka's daughter Chārumati was married to a kshatriya, called Devapāla who settled in Nepal and founded Devapātana (near Paśupati).

The 28th king, Patuka, was attacked by Somavaṁśi Rajputs from the west. He left the *durbār* at Gokarṇa and moved to the south, across the Saṅkhamula Tīrtha where he built another durbār. The 29th and the last king, Gasti, being hard-pressed by the Somavaṁśis, fled from the new durbār. Then, the Somavaṁśis built a new capital near the Godavari at the foot of the Phūlochcha Mountain (visible from Lalitapaṭṭana).

### Distortion by Colonial Historians

In the time of Jitedāsti who fought in the Mahābhārata War, Sakyasiṁha Buddha (not Gautama Buddha) visited Nepal. The 19th century European historians knew only one Buddha, Gautama Buddha. Gautama Buddha was often called Sakya Muni but never Sakyasiṁha Buddha. The European historians wrongly identified Sakyasiṁha Buddha mentioned in the Nepal Rāja Vaṁśāvali, who visited Nepal during the reign of Jitedāsti, as Gautama Buddha and questioned the authenticity of the entire Nepal Rāja Vaṁśāvali. Once we recognize that Sakyasiṁha and Sakya Muni were different, there is neither inconsistency nor confusion in the Vaṁśāvali.

## Somavaṁśi Dynasty, up to Kaliyuga 1389 (1713 BC)

1. Nimisha
2. Matāksha
3. Kākavarman
4. Paśuprekshadeva – populated his country with people of all four *varṇas* (occupations) and rebuilt the dilapidated Paśupati temple, roofing it with golden plates, and finishing it with a *gajara* on the top in **Kaliyuga 1234** (1868 BC).
5. Bhāskaravarman – conquered the whole of India, up to the Setubandha (Rameswaram), enlarged Devapāṭana, and had the rules for the worship of Paśupati engraved on a copper plate, which he deposited

in the Chārumativihāra.

The years of reigns for individual kings of the Somavaṁśi Dynasty are not given. The year mentioned in the fourth king's reign is Kaliyuga 1234 (1868 BC). The fifth king, Bhāskaravarman, being childless adopted a Sūryavaṁśi prince, Bhumivarman, who was crowned king in **Kaliyuga 1389** (1713 BC). He transferred his capital to Bāneśvara.

The interval of 155 years between the two dates is large for the two kings. Additional kings might have reigned during this interval and those names have likely been lost. The omission of some of the kings can't be used to question the authenticity of the two dates mentioned clearly in the Vaṁśāvali and thereby discard the Vaṁśāvali completely as done by the 19th century European historians. The establishment of the Sūryavaṁśi Dynasty in Kali 1389 (1713 BC), the crowning of the first king of the dynasty, Bhumivarman, and the transfer of capital to the Bānesvara city are important historic events so the dates of these events were recorded.

## Sūryavaṁśi Dynasty, Kaliyuga 1389–3000 (1713–102 BC)

The names and the years of the reign (exceptions discussed later) of the 31 kings of the Sūryavaṁśi Dynasty according to the Nepal Rāj Vaṁśāvali (Indraji and Bühler, 1884, p. 412; Wright, 1877/1990, p. 113) are given in Table 41. The reigns of the first 18 kings of the dynasty extend over 50–80 years each. There may have been more kings in the dynasty but probably only the names of the important kings have been retained while the other names might have been lost over time.

Vrishadevavarman, the 18th king, was a very pious king. He built *vihāras* and erected images of Lokeśvara and other Buddhist divinities. After a miraculous escape from death, Vrishadevavarman retired and handed over the reign to his brother Bālārchanadeva. According to the Vaṁśāvali, Ādi Śaṅkarāchārya visited Nepal shortly afterward, defeated Buddhist priests in debates and repelled the Buddhist faith there. At the time of Ādi Śaṅkarāchārya's visit, Vrishadevavarman had died, leaving his queen pregnant. A son was soon born to the queen and named **Śaṅkaradeva** after Śaṅkarāchārya.

As discussed in Chapter 9, Ādi Śaṅkarāchārya lived from Kaliyuga 2593 to 2625 (509–477 BC) and visited Nepal in about Kaliyuga 2614–2615. The interval between Bhumivarman's crowning in Kaliyuga 1389 and Ādi Śaṅkarāchārya's visit to Nepal is 1,225 years. The years of the reign of the first king are missing in the Vaṁśāvali. The total years of reign for the 2nd to the 18th king as given in

Thus, the accounts of Vrishadevavarman and **Śaṅkaradeva** (the 18th and 19th kings in Table 41) in the Nepal Rāj Vaṁśāvali corroborate the time of Ādi Śaṅkarāchārya (509-477 BC) proved in **Chapter 9**.

**Table 41: Kings of the Sūryavaṁśi Dynasty, Kaliyuga 1389–3000 (1713–102 BC)**

| Sr. No. | Name of the King | Years of Reign |
|---|---|---|
| 1 | Bhumivarman | 66 |
| 2 | Chandravarman | 61 |
| 3 | Jayavarman | 82 |
| 4 | Varṣavarman | 61 |
| 5 | Sarvavarman | 78 |
| 6 | Prithvivarman | 76 |
| 7 | Jyeshṭhavarman | 75 |
| 8 | Harivarman | 76 |
| 9 | Kuberavarman | 88 |
| 10 | Siddhivarman | 61 |
| 11 | Haridattavarman – built temples for the four Nārāyaṇas – Chāṅgu, Chaiñju, Ichaṅgu, and Śikhara; and a temple of Jalāśayana at Buddha Nilakaṇṭha | 81 |
| 12 | Vasudattavarman | 63 |
| 13 | Pativarman | 53 |
| 14 | Śivavriddhivarman | 54 |
| 15 | Vasantavarman | 61 |
| 16 | Śivavarman | 62 |
| 17 | Rudradevavarman | 66 |
| 18 | **Vrishadevavarman** – shortly after his death, Ādi Śaṅkarāchārya came from the south and repelled the Buddhist faith (ca. Kaliyuga 2614–2615) | 61 |

*Table continued*

| Sr. No. | Name of the King | Years of Reign |
|---|---|---|
| 19 | **Śaṅkaradeva,** son of Vrishadevavarman (No. 18) – named after Ādi Śaṅkarāchārya, erected *triśul* (trident) of iron at the Paśupati Temple | 25* |
| 20 | Dharmadeva | 24* |
| 21 | Mānadeva – built the *Chakra Vihāra* near Matirājya and according to some, the *Khāsa Chaitya* | 20* |
| 22 | Mahīdeva | 20* |
| 23 | Vasantadeva – crowned in Kaliyuga 2800 (301 BC) (the year is questionable) | 15* |
| 24 | Udayadevavarman – became a *bhikṣu* | 6* |
| 25 | Mānadevavarman | 30* |
| 26 | Guṇakāmadevavarman | 10* |
| 27 | Śivadevavarman – made Devapātana his capital, restored the Śākta rites, and became a *bhikṣu*. His son Puṇyadevavarman followed his example. | 61 |
| 28 | Narendradevavarman (brother of Śivadevavarman) | 42 |
| 29 | Bhimadevavarman | 36 |
| 30 | Viṣṇudevavarman | 47 |
| 31 | Viśvadevavarman – did not have a son, gave his daughter in marriage to a Thākuri, Aṁśuvarman, and died shortly afterward. | 51 |
| | **Total** | **1,612** |

**reign periods adjusted to meet the milestone event*

the Vaṁśāvali (Table 41) are 1,159 years. The difference of 66 years is assigned to the first king. Thus, using Ādi Śaṅkarāchārya's true time with Nepal Rāj Vaṁśāvali gives reasonable years of reign for the first king.

An inscription of Mānadeva, dated Samvat 386 (Indraji and Bühler, 1880, p. 163) lists the 18th–21st kings of this dynasty. Three inscriptions of Śivadevavarman, the 27th king, have been discovered. Of these inscriptions numbered 12, 13, and 14, inscription 12 is dated as Samvat 119 (of Śrī Harṣa Era). As discussed in Chapter 4, Alberuni has recorded (Sachau, 1910, p. 5–7) that the Śrī Harṣa Vikramāditya Era commenced in 457 BC. Accordingly, the year of Śivadevavarman's inscription is 457 BC + 119 = 338 BC or Kaliyuga 2764.

The total of the years of reign for the 27th–31st kings, given in the Vaṁśāvali (Indraji and Bühler, 1884, p. 411–428) is 227 years. Going backward by 227 years from the crowning of Aṁśuvarman in Kaliyuga 3000 (102 BC) brings us to Kaliyuga 2773 (329 BC) which is only 9 years away from 338 BC, the true date of the inscription. The reigning periods of the 19th to the 27th kings have been adjusted (decreased) from those given in the Vaṁśāvali to fit with the date of Śivadevavarman's inscription date of Kaliyuga 2764 (338 BC), as done by Pandit Venkatachelam (1953a, p. 66). With this adjustment, the date of Kaliyuga 2800 given in the Vaṁśāvali for the crowning of the 23rd king Vasantadeva appears erroneous.

Nepal Rāja Vaṁśāvali states that either shortly before or after the death of Viśvadevavarman, the 31st and the last king of this dynasty, Vikramāditya, a very powerful monarch from Ujjain came to Nepal, paid off all of Nepal's debt and introduced his new era Vikrama Samvat in Nepal (Wright, 1877/1990, p. 131; Indraji and Bühler, 1884, p. 411). Emperor Vikramāditya reigned from Kaliyuga 3020 to 3120 (82 BC–AD 18) as described in detail in Chapter 10. Aṁśuvarman, the son-in-law of Viśvadevavarman, was crowned soon after Vikramāditya visited Nepal. Therefore, accordingly, the reign of the Viśvadevavarman would have ended in Kaliyuga 3045–3046 (57–56 BC). On the other hand, Pandit Bhagavānlāl Indraji and Dr. G. Bühler (1884, p. 411) state: “Aṁśuvarman ... crowned in Kaliyuga 3000 or 101 B.C.”

## Distortions by Pandit Bhagavānlāl Indraji and Dr. Bühler

Pandit Indraji and Dr. Bühler, the 19th century Indologists, rejected the visit of Emperor Vikramāditya to Nepal and the inauguration of the Vikrama Samvat stated in the Nepal Rāja Vaṁśāvali because the reigns of the kings stated in the Vaṁśāvali were too long for them to believe. They alleged that the years of the event mentioned in the Nepali inscriptions were wrongly attributed to the Vikrama Era by the author of the Vaṁśāvali. Similarly, they rejected other kings of the Sūryavaṁśi Dynasty and their dates as follows (1884, p. 418):

> “According to the latter [the inscriptions], the twenty-first king of the Sūryavaṁśi dynasty, Mānadeva, reigned from between the years 386–413 of an unnamed era and the characters show that this period falls in the fourth or fifth century of our era [Christian era]. Yet the *Vaṁśāvali* asserts that Mānadeva's grandson, Vasantadevavarman was crowned in Kali 2800 or 301 BC.”

The colonial era Indologists, having started with a grossly erroneous basis, dated the characters of inscriptions falsely, and then, used the false post-dating of the characters to negate the true chronologies. Dr. Bühler ignored the Śrī Harṣa Era of 457 BC recorded by Alberuni on the ground that Alberuni has not given details of the era or its inauguration. He identified the era with Harṣa Śiladitya (Harṣavardhana) of AD 606 who never started an era as discussed in Chapter 4. Then, he dated the Śrī Harṣa Samvat year 119 on the inscription of Śivadevavarman to AD 606 + 119 = AD 725 instead of its true date of 457 BC + 119 = 338 BC. Thus, he cut short the antiquity of the royal dynasties of Nepal recorded in the Nepal Rāja Vaṁśāvali by 1,063 years!

### Eliminated kings from the Vaṁśāvali

After having shrunk the chronology by more than a thousand years, Pandit Indraji and Dr. Bühler (1884, p. 427 footnote) needed to eliminate some of the kings from the Vaṁśāvali as stated in the footnote of the paper:

> "As the *Vaṁśāvali* has three princes more between Jayadeva-Jayavarman and Vṛishadeva than In. 15, three names have probably to be eliminated. One of these is probably Pativarman, whose name is suspicious, another either Śivavarman or Rudradeva, whose names are synonymous; the third is doubtful."

## Thākuri Dynasty, Kaliyuga 3000–3874+ (102 BC–AD 772+)

Aṁśuvarman, the son-in-law of the last king of the Sūryavaṁśi Dynasty, was the first king of this dynasty. Use of the new era (Vikrama Samvat) by Aṁśuvarman can be seen in the inscriptions numbered 6, 7, and 8 described in the *Indian Antiquary* (Indraji and Bühler, 1880, p. 163 ff) where Samvat years 34, 39, and 45 have been used, respectively. The inscription number 8, dated Samvat 45, was produced by Aṁśuvarman's son, Vibhuvarman, in memory of his father. The authors of the paper, Pandit Bhagavānlāl Indraji, and Dr. Bühler, have wrongly claimed the Samvat of the inscription as Harṣa Samvat. As discussed in the preceding section, there is uncertainty regarding the exact year of the crowning of Aṁśuvarman, whether it was Kaliyuga 3000 (102 BC) or Kaliyuga 3046 (56 BC), or any year between the two. Table 42 shows the genealogy of the Thākuri Dynasty, assuming Aṁśuvarman was crowned in Kaliyuga 3000.

The first king, Aṁśuvarman, was crowned in Kaliyuga 3000 (102 BC) or in Kaliyuga 3046 (56 BC), or any time between the two dates. The fifth

**Table 42: Thākuri Dynasty, Kaliyuga 3000–3874+ (102 BC–AD 772+)**

| Sr. No. | Name of the King | Years of Reign |
|---|---|---|
| 1 | Aṁśuvarman – moved the *durbār* (capital) from Devapāṭana to Madhyalakhu; his son, Vibhuvarman built an aqueduct with seven spouts and inscribed on it (Indraji and Bühler, 1880, p. 171, Inscription No. 8). | 68 |
| | Vibhuvarman – described in the inscription | |
| 2 | Kritavarman | 87 |
| 3 | Bhimārjunavarman | 93 |
| 4 | Nandadeva – introduced Śālivāhana Śaka in Nepal | 25 |
| | *kings missing from the list* | |
| 5 | Viradeva – crowned when **3400 years of Kaliyuga** (AD 298–299) had passed, founded Lalitapaṭṭana (Lalitpāṭan or Lalitpur) naming it after a grass-seller Lalit; built a tank and watercourses as well as temples, lingas, etc. which were called Manitalāv, after the king's *Īṣtadevata*, Maṇiyogini. | 95 |
| 6 | Chandraketuḍeva – enemies from all sides attacked and plundered the country during his reign | |
| 7 | Narendradeva – built *Tirtha* vihāra near Lomri-Devi and gave it to Bandhudatta Āchārya, his father's spiritual guide. The first two of his three sons – Padmadeva, Ratnadeva, and Varadeva, became ascetics, and the third succeeded his father, who before his death retired in Alag-bahal or Ak-bahal vihāra. | 7 |
| 8 | Varadeva, son of Narendradeva – moved the capital to Lalitapaṭṭana; during his reign, Śaṅkarāchārya (not Ādi Śaṅkarāchārya but a *Pīṭhādhipati*) visited Nepal; Avalokiteśvara came to Nepal in **Kaliyuga 3623 (AD 521–522)** | 8 |
| 9 | Śaṅkaradeva, named in honor of Śaṅkarāchārya – built the town of Saṅkhu (in the shape of a Śaṅkha) | 12 |
| 10 | Vardhamānadeva | 13 |
| 11 | Balideva | 13 |
| 12 | Jayadeva | 15 |
| 13 | Bālārjunadeva | 17 |
| 14 | Vikramadeva | 12 |
| 15 | Guṇakāmadeva – built Kāntipura (modern-day **Kāthamandu**, the present capital of Nepal) in **Kaliyuga 3824** (AD 722) and moved the capital there. | 51 |
| 16 | Bhojadeva | 8 |
| 17 | Lakshmikāmadeva | 22 |
| 18 | Jayakāmadeva – died without a child and was succeeded by a member of the Navākot Thākuri Dynasty | 20 |

king, Viradeva, was crowned in Kaliyuga 3400. The period between the two events is 400 or 355 years. The total years of reign for the first four kings are 273, leaving a gap of 127 or 82 years. Therefore, there were likely more kings for the unaccounted years. Vibhuvarman's inscription describes that he built the aqueduct for his father's spiritual merit but his name and years of reign are not included in the Vaṁśavali.

Nandadeva, the fourth king, heard that the Śālivāhana Śaka (Era) was being used in the other states and introduced it in Nepal. Some people, however, in gratitude to Vikramāditya, who had paid off the debt of the country and introduced his era, were averse to giving up the Vikrama Samvat. Others, out of deference to the king's wishes started using the Śālivāhana Śaka. This fits well with the fact that the Śālivāhana Śaka started in AD 79 and was already in use in other states by the time of Nandadeva. The Vaṁśāvali shown in the *Indian Antiquary* (1884, p. 411) does not show years of reign for the sixth, seventh, and eighth king, whereas the Vaṁśāvali in the *History of Nepal* by Daniel Wright (1877/1990, p. 139) gives years of reign for the seventh and the eighth kings as shown in Table 42.

Another important year in the history of Nepal is Kaliyuga 3824 (AD 722). In that year, the 15th king of the Thākuri Dynasty, Guṇakāmadeva, founded Kāntipura and transferred the capital from Madhyalakhu to the newly built Kāntipura (present-day Kāthamandu). The two dates, Kaliyuga 3400 and Kaliyuga 3824, are important, hence, proudly remembered by the kings and their descendants and duly preserved in the records of the royal archives. These dates must not be meddled with.

### Aramudi

Kalhaṇa's (1148/1985) *Rājataraṅgiṇī* (4.544) states that Aramudi, the king of Nepal, captured Jayāpiḍa, the king of Kashmir, in a battle and imprisoned him during Jayāpiḍa's march through India. Jayāpiḍa later escaped from prison and defeated Aramudi. The Nepal Rāja Vaṁśāvali does not mention Aramudi. As discussed in Chapter 11, Jayāpiḍa's time was about AD 751–782. Hence, Aramudi's time should be around the same time.

## Navākot Thākuri Dynasty

Jayakāmadeva, the 18th and the last king of the Thākuri Dynasty did not have a child. After his death, the Thākuris of the Navākot mountain came and elected a *Rājā* (king) from among themselves. This king's name was

Bhāskaradeva. There were five kings from this dynasty as follows:

1. Bhāskaradeva
2. Baladeva
3. Padmadeva
4. Nāgārjunadeva
5. Śaṅkaradeva

## Second Thākuri Dynasty of Aṁśuvarman, up to Nepal Samvat 9 (AD 889)

Vāmadva, a descendant from the family of the former King Aṁśuvarman (the first king of the prior Thākuri Dynasty), assisted by the chiefs of Lalitapaṭṭana and Kāntipura, expelled the Navākot Thākuris and drove them back to their

**Table 43: The second Thākuri Dynasty of Aṁśuvarman**

| Sr. No. | Name of the King | Years of Reign |
|---|---|---|
| 1 | Vāmadeva | |
| 2 | Harshadeva | |
| 3 | Sadāśivadeva – founded Kirtipura on a hill, southwest of Kāthamandu, conquered many kingdoms, and made a new golden roof for Paśupatinath Temple in **Kaliyuga 3851 (AD 749)** | |
| 4 | Mānadeva – abdicated the throne in favor of his son | 10 |
| 5 | Narasiṁhadeva | 22 |
| 6 | Nandadeva | 21 |
| 7 | Rudradeva | 7 or 19* |
| 8 | Mitradeva | 21 |
| 9 | Arideva | 22 |
| 10 | Abhayamalla – had two sons | |
| 11 | Jayadevamalla, elder son of Abhayamalla (No. 10) – ruled over Kāntipura and Lalitapaṭṭana (or Lalitpāṭan); established the Nepal Samvat beginning in **AD 880** | 10 |
| 12 | Anandamalla, younger brother of Jayadevamalla (No.11) – founded Bhaktapur (Bhātgām) and the seven towns; resided in Bhātgām | 25 |

**19 years per Indraji and Bühler (1884, p. 411),*
*7 years per History of Nepal by Daniel Wright (1877/1990)*

original seat. He then made himself the king. Thus began, the second Thākuri Dynasty of Aṁśuvarman. The kings of this dynasty are listed in Table 43.

It appears that this dynasty may have existed separately with a separate kingdom, somewhat overlapping with the previous one or two dynasties because there is only 27 years gap between the founding of Kāntipura (Kāthamandu) in Kaliyuga 3824 by Gunkāmadeva, the 15th king of the previous Thākuri Dynasty, and the founding of Kirtipura in Kaliyuga 3851 by Sadāśivadeva, the third king of this dynasty.

## Karṇātaka Dynasty, AD 889 onwards

At the time when King Jayadevamalla was ruling over Lalitpāṭan and Kāntipura, and Anandamalla over Bhaktapur, the last two kings in Table 43, in the Śaka 811 or Nepal Samvat 9 (AD 889) on Śrāvana Sudi 7, Nānyadeva from South Karṇātaka came and drove the two Mallas to Tirhut. Nānyadeva ruled from Bhaktapur, and also over Lalitpāṭan and Kāntipura. He ruled for 50 years.

Further details of this dynasty, the succeeding dynasties, and the kings of Nepal at least up to AD 1768 can be found in the Nepal Rāja Vaṁśāvali. Thus, Nepal Rāja Vaṁśāvali is a goldmine for the chronology of the kings of Nepal, including several event-specific dates starting from centuries before the Mahābhārata War to the last millennium with only some missing kings as shown in Figure 35.

Pandit Bhagavānlāl Indraji and Dr. Bühler (1884, p. 417) were wrong in declaring that the Nepal Rāja Vaṁśāvali possesses no historical value whatsoever as a whole.

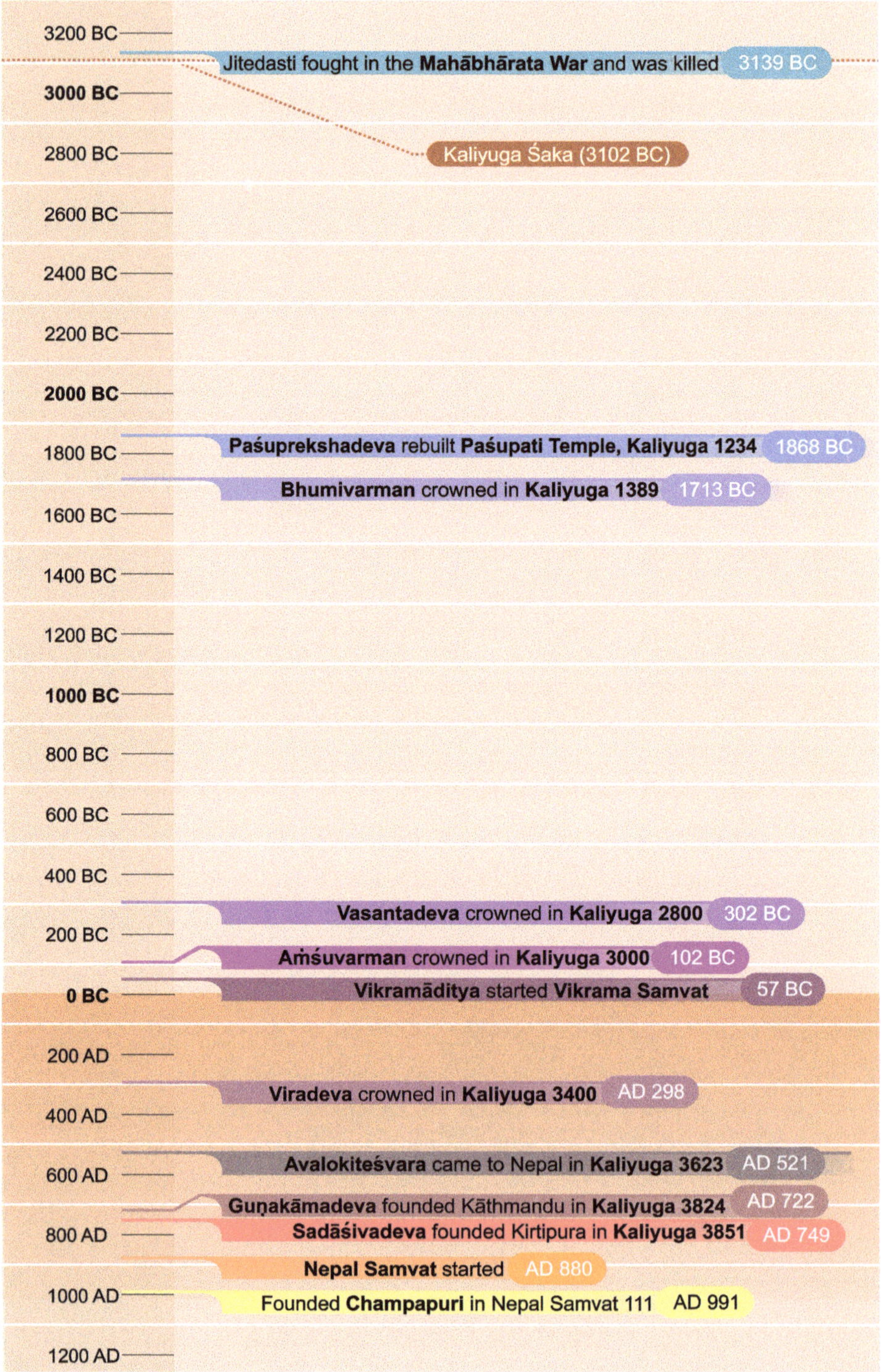


**Figure 35: Dates recorded in Nepal Rāja Vaṁśāvali**

## References

1. Indraji, Pandit Bhagavānlāl, and Dr. G. Bühler (1880). 'Inscriptions from Nepal.' *The Indian Antiquary: A Journal of Oriental Research in Archaeology, History, Literature, Languages, Philosophy, Religion, Folklore,* etc. *Vol. 9,* 163–194. Bombay.

2. Indraji, Pandit Bhagavānlāl, and Dr. G. Bühler (1884). 'Some Considerations on the History of Nepal.' *The Indian Antiquary: A Journal of Oriental Research in Archaeology, History, Literature, Languages, Philosophy, Religion, Folklore, etc. Vol. 13,* 411–428. Bombay.

3. Kalhaṇa (1148). *Rājataraṅgiṇī (Chronicle of the Kings of Kashmir) (Sanskrit text),* Edited with Hindi translation by Shri Ramtej Shastri Pandey (Vikrama Samvat 2017 (AD 1960), rpt. ed. 1985). Delhi & Varanasi: Chaukhamba Sanskrit Pratishthan.

4. Sachau, Dr. Edward C. (Ed.) (1910). *Alberuni's India: An Account of the Religion, Philosophy, Literature, Geography, Chronology, Astronomy, Customs, Laws and Astrology of India, about A.D. 1030* (English ed., Vol. 2). London: Trübner & Co.

5. Venkatachelam, Pandit Kota (Kali 5054, AD 1953a). *Chronology of Nepal History Reconstructed (Nepalraja Vamsavali).* Arya Vijnana, Publication 16. Vijayawada.

6. Wright, Daniel (1877). *History of Nepal: with an Introductory Sketch of the Country and People of Nepal* (Translated from Parbatiya by Munshi Shew Shunker Singh & Pandit Śhrī Gunanand, rpt. 1990). New Delhi: Asian Educational Services.

# 13

# AGE OF PATANJALI, MAHĀVIRA SWAMI, AND VARĀHAMIHIRA

## Age of Patanjali

Patanjali is known to have written *Mahābhāṣya* (the great commentary) on the *Sutras* of Pāṇini, the great ancient Sanskrit grammarian and the author of Aṣṭādhyāyi. Patanjali also wrote two other works on Yoga and *vaidya* (medicine). King Bhoja, in his commentary on Patanjali's *Yoga Sutras,* refers to him not only as a great philosopher but also as a great grammarian and physician. Patanjali is thus said to have prescribed medicine for the body, mind, and spirit – all three (Narayana Sastry, 1916/1971, p. 50–51).

The sentence '*Ihapuṣpamitram yajayamah*' is found in Patanjali's *Mahābhāṣya* on the Sutras of Pāṇini. Therefore, Vincent Smith inferred that Patanjali was a contemporary of Puṣyamitra Śuṅga and attended the *Aśvamedha yajña* performed by him. According to the true chronology of the kings of Magadha discussed in Chapter 7, Puṣyamitra Śuṅga ruled from 1218 to 1158 BC, but the colonial era European Indologists placed him and Patanjali in the second century BC because of their false foundation for the chronology of India (Venkatachelam, 1957a, p. 99).

*Rājataraṅgiṇī* (Kalhana, 1148/1985, 1.176) mentions *Mahābhāṣya* and *Vyākaraṇa* (grammar) as shown below while describing the reign of Abhimanyu, the 52nd king of Kashmir who reigned from 1234 to 1182 BC.

चन्द्राचार्यादिभिर्लब्ध्वा देशं तस्मात्तदागमम् ।
प्रवर्तितं महाभाष्यं स्वं च व्याकरणं कृतम् ।।

Candrācāryādibhirlabdhvā deśaṁ tasmāttadāgamam |
Pravartitaṁ mahābhāṣyaṁ svaṁ ca vyākaraṇaṁ kṛtam | |

Translation:

(During the reign of Abhimanyu of Kashmir), Chandrāchārya etc. came (to Kashmir) and propagated the study of Mahābhāṣya and wrote grammar.

From this, we can conclude that Patanjali, the author of the *Mahābhāṣya*, lived before 1234–1182 BC, the reigning period of Abhimanyu, since Patanjali's *Mahābhāṣya* already existed then. Thus, the two completely independent references to Patanjali's *Mahābhāṣya* have remarkably similar dates, as early as the 12th or 13th century BC.

## Age of Mahāvira Swami

Mahāvira Swami, the 24th and the last *Tirthankara* of Jains, was born in Kaliyuga 2503 (599 BC) and passed away in Kaliyuga 2574 (527 BC) according to *Jina Vijaya* (Narayana Sastry, 1916/1971, p. 136; Venkatachelam, 1955, p. 156). The Jains' Veera calendar started in 527 BC, the year of the nirvana of Mahāvira Swami. Some European Indologists (Dundas, 2002) have attempted to push down these dates to 425 or 540 BC. Wikipedia calls the 599 BC date traditional and the 540 BC date historical! It begs a question—why is the traditionally accepted date of 599 BC not historical?

Pārśvanātha was the 23rd Tirthankara and, according to the Jain tradition, he lived from 872 to 772 BC. See *The Age of Śankara* (Narayana Sastry, p. 136) for more details on Pārśvanātha. Neminātha was the 22nd Tirthankara and the Jain tradition holds him to be a contemporary of Śrī Krishna.

## Age of Varāhmihira

Varāhamihira, the great astronomer and mathematician of ancient India, was one of the nine gems in the court of Emperor Vikramāditya in Ujjain and a senior contemporary of the great Sanskrit poet Kālidāsa, as stated by Kālidāsa in *Jyotirvidābharaṇa*. Kālidāsa states that he wrote *Jyotirvidābharaṇa* when 3,068 years of Kaliyuga had elapsed (33 BC) and Varāhamihira had passed away in 41 BC. Vikramāditya ruled from 82 BC to AD 18 as discussed in Chapter 10.

As shown in the verse under Cyrus Śaka in Chapter 4, Varāhamihira has given his time in Śaka Kāla in *Pañcasiddhāntikā* (2nd century BC/1993, Shloka 8), stating that he was writing it in the year 427 of the Śaka Kāla (of 550 BC) which gives his date as 550 BC + 427 = 123 BC (Venkatachelam, 1955, p. 242; 1991, p. 36). Also, as discussed in the same chapter under Yudhiṣṭhira Kāla, Varāhamihira (1st century BC/1959) has stated in *Brihat Samhitā* (13.3) that by adding 2,526 years to the Śaka Kāla, we get the starting year of Yudhiṣṭhira Kāla Śaka of 3076 BC. Figure 36 shows a photo of a 13th century AD palm leaf manuscript of *Brihat Samhitā* of Varāhamihira in Sanskrit, in Nepalakṣara script from a Buddhist monastery.

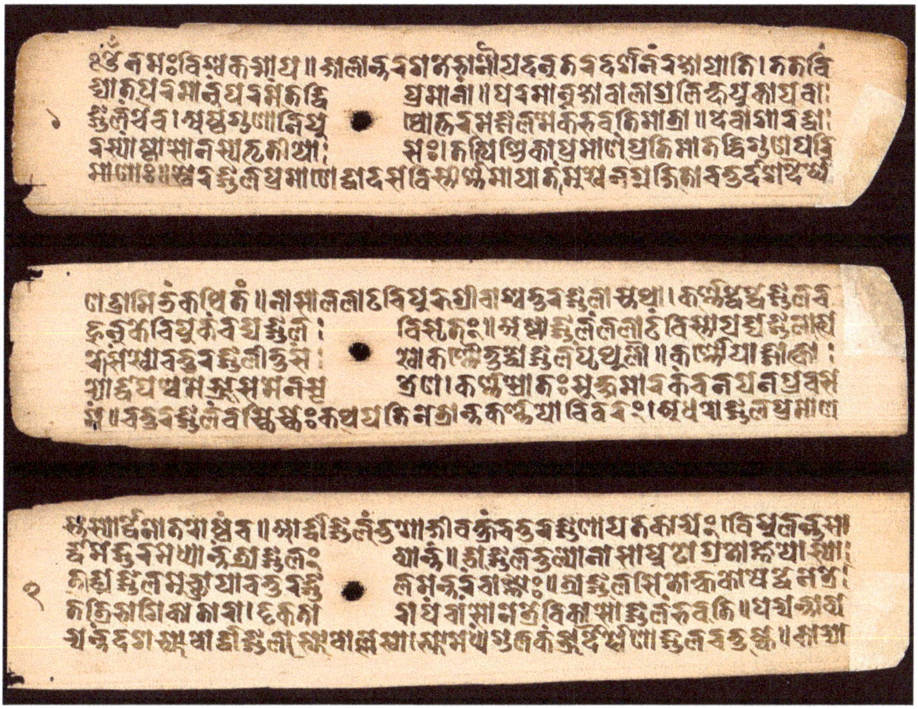

**Figure 36: 13th century palm leaf manuscript of Brihat Samhitā of Varāhamihira**
*Photo courtesy: Sarah Welch, Wikimedia Commons, CC BY-SA-4.0*

## Distortion by Colonial Era Indologists

As discussed earlier, the colonial era historians interpreted the Śaka Kāla as Śālivāhana Śaka of AD 79 instead of Śaka Kāla of 550 BC and fixed the date of Varāhamihira's *Pañcasiddhāntikā* to AD 78 (completed) + 427 = AD 505 instead of its true date of 550 BC + 427 = 123 BC. The word 'Śaka' in Śālivāhana Śaka means era or kāla and in 'Śaka Kāla' it refers to the Śaka people. So, Śaka Kāla means the era of Śakas. The AD 505 date assigned to Varāhamihira by the colonials, makes him neither a contemporary of Kālidāsa who has been placed in the fourth–fifth century AD nor of Emperor Vikramāditya whose existence has been denied.

## References

1. Dundas, Paul (2002). *The Jains* (2nd ed.). London and New York.
2. Kalhaṇa (1148). *Rājataraṅgiṇī (Chronicle of the Kings of Kashmir) (Sanskrit text),* Edited with Hindi translation by Shri Ramtej Shastri Pandey (Vikrama Samvat 2017 (AD 1960), rpt. ed. 1985). Delhi & Varanasi: Chaukhamba Sanskrit Pratishthan.
3. Narayana Sastry, T. S. (1916). *The Age of Śankara* (2nd ed. 1971, edited by T. N. Kumaraswamy). Madras: B. G. Paul & Co.
4. *Pañcasiddhāntikā of Varāhamihira (in Sanskrit) with translation and notes:* K.V. Sarma (Ed.), T. S. Kuppanna Sastry (English trans. 1993). Madras: P.P.S.T. Foundation Adyar (Originally written in the 2nd century BC).
5. *Varahamihira's Brihat Samhita (Sanskrit):* with Hindi translation by Pandit Śrī Achutānanda Jhā Śarmaṇā, (Vikrama Samvat 2015 (AD 1959)), Adhyay XIII, Shloka 3. Varanasi: Chaukhamba Vidyabhavan (Originally written in the 1st century BC).
6. Venkatachelam, Pandit Kota (1955). *Chronology of Kashmir History Reconstructed*. Arya Vijnana Series, Publication 18. Vijayawada.
7. Venkatachelam, Pandit Kota (Kali 5058, AD 1957a). *Chronology of Ancient Hindu History Part I*. Arya Vijnana Grandhamala, Publication 23. Vijayawada.
8. Venkatachelam, Pandit Kota (Kali 5092, AD 1991). *Age of The Mahabharata War*. Arya Vijnana Grandhamala, Publication 25. Vijayawada.

# 14

# INSCRIPTIONS AND ARCHAEOLOGICAL EVIDENCE

## The Oldest Inscriptions

Thousands of inscriptions of various kinds such as on rocks, pillars, temple walls, and copper plates have been found throughout the Indian subcontinent and cataloged by archaeologists. Many of these have been reproduced in the publications of the Archaeological Survey of India, including the journals such as 'Indian Antiquaries' and several books. Some of the very important inscriptions among these have been discussed in the various chapters of this book. A few of the oldest and rarest are described in further detail in this chapter.

### Emperor Janamejaya's First Gift Deed

As discussed briefly in Chapter 5, this is the first known inscription using the Jayābhyudaya Yudhiṣṭhira Śaka that started in the first year of Kaliyuga. The inscription was published in *Indian Antiquary* (Fleet, 1875, p. 333–334). The complete text of the inscription in the Devanāgarī script is as follows:

"श्रीगणाधिपतये नमः।

श्लो ।। पांतु वो जलदस्यामाः शार्ङ्गज्याघातकर्कशाः ।

त्रैलोक्यमंडपस्तंभाश्चत्वारो हरिबाहवः ।। (१)

स्वस्ति श्रीजयाभ्युदये युधिष्ठिरशके प्लवंगाख्ये एकोननवति (८९) वत्सरे सहस्यमासि अमावास्यायां

सौम्यवासरे श्रीमन्महाराजाधिराजपरमश्वरो वीरप्रतापशाली कुरुकुलोद्भावो वैयग्रणीपादगोत्रजः

श्रीजनमेजयभूपः किष्किंद्यानगर्या सिंहासनस्थः सकलवर्णाश्रमधर्मप्रतिपालकः
पश्चिमदेशस्थ सीतापुरवृकोदरक्षेत्रे तत्रत्यमुनिवृन्दमठस्य गरुडवाहनतीर्थ
श्रीमच्छिष्यकैकयनाथैराराधितसीतारामस्य पूजार्थं कृतभूदानसाधनं
अस्मत्प्रपितामहयुधिष्ठिराधिस्थितमुनिवृन्दक्षेत्रे स्य चतुःसीमापरिमितिक्रमः :-

पूर्वभागे उत्तरवाहिन्याः तुंगभद्रायाः पश्चिमे दक्षिणभागे अगस्त्याश्रमसंगमादुत्तरे ।
पश्चिमे पाषाणनद्याः पूर्वे उत्तरभागे भिन्ननद्या दक्षिणे एतन्मध्यस्थितमुनिवृंदक्षेत्रं
भवच्छिष्यपारंपरया आचंद्रार्कपर्यंतं निधिनिक्षेपजलपाषाणक्षिण्या गामिसिद्धसाध्यतेजः
स्वाम्यसहितं स्वबुध्याऽनुकूलेन अस्मन्मातापितृणां विष्णुलोकप्राप्त्यर्थं
हरिहरसंनिधौ उपरागसमये सहिरण्येन तुंगभद्राजलधारापूर्वकं क्षेत्रं यतिहस्ते दत्तोस्मि अहं ।
एतद्धर्मैसाधनस्य साक्षिणः ।।

श्लो ।। आदित्यचंद्रावनिलो च ध्यौर्भूमिरापो हृदयं मनश्च ।
अहश्च रात्रिश्च उभे च संध्ये धर्मश्च जानाति नरस्य वृत्तिं ।। (२)

दानपालनयोर्मध्ये दानाच्छ्रेयो नुपालनं ।
दानात्स्वर्गमवाप्नोति पालनादच्युतं पदं ।। (३)

स्वदत्ताद्विगुणं पुण्यं परदत्तानुपालनं ।
परदत्तापहारेण स्वदत्तं निष्फलं भवेत् ।। (४)

मद्दत्ता पुत्रिका ज्ञेया पितृदत्ता सहोदरा ।
अन्यदत्ता तु जननी दत्तभूमीं परित्यजेत् ।। (५)

अन्यैस्तु च्छदितं भुक्षुद्रैश्वभिश्च छर्दितं न तु ।
ततः कष्टो ततो नीचः स्वयं दत्तापहारकः ।। (६)

स्वदत्तां परदत्तां वा ब्रह्मवृत्तिं हरेत यः ।
षष्ठिर्वर्षसहस्राणि विष्ठायां जायते क्रिमिः ।। (७)"

The inscription is for the gift of the land on the bank of the Tungabhadra River in the present-day Karnataka state for the worship of Sitā-Rāma. Since the colonial era Indologists did not believe in the real antiquity of India's history, J. F. Fleet (1875, p. 333), the publisher of the inscription called this inscription a forgery, stating:

> "This is from No. 10 of the photographs of copper-plate inscriptions at the end of Major Dixon's collection. The original belongs to the Bhīmanakaṭṭi Maṭha near Tirthahalli in Maisur. I publish this inscription chiefly as a curiosity, for it is manifestly a forgery. It purports to belong to the time of Janamejaya, the great-grandson of Yudhishṭhira of the *Mahābhārata*, and it is dated in the year of the Yudhishṭhira Śaka 89, the Plavaṅga *saṁvatsara*. The real date of it cannot be fixed ;"

## Emperor Janamejaya's Second Gift Deed

This is the second inscription of Janamejaya. It was not published in the Indian Antiquary but in Masulipatnam, Āndhra Pradesh, from where Pandit Venkatachelam (1991, p. 49) obtained a copy. The following is the text of the inscription in the Devanāgarī script. See *Age of the Mahabharata War* (Venkatachelam, 1991) for further details.

"स्वस्तिश्री जयाभ्युदययुधिष्ठिरशके प्लवंगाख्ये एकोननवतितम (८९) वत्सरे सहसिमासि अमावास्यायां सोमवासरे श्रीमन्महाराजाधिराजपरमेश्वर वैयाघ्रपदगोत्रज श्रीजनमेजयभूपो इंद्रप्रस्थनगरीसिंहासनस्थः सकलवर्णाश्रमधर्मप्रतिपालको उत्तरहिमालये श्रीकेदारक्षेत्रं तत्रत्यमुनयः उषामठस्य श्रीगोस्वामिआनंदलिंगजंगमाय श्रीमच्छिष्यज्ञानलिङ्गजङ्गमद्वाराराधितश्रीकेदारनाथस्य पूजार्थं दत्तवंतः चतुस्सीमा परिमितिक्रमः ।। पूर्वभागे दक्षिणवाहिनी मंदाकिनी । पश्चिमदक्षिणभागे क्षीरगंगा उत्तरपश्चिमे मधुगंगा, पूर्वोत्तरभागे स्वर्गद्वारनदी, दक्षिणे सरस्वती, मंदाकिन्योः संगमः, एतन्मध्ये श्रीकेदारक्षेत्रं भवच्छिष्यपरंपरया चंद्रार्कपर्यंतं निधिनिक्षेप जलपाषाणगामि सिद्धसाध्यतेजःस्वाम्यसहित मनुभोक्तुं स्वबुध्यानुकूल्ये नास्मन्मातृपितॄणां शिवलोकप्राप्त्यर्थं श्रीकेदारेश्वरसन्निध उपरागसमये सहिरण्यमंदाकिनी जलधारापूर्वकं क्षेत्रमिदं हस्ते दत्तवानस्मि । एतद्धर्मसाधनस्य साक्षिणः ।

श्लो ।। आदित्यचंद्रावनिलोऽनलश्च ध्यौर्भूमिरापोहृदयं यमश्च ।
अहश्च रात्रिश्च उभे च संध्ये धर्मश्च जानाति नरस्य वृत्तं ।। (२)

दानपालनयोर्मध्ये दानाच्छ्रेयोऽनुपालनं ।
दानात्स्वर्गमवाप्नोति पालनाद् द्विगुणं फलं ।। (३)

स्वदत्ता पुत्रिका ज्ञेया पितृदत्ता सहोदरी ।
अन्यदत्ता तु जननी दत्तभूमिं परित्यजेत् ।। (४)

स्वदत्तां परदत्तांवा ब्रह्मवृत्तिं हरेतयः ।
षष्ठिर्वर्षसहस्राणि विष्ठायां जायते कृमिः ।। (५)

Both these inscriptions record a gift of land in two separate places on the same day. In the first grant, the emperor is described as seated on the throne in the city of Kishkindhā; in the second grant, the Emperor is described as seated on the throne in the city of Indraprastha. This may raise a question—how could the emperor be in the two far-away places on the same day? Well, it was a tradition at that time to describe the emperor as seated in the main city of the province in a gift deed, although both gifts were made in one place (Venkatachelam, 1991, p. 50).

## Aihole Inscription

This inscription is on a stone tablet on the outside of the eastern wall of a Meguti Jain temple on top of the hill at Aihole, Karnataka. It records the construction of the temple in AD 634 during the reign of Pulakeshi II, and his achievements. Pulakeshi II defeated and checked the southward advance of Emperor Harṣavardhana's armies south of the Vindya mountains. The inscription was published in the *Indian Antiquary* (Fleet, 1876). This is one of the most important inscriptions as it contains the date of the inscription as well as the date of the Mahābhārata War and Kaliyuga, as shown in the following verses quoted from the inscription.

त्रिंशत्सु त्रिसहस्त्रेषु भारतादाहवादितः ।
सप्ताब्दशतयुक्तेषु श(ग)तेष्वब्देषु पञ्चसु ।।

पञ्चाशत्सु कलौ काले षट्सु पञ्चशतासु च ।
समासु समतीतासु शकानामपि भूभुजाम् ।।

The following is the widely accepted interpretation of the dates given in the inscription (Venkatachelam, 1957b, p. 50; Kushwaha, 2003, p. 94).

> From the Mahābhārata War, and after 30 + 3000 + 700 + 5 years elapsed in the Kali Era, and 50 + 6 + 500 years after the destruction of the Śaka kings, (this temple of Jinendra was constructed).

Accordingly, 3,735 years of Kaliyuga had elapsed (the current Kaliyuga year was 3736) when 556 years of (Śālivāhana) Śaka (Era) were completed in AD 635 (= 556 + 79). This means that 3,736 – 635 = 3101 years of Kaliyuga had elapsed before Christ. Hence, Kaliyuga started in 3102 BC. However, J. F. Fleet (1876, p. 73) interpreted the verse as follows:

> "—three thousand seven hundred and thirty years having elapsed since the war of the Bharatas, and (three thousand) five hundred and fifty years having elapsed in the Kali age, and five hundred and six years of the Śaka kings having elapsed,"

Fleet, in his interpretation, used the same numbers in more than one calculation and computed three separate numbers. According to Fleet's interpretation,

(1) The year of the Mahābhārata War works out to 3,730 – 506 years of the Śaka (AD 584) = 3146 BC.

(2) The year of the beginning of the Kaliyuga works out to 3,550 – AD 584 = 2966 BC. This is an utter contradiction to 3102 BC as the unanimously accepted date for the beginning of the Kaliyuga.

(3) The Śaka 506 equates to AD 584 but Pulakeshi, a contemporary of Harṣa Śilāditya (Harṣavardhana) of AD 606–647, belongs to Śaka 556 (AD 634). Therefore, the AD 584 date is contradictory to the fact.

Thus, Fleet's interpretation leads to absurd results. See *Age of the Mahabharata War* (Venkatachelam, 1991, p. 51) for additional interpretations by others and further discussion.

## Inscription Dated Yudhiṣṭhira Śaka 168 (2970 BC)

Francis Buchanan found many inscriptions during his roaming in Karnataka and the surrounding areas in the early 1800s. Francis met a brahmana whose name was Madhu Linga Butta, in a village named Banawāsi. Buchanan states (1807/1988, p. 231):

> “*Madu Linga* gave me copies of the following inscriptions, which have been delivered to the Bengal government.
>
> The most ancient by far, and, unless there be some mistake in the matter, which indeed is almost certain, the most ancient inscription anywhere existing, is at the temple *Madugeswara*, and contains a grant of lands to the god *Maducanta*, by *Simhunna Bupa* of *Yudishtara's* family, dated in the year of the era of *Yudishtara* 168. As the Christian era, according to the usual reckoning of the *Brahmanas*, commences in the 3102 year of *Yudishtara**, this inscription was made 4735 years ago.”

* The Yudhiṣṭhira Śaka started in 3138 BC (See Chapter 4). Hence the correct year of the inscription is 3138 BC – 168 = 2970 BC.

## Inscription Dated Kaliyuga 600

Francis Buchanan (1807/1988, p. 411) writes further:

> “Having assembled the most learned *Jain* here, they gave me a copy of a writing on *Palmira* leaves, which they said was a copy of an inscription on copper belonging to the *Sannyāsi*, their *Guru*. It is dated in the year of the *Kaliyugam* 600, and in the reign of *Rājā Mulla*, king of the south. A copy has been delivered to the Bengal government.”

## Inscription Dated Vikrama Samvat 96

Francis Buchanan (1807/1988, p. 231) quotes another inscription of a much later date, but very important as follows:

> “Another very ancient inscription, but following the other at a great interval, is also at the temple of *Maducanta*. It is dated in the year *Jeya* of the era of *Vicrama* 96, in the reign of *Vicrama Ditya*. This answers to the 39th year of our Lord.”

The above inscription is one of the earliest known inscriptions recorded using the Vikrama Samvat. The inscription proves that the Vikrama Samvat started in 57 BC and has existed by that name at least since AD 39.

## The Ancient Sarasvati River

The legend of the River Sarasvati having gone underground has been passed down in India since ancient times. Sarasvati is the most important of the rivers in Ṛgveda (Frawley, 1991, p. 69), “the most frequently and intimately mentioned.” The *Mahābhārata* (Vol. 4, Śalya Parva, Adhyay 35, 37, 38) also refers to Sarasvati frequently including even the change in the course of the river (Śalya Parva 35.39–40). A few verses describe the disappearance of Sarasvati in some places which indicates that the mighty river had already begun to decline by the time of the Mahābhārata. In the 1970s, M. R. Mughal (1982) found that most of the Indus valley civilization towns were located on the banks of the ancient Sarasvati River as shown on the map at the Dholavira archaeological site. See Figure 37.

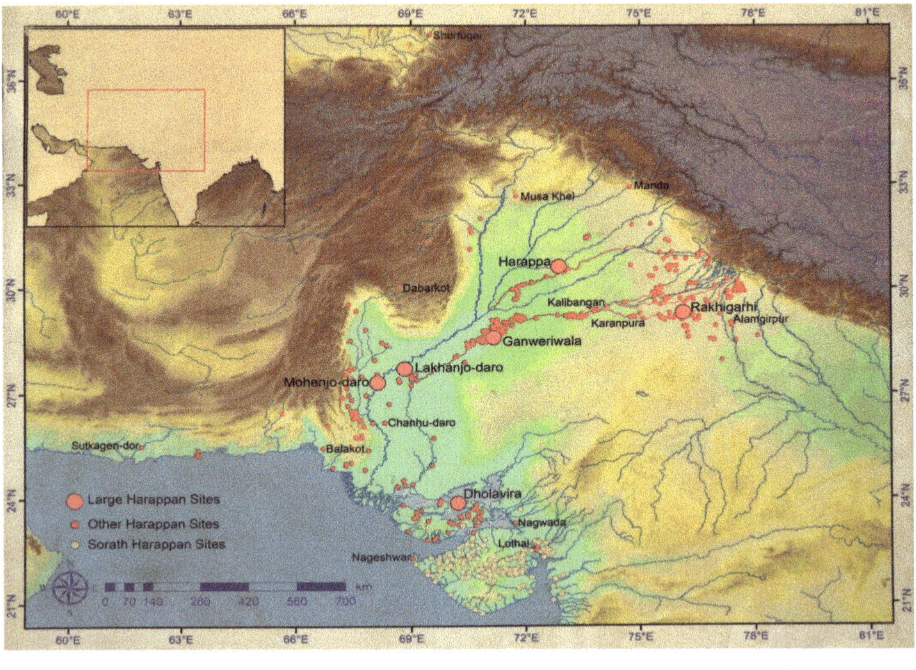


**Figure 37: Harappan sites on the banks of the ancient Sarasvati River**

Modern research has established that this river dried up around 1900 BC. This is another evidence that the Mahābhārata was written before 1900 BC since it mentions the ancient Sarasvati River. Numerous research papers and books have been published on mapping this lost, ancient river (Valdiya, 2002; Danino, 2010). Figure 38 shows a map of the lost river (Ghose et al., 1979). Extensive Landsat imagery was employed to ascertain the paleo-channels of the Satalaj, the Sarasvati, and the Yamuna (Lal et al., 2003).

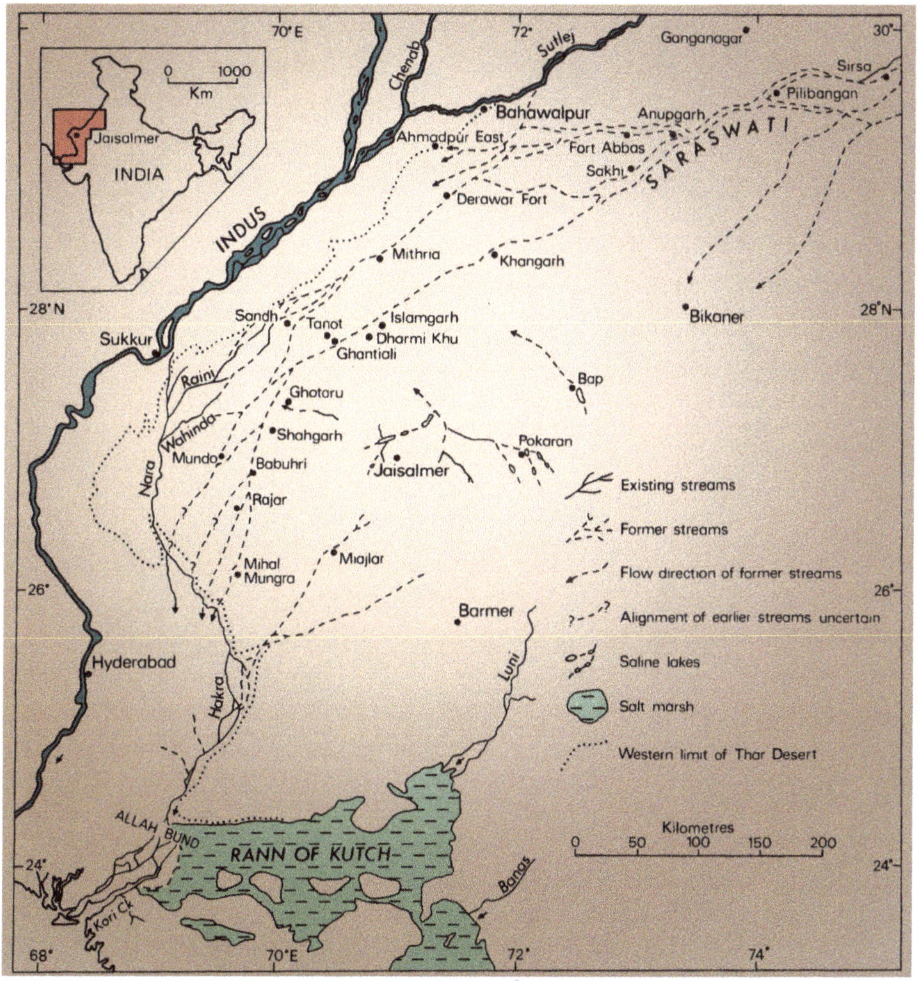


**Figure 38: The lost courses of the Sarasvati River**
*Chart adapted from: The Lost Courses of the Saraswati River in the Great Indian Desert: New Evidence from Landsat Imagery (Ghose et al., 1979)*

The seasonal Ghaggar-Hakra River in Haryana and Rajasthan is believed to be the ancient Sarasvati which flowed into Kaccha (कच्छ), Gujarat. There is a consensus that both Satalaj and Yamuna at one time drained into the Sarasvati and made it a mighty river. Satalaj and Yamuna have changed their courses several times before occupying their present paths. 'Kaccha' is a Sanskrit word for marshland. This suggests that the Kaccha district was likely the delta and marshland of the ancient Sarasvati. The Dholavira archaeological site located in Kaccha, dated to the late fourth and early third millennium, adds further support that Kaccha was likely a fertile area before the ancient Sarasvati dried up. The Banas and Sarasvati, the two biggest rivers of North Gujarat which disappear in the desert of Kaccha, may have been connected with the ancient Sarasvati River.

## Archaeological Evidence

Most people have heard of the archaeological findings from Harappa and Mohenjo-daro, the two famous sites of the Sindhu valley, located in Pakistan, because these were some of the first sites excavated in the Indian subcontinent in the 1920s and are included in the history textbooks. Excavations since independence have uncovered numerous sites in the Sarasvati-Ghaggar-Hakra-Drishādvati valley, in the upper reaches of the Yamuna-Hindon divide, in Gujarat and the upper reaches of the Godavari in Maharashtra.

The signature of the Harappan civilization extends over a vast area covering the northwestern part of the subcontinent. It extends in the north to Manda in lower Jammu and Kashmir, Shortughai in upper Afghanistan, and in the south to Daimabad, Maharashtra—covering more than 1,600 km north to south. It extends from Alamgirpur in Uttar Pradesh in the east to Sutkagan Dor in the Balochistan province of Pakistan (near the border with Iran) in the west—covering more than 1,600 km. The area covered by the Sindhu-Sarasvati civilization is much larger than the area of the contemporary civilizations of Egypt and Mesopotamia combined (Johnsen, 2009, p. 20). More sites have come to light on the paleochannels (remnants of the old river buried by younger sediment) of Sarasvati-Ghaggar-Drishādvati (Chitang)-Hakra than on any other river system of the sub-continent. (Amarendra Nath, 2014).

Subhash Kak (1992, p. 141) provides a summary of the archaeological findings in India dating up to about 6500 BC. Figure 39 show the location of some of the major archaeological sites of the Sarasvati-Sindhu civilization: Mohenjo-daro, Harappa, Dholavira, Lothal, Rakhigarhi, Kalibangan, Sinauli,

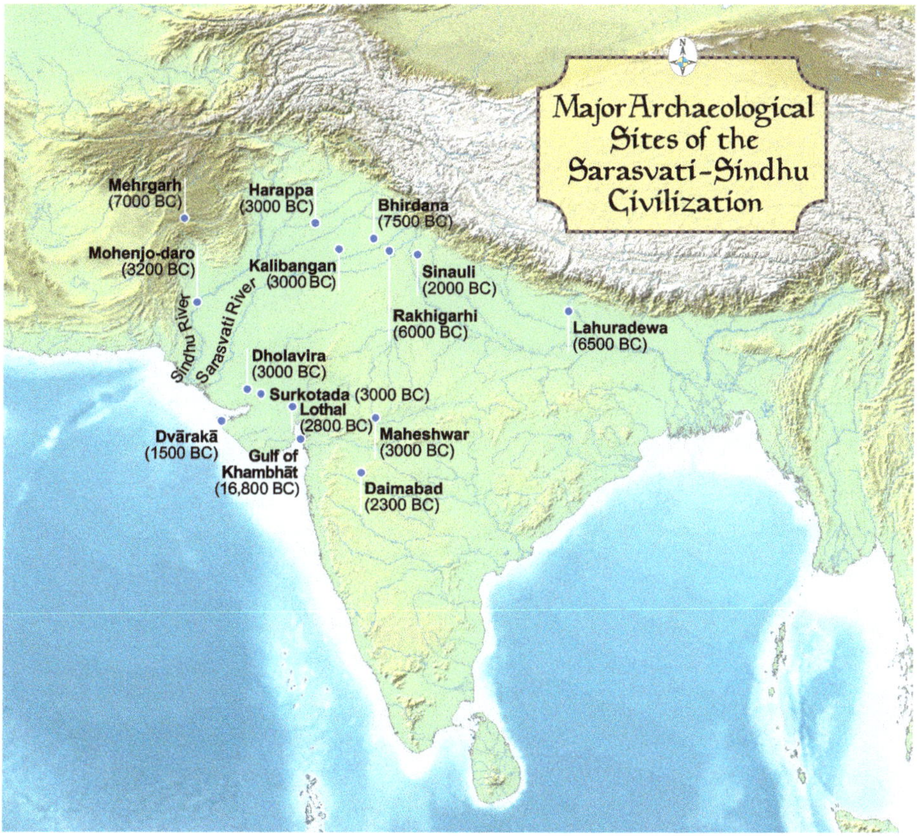


**Figure 39: Major archaeological sites of the Sarasvati-Sindhu Civilization**
*Blank map courtesy: DEMIS Mapserver, Wikimedia Commons, CC BY-SA 3.0*

Mehrgarh, and more. Archaeological finds from these sites are briefly discussed in the following paragraphs.

## Mohenjo-daro, Sindh

Excavation of Mohenjo-daro (Marshall, 1931; *Dholavira Report, 1.1.5*) site in Sindh, Pakistan, in 1922 led by R. D. Banerjee of the Archaeological Survey of India, found a great ancient city, well laid out with wide streets running at right angles. The houses are built of bricks, often several stories high, with flat roofs, drains, and bathrooms. According to John Marshall (1931, p. v), then the Director General of the Archaeological Survey of India, 5,000 years ago, Panjab and Sindh, if not other parts of India as well, were enjoying an advanced and singularly uniform civilization of their own, closely akin to, and in some respects, even superior to that of contemporary Mesopotamia and Egypt. Marshall (p. 104) estimated the occupation of Mohenjo-daro between 3250 and

2750 BC. Marshall wrote:

> “The use of cotton for textiles was exclusively restricted to India and was not extended to the Western world until two or three thousand years later. Again, there is nothing that we know of in prehistoric Egypt or Mesopotamia or anywhere else in Western Asia to compare with the well-built baths and commodious houses of the citizens. ... with their ubiquitous wells and bathrooms and elaborate system of drainage, ordinary townspeople enjoyed a degree of comfort and luxury unexampled in other parts of the then civilized world.” (p. vi).

> “One thing that stands out clear and unmistakable both at Mohenjo-daro and Harappa, is that the civilization hitherto revealed at these two places is not an incipient civilization, but one already age-old and stereotyped on Indian soil, with many millennia of human endeavour behind it.” (p. viii)

Figure 40 shows a variety of seals including the Swastika seal found from the Indus civilization. The Swastika symbol is considered auspicious and has been widely used in India for millennia.

**Figure 40: Seals from Indus valley civilization in the British Museum, London**
*Photo adapted from: World Imaging, Wikimedia Commons, CC BY-SA 3.0*

Figure 41 shows an impression of the Paśupati seal of a deity seated in a yogic pose amid animals, found from Mohenjo-daro. The seal is partially broken in the bottom left-hand corner. The Swastika and the Paśupati seals show a continuation of the ancient civilization to the present time. The seals also show evidence of a writing system prevalent then. Clay and stone tablets found at Harappa were carbon-dated to 3300–3200 BC.

**Figure 41: Impression of the Paśupati Seal from Mohenjo-daro.** *Photo courtesy: Ismoon, Wikimedia Commons, CCO 1.0 Public domain*

## Kalibangan, Rajasthan

Kalibangan in the Hanumangarh district of Rajasthan lies on the left bank of the seasonal Ghaggar (ancient Sarasvati) River in North Rajasthan. Kālibangan literally means black bangle. The name comes from the sight of the countless fragments of black bangles found at the site. The site, excavated from 1961 to 1969 by B. B. Lal et al. (2003) has revealed a pre-Harappan or early Harappan period culture (3500–2600 BC), and mature Harappan period culture (2600–1900 BC). The pre-Harappan settlement was fortified, and designed in the form of a parallelogram, measuring 240–250 meters from north to south and 170 meters from east to west. Kalibangan is distinguished by its unique fire altars and the **world's earliest plowed field of 2800 BC.** Kalibangan was abandoned around 2000–1900 BC when the River Sarasvati dried up. B. B. Lal states that an earthquake occurred around 2600 BC (Joshi and Bisht, 1994, p. 6–12; *Dholavira report*, 2015, 1.1.7).

## Dvārakā, Gujarat

See the archaeological evidence in Chapter 6.

## Lothal, Gujarat

Lothal is located about 80 km southwest of Ahmedabad and 30 km from the Gulf of Khambhat, situated along the Bhogava River, a tributary of Sabarmati (Joshi and Bisht, 1994, p. 36–40). It was excavated from 1955 to 1962 by a team led by Dr. S. R. Rao (1979) of the Archaeological Survey of India. Phase I of Lothal was dated to 2450 BC. Ancient Lothal is noted for its planning, dockyard, warehouse, bead factory, cemetery, and stratigraphic evidence which revealed the evolution of the Indus script and the gradual decline of the Harappan culture after 1900 BC. The clear evidence of destruction by floods at Lothal set archaeologists thinking about natural calamities that must have struck Mohenjo-daro. The name Lothal means the mound of the dead in the local area (Nayak and Ghosh, 1992, Vol. 1, p. xxv).

Lothal was a major port town with the oldest known tidal dockyard in the world with a unique lock-gate system. The artificial basin lined with brick walls, built in 2800 BC and measuring 210 x 35 meters, shown in Figure 42, is a monumental example of the engineering skills of the ancient people (Rao, 2001).

**Figure 42: World's oldest tidal dock with a lock-gate system (ca. 2800 BC), Lothal, Gujarat**

The simplification of the Indus script noticed at Lothal enabled Dr. Rao to decipher the script. The largest collection of archaeological artifacts in Indian archaeology comes from Lothal. The remains found here include metal tools, weights, measures, and seals. Lothal displays many features of the Harrapan civilization.

## Dholavira, Gujarat

The ancient city found at Dholavira in the Kaccha (कच्छ) district of Gujarat state is one of the five largest cities of the Indus valley civilization. The ancient ruins are spread over an area of 100 hectares. It was discovered in 1966 by Jagat Pati Joshi and excavated by R.S. Bisht of Archaeological Survey of India for 13 field seasons since 1989 (Joshi and Bisht, 1994, p. 23–31; *Dholavira Report*, 2015). The site provides a long cultural sequence, starting from the late fourth or early third millennium BC to the middle of the second millennium BC.

The excavations have revealed a major model city with exquisite planning, monumental structures, aesthetic architecture, a very intricate system of fortifications, and an amazing water-management system. The area reserved for the water storage was immense, approximately 750 m x 70–80 m. Water harvesting is of critical importance in the present world. Figure 43 shows a section of the multi-stage water harvesting and treatment system.

**Figure 43: A section of the water harvesting system (ca. 3000 BC), Dholavira, Gujarat**

In addition, two multipurpose grounds or plazas were revealed which were also used as stadiums where the larger one was furnished with stands for seating spectators. The site enjoys the unique distinction of yielding an inscription made of ten large-sized signs of the Indus script. A rich harvest of antiquities includes limestone pillar remnants of superb workmanship. Besides, there are seals, weights, and a wide variety of jewelry of gold, silver, copper, semi-precious stones, ivory, tools of copper, stone, shell, etc.

## Maheshwar, Madhya Pradesh

Rawlinson writes in *The Oxford Student's History of India* (Smith, 1951, p. 9):

> "At Maheswar in the Indore State, an entire city, a mile-long has been excavated, dating from 3000 B.C., and complete with artefacts (implements made by man), beads and brick structures.
>
> **The Copper Age**. In Northern India one of the first metals to become known was copper. Hundreds of curious implements made of pure copper have been found in the Central Provinces, in old beds of the Ganges near Cawnpore [Kanpur], and in other places from Eastern Bengal to Sind and the Kurram valley. They are supposed to date from about 2000 B.C., more or less. The time when iron being unknown, tempered or hardened pure copper, not bronze, was used to make tools is called the Copper Age. It is possible that some of the Rigveda hymns may date from that age, but commentators differ."

## Mehrgarh, Balochistan

Mehrgarh is located at the foot of the Bolan pass, on the banks of the Bolan River, not far from Quetta, Balochistan. Archaeological exploration of the site from 1975 to 1985 (Jarrige, 2006) by the French Archaeological Mission, in collaboration with the Department of Archaeology of Pakistan, found a vast area of about 300 hectares covered with archaeological remains left by a continuous sequence of occupation from the eighth to the third millennium BC.

## Rakhigarhi, Haryana

Rakhigarhi (Rakhigaḍhi) in Haryana lies on a channel of ancient Drishādvati which is now represented by Chatang Nala in Haryana and northern Rajasthan (*Dholāvira Report* 1.1.16). The site was excavated from 1997 to 2001. The site has several mounds. The discovery of two new mounds in January 2014, in addition to the seven mounds already discovered, makes it the largest archaeological site of the Indus valley, even bigger than the Mohenjo-daro site which extends around 300 hectares. In Rakhigarhi, a citadel was found with massive walls, typical of Indus planning. The site has yielded huge amounts of antiquities, and ceramics.

Rakhigarhi (Amarendra Nath, 2014) has an unbroken history of settlement—early farming communities from 6000–4500 BC, followed by the mature urbanization phase from 4500–3000 BC and then the highly urbanized mature phase from 3000 BC to its collapse around 1800 BC.

## Bhirdana, Haryana

Archaeological Survey of India report submitted in December 2014 (Dua, 2015), has revealed that the mounds at Bhirrana village, on the banks of Ghaggar (ancient Sarasvati) River, in Fatehabad district of Haryana date back to 7570–6200 BC. This makes it the oldest Sindhu-Sarasvati archaeological site. See also Bhirrana in *Dholavira Report* (1.1.14).

## Sinauli, Uttar Pradesh

The Sinauli archaeological site in the Baghpat district in Uttar Pradesh, 67 km north of Delhi, was an accidental find in 2005–2006 when a farmer was leveling his field. The excavations in 2018 by the Archaeological Survey of India (Rai, 2018; Kumar, 2018) have found chariots, copper engraved shields, and antenna swords with copper-covered wooden hilts dated to about 2000 BC.

## Lahuradewa, Uttar Pradesh

Excavations carried out at the lakeside settlement of Lahuradewa (Tewari et al., 2006), from 2001 to 2006, in the Sant Kabirnagar district, Uttar Pradesh, have found carbonized grains of domesticated rice dated to 6400 BC, indicating rice cultivation at that time.

## Maritime Trade of the Sindhu-Sarasvati Civilization

Late Dr. S. R. Rao (2001), an eminent archaeologist of the Archaeological Survey of India, states the following about the maritime activity of the Indus civilization:

> “The Harappan seals, stone weights and beads of gemstones are some of the unperishable articles found in the excavations in Bahrain, Failaka and Oman in the Arabian Peninsula, and at Ur, Kish, and Brak in Iraq, and Hissar and Suse in Iran. ... The occurrence of the Harappan chessmen in the tomb of Queen Hatchepsout and Egyptian terracotta models of mummies and gorillas in the excavations at Lothal ... are clear indications of extensive overseas trade between India and Africa in the third millennium B.C.” (p. 3)

> “The discovery of a Bahraini seal at Lothal dated 2300 BC ... and a seal of west Asian origin in Late Harappan levels at Prabhasa signifies brisk overseas trade between India and Mesopotamia in the 3rd and 2nd millennium B.C.” (p. 5)

## Evidence From Marine Archaeology

Sea level all over the world has gone up by about 130 meters after reaching the lowest level at the peak of the last Glacial Age around 20,000 years ago. Therefore, it is logical that any coastal settlements or cities from thousands of years ago would be underwater now.

In the Marine Archaeological expedition in 1992 near the submerged city of Poompuhar in Tamilnadu, a shipwreck was excavated and a stone structure at 23 m depth was identified (Rao, 2001, p. 175). The sea level was 23 meters lower than the present level more than 8,000 years ago which suggests that the stone structure would be at least 8,000 years old.

The National Institute of Ocean Technology (NIOT) of India, has been carrying out multidisciplinary marine surveys all along the Indian coast for various purposes. In the Gulf of Khambhat, NIOT has found evidence of a well-developed urban settlement at a water depth of 20–40 meters, and ancient people making fired clay pottery from about 16,800 BC, the oldest in the world so far (Badrinaryan, n.d., 2006, 2010). The ancient civilization knew the art of constructing towns and houses in neat straight lines as seen by the side-scan sonar images.

## Similarities between the Brahmi and the Indus Valley Scripts

We often hear that ancient India did not have a writing system and that knowledge was only orally passed. However, it is stated in the Mahābhārata that it was entirely written to Veda Vyāsa's dictation. Evidence of the writing system has been found from the archaeological sites in the Sarasvati-Sindhu valley. Contrary to the prevailing understanding among the general population that the Indus valley script has not been deciphered, noteworthy progress has been made over the last several decades in deciphering the script (Mathur, 1992, p. 103–122; Priyanka, 1992, p. 123–131). S. R. Rao has deciphered several names such as MANU. Figure 44 (Priyanka, 1992, p. 129), shows a remarkable similarity between the ancient Brahmi script of Aśokan inscriptions (15th century BC) and the Harappan characters. Many signs in Brahmi look almost identical to the Harappan signs which indicates that the Brahmi script evolved from the Harappan script. In the same book, Subhash Kak (1992, p. 149) states:

> “My analysis of Indus and Brahmi based on computer created concordances, revealed obvious connections between the two scripts that could not be explained as arising out of chance (Kak 1987a, 1988, 1989, 1990).”

Recently, Dr. S. Kalyanaraman (2010, 2012) has published several books on decoding the Indus civilization script.

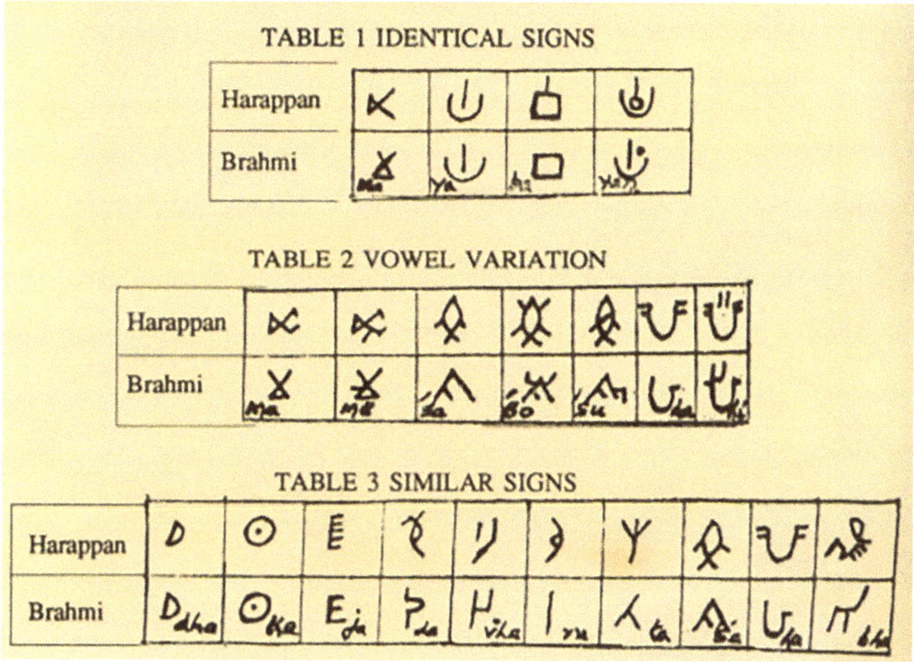


**Figure 44: Similarity between Harappan and Brahmi characters**

*Chart courtesy: Decipherment of Indus Script: A New Attempt* (Priyanka, 1992, p. 129)

## The True Dating of the Brahmi Script

Based on the wrong dating of the Maurya Dynasty, the Brahmi script of the Maurya Emperor Aśoka's inscriptions all over India has been dated to the 3rd century BC. Based on the true chronology, the Brahmi script used in the Aśokan inscriptions should be dated to the 15th century BC, the true time of Aśoka. The history written in the colonial era has been the story of one false justifying another false. The false dating of the script was in turn used to date other inscriptions to a much later date!

## References


1. Amarendra Nath, Dr. (2014). *Excavations at Rakhigarhi: 1997–98 to 1999–2000*. Archaeological Survey of India.
2. Badrinaryan, S. (n.d.). 'Gulf of Cambay: Cradle of Ancient Civilization.', Archaeology Online. www.archaeologyonline.net/artifacts/cambay (Accessed on January 30, 2023).
3. Badrinaryan, S. (2006, February 1). 'Gulf of Cambay: Cradle of Ancient Civilization.', Graham Hancock. https://grahamhancock.com/badrinaryanb1/ (Accessed on January 30, 2023).
4. Badrinaryan, S. (2010). 'The Gulf of Khambhat: Does the Cradle of Ancient Civilization lie off the coast of India?' in Glenn Kreisberg (Ed.), *Lost Knowledge of the Ancients: A Graham Hancock Reader* (Ch. 11). Toronto & Vermont: Bear & Company.
5. Buchanan, Francis (1807). *A Journey from Madras Through the Countries of Mysore, Canara and Malabar: For the express purpose of investigating the state of Agriculture, Arts and Commerce; The Religion, Manners, and Customs; The History Natural and Civil and Antiquities* (Vol.3, rpt. 1988). New Delhi: Asian Educational Services.
6. Danino, Michel (2010). *The Lost River: On the trail of the Sarasvati*. New Delhi: Penguin India.
7. *Dholavira Report: (preliminary, January 2015)*. Archaeological Survey of India.
8. Dua, Rohan (2015, April 15). 'Haryana's Bhirrana Oldest Harrapan Site, Rakhigarhi Asia's Largest: ASI.' *The Times of India*. https://timesofindia.indiatimes.com/city/chandigarh/haryanas-bhirrana-oldest-harappan-site-rakhigarhi-asias-largest-asi/articleshow/46926693.cms
9. Fleet, J. F. (1875). 'Sanskrit and Old Canarese Inscriptions: No. VIII (of Janamejaya).' *The Indian Antiquary: A Journal of Oriental Research in Archaeology, History, Literature, Language, Philosophy, Religion, Folklore etc., Vol. 4*, 333–335. Bombay.
10. Fleet, J. F. (1876). 'Sanskrit and Old Canarese Inscriptions: No. XIII.' *The Indian Antiquary: A Journal of Oriental Research in Archaeology, History, Literature, Language, Philosophy, Religion, Folklore etc., Vol. 5*, 67–73. Bombay.
11. Frawley, David (1991). *Gods, Sages and Kings: Vedic Secrets of Ancient*

*Civilization*. Twin Lakes, WI: Lotus Press.

12. Ghose, Bimal; Amal Kar, and Zahid Husain (1979, November). 'The Lost Courses of the Saraswati River in the Great Indian Desert: New Evidence from Landsat Imagery.' *The Geographical Journal, Vol. 145(*3), 446–451. London: The Royal Geographical Society (with IBG).

13. Jarrige, Jean-Francois (2006, January 18–20). *Mehrgarh Neolithic* [Paper presentation]. International Seminar on the 'First Farmers in Global Perspective', Lucknow, India.

14. Johnsen, Linda (2009). *The Complete Idiot's Guide to Hinduism* (2nd ed.). Alpha Books.

15. Joshi, Jagat Pati, and R. S. Bisht (1994). *India and The Indus Civilisation*. New Delhi: National Museums Institute.

16. Kak, Subhas (1992). 'The Indus Maṇḍala and the Indo-Aryans.' in B. U. Nayak and N. C. Ghosh (Eds.) *New Trends in Indian Art and Archaeology: S.R. Rao's 70th Birthday Felicitation Volume* (Vol. 1, Ch. III.4). New Delhi: Aditya Prakashan.

17. Kalyanaraman, S. (2010). *Indus Script Cipher: Hieroglyphs of Indian linguistic area*. Sarasvati Research Center.

18. Kalyanaraman, S. (2012). *Indian Hieroglyphs: Invention of Writing*. Sarasvati Research Center.

19. Kumar, Vijay (2018). 'A Note on Chariot Burials Found at Sinauli District Baghpat, U.P.' *Indian Journal of Archaeology,* 3(2): http://ijarch.org/Admin/Articles/9-Note%20on%20Chariots.pdf

20. Kushwaha, Dr. Rajendra Singh (2003). *Glimpses of Bhāratiya History*. New Delhi: Ocean Books.

21. Lal, B. B., B. K. Thapar, Jagat Pati Joshi, and Madhu Bala (2003). *Excavations at Kalibangan: The Early Harappans (1960–1969)*. Memoirs of the Archaeological Survey of India, no. 98.

22. *Mahābhārata: (Sanskrit) with Hindi translation* by Pandit Rāmanārāyaṇadatta Śastri Pāṇdeya, 6 vols. Gorakhpur: Gita Press.

23. Marshall, Sir John (Ed.) (1931). *Mohenjo-daro and The Indus Civilization: Being an official account of the Archaeological Excavations at Mohenjo-daro carried out by the Government of India between the years 1922 and 1927* (Vol. 1). London: Arthur Probsthain.

24. Mathur, P. N. (1992). 'Decipherment of Indus Script and Traditional Indian History.' in B. U. Nayak and N. C. Ghosh (Eds.), *New Trends in Indian Art and Archaeology: S. R. Rao's 70th Birthday Felicitation Volume:* (Vol. 1, Ch. III.1). New Delhi: Aditya Prakashan.

25. Mughal, M. Rafique (1982). 'Recent Archaeological Research in the Cholistan Desert.' Reprinted from Gregory L. Possehl (Ed.) *Harappan Civilization*. New Delhi: Oxford & IBH Publishing.

26. Nayak, B. U., and N. C. Ghosh (Eds.) (1992). 'Life Sketch of Dr. S. R. Rao.' in *New Trends in Indian Art and Archaeology: S.R. Rao's 70th Birthday Felicitation Volume* (Vol. 1). New Delhi: Aditya Prakashan.

27. Priyanka, Benille (1992). 'Decipherment of Indus Script: A New Attempt.' in B. U. Nayak and N. C. Ghosh (Eds.), *New Trends in Indian Art and Archaeology: S. R. Rao's 70th Birthday Felicitation Volume* (Vol. 1, Ch. III.2). New Delhi: Aditya Prakashan.

28. Rai, Sandeep (2018, June 6). 'ASI unearths 'first-ever' physical evidence of chariots in Copper-Bronze age.' *The Times of India.* https://timesofindia.indiatimes.com/city/meerut/asi-unearths-first-ever-physical-evidence-of-chariots-in-copper-bronze-age/articleshow/64469616.cms

29. Rao, S. R. (1979). *Lothal: A Harappan Port Town (1955-62)* (Vol. I.) Memoirs of the Archaeological Survey of India, No. 78. New Delhi.

30. Rao, S. R. (2001). *Marine Archaeology in India.* Ministry of Information and Broadcasting, Government of India.

31. Smith, Vincent A. (1951). *The Oxford Student's History of India* (15th ed. Revised by H.G. Rawlinson). Oxford University Press.

32. Tewari, Rakesh; R.K. Srivastava, K.S. Saraswat, I.B. Singh, and K.K. Singh (2006, January 18–20). *Early farming at Lahuradewa* [Paper presentation]. International Seminar on the 'First Farmers in Global Perspective', Lucknow, India.

33. Valdiya, K. S. (2002). *Saraswati: The River that Disappeared.* Hyderabad: Universities Press.

34. Venkatachelam, Pandit Kota (Kali 5058, AD 1957b). *Chronology of Ancient Hindu History Part II.* Arya Vijnana Grandhamala, Publication 24. Vijayawada

35. Venkatachelam, Pandit Kota (Kali 5092, AD 1991). *Age of The Mahabharata War.* Arya Vijnana Grandhamala, Publication 25. Vijayawada.

# 15

# THE FALLACY OF THE ARYAN INVASION OF INDIA

## What is the Aryan Invasion Theory?

The Aryan invasion theory was conjectured by European Indologists during the colonial rule of India and thrust upon India in the second half of the 19th century. The theory states that around 1500 BC (3,500 years ago), Sanskrit speaking fair-skinned people called Aryans from central Asia, invaded India and took over the entire northern part of the Indian subcontinent, furthermore, they then pushed the dark-skinned Dravidian people living in northern India into southern India.

The crux of the Aryan invasion theory:

1. Sanskrit did not originate in India but came through the Sanskrit-speaking Aryans from central Asia who invaded India around 1500 BC.
2. All of ancient India's works such as the Vedas, Purāṇas, Mahābhārata, Rāmāyana, etc. were composed by these Aryans after they arrived in India in 1500 BC; the four Vedas were composed in the 1200–400 BC period and the Rāmāyana, Mahābhārata, and Bhagavadgītā were composed even later.
3. Divided the Indian population into two groups—the people and the languages of North India were called of Aryan origin and the people and the languages of South India were called of Dravidian origin.

## Origin of the Aryan Invasion Theory

William Jones, the late 18th century British scholar, working for the British East India Company, learned Sanskrit and noticed a strong similarity between

Sanskrit and European languages. Jones, not believing in the greater antiquity of India, began to think that the European languages and Sanskrit must have come from a common source. In the discourse delivered as president of the Asiatic Society on Feb 2, 1786, in Kolkata, on the Asiatic Society's third anniversary, William Jones stated (1884/1972, p. 348–349):

> " The *Sanscrit* language, whatever be its antiquity, is of a wonderful structure ; more perfect than the *Greek*, more copious than the *Latin* and more exquisitely refined than either ; yet bearing to both of them a stronger affinity, both in the roots of verbs, and in the forms of grammar, than could possibly have been produced by accident ; so strong, indeed, that no philologer could examine them all three, without believing them to have sprung from some common source, which, perhaps, no longer exists. There is a similar reason, though not quite so forcible, for supposing that both the *Gothic* and the *Celtic*, though blended with a very different idiom, had the same origin with the *Sanscrit* ; and the old *Persian* might be added to the same family, if this were the place for discussing any questions concerning the antiquities of *Persia*. "

The following are a few examples of some of the most basic English words which sound similar to the corresponding Sanskrit words. The English language is about a thousand years old, Latin is about 2,000–2,500 years old, Greek is about 2,500–3,000 years old, whereas Sanskrit literature can be traced back to more than 5,000 years ago. Therefore, arguably, the origin of these English words can be traced back to Sanskrit. There are hundreds of other English words which sound similar to the words in Sanskrit but that is outside the scope of this book, hence only a few examples will suffice to illustrate William Jones's observation.

Father – Pāter in Latin – Pitar (पितर्) in Sanskrit

Mother – Māter in Latin – Mātar (मातर्) in Sanskrit

Brother – Frater in Latin – Bhrātar (भ्रातर्) in Sanskrit

Sister – Schwester in German – Svasār (स्वसार्) in Sanskrit

Daughter – Dauhitar (दौहितर्) in Sanskrit

Divine – Divya (दिव्य) in Sanskrit

Omni in Omnipresent, Omniscient – Om (ओम) in Sanskrit

Adam – Ādi (आदि) in Sanskrit

Mortal – Mṛta (मृत) in Sanskrit

That – Tat (तत्) in Sanskrit

Star – Tārā (तारा) in Sanskrit

Center – spelled centre in British style – Kendra (केन्द्र) in Sanskrit

Meter – spelled metre in British style – Mātrā (मात्रा) in Sanskrit

Door – Dvāra (द्वार) in Sanskrit

Wrath – Krodha (क्रोध) in Sanskrit

Cruel – Krur (क्रुर्) in Sanskrit

Myth – Mithyā (मिथ्या) in Sanskrit

In the same discourse, William Jones (1884/1972, p. 354–355) said:

> “ The philosopher whose works are said to include a System of the Universe, founded on the principle of *Attraction* and the *central* Position of the Sun, is named YAVAN ACHA'RYA, because he had travelled, we are told, into Ionia. If this be true, he might have been one of those who conversed with PYTHAGORAS. This at least is undeniable, that a book on astronomy in *Sanscrit* bears the title of *Yavana Jatica*, which may signify the *Ionic Sect*. Nor is it improbable, that the names of the Planets and *Zodiacal* Stars, which the *Arabs* borrowed from the *Greeks*, but which we find in the oldest *Indian* records, were originally devised by the same ingenious and enterprizing race, from whom both *Greece* and *India* were peopled ; ...
>
> Of these cursory observations on the *Hindus*, which it would require volumes to expand and illustrate, this is the result : that they had an immemorial affinity with the old *Persians, Ethiopians*, and *Egyptians* ; the *Phenicians, Greeks*, and *Tuscans* ; the *Scythians* or *Goths*, and *Celts* ; the *Chinese, Japanese*, and *Peruvians* ; whence as no reason appears for believing that they were a colony from any of those nations, or any of those nations from them, we may fairly conclude that they all proceeded from some *central* country, to investigate which will be the object of my future discourses ; ”

According to the above-quoted paragraphs, William Jones noticed similarities not only in the languages but also in the science and astronomy knowledge of the Greeks and Indians and mooted the idea that Indian people came from outside of India, thus planting the seeds of the Aryan invasion theory.

As described in Chapter 2, William Jones, like most Europeans of his time, firmly believed in the biblical version of history that the world started in 4006 BC and the 'deluge' happened in 2350 BC. Jones was familiar with Greek history and believed it to be the oldest and knew that it did not go beyond about 600 BC. As a result, he did not accept India's historical tradition recorded in the Purāṇas, going back beyond 3100 BC. He imagined a much less antiquated timeline of India's history. Other European historians following him continued on the same path, shrinking India's chronology and rewriting India's history starting only from about 600 BC, making it not older than Greek history.

Postdating India's history from 3100+ BC to no earlier than 600 BC, created a gap in India's chronology for the time before 600 BC. This gap was filled with the Aryan invasion theory in the second half of the 19th century by Max Müller, to justify the similarity between the European languages and Sanskrit. Max Müller was hired by the East India Company in 1847 to translate a *Rig-Veda-Sanhita*. While translating the work, he interpreted the battle between light (of knowledge) and darkness (of ignorance) as a fight between light-skinned and dark-skinned people.

Max Müller moved to Britain at the age of 23 years and lived there for the rest of his life. He never visited India. Since the biblical deluge (floods) was believed to have occurred in about 2350 BC, the Aryans' invasion could not be placed earlier than 1500 BC; thus, the date of the Aryan invasion of India was fixed at 1500 BC. Max Müller assumed that the four Vedas and the Upanishads were composed after this event and by Gautama Buddha's time in 500 BC which is the wrong date as discussed in Chapter 8. Thus, the composition of the four Vedas was arbitrarily assumed to be in the 1200–400 BC period.

## Aryan Invasion Theory Debunked

The Aryan Invasion theory has been seriously questioned for decades and now stands discredited (Frawley, 1991; Allur, 1992, Ch. VIII.5; Danino and Nahar, 1996; Knapp, 2008).

1. There is no mention in India's historical and literary traditions of Aryans invading India, sweeping all original inhabitants of the vast areas of North India into South India. If Aryans came into India from outside through the passes in the northwest of the Indian subcontinent, pushed the native inhabitants of all of North India to South India, and then composed all the Vedas, Purāṇas, etc., why wouldn't they write about such a huge

historical event in the texts composed by them?

2. When excavations in the Indus valley led by R.D. Banerjee, in the early 1920s, revealed evidence of an advanced civilization (from Mohenjo-daro and Harappa) dating to about 3000 BC, it posed a direct challenge to the Aryan invasion theory which stated that the civilization of India began only after the Aryans came in 1500 BC. Then, the die-hard supporters of the theory simply modified their theory to state that the more powerful Aryans destroyed the earlier advanced civilization.

3. The unearthing of Dholavira, Lothal in Gujarat, and hundreds of other archaeological sites made the theory of the destruction of the Indus cities by invading Aryans and the sudden disappearance of the Indus Civilization unsustainable (Nayak and Ghosh, 1992, Editorial).

4. As pointed out by David Frawley (1998) and discussed in Chapter 14, the great majority of the sites of the Indus valley culture are in the east, not west of the Indus River. The largest concentration of the sites is near the dry banks of the ancient Sarasvati and Drishādvati Rivers in present-day Haryana and Rajasthan. The Sarasvati River is lauded as the main river in Ṛgveda and is the most frequently mentioned river in the text. It was said to be very wide, even endless in size, a great flood. It dried up around 1900 BC according to modern research (Kak, 1992, p. 141). If the Aryans invaded India in 1500 BC and wrote all the Vedas, Purāṇas, and Mahābhārata in the 1200–200 BC period, how could they have known about River Sarasvati which dried up in 1900 BC?

5. It is now widely accepted that most of India's modern languages are derived from Sanskrit. Even Tamil has many Sanskrit words and most of the Tamilian names are from Sanskrit. Kannada, Telugu, and Malayalam, the three southern languages, appear to be derived from both Sanskrit and Tamil. This fact contradicts the claim of the Aryan invasion theory that the languages of South India are not derived from Sanskrit.

6. If Sanskrit was brought into India from central Asia, why are the present-day Indian languages the closest to Sanskrit, compared with languages outside of the Indian subcontinent?

7. Is it even conceivable that a few thousand or tens of thousands of Aryans swept the vast northern part of the Indian subcontinent stretching 2,000 miles from Pakistan in the west to Assam in the east, and pushed a much larger population living there into South India? What an absurd proposition!

8. The colonial era Indologists lacked sufficient knowledge of India's history, language, and culture. Many of the European Indologists were Christian missionaries and very unsympathetic to India's Vedas and other literature as discussed in Chapter 2.

9. The word 'Ārya', appearing in the Vedas and the Purāṇas is a Sanskrit word which means a cultured person. Max Müller, after learning this word, introduced it to the outside world in the 1850s, falsely propagating it as referring to a race. However, when challenged later by other scholars of such wrong interpretation, Max Müller (1888, p. 120) responded:

   > "I have declared again and again that if I say Aryas, I mean neither blood nor bones, nor hair nor skull ; I mean simply those who speak an Aryan language. ... To me an ethnologist who speaks of Aryan race, Aryan blood, Aryan eyes and hair, is as great a sinner as a linguist who speaks of a dolichocephalic dictionary or a brachycephalic grammar. It is worse than a Babylonian confusion of tongues—it is downright theft."

10. The word 'Travida' was used by Śrī Ādi Śaṅkarāchārya when he introduced himself as a *Travida* Śiśu for the famous debate with Mandana Misra. The word *Travida* means the land surrounded by three seas – the Arabian Sea in the west, the Bay of Bengal in the east, and the Indian Ocean in the south. Thus, the word 'Dravida (Travida)' is a geographical description of South India and has nothing to do with race.

11. There is a remarkable similarity between the Brahmi and the Harappan scripts as discussed in Chapter 14 which shows that the ancient Brahmi script evolved from the Harappan script of about 3000 BC.

12. Finally, we have a continuous chronology of Magadha/Ujjain, Kashmir, and Nepal from centuries before the time of the Mahābhārata War in 3139 BC to AD 1192, leaving no place for the Aryan invasion theory.

Highly respected Indian Vedic scholars such as Dayānanda Sarasvati (Danino and Nahar, 1996, p. 34), Bāl Gangādhar Tilak, Swami Vivekananda, Aurobindo Ghosh, and many such intellectuals rejected the Aryan invasion theory. Dr. Ambedkar, who chaired the constitution assembly of India, after its freedom in 1947, also rejected this theory. The following comments from Swami Vivekananda (1863–1902) and Aurobindo Ghosh show their rejection of this theory outright.

Swami Vivekananda (Advaita Ashrama, 1964, p. 534–535) stated:

> “ And what your European Pundits say about the Aryan's swooping down from some foreign land, snatching away the lands of the aborigines and settling in India by exterminating them, is all pure nonsense, foolish talk! Strange, that our Indian scholars, too, say amen to them ; and all these monstrous lies are being taught to our boys! This is very bad indeed. ”

Śrī Aurobindo Ghosh (1872–1950) wrote:

> “ In India we have fallen during the last few centuries into a fixed habit of unquestioning deference to authority. ... We are ready to accept all European theories, the theory of an 'Aryan' colonisation of a Dravidian India, the theory of Nature-worship. ” (as cited in Danino and Nahar, 1996, p. 40).

Thus, there is no basis for the theory of the Aryan invasion of India conjectured by European Indologists of the colonial era and it must be discarded completely. The Aryan race theory gave rise to Nazism in Germany with disastrous results (Danino and Nahar, p. 31). It is heartening to know that the Aryan invasion theory is not even mentioned in the school history textbooks published by the National Council of Educational Research and Training since 2006.

## References


1. Advaita Ashrama (1964). 'The East and the West.' in *The Complete Works of Swami Vivekananda: Mayavati Memorial Edition* (8th ed., Vol. 5). Calcutta.
2. Allur, K. R. (1992). 'Aryan Invasion of India, Indo-Gangetic Valley Cultures.' in B. U. Nayak and N.C. Ghosh (Eds), *New Trends in Indian Art and Archaeology: S.R. Rao's 70th Birthday Felicitation Volume* (Vol. 2). New Delhi: Aditya Prakashan.
3. Danino, Michel, and Sujata Nahar (1996). *The Invasion that Never Was.* New Delhi: Song of Humanity.
4. Frawley, David (1991). *Gods, Sages and Kings: Vedic Secrets of Ancient Civilization*. Twin Lakes, WI: Lotus Press.
5. Jones, William (1884). 'The Third Anniversary Discourse by The President.' *Asiatic Researches; or Transactions of the Society Instituted in Bengal for inquiring into the History and Antiquities, the Arts, Sciences, and Literature of Asia, Vol. 1*, 343–355 (rpt. 1972). Varanasi: Bharat-Bharati.
6. Kak, Subhas (1992). 'The Indus Maṇḍala and the Indo-Aryans.' in B. U. Nayak and N. C. Ghosh (Eds.) *New Trends in Indian Art and Archaeology: S.R. Rao's 70th Birthday Felicitation Volume* (Vol. 1, Ch. III.4). New Delhi: Aditya Prakashan.
7. Knapp, Stephen (2008). *Death of the Aryan Invasion Theory*. https://www.stephen-knapp.com/death_of_the_aryan_invasion_theory.htm (Accessed February 1, 2023).
8. Max Müller, F. (1888). *Biographies of Words and the Home of the Aryas.* London: Longmans, Green, and Co.
9. Nayak, B. U., and N. C. Ghosh (Eds.) (1992). 'Editorial.' in *New Trends in Indian Art and Archaeology: S.R. Rao's 70th Birthday Felicitation Volume, 2 vols*. New Delhi: Aditya Prakashan.

# 16

# SUMMARY AND CONCLUSION

It is not common knowledge, even within India, let alone the world, that the current history and chronology of ancient India which pervades the curricula in the schools and colleges of the world, is not the one recorded by Indians, but a distorted version created by European Indologists (mainly British and German) during the British colonial rule of India from the late 1700s to 1947.

A complete chronology of the kings, dynasties, and their years of reign from the time of the Mahābhārata War in 3139 BC to the end of the reign of Prithvirāj Chauhan in AD 1192 is given in our Purāṇas for the kings of Magadha, Ujjain, and other ancient centers of India. A complete chronology of the kings of Kashmir from before the time of the Mahābhārata War to AD 1148 is given in Rājataraṅgiṇī (a chronicle of the kings of Kashmir). Nepal Rāja Vaṁśāvali contains a complete chronology of the kings of Nepal from centuries before the Mahābhārata War to modern times. Thus, the Mahābhārata War is vouched for by three independent sources.

Rewriting of India's history began with the founding of the Asiatic Society in Kolkata in AD 1784 by William Jones, a Britisher working for the East India Company. Only Europeans were elected as members of the society until 1829 when Indians were first admitted as members. Jones was rooted in the biblical version of history that the world began in 4006 BC and believed the history of Greece to be the oldest. As a result, he dismissed the traditional high antiquity (3100+ BC) of India's chronology given in the Purāṇas and started shortening it arbitrarily to fit it into the biblical timeline so firmly believed by him and most

Europeans of his time. He then laid the foundation of the false chronology by misidentifying '*Sandracottus*', the contemporary of Alexander described by ancient Greek writers, with Chandragupta Maurya of 1534 BC instead of Chandragupta I of the Gupta Dynasty of 327 BC. This misidentification blunder erased over 1,200 years of ancient India's chronology.

Later European Indologists followed in Jones's footsteps. Max Müller (1859/1926), a German Sanskritist hired by the British East India Company in 1847 to translate a *Rig-Veda-Sanhita* from Sanskrit to English, concretized the false identification in about 1859 and made it the 'anchor sheet' for redating the entire history of India. Over the next 50–60 years, several colonial Indologists such as Vincent Smith, F. E. Pargiter, and several others completed rewriting of India's history. These colonial Indologists knew of the Purāṇas and wrote the history of India using them as guides. However, while they accepted the lists of kings given in the Purāṇas, they cherry-picked the information – rejected some of the kings and dynasties, and reduced the reigning periods of many kings and dynasties as it suited them to fit the chronology in the biblical timeline. They even altered verses in the Purāṇas to justify their distortions as discussed in the various chapters.

As discussed in Chapter 2, Megasthenes (McCrindle, 1877, p. 115) reported:

> "From the days of father Bacchus to Alexander the Great their kings are reckoned at 154, whose reigns extend over 6451 years and 3 months."

Since Alexander invaded India in 326 BC, going backward by 6,451 years takes the beginning of India's chronology to 6777 BC. Keeping track of an exact number of years and months elapsed is possible only with a calendar, and this calendar must have started at least in 6777 BC. As discussed in Chapter 4, Alexander Cunningham (1883, p. 15) concluded that the Saptarṣi cycle likely started in 6777 BC. Thus, we get the same year for the beginning of the calendar from two independent sources. This is momentous evidence of the use of calendars in India at least since 6777 BC.

As shown in Figure 8 (Chapter 4), India's Panchāngas are still tracking the Kaliyuga calendar of more than 5,100 years of age. Despite such strong evidence of time tracking by Indians, colonial Indologists claimed that ancient India did not have a system of reckoning time!

As discussed in Chapter 4, Dr. B. G. Sidharth (1999) proves in his book, *The Celestial Key to the Vedas*, that the earliest portions of the Ṛgveda, the world's oldest teachings, can be dated to as early as 7,300 BC, based on the astronomical positions described in the Veda.

The history documented in the Purāṇas and other historical texts of India is backed up with archaeological evidence from the vast areas of India as described in Chapter 14. A marine survey carried out by the National Institute of Ocean Technology (NIOT) of India in the Gulf of Khambhat has found evidence of a well-developed urban settlement at a water depth of 20-40 meters, and ancient people making fired clay pottery from about 16,800 BC (Badrinaryan, n.d., 2006, 2010). The ancient civilization knew the art of constructing towns and houses in neat straight lines as seen by the side-scan sonar images.

Thus, based on literary, genealogical, inscriptional, astronomical, and archaeological evidence, India has a continuous civilization going back to at least ten thousand years before the present. George Feuerstein, Subhash Kak, and David Frawley (1995) convincingly show in their book, *In Search of the Cradle of Civilization,* that India was the cradle of human civilization. It is high time indeed, to discard completely the false chronology and history and restore the true one.

## References


1. Badrinaryan, S. (2006, February 1). 'Gulf of Cambay: Cradle of Ancient Civilization.' Graham Hancock. https://grahamhancock.com/badrinaryanb1/ (Accessed on January 30, 2023).
2. Badrinaryan, S. (2010). 'The Gulf of Khambhat: Does the Cradle of Ancient Civilization lie off the coast of India?' in Glenn Kreisberg (Ed.), *Lost Knowledge of the Ancients: A Graham Hancock Reader* (Ch. 11). Toronto & Vermont: Bear & Company.
3. Badrinaryan, S. (n.d.). 'Gulf of Cambay: Cradle of Ancient Civilization.' Archaeology Online. www.archaeologyonline.net/artifacts/cambay (Accessed on January 30, 2023).
4. Cunningham, Alexander (1883). *Book of Indian Eras: with Tables for Calculating Indian Dates*. Calcutta: Thacker, Spink and Co.
5. Feuerstein, George; Subhash Kak, and David Frawley (1995). *In Search of the Cradle of Civilization: New Light on Ancient India*. Madras & Wheaton: Quest Books.
6. Max Müller (1859). *A History of Ancient Sanskrit Literature: So far as it illustrates the Primitive Religion of the Brahmans* (Allahabad ed. 1926). London: Williams and Norgate.
7. McCrindle, J. W. (1877). *Ancient India as Described by Megasthenes and Arrian: a translation of the Fragments of the Indika of Megasthenes collected by Dr. Schwanbeck, and of the First part of the Indika of Arrian*. London: Trübner & Co.
8. Sidharth, B. G. (1999). *The Celestial key to the Vedas: Discovering the Origins of the World's Oldest Civilization*. Rochester: Inner Traditions Bear and Co. http://www.Innertraditions.com

# Appendix I
# Genealogy of the Chandra Dynasty – up to King Kuru

(*Viṣṇu Purāṇa*, 4th Aṁśa, Adhyay 6, 10, 19;
*Bhāgavata Purāṇa*, Skandha 9, Adhyay 14, 17–22)

1. Atri Prajāpati (अत्रि प्रजापति)
2. Chandramā (चन्द्रमा) or Soma (सोम)
3. Budha (बुध) – married Ilā (इला)
4. Purūravā (पुरूरवा) – had six sons – Āyu, Amāvasu, Viśvavasu, Śrutāyu, Śatāyu, and Ayutāyu
5. Āyu (आयु) – had four sons – Nahuṣa, Khatravṛddha, Raji, Rambha, and Anena
6. **Nahuṣa** (नहुष) – had six sons – Yati, Yayāti, Saṁyāti, Āyāti, Viyāti, and Kṛti
7. **Yayāti** (ययाति) – had five sons – **Yadu** (यदु) and **Turvasu** (तुर्वसु) from Devyāni; **Druhyu** (द्रुह्यु), **Anu** (अनु), **and Pūru** (पूरु) from Śarmiṣthā – See **Appendix III** for another branch from this point
8. **Pūru** (पूरु) – the following is the Pūru line from this point onwards
9. Janamejaya (जनमेजय)
10. Pracinvān (प्रचिन्वान्)
11. Pravīra (प्रवीर)
12. Manasyu (मनस्यु)
13. Abhayada (अभयद)
14. Sudhyu (सुद्यु)
15. Bahugata (बहुगत)
16. Saṁyāti (संयाति)
17. Ahaṁyāti (अहंयाति)
18. Raudrāśva (रौद्राश्व)
19. Ṛteṣu (ऋतेषु)
20. Antināra (अन्तिनार) – had three sons – Sumati, Dhruva, and Apratiratha

Names highlighted in bold were the famous kings.

21. Apratiratha (अप्रतिरथ) – Kaṇva and Elīna
22. Elīna (ऐलीन)
23. **Duṣyanta** (दुष्यन्त) – married Śakuntalā (शकुन्तला), daughter of Viśvamitra and Menaka, raised by *Ṛṣi* Kaṇva
24. **Bharata** (भरत) **– was emperor, India came to be known as 'Bhārata' after him**
25. Bharadvāja (Vitatha) (भरद्वाज वितथ)
26. Manyu (मन्यु)
27. Bṛhatkṣatra (बृहत्क्षत्र)
28. Suhotra (सुहोत्र)
29. **Hasti** (हस्ती) **– founded Hastināpura**, had three sons – Ajamīḍha, Dvijamīḍha, and Purūmīḍha
30. Ajamīḍha (अजमीढ) – Kaṇva, Bṛhadiśu, Ṛkṣa, Nīla – See **Appendix II** for another branch from this point
31. Ṛkṣa (ऋक्ष)
32. Saṁvaraṇa (संवरण)
33. **Kuru** (कुरु)

The genealogy after Kuru is continued in Chapter 5.

# Appendix II
# Genealogy of King Drupada

(*Viṣṇu Purāṇa*, 4th Aṁśa, Adhyay 19; *Bhāgavata Purāṇa*, Skandha 9, Adhyay 21 has a similar list but differs a little)

30. Ajamīḍha (अजमीढ) – continuing from Ajamīḍha (30th king in Appendix I)
31. Nīla (नील) – from Ajamīḍha's second wife Nalinī (नलिनी)
32. Śānti (शान्ति)
33. Suśānti (सुशान्ति)
34. Puruñjaya (पुरुञ्जय)
35. Ṛkṣa (ऋक्ष) or Arka (अर्क)
36. Haryaśva (हर्यश्व) – had five sons – Mudgal, Yavīnar, Bṛhadiśu, Kāmpilya, and Sanjay – Haryaśva said that his five sons are capable of ruling five countries, hence they were called **Pāñcāla** (पांचाल)
37. Mudgala (मुद्गल)
38. Bṛhadaśva (ब्रुहदश्व)
39. Divodāsa (दिवोदास)
40. Mitrāyu (मित्रायु)
41. Cyavana (च्यवन)
42. Saudāsa (सौदास)
43. Sahadeva (सहदेव)
44. Somaka (सोमक)
45. Pṛṣata (पृषत)
46. **Drupada** (द्रुपद)
47. **Dhṛṣtadhyumna** (धृष्टध्युम्न) **and Krishnā (better known as Draupadī)** (द्रौपदी)
48. Dhṛṣtaketu (धृष्टकेतु)

## Appendix III
# Genealogy of the Early Eastern Kings

(*Viṣṇu Purāṇa*, 4th Aṁśa, Adhyay 18;
*Bhāgavata Purāṇa*, Skandha 9, Adhyay 17–22)

7. Yayāti (ययाति) – the seventh king in Appendix I
8. Anu (अनु) – fourth son of Yayāti
9. Sabhānala (सभानल) or Sabhānara in Bhāgavata Purāṇa – brothers Cakṣu and Parokṣa or Parameśu in Bhāgavata Purāṇa
10. Kālānala (कालानल) or Kālanar (कालनर) in Bhāgavata Purāṇa
11. Sṛñjaya (सृञ्जय)
12. Puruñjaya (पुरुञ्जय) – missing in Bhāgavata Purāṇa
13. Janamejaya (जनमेजय)
14. Mahāśāla (महाशाल) or Mahāśīla (महाशील) in Bhāgavata Purāṇa
15. Mahāmanā (महामना)
16. Titikṣu (तितिक्षु) – brother Uśinara (उशीनर)
17. Ruśadratha (रुशद्रथ)
18. Hema (हेम)
19. Sutapā (सुतपा)
20. Bali (बलि)
21. **Aṅga (अंग), Vaṅga (वंग), Kaliṅga (कलिंग), Suhma (सुह्म), Puṇdra (पुण्ड्र), and Āndhra (आन्ध्र)** (Viṣṇu Purāṇa lists only the first five sons) – The six princes established six kingdoms in their name in the east. Some of these names are still in use.

Uśinara, the 16th in the list above, brother of Titikṣu, had Śibi (शिबि) and four other sons. Śibi had four sons – Pṛṣadarbha (पृषदर्भ), Suvīra (सुवीर), Kekaya (केकय), and Madraka (मद्रक) or Madra (मद्र) by Bhāgavata Purāṇa. Thus, we can see the origin of the names **Kekaya** and **Madra** kingdoms which appear in Rāmāyaṇa and Mahābhārata, respectively. **Kaikeyi,** one of King Daśaratha's three queens, was from Kekaya. **Mādri**, the second queen of Pāṇḍu was from Madra Deśa. See these places in the map in Figure 14.

# Appendix IV
## Genealogy of the Ikṣvāku Dynasty and Śrī Rāma

(*Viṣṇu Purāṇa*, 4th Aṁśa, Adhyay 1–4;
*Brahmāṇḍa Purāṇa*, Adhyay 63)

1. Ikṣvāku (इक्ष्वाकु) – had many sons
2. Vikukṣi (विकुक्षि)
3. Kakutstha (ककुत्स्थ) or Purañjaya (पुरञ्जय)
4. Anenā (अनेना)
5. Pṛthu (पृथु)
6. Viṣṭarāśva (विष्टराश्व)
7. Cāndra Yuvanāśva (चान्द्र युवनाश्व)
8. **Śāvasta (शावस्त)** – founded **Śāvastī (शावस्ती)** – later grew into a large city during Gautama Buddha's time
9. Bṛhadaśva (बृहदश्व)
10. Kuvalayāśva (कुवलयाश्व) or Dhundhumāra (धुन्धुमार)
11. Dṛḍhāśva (दृढाश्व)
12. Haryaśva (हर्यश्व)
13. Nikumbha (निकुम्भ)
14. Amitāśva (अमिताश्व)
15. Kṛśāśva (कृशाश्व)
16. Prasenajit (प्रसेनजित्)
17. Yuvanāśva (युवनाश्व)
18. **Māndhātā** (मान्धाता) – was emperor
19. Ambarīṣa (अम्बरीष)
20. Yuvanāśva (युवनाश्व)
21. Hārīta (हारीत)
22. Purukutsa (पुरुकुत्स)
23. Trasadasyu (त्रसदस्यु)
24. Anaraṇya (अनरण्य)

Omkareshwar is located on Māndhātā island in the Narmada river.

Names highlighted in bold were the famous kings.

25. Pṛṣadaśva (पृषदश्व)
26. Haryśava (हर्यश्व)
27. Hasta (हस्त)
28. Sumanā (सुमना) or Sumati (सुमति) in Brahmāṇḍa Purāṇa
29. Tridhanvā (त्रिधन्वा)
30. Trayyāruṇi (त्रय्यारुणि)
31. Satyavrata (सत्यव्रत), later called Triśanku (त्रिशंकु)
32. **Hariścandra (हरिशचन्द्र)**
33. Rohitāśva (रोहिताश्व)
34. Harita (हरित)
35. Cañcu (चञ्चु)
36. Vijaya (विजय) or Vinaya (विनय) in Brahmāṇḍa Purāṇa
37. Ruruka (रुरुक)
38. Vṛka (वृक)
39. Bāhu (बाहु)
40. **Sagara (सगर)**
41. Asamañjasa (असमञ्जस) – ill-mannered since childhood
42. Aṁśumāna (अंशुमान)
43. Dilīpa (दिलीप)
44. **Bhagīratha (भगीरथ) – was emperor**
45. Suhotra (सुहोत्र)
46. Śruti (श्रुति) or Śruta (श्रुत) in Brahmāṇḍa Purāṇa
47. Nābhāga (नाभाग)
48. **Ambarīṣa (अम्बरीष)**
49. Sindhudvīpa (सिन्धुद्वीप)
50. Ayutāyu (अयुतायु)
51. Ṛtuparṇa (ऋतुपर्ण) – helped king Nala
52. Sarvakāma (सर्वकाम)
53. Sudāsa (सुदास) or Sudāma (सुदाम) in Brahmāṇḍa Purāṇa

54. Saudāsa Mitrasaha (सौदास मित्रसह), later called Kalmāṣapāda (कल्माषपाद)

55. Aśmaka (अश्मक)

56. Mūlaka (मूलक)

57. Daśaratha (दशरथ) or Śataratha (शतरथ) in Brahmāṇḍa Purāṇa

58. Ilivila (इलिविल) or Labiḍa (लबिड) in Brahmāṇḍa Purāṇa

59. Viśvasaha (विश्वसह) or Kṛśaśarmā (कृशशर्मा) in Brahmāṇḍa Purāṇa

60. Khaṭvāṅga (खट्वाङ्ग)

61. Dīrghabāhu (दीर्घबाहु)

**62. Raghu (रघु)**

63. Aja (अज)

**64. Daśaratha (दशरथ)**

**65. Rāma (राम), Lakṣamaṇa (लक्ष्मण), Bharata (भरत), and Śatrughna (शत्रुघ्न)**

The names highlighted in **bold** are the famous kings, mentioned in the *Mahābhārata* (Vol. 1, Sabhā Parva 52.20–22) and Rāmāyaṇa. Bāhu, the 39th king, after getting defeated by an alliance of Haihayas and Tālajangha, went to the forest with his pregnant queen and died of old age. Years later, Sagara, Bāhu's son, learning of his father's defeat and humiliation by his enemies, vowed to destroy them. He raised an army and destroyed the Haihaya and Tālajangha kings. Then, the Śaka, Yavana, Kamboja, Parada, and Pahlava kings were afraid of Sagara and sought the protection of *Ṛṣi* Vasishta, the family priest of Sagara. They were then left alive but ex-communicated (*Viṣṇu Purāṇa* 4.3.42–49; Venkatachelam, 1956b, p. 82).

Śrī Rāma's youngest brother, Śatrughna, killed the very powerful demon Lavaṇa (लवण) and founded the city of Mathura. His sons Subāhu (सुबाहु) and Śūrasena (शूरसेन) succeeded him. Lakṣamaṇa's sons were Aṅgada (अङ्गद) and Chandraketu (चन्द्रकेतू). They ruled over the Himalayan regions. Aṅgada's capital was Aṅgadapuri (अङ्गदपुरी) and Chandrachakrapuri (चन्द्रचक्रपुरी) was Chandraketu's. The portions in Kośala that fell to the share of Lakṣamaṇa's sons are in present-day Nepal. Takṣa (तक्ष) and Puṣkala (पुष्कल) were Bharata's sons. Gāndhāra (गांधार) came under their rule. Takṣa had Takṣaśilā (तक्षशिला), and Puṣkara had Puṣkarāvati (पुष्करावति) as their capital. Kuśa and Lava were Rāma's sons and became the kings of Kośala. Dakṣina (South) Kośala was under Kuśa with Kuśasthali as the capital. Uttara (North) Kośala was under Lava with Śrāvasti as the capital (Visnu Purana 4.4.100-104).

### Dynasty of Kuśa (Capital Kuśasthali)

66. Kuśa (कुश) and Lava (लव)
67. Atithi (अतिथि)
68. Niṣadha (निषध)
69. Anala (अनल)
70. Nabha (नभ)
71. Puṇḍarīka (पुण्डरीक)
72. Kṣemadhanvā (क्षेमधन्वा)
73. Devānīka (देवानीक)
74. Ahīnaka (अहीनक)
75. Ruru (रुरु)
76. Pāriyātraka (पारियात्रक)
77. Devala (देवल)
78. Vaccala (वच्चल)
79. Ulka (उल्क)
80. Vajranābha (वज्रनाभ)
81. Śaṅkhaṇa (शङ्खण)
82. Yuṣitāśva (युषिताश्व)
83. Viśvasaha (विश्वसह)
84. Hiraṇyanābha (हिरण्यनाभ) – learned from Yajñavalkya (याज्ञवल्क्य)
85. Puṣya (पुष्य)
86. Dhruvasandhi (ध्रुवसन्धि)
87. Sudarśana (सुदर्शन)
88. Agnivarṇa (अग्निवर्ण)
89. Śīghraga (शीघ्रग)
90. Maru (मरु)
91. Prasuśruta (प्रसुश्रुत)
92. Susandhi (सुसन्धि)
93. Amarṣa (अमर्ष)
94. Sahasvāna (सहस्वान)
95. Viśvabhava (विश्वभव)
96. Bṛhadbala (बृहद्बल) – was killed by Abhimanyu in the Mahābhārata War in 3139 BC.

Thus, the above list has 31 kings starting from Kuśa to Bṛhadbala. The list in Bhāgavata Purāṇa, (Skandha 9, Adhyay 12) is slightly different with a total of 28 kings from Kuśa to Bṛhadbala.

## Dating of Śrī Rāma

The recent research by the Institute of Scientific Research on Vedas (Vedveer Arya, 2015, p. 4) has concluded, based on the sky views generated through Planetarium software and the astronomical positions described in the Vālmiki Rāmāyana, that Śrī Rāma was probably born in 5114 BC. This is, approximately, 2,000 years before the Mahābhārata War in 3139 BC.

## References

1. Arya, Vedveer (2015). *The Chronology of Ancient India: Victim of Concoctions and Distortions*. Hyderabad: Aryabhata Publications.

2. Venkatachelam, Pandit Kota (Kali 5057, AD 1956b). *The Age of Buddha, Milinda & Amtiyoka and Yugapurana*. Arya Vijnana Series, Publication 20. Vijayawada.

3. *Viṣṇu Purāṇa: (Sanskrit) with Hindi translation by* Śrī Munilāl Gupta (6th ed., Samvat 2024; 1st ed., Samvat 1990). Gorakhpur: Gita Press.

# Index

www.ingramcontent.com/pod-product-compliance
Lightning Source LLC
Chambersburg PA
CBHW051505120626
46551CB00012B/783
*9798987436929*